GRID

THE LIFE AND TIMES OF FIRST WORLD WAR
FIGHTER ACE KEITH CALDWELL

GRID

ADAM CLAASEN

MASSEY UNIVERSITY PRESS

For Sandra

A flight of five Royal Aircraft Factory SE5a scouts of 1 Squadron flying in formation from St Omer aerodrome, 21 June 1918.

Tell me about a complicated man.
Muse, tell me how he wandered and was lost
when he had wrecked the holy town of Troy,
and where he went, and who he met, the pain
he suffered in the storms at sea . . . tell the old
story for our modern times. Find the beginning.

Homer, *The Odyssey* (translated by Emily Wilson)

Contents

Foreword

I t is an honour to be asked to write the foreword for *Grid*, a biography about the life
and times of New Zealand First World War fighter ace Air Commodore Keith 'Grid'
Caldwell, brilliantly researched and written by Dr Adam Claasen.

As a young lad growing up at RNZAF Base Woodbourne, I learnt to drive on the
streets of the base's married-quarters and often found myself in Caldwell Crescent,
learning to handle and park my own land-based 'grid' (slang for aircraft). I knew
nothing about the man it was named for or about the exceptional leadership and
fighting spirit of this 'big man, with jet black hair, swarthy complexion, deep-set blue
eyes and a prominent chin which was a good index to his determined character'.

Although it is focused on Caldwell's exploits, *Grid* is more than a biography.
Dr Claasen's four-year journey to bring this story to life, using first-hand accounts
of early aerial combat, letters home to loved ones and a vast array of photographs
matched by vivid descriptions, demonstrates a meticulous attention to detail — a
worthy tribute to one of our finest, if somewhat lesser known, war heroes.

Grid Caldwell was a phenomenal wartime leader. With 26 aerial victories,
he was New Zealand's highest scoring pilot of the First World War. Grid led by
example, taking great care of his new charges and always putting them and the
needs of the squadron first. Death and close calls were ever present — a miraculous
escape from a mid-air collision and likely encounter with Baron von Richthofen

are two notable examples of the precarious nature of life as a fighter pilot over the Western Front.

The majority of *Grid* rightly focuses on his First World War exploits, however his indomitable spirit and desire to serve would also see Wing Commander Caldwell called up to help lead the massive expansion of military aviation that got underway in New Zealand in the 1930s. First at RNZAF Base Woodbourne, and subsequently as Station Commander of RNZAF Base Wigram, he drove that same operationally focused, no-nonsense approach.

Upon promotion to Air Commodore, his missions to India and the UK to help manage deployed personnel and the enormous repatriation efforts rounded out an incredible contribution to New Zealand's military and aviation history.

It's worth considering why a comprehensive account of Air Commodore Caldwell has taken this long to compile. In *Grid*, Dr Claasen expertly describes the absolute modesty of a man who did his utmost to avoid personal publicity, 'especially if it reflects skill or courage to some degree. One does not talk about these matters to anyone' — traits not always obvious in some of his colleagues.

As old age crept up, many tried to pry those memories out of him, but Grid was not one for sentimental storytelling. We should therefore be even more grateful for the support of the Caldwell family and the persistence demonstrated by Dr Claasen in carefully and accurately bringing to life this account of an extraordinary New Zealander who shaped a military aviation culture and an ethos that continues to resonate today.

Air Vice-Marshal Darryn Webb
Chief of Air Force
Wellington

Introduction

In Sally Gordon's inner city villa in Auckland, the central hallway is lined with photographs of four generations of her family. Among them are two striking images: one a studio portrait of a serious air commodore, all braid and ribbons, and the other a Kodak Brownie snapshot of a newly married groom and his bride, all smiles and unrestrained joy. They're photographs of her late grandfather Keith Caldwell, airman extraordinaire and family man.

I'm here to interview Sally's mother — and Keith's only surviving child — Mary Gordon (née Caldwell). Well into her nineties, she is a window into the life and times of one of the First World War's most important airmen and one of New Zealand's most significant contributors to its Second World War effort.

'Grid', as he was universally known on the Western Front, was widely acknowledged to have survived more aerial battles than any other Empire airman, including a heart-pounding tussle against Germany's most accomplished pilot, Werner Voss, and members of Manfred von Richthofen's Flying Circus. Caldwell's miraculous and famous 'leap' from his doomed aeroplane in September 1918, which opens the first chapter of this book, was just one of six crash-landings he survived over an incredible 27 months in a service in which many men's lives were counted in mere days.

His longevity as a pilot, from 1916 to 1918, meant he was one of the few airmen to witness first hand the rapid development of the war's single-seat fighters and aerial fighting tactics. While flying some of the war's most recognisable biplanes — the rudimentary Maurice Farman, the ubiquitous Royal Aircraft Factory BE2c, the French-designed Nieuport 17, the twitchy Sopwith Camel and the fleet-footed Royal Aircraft Factory SE5a — he served with and befriended a constellation of luminous individuals, including Albert Ball, Robert Smith-Barry, Frank Soden, Robert Chidlaw-Roberts, Henry Meintjes, William Fry, Alan 'Jack' Scott, Spencer Horn, William Molesworth, Sydney Pope, Billy Bishop, Benjamin Roxburgh-Smith, Ira Jones and Edward 'Mick' Mannock. In the final year of the war, aged 22, he was given command of a newly formed fighter formation: 74 'Tiger' Squadron. In France, under his leadership, this became, by many measures, the most successful British squadron and Caldwell one of the war's most effective commanders.

The Tigers accumulated victories in aerial combat more quickly than any other British fighter squadron in the same period: 225 (including 15 balloons) in only 206 days. And all of this was achieved with only 10 killed in action, four in accidents and eight taken as prisoners of war — one of the lowest casualty rates for a fighter squadron on the Western Front. Along the way Caldwell and his men accumulated a clutch of decorations: a Distinguished Service Order (DSO) medal and two bars; a Military Cross (MC); nine Distinguished Flying Crosses (DFC) and three bars; a Military Medal and three Belgian Croix de guerres. The large number of DFCs led at least one unit historian to dub the Tigers the 'DFC Squadron'.[1]

Caldwell was central to all of this. 'Major Caldwell had more guts than any other three men,' wrote 74 Squadron pilot Len Richardson. '[He was] without doubt the fairest, squarest and most beloved C.O. of any squadron in France.' Fellow airman Ira Jones was emphatic:

> Major Caldwell's success as a C.O. lay in example, both by words and deeds he inspired us to fight to kill. There were no half measures about him. He always led squadron patrols and his fearless leadership invariably took us far over the enemy's lines regardless of opposition. The more the enemy the more he revelled in the attack. Like the German [Oswald] Boelcke he had the rare ability of picking out promising fighters, while not hesitating to get rid of duds; by patience, practice and leadership, he welded together a unit which feared no foe. He possessed that indefinable quality called Personality.[2]

After taking command of 74 Squadron, Caldwell's modest personal tally in aerial combat rose prodigiously. During 1918, in disregard of general prohibitions against squadron commanders flying on operations with their men and specific orders he'd received, Caldwell regularly led late-afternoon offensive squadron patrols. Seventeen of his 26 victories in the First World War were at the helm of the Tigers, a remarkable achievement that made him not only his nation's highest scoring pilot of the war but also the fourth-highest in the British air service in victories acquired over the enemy *while* commanding a squadron.[3]

During the interwar period he helped to develop military and civil aviation, and he played important roles in New Zealand's nascent air force and the Auckland Aero Club before contributing to the Royal New Zealand Air Force's (RNZAF) efforts in the Second World War. As commander at RNZAF stations Woodbourne and Wigram he dispatched more New Zealand-trained air service personnel to Europe and the Pacific than any other antipodean, and in the war's latter stages he went on two important overseas postings. In India, he came to the rescue of forgotten and abandoned countrymen and in Britain he organised and managed the largest repatriation of New Zealanders from service in foreign forces in the nation's history. In the three decades that followed, Caldwell was a prominent figure in the remembrance of those who had served and fallen in both wars and in the global community dedicated to recalling and retelling the stories of the Great War airmen. His life is both a gripping tale and an illuminating study in leadership and resilience across two world wars.

Given all of this, it is surprising Caldwell had never been the subject of a biography, especially when memoirs and biographies of airmen of far lesser stature proliferated after the war and in the decades that followed. Towards the end of his life, surviving airmen of the Great War and air-power enthusiasts, researchers and historians begged Caldwell to give the world of military aviation a memoir. He demurred, citing declining memory, pedestrian typing and the difficulty of reconstructing the story from a hodgepodge of incomplete and scattered documentation.

Despite his protestations, by the 1970s he was one of the few airmen of his stature left who had their wits about them. Some suggested he record his story to cassette tape for later transcription but he was having none of it. Part of this was simply that in his advanced retirement he lacked the motivation for the demanding task. He was also possessed of excessive modesty. Caldwell was far more at ease talking about the brave deeds of his comrades-in-arms than of his own endeavours and, although he championed the publication of books about others, was not about to blow his own trumpet with a Caldwell memoir.

Caldwell's concern about his ability to locate, gather and order a sufficient body of materials to reconstruct his life was not misplaced. The biographical attempts of several researchers and historians wanting to tell this story have floundered on these rocks. For international writers, the tyranny of distance in the pre-internet age was a significant impediment to acquiring adequate material from far-flung New Zealand. Letters to his descendants were met with replies that hinted at assistance and possible sources but never bore fruit to bring a project into full focus.

Consequently, all that had been published on Caldwell during his lifetime and after his death in 1980 was a handful of short articles in aviation-related publications, and of course these were narrowly focused on his military exploits. In other words, although Caldwell was an eminent candidate for a rich biography, it was uncertain whether sufficient material existed to produce one that captured the times in which he lived, the forces that shaped him, and the institutions and people on which he had an impact in his public and private life.

My subsequent research involved locating and gathering materials from New Zealand and British archives and members of the Caldwell family. Domestically, the most important source was the Air Force Museum of New Zealand (AFMNZ), which not only holds Caldwell's all-important logbook but also a large collection of his personal photograph albums. Both bear Caldwell's imprint: he overwrote his fading wartime logbook pencil notations in ball-point pen after the Second World War and many of his snapshots are plastered with Dymo Label Maker black tape embossed with relevant information.

Among other important pieces of the Caldwell puzzle was a confidential file, held by the AFMNZ, that he compiled during his postings to Woodbourne and Wigram. The manila folder is surprisingly thick with paperwork and controversy. Crises and conspiracies abound alongside mundane matters. Archives New Zealand Te Rua Mahara o te Kāwanatanga (ANZ) holds Caldwell's 'Base Records' personnel file, which contains sketchy but useful materials on his post-First World War life with the New Zealand air service in its various guises and his involvement in the Second World War RNZAF.

In addition to ANZ's files on the establishment and running of the New Zealand Flying School, where Caldwell first learnt to fly, the Auckland Museum of Transport and Technology's (MOTAT) Walsh Memorial Library had useful material on the local instruction of men like Caldwell before their embarkation to Britain. Whanganui

Collegiate School archives has details of Caldwell's academic and sporting records, photographs and copies of the school's magazine. *The Wanganui Collegian* proved a rich source for Caldwell's formative years. The Auckland War Memorial Museum Tāmaki Paenga Hira, while lacking much in the way of Caldwell documentation, had two objects closely associated with him: his flying suit and a war trophy — a German machine gun extracted from a 'downed' Fokker DVII.

Of the British archives, three London-based repositories were extremely important for Caldwell's First World War service: the Imperial War Museum (IWM), the Royal Air Force Museum and The National Archives (TNA). The latter two institutions were foundational for fleshing out Caldwell's activities in 8 Squadron, 60 Squadron and 74 Squadron. For example, materials at TNA revealed that for all his bravery and leadership skills, Caldwell was never a stickler for personal record keeping. Caldwell's logbook records only a single sortie between 11 September and 11 October 1917, while his squadron officer record book details nearly 40 flights. Conflicting dates over engagements with the enemy and other important matters charted in his logbook required considerable checking against other materials.

Given the large number of individuals with whom Caldwell rubbed shoulders and who fell under his leadership in 74 Squadron, a significant number of War Office personnel files were collected. To put Caldwell's activities in context of the larger air war effort, I gathered the war diaries of relevant wings and battalions under which these respective squadrons operated, as well as the daily 'routine orders' that deal with such matters as personnel departures and arrivals, leave provisions, discipline enforcement and the myriad official strictures covering everything from sexually transmitted diseases and the treatment of French farmers' crops to the use of the squadron's motor pool. These orders have seldom been utilised by researchers and historians and they open a window to the difficulties and demands faced by squadron commanding officers.

Even with thousands of pages of documents, there were still gaps in his military service in both world wars and in his private family life. Mercifully, I discovered that although other writers had made little progress in locating documents from the family, I had a strong ally in Caldwell's granddaughter Sally Gordon. She was able to introduce me not only to her mother but also to other grandchildren, family members and individuals with links to her late grandfather.

It gradually became apparent that 'Werfer', as he was affectionately known among his descendants, had in fact left a considerable collection of personal papers and photographs and that these had been dispersed among his four children (Mary,

Peter, David and Virginia), and subsequently handed on to the next generation. Sally supplied me with a very large trove of long and fulsome letters written by Caldwell that filled in the details of his time in India and London between 1944 and 1946.

When I visited David's son, Andrew Caldwell, on his Glen Murray farm, he regretted that some materials had been lost in flooding on the farm decades earlier, yet he still produced two large suitcases filled with an eclectic range of indispensable documents and items related to his grandfather's civil and military life, including correspondence with family members, solicitors, government officials and First World War airmen; old passports charting world trips; papers associated with membership in the Auckland Aero Club and the Northern Club; and a vast amount of documentation to do with Caldwell's farm at Glen Murray and Papatoetoe.

Virginia's daughter Deborah Stovell was able to answer a question that lingered long into the project: Had Caldwell written letters during the First World War and, if he had, where were they? Deborah produced a cache of over two dozen letters written from the Western Front to his mother and sister when they were living in London in 1918. All this substantial primary material was supplemented by published and unpublished diaries and memoirs from airmen who had flown with Caldwell; extracts from interviews and letters that appeared in the journal dedicated to First World War aviation, the British and international editions of the *Cross and Cockade*; and correspondence between Caldwell and his former squadron members in the last two decades of his life.

I would encourage readers of this biography to set aside misapprehensions and easy tropes about the Great War and early military aviation. The term 'victories' used throughout this book covers a broad range of achievements over the enemy and not simply 'kills', as popularly conceived. During the 1914–1918 war, success against Central Power airmen in aerial combat encompassed a much wider range of possibilities including 'destroyed', 'out of control', 'captured' or 'forced to land'. In other words, a victory did not necessarily entail the death of the enemy airman. Nonetheless, all the proceeding categories were unquestionably 'victories' of one kind or another over the enemy and were seen that way during the war.

When fighting took place high up, between 12,000 and 18,000 feet, it was not always possible to confirm the result of what appeared to be a successful encounter, especially in a continuing dogfight or with low cloud cover. Undoubtedly, on many occasions enemy pilots feigned fatal injuries only to pull out of a death spiral at low altitude and flee east to fight another day. Moreover, given that the fighting took place for the most part on the German side of the lines, it was often impossible to conclusively verify a pilot's claim.

'The Germans,' wrote Caldwell to an aviation researcher in the 1970s, 'could be much more accurate in their claims because, as most of the air fighting was over their side, they were able to confirm the destruction of Allied aircraft.'[4] The character qualities of the British air service claimant, the supporting evidence from fellow airmen or observers on the ground all fed into the decision by a squadron's commanding officer to sign off and forward combat claims to higher authorities for addition to an airman's score.

Caldwell's total of 26 victories is chiefly derived from his 'combat in air' reports. Where possible, these were corroborated with other primary documents and compared with Caldwell's tallies that appear in several published works. With a few qualifications regarding dates and locations of claims, the list at the end of this book is close to the number given in the widely respected, if dated, work on the subject: Christopher Shores, Norman Franks and Russell Guest's *Above the Trenches: A complete record of the fighter aces and units of the British Empire air forces, 1915–1920*. Given the gaps in the surviving records and the assertion by several of his contemporaries that Caldwell passed some of his victories on to newly arrived airmen in 74 Squadron, it is entirely possible that his own calculation of '27 enemy machines down' — written in the last few pages of his logbook — is conservative.

Modern readers tend to place a lot of importance on the 'ace' status (five or more victories) and leaderboards of the war's top pilots, but Caldwell always emphasised that the total 'score of victories to this or that airman in the air lists of books . . . should not be regarded as the "be all" or "end all" of an airman's worth'.[5] On a number of occasions after the war he expressed his frustration with aviation buffs whose narrow focus on such matters ignored the greater body of men (air and ground crew) who made *any* victories possible and argued that an individual's contribution to a squadron could not be measured in such a crude manner. The ability to knock the enemy from the sky was extremely important but it was not the defining or sole quality of a good airman in Caldwell's eyes.

Moreover, the war was neither Rupert Brooke *nor* Wilfred Owen — idealism and glory versus cruelty and horror. As readers will discover, there is considerable truth to W. E. John's portrayal of the wondrously adventurous life on the Western Front of the airman he dubbed Biggles, but there was also an unequivocal ruthlessness to killing the enemy. Death and grief were as close as the next patrol. Through all of this, bonds were formed that would last a lifetime. For many, including Caldwell, the war proved to be the pivotal event of their lives, simultaneously marring and surprisingly enriching.

Likewise, it is fashionable to see the First World War aeroplanes as rickety wood, wire and fabric death-traps. Although there is considerable truth to the impression that early in the war great numbers of poorly trained airmen flying unreliable and unstable machines were quickly dispatched both at home and over the Western Front, and that throughout the war, fire was an ever-present danger in a service in which parachutes were inexplicably absent, it is also true that by mid-war the aeroplanes were extremely robust and purposeful in their lethality.

Stronger airframes, more powerful engines and increased weaponry meant Caldwell's SE5a of 1918 bore only a passing resemblance to the machines he learnt to fly in 1915. In preparation for writing this book I was fortunate to be offered the opportunity to fly in a First World War two-seat BE2c from Sir Peter Jackson's collection at Hood Aerodrome, Masterton. Unbeknown to me, my pilot, Dave Horrell, had arranged for us to be 'jumped' by an SE5a and Fokker DVII from The Vintage Aviator Limited's large aeroplane inventory. The rapidity and aggressiveness of the two single-seat fighters as they mercilessly swooped in behind us and peeled away at speed was as frightening as it was exhilarating. Make no mistake, these were the premier machines of their era and not the stuff of *Those Magnificent Men in their Flying Machines* and popular imagination. Think of them as the Supermarine Spitfire of the Second World War or the Lockheed Martin F-35 Lightening II of our own time.

The war was far from sepia-toned, and in the air even less so. The surviving photographs of the First World War mislead us. The multi-coloured fields and green forests of northwestern France fought with the riotous yellows, blues and reds of the German machines for the attention of the British air service pilots. As the inclusion of photographs of machines from The Vintage Aviator collection in the colour section of this book demonstrates, the air war was as colourful as its participants.

Little did I realise when I finished my interview with Mary Gordon that four years of research and writing lay ahead of me. I had planned to place the published copy of this book in her hands but, sadly, as the completion of the manuscript drew near, Sally told me that her mother had died, aged 98. It is my hope that this book will bring the story of Mary's father to life for a new generation.

CHAPTER ONE

Very Lucky Still

September 1918, France. Red fabric streamers fluttered from the spars of his single-seat fighter as Keith 'Grid' Caldwell led a three-strong offensive patrol high above north-western France. Behind him lay the verdant late-summer countryside of St Omer. Directly before him, under the nose of his spinning propeller, a wide gash in the earth stretched from the English Channel southward to the Franco–Swiss frontier. After four years of incessant, murderous warfare, the Western Front was an eviscerated no man's land flanked by a lacework of trenches.

At 16,000 feet, Caldwell and his wingmen, Sydney Carlin and George Hicks, pointed their Royal Aircraft Factory SE5s deep into enemy territory. In the distance, dark specks: German Fokker DVIIs. Caldwell alerted Carlin and Hicks before feeding fuel to the V8 Viper engine and turning his nose towards the enemy. As the trio collected speed, the dark smudges on the Fokkers crystallised into black German crosses. Caldwell lined up his twin machine guns on one of them, preparing to fire at close range.

Suddenly his SE5a jolted and twisted as Carlin's undercarriage ploughed into his upper left wing. Timber splintered and fabric tore in the ugly collision. Carlin managed to pull his machine away, limping towards Clairmarais with a portion of his tail torn off.

Hicks stayed close enough to see that Caldwell was in all kinds of hell. The buckled wing had upended the delicate aerodynamics of the SE5a and it was doing everything in its power to kill him. It fell, before entering a semi-flat spin, the altimeter unwinding rapidly in the unchecked descent.

Then Hicks saw Caldwell stand up in the cockpit. At 5000 feet, attempting to regain mastery over the machine, Caldwell placed his left foot on the right rudder pedal and leant out as far as he could, away from the damaged wing. As Hicks swung his machine away, Caldwell lifted a hand to wave. Hicks was sickened: his squadron commander was surely doomed.

But Caldwell was not done. Heading west in a long shallow dive, he leant into the full blast of the wind and the backwash of the churning propeller. He calculated his height, distance and speed. Reaching his own lines would be close.

The German trenches appeared and receded as the SE5a crossed no man's land, the roar of the engine alerting British infantry, who looked up as the aeroplane careened barely 10 feet above them. Impact was moments away.

Caldwell leapt. As the machine ploughed into the ground, he tumbled free, over and over. Then he stood up, flicked the dirt from his aviator's suit and strode to the nearest trench in search of a telephone.

Back at the aerodrome, Hicks delivered the dreadful news to the squadron: Grid was surely lost. Caldwell's men were stricken and Carlin inconsolable. Hours passed and no word came. It appeared that the 'bravest of the brave' had fallen. Distraught, Carlin declared he'd go back and shoot up an enemy aerodrome. Mechanics slipped out to discreetly disable his aeroplane. Airmen from neighbouring squadrons arrived to offer moral support. They tried to liven up the after-dinner gathering but it was more like a wake. The men barely looked at each other as they recalled the courageous exploits of their commanding officer.

Then into this mournful gloom bounded the unit's recording officer: Caldwell was alive and on his way back to the squadron. The news was met with a cacophonous roar. By the time a grinning Caldwell swaggered into the mess, a party was in full swing. Later in the evening, Carlin passed out in 'complete happiness'. It was a knees-up to end all knees-ups. The dead lived. The 'miracle' story spread through the aerodromes of the Western Front, across the channel to Britain, and finally appeared in the newspapers of Caldwell's New Zealand homeland under the headline 'Caldwell's Great Escape'. That night he wrote in his pilot's logbook: 'Very lucky still.'[1]

Keith Logan Caldwell grew up in the small rural New Zealand town of Cambridge. His family arrived there from Wellington, where he was born in 1895, and settled into Green Hedges, a property that covered nearly half a town block and was staffed by servants, a cook and chauffeur.[2]

Keith's father, David Robert Caldwell, was from Ayr, Scotland, and his mother, Mary Dunlop McKerrow, was the daughter of the chief commissioner of New Zealand Railways Corporation. Keith and his sister, Vida, were raised in Edwardian fashion by a sometimes stern father and an empathic mother.[3] Cambridge offered many opportunities for David to play golf and his son to ride, but it was some distance from his Auckland workplace: the retail stores and warehouses of one of the dominion's largest manufacturers and importers of soft goods, Macky, Logan, Caldwell and Company.[4]

The senior partner, Joseph Macky, was the personable and friendly face of the institution. 'Mr Caldwell', as he was known even to Macky, was the forbidding and uncompromising bookkeeper and financial officer.[5] The two men had built the company from a handful of workers in the 1890s to nearly 600 employees by 1910, with warehouses and stores in Auckland, Napier, Gisborne, New Plymouth, Whanganui and Christchurch.[6] In addition to their own Cambridge clothing range, the enterprise supported local manufacturers and imported a wide range of goods: hat-pins, millinery, drapery, boots and clothing. Its storefront windows displayed items selected by David Caldwell on overseas buying excursions.

'I had long letters from Mr. Caldwell from Montreal, Toronto, Quebec, Boston and New York,' Macky recalled. 'He was immediately struck with the value of the Canadian and American boots, shirts, felt hats, braces and some of their cotton goods.'[7] When he was required to spend extended periods in Britain sourcing fabrics and soft goods, Caldwell would take the family; some of Keith's early education was completed in England.

To be closer to Auckland, the family bought a second home in Arney Road, Remuera, a large house in a wealthy neighbourhood.[8] David Caldwell became president of the Remuera Bowling Club and the Caldwells were popular socially.[9] Keith often accompanied his father on the 100-mile drive from Green Hedges to Auckland in the large chauffeur-driven Buick. Along the way, David passed on fatherly wisdom and regaled his son with travel stories, including an oft-retold chronicle of his visit to Washington DC in 1902, when, as a leading member of the Auckland Chamber of Commerce, he met President Theodore Roosevelt, who embodied just the qualities David hoped to instill in his only son: 'self-reliance' and the powers of 'push and "hustling" as the Yankees called it'. Rather than relying on an inheritance,

he told Macky, which would not be a blessing 'especially [to] his boy Keith', Caldwell wanted both of his children to develop qualities of character that would endure life's vicissitudes.[10] With this in mind, in 1910, he shipped his 15-year-old son from King's College in Auckland to board at Wanganui Collegiate School.

D uring this period, it was common for the sons of well-heeled politicians, lawyers, doctors, engineers, farmers and businessmen to be dispatched to New Zealand's elite schools, which transplanted the aesthetics, manners and teaching practices and philosophies — and even the building styles — of English public schools.[11] Their grounds were planted with oaks and elms, and gowned masters taught boys who wore Edwardian jackets, white shirts with Eton collars and ties.

Established in 1854 by a land grant from Governor Sir George Grey to the Bishop of New Zealand, George Augustus Selwyn, Wanganui Collegiate was one of the colony's first schools, and as the New Zealand economy prospered in the wake of refrigerated shipping and improved rail services, its wealthier citizens increasingly sent their sons there. When Caldwell arrived, a sizeable building programme was under way. Within 18 months, he and his classmates were transferred from timber buildings situated close to the Whanganui River to substantial new red-brick structures. The boys were all part of the building work: along with other pupils, Caldwell periodically helped to prepare new sports fields, a tennis court and house gardens and to dig the new swimming pool.[12]

The Reverend Julian Dove, the school's headmaster, a product of Marlborough College and the University of Cambridge, had been recruited under the received wisdom that headmasters born and educated in New Zealand simply lacked the gravitas to meet the expectations of rising professional and middle-class parents. Building on the example of his predecessor, Walter Empson, Dove oversaw not just the building of the new school but the building of character in boys like Caldwell.[13]

At his first prize-giving assembly, Caldwell joined in rousing renditions of such English public school anthems as the 'Eton Boating Song' and heard the Bishop of Wellington, Dr Thomas Sprott, commend the school for its agreeable transportation of 'all the noble traditions and high ideals of the public schools of the old country into this land'. Dove reminded everyone that the school's supreme calling was to

Keith Caldwell, aged four, in 1899. The family's successful soft-goods business ensured he always looked his best.

'train men to be good citizens, to make able servants of God, and King and Country'.[14]

The classrooms reinforced this message. Ten-point stag trophies loomed over a wall lined with photographs and prints of the British Empire's famous individuals. Men like Horatio Nelson, the Duke of Wellington and Herbert Kitchener were not only victors in great conflicts but also personifications of bravery, honour and sacrifice.

I n class, Caldwell, who was a middling student, scrawled down lessons from the school's masters in his angular longhand.[15] From his English and mathematics teachers he learnt not to mix his metaphors or split his infinitives and the trigonometric ratios in right triangles and arcane algebraic formulas. French, geography, divinity, and Latin filled out the curriculum. In 1912, Caldwell was confirmed in the newly dedicated chapel, where the Bishop of Wellington delivered a 'wonderfully inspiring address on the subject of "Strength"', according to the school's magazine, the *Wanganui Collegian*. 'The real gain of Christianity . . . was the moral strength he knew he could get, if he wanted it, from Jesus Christ', he declared. He exhorted the boys to 'seek those things which are above', for 'something more than body or mind — 'the development of soul'.[16] As Cabinet minister Dr John Findlay had emphasised to the students a year earlier, 'Worldly success too often permits a man to adopt methods which, while allowed by the police, are not sanctioned by honour or honesty', but the outcome would only be dishonour.[17]

Sacrifice, on the other hand, was to be embraced, and it came in many forms. There were regular reports of old boys taking holy orders and of the numerous visitors 'of the cloth' who spoke to the pupils about missionary efforts abroad: 'The development of Christianity in China and Japan', 'Fighting the Good Fight' in Melanesia and 'In Darkest Africa with Bible, Knapsack and Gun'.[18] In his final year, Caldwell put his divinity instruction to good use at a local school, Mosston, as a Sunday school teacher. Though never demonstrably religious in later life, Caldwell embraced the ethos and nobility of sacrifice for the greater good.[19]

This link between sacrifice and war was nowhere more evident than in the school's chapel, where the morning sun shone through the 1899–1902 Second Anglo–Boer War memorial window. Eighty-five old boys had served and nine had lost their lives in South Africa; a brass plaque close to the altar listed their names.[20] In his speech

Keith Caldwell's mother, Mary, his sister, Vida, and his father, David, at ease in Territet, Switzerland, in 1908. David Caldwell often took his family on extended overseas trips that combined work with sightseeing.

at the prize-giving of 1900, Walter Empson had prophetically concluded that 'if ever the occasion should arise, and their country should have real need of them, not forty-six [the number of former pupils then in South Africa] only of those who have been educated here, but double, and treble, aye and twenty times that number will muster at her call'.[21]

The Graeco-Roman world figured heavily at a school where final-year students traditionally carried around a life-sized bust of Julius Caesar, and where a statue of *The Dying Gladiator* sat on one of the classroom mantelpieces.[22] Caldwell's class listened to tales of the classical realm: Zeus and Hera and their unruly siblings and offspring; Hercules and his 12 labours; Prometheus and the theft of fire; and Icarus's prideful encounter with the sun. Most loved, though, were the Homeric epics, especially the story of Odysseus. Through this mythical hero the masters reinforced to impressionable boys the importance of being remembered by doing great deeds. During Caldwell's years at Wanganui Collegiate, this was no better epitomised than in Captain Robert Falcon Scott's attempt on the South Pole.

The dashing British Royal Navy officer and his teams of men and animals were in a magnificent arm wrestle with the frozen wastes of Antarctica. When Scott had departed from Lyttelton on the *Terra Nova* in late 1910, a Wanganui Collegiate old boy, James Dennistoun, was charged with looking after the mules that would be used by the relief party during the return from the Pole.[23] Dennistoun was already well known to the school as a fine mountaineer, notably as the conqueror of Fiordland's supposedly 'unassailable' Mitre Peak. The boys bent over the local newspapers, perusing grainy pictures of huts, muffled-up adventurers, waddling penguins and *Terra Nova* casting shadows on the snow and ice. Caldwell attended a lecture given by French teacher, drama instructor and drawing master John Neame in aid of Scott's expedition, which, he said, 'kept alive the spirit of adventure which was characteristic of the British race [and had] made the Empire what it is'.[24] A sum of £9 12s 6d was collected in a fundraising drive. That Scott's expedition was one of three racing for South-Pole laurels only added to the drama.[25]

On 17 January 1912, Scott and four others reached the South Pole, only to find that the Norwegian Roald Amundsen had got there five weeks earlier. When the boys were told that the entire party had died on the return journey, the 'School expressed its feelings in the best of ways — by absolute silence'.[26] At the end of the year, Dove unveiled a memorial tablet to those who 'after enduring together as loyal comrades untold privation and hardship . . . fell asleep amid the eternal snow'.[27]

Scott's last diary entry was on the lips of many a school assembly across the empire: 'Had we lived I should have a tale to tell of the hardihood, endurance and courage of my companions, which would have stirred the heart of every Englishman.' The boys at Wanganui Collegiate School were 'proud to think that we were members of a race that could produce such men'.[28] The message was clear: Scott, even in defeat, would not be easily forgotten.

CHAPTER TWO

Favoured Ones

I n Wanganui Collegiate's Big School room, alongside photographs of King George V and various nineteenth-century admirals and generals, were two images of the near-naked torso of Eugen Sandow. A native of Königsberg, Prussia, Sandow had avoided military service to become a circus performer before gravitating to strongman competitions. By the time Caldwell entered school, the Prussian was the toast of the world, the father of modern bodybuilding, captivating crowds everywhere. When he visited New Zealand in 1902 for seven weeks, as part of a world tour showcasing the 'Sandow System', he was a global celebrity. In San Francisco he had subdued a 650-pound lion in a contest in which the lion, dubbed 'The Commodore', piteously 'drew his tail carefully beneath him and lay down with his nose buried in the earth'.[1]

Clothed, Sandow looked like anyone. As one woman exclaimed upon spotting him on the streets of Wellington, 'Why, he's just a MAN!'[2] But arrayed in tights, sandals and a leopard skin, the powdered Sandow was an Olympian, a Grecian statue brought to life, 'A Hercules Indeed!'[3] One reporter gushed over 'the great rows of

---

By the time Keith Caldwell arrived at Wanganui Collegiate School, the Big School room had been transported to the school's new location and converted into a gymnasium. The values enshrined in the room's large number of photographs dedicated to the king, the empire and muscular Christianity underpinned the school's educational approach in the years leading up to the First World War.

muscles which stand out like coils of cordage . . . [and] in the inflation of his chest Mr Sandow seemed to grow into gigantic proportions.'[4] The Wanganui Collegiate boys were delighted when he visited the school, and in the evening, at the opera house, they saw the 'mighty Sandow in all of his glory'. Dove and others dubbed him the 'apostle of physical culture'.[5]

Sandow's gospel was the advancement of fitness and health. 'If in your New Zealand schools you paid more attention to the development of physical prowess in the children, better results, mentally speaking, would be obtained, and the human race would be the gainer,' he told the *Otago Daily Times*.[6] The message echoed the 'muscular' Christianity of the period that emphasised not only virtue but also the physical beauty of athleticism, masculinity and discipline.

Politicians and school masters wanted young men and woman fit to advance imperial and national causes. British and New Zealand eugenicists fretted over declining fertility rates of the 'better' classes and the bodily atrophy resulting from modern sedentary lifestyles and technological advances.[7] The all-too-recent war in South Africa had exposed a nation possessed of less physical vitality than had been imagined.

Sandow's gospel found a receptive audience in New Zealand schools, and led to the replacement of constricting uniforms in order to facilitate the introduction of compulsory exercise. At Wanganui Collegiate, the more casual blue socks and shorts, and grey flannel shirts of the school's new 'Loretto garb', spoke of a nation invigorated by clean air and a 'physical culture'.[8] The original Big School room was appropriately converted into the gymnasium on the school's new grounds in 1912.

W ithin days of his arrival, Caldwell was embracing the school's demanding physical regime. He began each day with pre-dawn compulsory exercises in the gymnasium, a half-mile run, followed by a cold bath and then breakfast. And there was 'no eating between meals except plain cake at 11 am'. On Sundays a 5-mile walk after chapel had the advantage of combining spiritual reflection and physical exercise.[9] Each year the school published the physical measurements of its students, tabulating columns of heights, weights and bicep and chest dimensions. As the *Wanganui Collegian* noted, not only was the school increasing in size numerically

Keith Caldwell, right, and his good mate Trevor Bloomfield overseeing Wanganui Collegiate School's annual sports day events. Caldwell was one of the school's great sporting all-rounders, equally at home with a cricket bat in his hand or kicking a rugby ball.

and geographically, but the boys were also stronger and healthier. Caldwell was notably taller than his peers and whether wielding a cricket bat, kicking a rugby ball or donning boxing gloves, he spent his last two years accumulating athletic laurels. Sporting competition and the amateur ethos of the era gave Caldwell an 'internal discipline and a code' that he carried for the rest of his life.[10]

Dove believed that what the pupils did in the classroom was less than half as important as what took place on the sports field. In the spartan dormitories of the boarding house and on the playing field the boys learnt 'habits of self-control, comradeship, loyalty . . . and that wholesome habit of keeping the pores of the skin open and the mouth shut, without all of which a man can be of little use in the service of Church and State'.[11] The school also deliberately linked sporting achievement with military endeavour. Caldwell's generation was steeped in the ideas vividly expressed in Henry Newbolt's poem 'Vitai Lampada', which linked the Battle of Abu Klea in the Sudan with the selfless commitment required on the cricket pitch: 'Play up! play up! and play the game!'[12]

The boys gained many of their lifelong values and much of their self-discipline from the two principal games of the empire: cricket and rugby. The former 'crafted gentlemen'; the latter 'made men'.[13] In the summer of 1912–13, Caldwell was one of the school's top cricketers and he confirmed his status the following season in victories over Wanganui Collegiate's main sporting opposition: Wellington College and Christ's College, Christchurch. Against the latter he took two wickets off the first and last ball of just his second over. He was the school's best all-rounder, with 37 wickets for the season.[14] He could wield 'anything with a handle', as testified to by his adroitness with both a tennis racket and a golf club.[15]

After joining the First XV in 1913, Caldwell improved 'greatly during the season', even if he was sometimes inclined to 'run across field' too much. He had a good place kick and looked for 'work and [was] game at tackling and stopping rushes'. By the end of 1914 he had gained a solid reputation with the boot — he had punted and place-kicked accurately and 'brought off some magnificent goals'. He could have improved defensively, one assessment noted, but his quick hands 'made good openings for the wings'. Caldwell was also a useful boxer with a sharp, punishing left hook. During the in-school tournament he completed two bouts in the heavyweight division.[16]

I f the school's sporting endeavours were replete with implicit martial overtones, then its Naval League and army cadets were explicit war-committed enterprises.

The local Whanganui branch of the league was the gathering place for worship of the Royal Navy, the most potent sea-going force in the world, which had secured and maintained Britain's empire throughout the nineteenth century. It had kept New Zealand safe from foreign threats and protected the sea lanes on which it depended for its trade.

At the annual general meeting of 1912, the league's secretary reminded the boys that 'England depended on the sea for everything and if she once lost command of the sea she would very soon starve. The object of the Navy League was to keep . . . [New Zealand] alive to this fact and to urge on the government the necessity for keeping up our naval supremacy.'[17] The presentation concluded with lantern slides of foreign and British warships. A little over 12 months later, one of the latter came to New Zealand waters.

Launched in 1911, HMS *New Zealand* was the incarnation of the dominion's military commitment to empire in time of war, a £2 million gift to Britain. In the words of Prime Minister Sir Joseph Ward, 'We distant sons desire to stand in any peril beside the lion mother of our race, and to the utmost of our resources prove to her and to the world how dear to us is Britain's name and greatness.'[18] When, in 1913, HMS *New Zealand* undertook a 10-month circuit of the New Zealand coast, nearly half of the nation's citizenry — 500,000 — came out to inspect the battlecruiser.

On a wintery 16 June day, bundled up against the cold, Caldwell and his fellow pupils competed for the best view with over a thousand other school children and swarms of flag-waving Whanganui residents. HMS *New Zealand* truly was the 'grim and formidable fighting machine' of which the papers spoke.[19] Much of the throng had high hopes of walking the ship's deck but were to be disappointed. The choppy seas prevented nearly anyone boarding, so many simply circled the ship in local tenders and launches, becoming increasingly seasick.

The only visitors to go aboard were the civic party, who brought a feast of game — five deer, two swans, 32 brace of pigeons, hares and 20 lambs — and some 'favoured ones': jubilant Wanganui Collegiate boys, including Caldwell, who waved at the envious crowd of boats milling and swirling around the warship, which suddenly loomed over them, a vast cliff of steel.[20] When his turn came, Caldwell ascended, grabbed the rail and pulled himself onto the vessel.

Overleaf: **HMS *New Zealand*** was the dominion's most highly visible martial link to the greater empire. Tens of thousands of New Zealanders, including Keith Caldwell, turned out to admire its warlike lines when it toured the nation in 1913. Here a flotilla of small boats surrounds the great man-of-war in Auckland.

The boys oohed and aahed. The vessel exceeded the length of a rugby field by a good margin. Its defensive deck armour was 2 inches thick and its armament included torpedo tubes and 16 single 4-inch guns with twin 12-inch guns fore and aft. After their short excursion, the students were bundled onto the returning ferry, many reasoning that with such steel titans the empire was surely unassailable. One, however, was left behind. Trevor Bloomfield, an 'accidental' stowaway, was later duly offloaded when the ship docked in New Plymouth. When he returned to the school, he was greeted by the admiration of his classmates — and six of the best from one of the masters.[21]

Despite the talk of naval strength, New Zealand's elite schools recognised that if war broke out, most of it would be fought on land and that it was the nationwide army cadet system that offered the skills and ethos they needed. Caldwell was a colour sergeant in one of the school battalion's three companies. On wet days he sat listening to lectures on musketry and skirmishing, but when the skies cleared, he made war in the local sandhills. The signalling boys and company scouts were trained in semaphore and the use of compass and map. More formal war gaming involved practising advanced guard operations and the art of scouts maintaining contact with a main body of men.

On other occasions Caldwell was involved in well-planned exercises, such as the 'Field Operations around the Golf Links' at Belmont in 1913. 'The attacking party, No. 1 Company, was the advance party of a foreign army supposed to have landed near the Heads with the object of taking Wanganui. The defending force, No. 2 and 3 Companies, took up a strong position on the hills to the west of the Golf Links. After some hours of severe fighting in a fog the "cease fire" sounded with neither side gaining much advantage. Battalion assembled at the Gold House for lunch.'[22]

Training camps were held at the Feilding racecourse, 35 miles south-east of the school: 6 a.m. reveille, 45 minutes cleaning tents, boots, buttons and guns and an hour of physical drill — all before breakfast. The remainder of the morning was consumed by a parade and monotonous drill, broken by a single 15-minute break. The afternoon was similarly occupied. In the evening the boys listened to lectures from the instructing officers on elementary tactics such as a 'company in attack', cooperation with cavalry, how to form a picket and how to protect themselves from a night attack.[23]

Caldwell and his fellow cadets were regularly inspected and inspired by various senior officers, including, in mid-1914, General Sir Ian Hamilton, Inspector General of Overseas Forces, who was pleased with the 26,000 senior New Zealand boys he reviewed, including the Wanganui Collegiate lads.[24] He was also pleasantly surprised by the military advances made by Major General Alexander Godley, Commandant of the New Zealand Defence Forces. In the wake of the 1909 Defence Act, which had introduced compulsory military training and school cadets, and a 1910 advisory visit by Field Marshal Lord Kitchener, in 1911 Godley had professionalised and reorganised the Territorial Force and the cadets. When Godley spoke at Wanganui Collegiate's 1912 prize-giving, he gave the boys some 'sound advice', particularly regarding the part they would have to play as 'soldiers of the Empire'. The great privileges they enjoyed meant 'their future responsibilities would be correspondingly great . . . If — God forbid it — the evil day came when it was necessary to defend this little bit of the Empire, the boys of the public schools would be expected to set an example to the soldiers of the country.'[25]

Early in August 1914, Caldwell's academic and sporting world was interrupted by war. Following the assassination of Archduke Franz Ferdinand had come the Austro-Hungarian and Russian mobilisations and then the German invasion of Belgium and France. What had begun as a localised contest in eastern Europe — the competition between Austria–Hungary and Russia for suzerainty over the Balkans — had quickly metastasised into a broader European war as expansionist Kaiser Wilhelm II sought to assert Germanic dominance in the heart of Europe. Britain could not allow this to happen and declared war on Germany on 4 August.

The news reached New Zealand at lunchtime on 5 August, and later that afternoon thousands of Wellingtonians had gathered on the steps of Parliament to hear the British government's declaration of war and the statement of the governor, Lord Liverpool, in support of King George V and the war: 'New Zealand . . . is prepared to make any sacrifice to maintain her heritage and her birthright.'[26] As requested by Britain, New Zealand pounced on the colony of German Sāmoa, landing at Apia on 29 August. An old boy participated in the bloodless seizure. He appropriated a German flag from the radio station at Apia and offered it to his alma mater.[27]

The senior boys were eager to fight and, when the formation of a New Zealand Expeditionary Force was announced, they assembled excitedly for a meeting. 'The result was a terrific writing home to parents,' recalled one old boy, 'in many cases the letter being explanatory of a preceding telegram.'[28] The editorial in the student magazine in December 1914 stated, 'We think of war by day and dream of war by night.' Of the some 700 old boys who would serve in all services and theatres, 162 would never return.[29]

CHAPTER THREE

Clear-eyed Young Men

Caldwell's schooling had kept him abreast of international affairs and the concerns of the wider empire. Informal 'parliamentary' debates at Wanganui Collegiate had covered matters of 'Coloured Immigration', global free trade, the Anglo-Japanese Alliance, 'Drink and Grand Dukes are the two great curses of Russia' and imperial naval defence. The boys were well aware of Germany's maritime expansion, and its empire-building in Africa and elsewhere.[1]

Many of the letters written to their parents by students at Wanganui Collegiate, and other similar schools throughout New Zealand, were impassioned and sometimes intemperate. 'You seem very perturbed about the war,' wrote one Waitaki Boys' High School pupil to his concerned mother, 'I tell you I don't care a scrap for the Germans and their battleships. You need not entertain the slightest fears as to the result of the war. . . the Germans are in the wrong, and do you believe the "wrong" will win, and has it ever won? . . . Surely you can put your trust in the British Empire and what it stands for, and not worry your head off.'[2]

Predictably, such jingoistic rhetoric from their young sons was not always well received by men and women who had experienced the Second Anglo–Boer War and its aftermath. 'Needless to say, practically everyone received cold replies from parents who — so it was thought — had not a drop of patriotic blood in them,' recalled one Wanganui Collegiate old boy.[3]

Just shy of 6 feet tall, with a sterling sporting record and two years in the Territorial Force behind him, Caldwell was ideal army officer material. He was offered a commission as a second lieutenant in the New Zealand Expeditionary Force (NZEF). Official documents slated him for the 10th Reinforcements to coincide with his twentieth birthday. But Caldwell, now in a stifling clerical position at the Bank of New Zealand in Auckland, was unconvinced.[4] He wanted to fly.

Although New Zealand had been relatively late to the flying craze due to its isolation, there had been a flurry of aviation activity in the pre-war years. In 1911, two Auckland engineers, Leo and Vivian Walsh, completed the nation's first sustained flight in a box-kite-designed biplane, and in the months leading up to the war, New Zealand pioneer aeronauts Joseph Hammond and James Scotland captured the imagination of Caldwell's generation.

In the second week of January 1914, Hammond, the first New Zealander to gain a flying certificate, from the Aéro-Club de France, dazzled Auckland's residents with the first ever flight over the city, in a Blériot monoplane. 'People were dressing for church . . . when they heard a rhythmic throbbing which set them wondering. They rushed to windows and doorways to investigate the phenomenon, and there poised gracefully between Earth and blue sky, was *Britannia* in rapid flight,' recorded the *New Zealand Times*. 'Auckland talked of aeroplanes for the rest of the day.'[5]

Hammond was lauded as a classical god astride a modern Pegasus, as was Scotland, who in a series of long flights flew half the length of the South Island, finishing in Christchurch. Vast throngs followed the journey and attended exhibition flights in Canterbury. After disembarking from his French Caudron biplane, the youthful Scotland was swamped with adoring crowds of all ages. 'An old man of 98 years of age greeted him and thanked the aviator for allowing him to see the wonder of the age before he died,' the *Sun* reported. 'Mothers brought up their children to speak to the birdman. And even policemen seemed to lose their heads. It was a scene of magnificent enthusiasm.'[6]

With flying fever running high, Wanganui Collegiate graduates rushed headlong to enter the air service. The first young man to go to war was a 17-year-old heading to Gallipoli, but the 'next fellows to actually leave School to go to war were J. D. Canning,

J. S. Smith and D. W. Gray, all of whom went Home to England and joined the RFC'.[7] Letters from these new airmen were published in both the school magazine and in New Zealand newspapers. Rainsford Balcombe-Brown, for example, joined the Royal Field Artillery but in 1915 was seconded to fly as an observer.

> I had my first ride in an aeroplane. Between here and Armentieres by zigzagging about we climbed to 6500 feet, and then set off over the German lines . . . The object was to see what troops, transport and trains were moving about behind the German lines . . . I was utterly astonished by the distance one could see. The cliffs on the south coast of England were actually visible . . . [but I] didn't bother very much about observing, because I was so engrossed in looking all round (instead of down), and enjoying to the full a new sensation . . . At Wervicq two shells were fired at us, but were miles away. At Comines the shooting was a little better . . . the shells bursting above and below and all over the place.[8]

Wanganui Collegiate would supply more airmen than any other New Zealand school.[9]

In the first year of the war, New Zealanders who wanted to train for a position in either the Royal Flying Corps (RFC) or the Royal Naval Air Service (RNAS) had to do so in Britain. But the Walsh brothers were keen to meet the demand of their countrymen for flying instruction. When Caldwell heard this, he applied to have his name withdrawn from the NZEF on the grounds that he wished to join the RFC.[10]

In May 1915, Joseph and Mary Macky had been travelling through Canada and the United States on business. After they arrived in New York, Macky sought passage across the Atlantic to Britain but a berth was difficult to secure. The Germans were intensifying their submarine war and had declared the waters off Britain a war zone. The German Embassy in Washington placed advertisements in American newspapers warning potential travellers of the danger, but Joseph Macky considered the journey low-risk: 'indeed we have little fear,' he wrote in a letter home. 'There is a warning from the German Govt not to travel across the Atlantic, but we think we are safe in this good fast ship . . . Anyway we are in God's hands and are content to leave with Him "our going out and our coming in".'[11]

Eventually he found them a berth on the Cunard ocean liner, *Lusitania*, for a time the world's largest passenger vessel, which held the speed record for crossing the Atlantic. Some called it the 'ocean greyhound'; Macky dubbed it the 'leviathan'.

On 1 May 1915, Joseph and Mary Macky, along with nearly 2000 fellow passengers, watched the Manhattan skyline shrink into the distance as the ship headed out into the Atlantic. Their first-class accommodation, and the ship's lounges and dining rooms, were of unparalleled luxury but, unbeknown to the passengers, below decks were munitions and weapons destined for Britain and its allies.

The Atlantic crossing was uneventful, and on 7 May *Lusitania* was running parallel to the south Irish coast with Liverpool only hours away. At 2.10 p.m., an 18-year-old lookout spotted track marks of foam streaking towards the hull on the starboard side. Shortly thereafter, *Lusitania* was struck by a single U-boat torpedo just behind its bridge.[12] A second larger explosion followed, and the ship rapidly lost speed and began listing. Within minutes, the electrical power failed and the interior went dark. Those who had scrambled to the open deck found chaos. A 15-degree list made launching lifeboats difficult; some overturned in the descent, spilling people into the sea. In all, only six of the 48 lifeboats reached the water intact.

Mary Macky was among those offered a seat on a boat. She declined in favour of another passenger: 'I am getting old, and would rather stay with my husband. You are a younger woman, and have life before you,' she told the fellow passenger.[13] The woman was one of only 761 survivors, a number of whom later reported seeing the elderly Macky couple standing together 'with calmness' in the ship's last moments. Just 18 minutes after being hit, the bow sank, the propellers rose out of the water and *Lusitania* slipped into the deep.

When the news broke throughout the British Empire, it was one of the biggest stories of the year. The newspapers raged against Germany for its callous disregard for the rules of war, while the Germans defended the actions of the U-boat commander, arguing that the *Lusitania* was armed and therefore a legitimate target. Others questioned the culpability of the Cunard Line and the captain. For the Auckland business community, the loss of the popular and influential Mackys was a blow.

A few weeks later Auckland businesses shut their doors and flags were flown at half-mast as a crowd of 3000, including Keith Caldwell and his parents, sitting near the front, attended their memorial service in the town hall.[14] With time, it was revealed that Macky had left a string of bequests to orphanages, the Unitarian church, childhood education, infant health and the blind. To his employees he left a fortune of nearly £20,000.[15] 'Joe and Mary Macky had enshrined themselves in the hearts of Auckland, as probably few had done before,' said the mayor, James Gunson.[16] Their deaths and the sinking of the *Lusitania* steeled the hearts of many young Aucklanders against the Germans in the war ahead of them.

In the second week of July 1915, Leo and Vivian Walsh and Reuben Dexter, who had a Cadillac car agency in Auckland, announced the establishment of their New Zealand Flying School. Caldwell was one of the early respondents to an *Auckland Star* advertisement: 'NZ Flying Corps . . . Training our own Pilots. Aeroplane Building in Auckland.'[17] The £100 tuition fee, a sum almost equivalent to the average annual wage, made the training the preserve of the sons of the wealthy.[18] Within two months, Caldwell was seated in front of the newly created flying school's ad hoc selection panel — the Walshes' father, Austin, and Dexter — and on 2 October 1915 he began his flight training, one of the lucky six chosen from numerous candidates. With these half a dozen trainees, one self-taught instructor (Vivian Walsh) and a homemade machine, the school was under way.

Caldwell found the setting to his liking. The school's base was at Mission Bay, then known as Kohimarama or simply Kohi. Like most students, he arrived on a motorcycle over undulating farmland. The first sign that he was closing in on the school were the two towering Norfolk pines, planted by missionaries in the 1860s, which dominated the bay. Beneath them were the stone buildings of the former Melanesian Mission, established by Bishop Selwyn and now the flying school's headquarters, dining hall and staff accommodation.[19]

Student lodging was less salubrious: tents pitched on the grass above the white-sand beach. Caldwell and his fellow trainees — Geoffrey Callender, Bertram Dawson, Werner Langguth, Joe Banks and Gordon Martin — woke up and went to sleep to the sound of lapping waves. They had a stunning view over the Waitematā Harbour to North Head and Rangitoto Island, the vast, dormant volcano cone that rose from the Hauraki Gulf.

The young men got up early each day, shaking Vivian Walsh awake if the weather was conducive to taking the seaplane out. Until iron rails were laid to make launching and retrieval easier, Caldwell and the others had to manhandle the machine down to the water. Rather than import an aeroplane, the Walsh brothers had styled their homemade machine on a model designed by the New York-based Curtiss Aeroplane and Motor Company for the United States Navy.[20] A biplane powered by a single

Seaplanes of the Walsh brothers' New Zealand Flying School at rest at Mission Bay in Auckland. Keith Caldwell was the school's most celebrated alumnus.

Overleaf: The Walsh brothers' flying boat landing off Mission Bay with Devonport's North Head in the background. Underpowered and slow, the plane was nonetheless instrumental in teaching Caldwell the rudiments of flight without killing him in the process, an all-too-common event at British flying schools.

engine mounted on struts that separated the upper and lower wings, it was a pusher-machine, which meant that, unlike the more common tractor configuration, the propeller sat behind the engine and 'pushed' the aeroplane along. The pilot and passenger sat side by side in an open cockpit at the front.

With Walsh sitting next to him overseeing proceedings, Caldwell had to stand, turn around and perch himself on the swaying seat to reach up and turn the heavy crank over, a tricky task in calm conditions, and arduous when the wind picked up. The pupils endured many a dunking. The motor was always only too willing to foul the plug of the bottom radial cylinder with excess oil, thwarting even the most determined young arms. More times than Caldwell hoped to remember, he, or another trainee, was unable to get the engine to start and had to signal for the school's motorboat to bring them back in, cold, wet, oil-smeared and with aching shoulders and burning arms.

When the engine did turn over, barking as the cylinders fired off, and the nose lifted as the flying boat gathered speed, it was clear that separating hull from water was going to be a close-run thing. The low-powered Italian Anzani engine struggled to get machine and men airborne. The tail section could drag in the water, and whenever this happened Caldwell would have to slide out on his belly onto the nose, his face overhanging the leading edge. This pushed the nose down and the rear up. In the meantime, Walsh would open the throttle and rock the aeroplane as far as he could, so that the shallow hull would escape not just the bonds of gravity but also the resistant surface tension of the water.

Smooth, glass-like water was the machine's bane, and sometimes a motorboat was required to zigzag in front of the seaplane to break up the water and grant a release. The 'flying boat was strong, but overweight and underpowered,' noted Caldwell, 'and it rarely left the water with two up.'[21] When it did, Caldwell would let go of the nose thrust-post and allow the slipstream to blow him back into the cockpit. He would then grasp the dual control as the seaplane flew just above the waves.

When the weather precluded flying, Caldwell donned overalls and headed to the workshops for instruction with the mechanics, his hands accumulating glue, splinters and grease. The flying boat's engine required a lot of maintenance and an overhaul every 50 or so flying hours.[22] The school purchased Scotland's record-setting Caudron and began converting it to a floatplane with slender pontoons mounted under the fuselage. In addition to these two dual-control machines, the Walsh brothers were also building a single-seat flying boat for solo flights. Housing all this was a growing expanse of hangars, workshops and a fitting shed, much of it built out of car-packing cases supplied by Dexter. An ever-expanding spider's web of rail lines and a turntable linked the hangars to the harbour.

In his free time, Caldwell enjoyed the holiday camp-like surroundings and local wildlife. Cows were often dropped off in the bay to graze and by night would sniff around the tents. The men kept a shotgun on hand to send them loping away.[23] The school collected several dogs, including a playful long-haired Collie called Landy, but nicknamed Fleabag, a dull-witted retriever and a pugnacious bulldog dubbed Bully, who spent most of his days within two yards of the cookhouse door, protecting his patch. Some of the students had horses brought in and stabled at Kohi. However, if speed was required, the students had their growing fleet of motorcycles.

Cars, but more commonly motorcycles, offered the opportunity for constant tinkering (on his entry papers to the RFC, Caldwell stated he had worked on the family Daimler) and absorbed many hours of the students' time. Motorcycles were easily stored and were an affordable means of getting around Auckland. The pupils would race the narrow roads and lanes that snaked between the bay, Remuera, Epsom and downtown Auckland. The locals were less impressed with Kohimarama's goggled and gloved gang.[24]

On 25 November 1915, Minister of Defence James Allen, accompanied by a clutch of dignitaries and reporters, arrived to inspect the school at Kohimarama.[25] The blustery Auckland day had grounded the flying boat, but Allen chatted with Caldwell and other students while he surveyed the flapping tents and creaking buildings. The minister examined the flying boat at close quarters and cast his eyes over the Caudron undergoing conversion. Allen thought the brothers 'fine young fellows, who had persevered with their flying machines in the face of considerable difficulties'. The Walsh brothers happily told a reporter that the school's pupils 'would attempt shortly to pass the [final] test'.[26]

By now, though, there were only five, as Joe Banks had withdrawn, 'fed up' with the slow pace of instruction. Bertram Dawson and Gordon Martin would eventually be forced to delay their training.[27] What most disturbed Caldwell was the dramatic and unfair departure of Werner Langguth, whose prominent father, Eugene Langguth, was the former Austrian consul in Auckland.[28]

Since emigrating to New Zealand, Langguth had become one of Auckland's more prominent businessmen, who had made his fortune importing and wholesaling German beer, Scotch whisky and American canned fish and fruit. Langguth and his

wife attended numerous civic affairs and business gatherings with David and Mary Caldwell, and the two families went to the same Northern Club balls, fashionable society weddings and Government House garden parties.[29]

At Kohi, Keith Caldwell shared training, meals and a beachside tent with Werner Langguth and with Callender, who had returned home to enrol in the flying school after graduating with a degree in electrical engineering from the University of Sydney. They entered the Queen Carnival shooting competitions in December 1915.[30] But Langguth, who was born in New Zealand, educated at King's College and was a lieutenant of good standing in the New Zealand Garrison Artillery, was a lightning rod for the xenophobia that grew as the war went on. Only weeks into his training, the local newspaper headlined an article 'Germans in our forces'. Apparently, the paradisiacal Garden of Eden at Kohimarama had a snake among its students.

'These appointments of persons of alien enemy blood to commissions in our forces are apparently still going on in defiance of public opinion and the laws of propriety,' said the *New Zealand Times* on 19 November 1915. In the months and years that followed, Langguth was subjected to unfounded rumours spread by the Women's Anti-German League in Wellington, and his request to travel to the United States in another attempt to join the Allied cause was rejected by the New Zealand authorities. In 1918, James Allen cancelled Langguth's commission and attempts were made to recover his uniform and even extract a refund for a portion of its original cost.[31]

A t the school, training proceeded at a steady if frustratingly slow pace. The original flying boat was still disdainful of its intended task, but while taxiing flat out on the surface Caldwell gained good experience with the controls, and when the aircraft did sluggishly break free of the water it gave him a good sense of the demands of flying.

On 13 December 1915, just in time for sustained solo flights, the school's newly converted Caudron floatplane was commissioned. It was a relief for the two remaining students, Caldwell and Callender, to see Vivian Walsh christen the new machine. With so little flight training in the flying boat, he was reluctant to send the two students up in the Caudron. On the other hand, any further delay would mean putting off a new intake of students and endangering the future of the school. The

Geoffery Callender, the son of the general manager of the Bank of New Zealand and a former Bachelor of Engineering student at the University of Sydney, entered the Royal Flying Corps with Keith Caldwell.

Walsh brothers made what Caldwell called 'a very brave decision' and sent him and Callender up in the Caudron later that same day.[32]

The flights were suitably uneventful. With a speed of only 60 miles per hour, the Caudron was an ideal solo machine for trainees, and over the next nine days, Caldwell quickly accumulated three hours in the Caudron.[33] (It had taken 11 weeks to accrue five hours in the flying boat.) Adverse weather prevented them from taking the test for the Royal Aero Club aviator's certificate, but it did not matter: they could fly.

Three days before Christmas, Caldwell emptied his tent of his possessions and farewelled the Walsh brothers, who had provided him with a reference:

> We sincerely trust you will be successful in securing early admission to the Royal Flying Corps and that the knowledge gained at our flying school here . . . will assist you in support of the application . . . We have the pleasure in stating that you proved a very apt pupil and that in addition to straight flights on our 'Walsh' flying boat, you have made circuits and figure of eights on the 'Caudron' hydro-plane.[34]

The twin Norfolk pines receded in his rear-vision mirror as he rode out of the bay. He was on his way to war.

CHAPTER FOUR

Magnificent

K eith Caldwell spent the next two weeks with family and friends, celebrating Christmas and the New Year, and finalising travel plans. As was not uncommon for prosperous New Zealand families, his mother and sister would be sailing with him to Britain and would remain there for the entirety of his service. In anticipation of a bleak northern hemisphere winter, copious travel trunks and bags were filled with the best Macky, Logan and Caldwell soft goods.

On 6 January 1916, barely three weeks since finishing his training at Kohimarama, Caldwell was at the railing of the New Zealand Shipping Company's RMS *Remuera* as it slipped its Wellington berth.[1] The family was travelling first class saloon, as was Geoffrey Callender. As well as 280 passengers, the liner was carrying New Zealand produce: cheese, butter, wool, kauri gum, tallow, hemp and pelts, plus 20,000 mutton and 34,000 lamb carcasses in the freezing hold.[2] The antipodes would be doing their part for the war and then some: around 10 per cent of New Zealand's population served in uniform during the war, and a full quarter of its military-aged men were either killed or wounded.

Taking the long route, *Remuera* sailed west, around the Cape of Good Hope. Caldwell would have liked to have seen the newly opened Panama Canal, but mud slips had clogged the channel, and, besides, the threat of German U-boats was diverting vessels away from the area. The voyage was largely uneventful, save for the obligatory and semi-regular emergency drill. When the ship's foghorn blew, the engine stopped 'and from both ends of the ship sailors flocked, lifebelts in hand'. The deaths of the Mackys were not far from the minds of the Caldwells and added gravity to the proceedings.

For the most part, they filled their days with a lazy routine of eating and sleeping. As one *Remuera* passenger that year scrawled in their diary, soon after an early tea, a 'stewardess announces bath is ready. On going to bathroom, one finds water is run (salt) and basin with hot fresh water also ready. Then dress leisurely for 8.30 breakfast. After lying in deckchair, talking, reading or sleeping whiles the hours away or an occasional walk thrown in.'[3] Periodic games of quoits and deck billiards satisfied Caldwell and Callender's competitive spirits, and the evenings were filled with dances, choir practices and amateur theatrics. Sporadically, news of the wider world was snatched from the ether by the ship's wireless radio or found in large bundles of newspapers scooped up at visiting ports.

T he news was bleak: the Gallipoli campaign, Winston Churchill's grand plan to weaken the Ottoman Empire by securing the Dardanelles, had faltered and failed. Eight long months after the first Anzacs arrived on the peninsula, and with more than 2700 New Zealanders dead and over 4800 wounded, they abandoned it. The British would stay another month. Constantinople was 'dressed with flags and illuminated in celebration of the evacuation'.[4] The survivors and reinforcements, reorganised into the New Zealand Division, had been relocated to France to fight on the Western Front.

Letters written by former Wanganui Collegiate students described the horrors of Gallipoli — carving 'dug outs' out of steep-sided gullies and digging latrines that filled as fast as they were made. 'There is endless digging, digging, and still digging of trenches, saps and bomb-proofs,' wrote one weary old boy. 'The weather gets hotter and hotter, and the flies are so thick that we have quite a race to get our biscuits eaten before all the jam disappears.'

When the oppressive heat soared to unbearable levels, the men had sometimes stripped off and run into the water. 'We were having great sport, thoroughly enjoying the change from heat and flies, when we heard the "zip," "zip" of a couple of bullets low down, and the soft "thud" as they struck the water . . . in quicker time than crabs disappear into their holes' a hundred men cleared the beach and huddled naked under an earthen bank.[5]

Another old boy's troop of 36 was reduced to 13 by death, wounds and illness. 'One man had nearly half his lower jaw blown away; the doctor asked him how he was feeling, but of course he could not speak, so [beckoned] for a piece of paper and a pencil, and he wrote down "Fine, thanks and we took the trench."' Another Wanganui Collegiate man was hit in the head as he peered over the edge of his trench: 'He lay, half conscious, from 10am to 10pm in a narrow trench exposed to the heat of the sun. It was impossible to get him away as the Turks had practically surrounded us. We got him out that night when we were relieved, and the stretcher-bearers carried him 2½ miles to the landing where he was put on the Hospital boat. The next morning, they operated, but he was too far gone to live and about 24 hours later he died.'[6]

'Of 300 Old Boys at present serving, fully a third have appeared in the casualty lists,' said the last edition of the *Wanganui Collegian* Caldwell secured just before he left.[7] At Gallipoli, Edward Barnard-Brown had been killed in a 'night attack by the Turks'; Gerald Williams had 'died of enteric fever' (paratyphoid); Herbert Knight had been 'shot by a sniper'; Noel Williams had 'died of dysentery after a week's illness'; Arthur Hume had 'died of wounds received in severe fighting'; Percival Fullerton-Smith 'fell in action'.[8] It was a shocking litany of death. The old boys of the elite New Zealand schools were being winnowed by the fan of war not just in the Middle East, but also in western Europe.

Caldwell was dismayed, also, to learn that one of his masters, Hugh Butterworth, had been killed in September 1915 while serving with a British regiment in Flanders. He had led the boys in sports and been attuned to literature — 'Dickens, Thackeray, Kipling and Bernard Shaw' — and great ideas. 'He would read a book on socialism, or even evolution, or religion, not with the superior man's itch for criticising or refuting, but with the pure impulse to explore realms of thought hitherto unknown.' Caldwell and his peers in Selwyn House remembered him for his perpetual kindness to everyone, from the 'nervous new-boy to his older school-fellow'. Though not military in temperament, he had 'allowed his sense of duty' to overcome his 'love of life.' His letters from the trenches were honest and unadorned.

> I've seen Fear in the faces of almost all a company, and I've felt my own inside go wrong, and heard the voice of temper saying, 'Now Butterworth, old son, that's the spot for you; if you're rushed, you'll be near the exit-door and able to fall back.' At those times the only thing to do is to take oneself by the neck and get right into the heart of things; swarm about and cheer up the men, and generally restore your own confidence — in yourself.[9]

Caldwell also spotted his own name in print: 'K. L. Caldwell has been learning aviation at the Walsh Flying School, Kohimarama and is already making ascents by himself.'[10]

On 19 February 1916, after six weeks at sea, *Remuera* docked at Plymouth in Devon, and the Caldwell family trio and Geoffrey Callender departed for London. The two men had their letters of proficiency from the Walsh brothers in their back pockets and acquired more supporting documentation in London. 'Both of them have been educated at the best colleges in NZ . . . They are healthy young men — good at football and other games, and Caldwell is a good motor driver, and also a good horseman. I can confidently recommend them to you as young men of high character, and temperate habits, and likely to develop as reliable and brave officers in His Majesty's Service.'

Caldwell had references from the defence minister and, his trump card, an introduction from Prime Minister William Massey. Being the son of a 'wealthy merchant', and what New Zealand's high commissioner in London called 'well connected', had distinct advantages. The correspondence was careful to point out that the 20-year-old New Zealander was free from military obligations at home, where he had been granted a dispensation to pursue a place in the RFC.[11] The target of Caldwell and Callender's ambitions was a well-placed staff officer in the Directorate of Military Aeronautics, Major William Ward Warner.

In the third week of February, Caldwell stepped out of the recently opened art deco Regency Hotel — the largest in Europe, with well over 1000 staff — just north of Piccadilly, and set off for the directorate. In his letter of introduction, he had laid out his bona fides and gilded the lily by telling Warner that Governor Liverpool had signed a paper to 'the effect that I'm to offer my services in the RFC'. In his application he declared that he had 'ridden and hunted for the last 12 years or so', significant information given the contemporary belief that horsemanship was not only an obligatory skill for an officer but also demonstrated an aptitude similar to that required when handling an aeroplane. He noted, too, five years' experience in 'looking after a car and motorcycle'.

Neither Caldwell nor Callender need have worried. Caldwell was duly notified

By 1916 large numbers of men such as Keith Caldwell were being funnelled into empire-wide training for the war in the air. This image shows a Royal Flying Corps class on air-attacking manoeuvres in Toronto, Canada.

that he had been selected for appointment as a second lieutenant on probation in the Special Reserve of Officers, Royal Flying Corps, with effect from 15 April 1916. He was directed to Christ Church College, University of Oxford, for aviation instruction.[12]

Caldwell and Callender departed London for the buttery stone walls of the University of Oxford and the School of Military Aeronautics. Established in the twelfth century, its buildings and traditions predated European settlement in the Americas and far reaches of the British Empire. Caldwell and his cohort were housed at Christ Church College, established by Henry VIII in 1546 and famed for its architecture and alumni: King Edward VII, Lewis Carroll, John Locke and a dozen British prime ministers. 'I don't think I have ever been so impressed in my life,' wrote one New Zealander, 'not all the graven images of Egypt, nor the beauty of the English woodland, could move me to such raptures. I stood on the top of New College tower and looked at Oxford with the sun upon her towers and it was magnificent.'[13]

Caldwell stowed his kit in shared sleeping accommodation with a handful of other entrants.[14] High ceilings and tall windows gave the rooms a light and pleasant air, while the raw wood floors and rough-hewn tables reminded them that Oxford was a brief and purposeful stopping point on their way to war. Chairs were rare in the 'barracks' and the men routinely pulled a table up to the foot of their bed or used a suitcase on the bed as a makeshift writing desk.

The room of greatest importance to most students was Christ Church's chapel-like dining hall, with its oil portraits, stained-glass windows and vaulted ceiling. Here was the inspiration for Wanganui Collegiate and hundreds of similar schools through-out the empire, but the reality was significantly grander than the imitations.[15] Each of the 12-man tables was attended by a pair of white-gloved waiters and champagne was a regular accompaniment to the silver-service meal. 'This is indeed the life,' wrote one student as he enjoyed a vintage from 1904.[16]

Caldwell found the other cadets an agreeable group — young men like himself, primed to advance on Berlin and personally remove the Kaiser's crown. The thousands of military cadets now passing through the university provided a much-needed fiscal fillip. The war had taken great swathes of students to the front and the university's coffers were in decline. The government paid a set rate to the institution for the teaching facilities and the housing and feeding of Caldwell and his companions.[17]

The animated throng was testament to the RFC's rapid growth and to the large numbers of men from the dominions being funnelled into its ranks. When war broke out, the RFC had numbered no more than 2000 personnel, including a mere six South Africans, a single Australian and one New Zealander.[18] By the war's end, about one in five came from outside the British Isles, with Canada, Australia, New Zealand, South Africa and Newfoundland the largest 'foreign' contingents. Of the close to 50 cadets in Caldwell's 1916 cohort, at least nine were New Zealanders, nine South African, eight Canadian, six Australian and there were one each from India, Ceylon and the Federated Malay States. Caldwell was happy to be among them. About 1800 men are currently 'waiting to join the corps', he wrote his father, 'but men with previous service are taken on first.'[19]

Like Caldwell, the New Zealanders were all white middle- and upper-class 'colonials'. (The racial attitudes of the time meant only a handful of Māori men succeeded in entering the RFC.)[20] Three of the trainees, Caldwell, Callender and George Aimer, had worked in banks before the war, and Robin Barlow and Douglas Sam came from farming backgrounds; the latter's father owned Balmoral Station in the South Island's Mackenzie country. Wesley Spragg was a partner in a motor engineering firm and William Shirtcliffe had managed a shipping and machinery branch for a large Wellington merchandise company.[21] James Hewitt, a Wanganui Collegiate old boy, had worked as a marine engineer before the war.

C aldwell spent four weeks at the School of Military Aeronautics.[22] If he hoped this would be a reintroduction to actual flying, he was sorely disappointed; it was a 'ground school', where cadets acquired some semblance of military bearing and gained knowledge about the machinery, weaponry and dark arts of aviation warfare. His school and cadet experience had prepared him for the demands of early mornings and interminable marching: parade and physical exercise from 6.15 a.m., breakfast at 8 a.m., a parade to morning lectures, lunch and more lectures.[23] Dinner was at 7.30 p.m. Mess etiquette and the proper method of saluting were impressed upon the men as they went about their daily business of classes and drill.

Caldwell filled his notebook with dense scrawl and pencil diagrams in bright primary colours. In the steeply raked lecture rooms and the dusty, oily workshops, he learnt about the dropping of bombs, the intricacies of rigging, the vagaries of European meteorology and how to fire Vickers, Lewis and Maxim machine guns.[24] To ensure graduates could carry out the all-important duty of observation, cadets discovered how to use maps in flight, take aerial photographs and direct artillery onto enemy positions. To facilitate this, a room in the university museum was eventually turned over to a large display of 'the Ypres salient, done in sand and clay', where you could 'stand in a gallery above it and make sketches'.[25]

Teams of students also regularly dismantled and reassembled a static display aircraft and familiarised themselves with a number of common engines.[26] In addition to the basic differences between the rotary and stationary engines, Caldwell was required to understand the workings of the carburettor, magneto, water pump, radiator, gauges, controls and the petrol and oil tanks. At a pinch, he could make simple adjustments and repairs to a faltering or damaged engine, or patch ripped and torn fabric on the fuselage or wings. The closest the men got to flying was taxiing wingless machines.

In the future, Oxford cadets would use a primitive flight simulator suspended from the ceiling above a cleverly designed rolling panorama. Surprisingly, the theory of flight was not taught systematically until 1917, but the students did learn about the arcane components of aneroid barometers. Many notebooks survived the war in better condition than their authors since they were often never consulted again.

To break the tedium, Caldwell and his close associates explored the university and its bucolic surroundings. As daffodils and tulips swayed in the early weeks of the English spring, students took to the water in punts and raced lightweight narrow Canadian canoes.[27] Bicycles could be 'borrowed' and hedge- and tree-lined roads traversed. Blenheim Palace, only 10 miles away, was a frequent destination for cadets in their different uniforms. Many wore the distinctive 'maternity' jacket of the RFC, but Caldwell preferred the cuffed rank tunic with pockets and burnished brass buttons. Like many officers' uniforms, his was tailor made.

Every 2 miles, en route to Blenheim, bikes were dismounted and leant against 'delightful' wayside inns and taverns, where 'English ale and Scotch whisky and cheese and bread' were consumed in copious quantities. At the palace a bottle of port and lunch might follow, and the return journey would be broken as before. Any opportunity to celebrate was an opportunity to imbibe. 'Everybody was teed up before they got there and then we had cocktails by the quart and champagne and then each man got a half-gallon pitcher of ale,' wrote one American later in the war. 'We sang that old song and made everybody do bottoms-up by turn.'[28] It was generally agreed that the prospective airmen were a 'wilder body of guests' than their infantry counterparts at the other Oxford colleges.[29]

Cadets taxiing on a de Havilland fuselage at No. 1 School of Military Aeronautics in Reading, University of Oxford.

Periodically, the importance of their training was brought home by visits from dignitaries and those who had already fought in France. One unexpected visitor was His Majesty King George V. 'We were all in our classes, and going on (officially) as usual, when he came in . . . covered with decoration ribbons — three layers of them with red all over him — hat and shoulder tabs, and not without much brass work.' The King said, "'carry on"; we carried on (with signalling Morse) and he vanished.'[30]

As a decorated British major reminded another cohort of cadets, they were 'starting on a long trip. It's a hard trip and will require a lot of courage. You'll all be frightened many times but most of you will be able conquer your fear and carry on. But if you find fear has got the best of you and you can't stick it and you are beyond bucking up, don't go on and cause the death of brave men through your failure.' One man who was 'yellow' could imperil others. Only 'devotion to duty and concerted effort and disciplined teamwork' would ensure victory. 'War is cruel, war is senseless and war is a plague, but we've got to win it and there's no better use of your life than to give it to help stop the eternal slaughter.'[31]

Caldwell was often confronted with the survivors of this 'eternal slaughter'. The local military hospital was home to hundreds of wounded men. Scarred and sometimes limbless and sightless, wearing their distinctive blue convalescent uniforms, they shuffled, or were wheeled and guided, through the streets of Oxford.[32]

At the completion of the course, Caldwell passed the final examination, one of the 87 who 'did specifically well'.[33] He was now ready for his last hurdle, the Elementary Flying School.

CHAPTER FIVE

Wings

C aldwell was about to enter one of the most dangerous periods in the life of a
First World War airman: initial flight training. Long before meeting the enemy
over trenches, prospective pilots had to face the home training fields, where students
often seemed hell-bent on killing themselves, aided and abetted by wayward
aeroplanes and complicit instructors. About a fifth of all Great War airmen were
killed while under instruction in Britain. Caldwell abandoned the comforts of Oxford
for East Anglia, 150 miles away. Over the month of May 1916, he did his elementary
flying instruction with 9 Reserve Squadron at Norwich, and from June to mid-July, he
underwent advanced instruction with 45 Squadron at Sedgeford. The airfields were
within 30 miles of each other, separated by a largely flat and undulating landscape
with the North Sea close by.

With Caldwell was Callender and another New Zealander, Neal Spragg, the son of a
wealthy Auckland businessman famed for modernising the nation's dairy enterprises
and introducing cooperative farm ownership.[1] The family's considerable fortune
rested on the popularisation of parchment to wrap butter. The Spragg patriarch was
also a confirmed prohibitionist and involved in the Auckland YMCA and the Red
Cross. Like the Caldwells, the Spragg family had two homes, one in the Waitākere
Ranges and one in Auckland. Like Callender, Spragg had attended King's College.

Neal Spragg gravitated to swimming and boating rather than the traditional sports of cricket, rugby and boxing. Tall and sinewy, he had overcome a delicate and sickly childhood by undertaking numerous treks through the Waitākere Ranges, where he demonstrated considerable bushcraft and ability with a rifle. Like Caldwell, he was an accomplished horseman and had a talent for mechanics. Although 'shy and reserved', the fair-skinned and red-haired Spragg possessed a frank and kindly personality.[2]

C aldwell flew for the first time in England on 14 May 1916, a 10-minute dual-control flight over the RFC's Norwich aerodrome in a Maurice Farman Longhorn.[3] His early flights resembled his rudimentary efforts at Kohimarama: taxiing, takeoffs, straights, landings, turns, controlled dives (volplaning). But the East Anglian aerodromes were flush with machines, most of which were more powerful — though not by much — than those belonging to the Walsh brothers.

The Longhorn and its sibling, the Shorthorn, were staples of the 1916 flying schools. Their descent from aviation pioneers Wilbur and Orville Wright's Flyer was immediately obvious. They were pusher biplanes with a box-kite structure of thin timber bones and almost translucent fabric skin and a web of wire sinews for lightness and structural strength. They were, however, slow, with a speed of only 50 to 60 miles per hour, and skittish.

Lift, the essential element for flight, is obtained by air flowing over the curved upper surface of the wing. Loss of that airflow at low attitudes can be fatal since the pilot has insufficient space and time to regain it. Once lift is lost, gravity takes over. 'Half our accidents, especially with learners,' wrote another New Zealand trainee, 'is flying too low over parts that are unsuitable for a landing, such as woods, villages, camps, etc. If you have height and anything goes wrong with the engine you can glide down at a gentle slope for miles and pick out a suitable landing-ground.'[4] Moreover, the 70 horsepower engines were notoriously unreliable and prone to failure at the most inopportune moments. 'At full power it was just enough to get one safely off the ground and to climb high enough for turning, but if you drove along at too great a speed the engine would overheat, and at the slightest loss of power the nose of the machine had to be pushed down to maintain flying-speed.'[5] The Farmans also lacked inherent stability for level and trouble-free flight, which 'meant you dare not let go of the controls for a second,' wrote trainee Edgar Garland, from Wellington,

A crashed Royal Aircraft Factory BE2c. Before facing the enemy over the trenches of the Western Front, trainees had to navigate the perilous waters of flight training at home.

who estimated that they killed five airmen over the nine weeks of his training.[6] Many of these accidents occurred at takeoff, when low air speed, engine failure and difficult handling combined in a deadly cocktail. As one airman concluded, 'The whole business [was] unpleasantly suggestive of tight rope walking, the margins of safety were so narrow.'[7]

Guiding the novices through all this should have been the instructor's job but, as Caldwell found, they offered little support. Because the pilot and instructor sat one behind the other in an exposed two-man nacelle, an elongated bathtub-like enclosure of wood, fabric and leather, communication was difficult. The blare of the engine and the shrill whistling of the wind through spars and wires forced instructors to shout their injunctions or commune with their pupils via increasing levels of violence: nudges, shoves and kicks.

Even more alarmingly, in 1916, the RFC had no formal training school for instructors. 'In other words, while there was a training syllabus — of sorts — there was little doctrine or method to back it up, and there were no professional flying instructors.'[8] Often the students were taught by men who had only just sewn on their own wings — teachers who barely grasped the rudiments of flight and whose only qualification was they had not been killed in the preceding weeks during their own lessons. One later Kohimarama student, Trevor Alderton, was appointed an instructor in England the day after completing his course. When the 24-year-old took up his first student, their machine stalled and crashed. The pupil survived, but Alderton was killed.[9] Other instructors were so psychologically damaged that they were sent to Blighty on Home Establishment — non-operational duties — to settle their jagged nerves. One man, 'a good pilot, with a fine record in France . . . finally cracked up under the stress of flying an aeroplane of poor performance and ineffective armament against the new German fighters'. After a rest, he was made an instructor, 'but was a nervous wreck for flying of any kind'.[10]

Western Front survivors dubbed the trainees 'Huns', regarding them as a menace as great as a German aeroplane spitting machine-gun bullets over no man's land. This fear meant that the instructors only reluctantly turned the controls over to the students before snatching them back at the slightest threat. Some men never felt the weight of the controls before being sent up for their first solo flight.[11]

For most trainees, the solo flight was their moment of truth, and many were undone by poor instruction, unreliable machines and nerves. Significant numbers of airmen flying alone for the first time were killed or maimed when they panicked on takeoff, tipped a wing to return to the airfield, lost air speed and hit the ground.

If they managed to get airborne without incident, however, there was always the problem of landing. Some landed too heavily, destroying machines in a single blow; others landed on hedges, hangars, in trees and even on other aeroplanes.

'First solos are generally a nightmare to pupils and crashes on these occasions frequently occur,' wrote New Zealander Melville White, who reduced his own aeroplane to matchwood on landing. On his second, more successful attempt, he even found time to survey the aerodrome below. The sight was disconcerting. The detritus of previous airmen's failed efforts was scattered across the area; a sergeant major was instructing men in a funeral march; and ambulance and medical personnel sat, vulture-like, ready to feast on the remains of 'unfortunate youths who descended much quicker than they ascend'.[12]

Surviving the first solo was no guarantee of avoiding later problems. Another New Zealand trainee, Thomas Quarles Back, told Caldwell about his 'most alarming' ninth solo, when a spark plug failed: 'Saw a large field, all one crop, into the wind, remembered too late "never land in standing crops" — when I regained consciousness the sound of the birds was lovely. Groggily, I got to my feet, and looking some distance back saw the tail standing up above the crop.'[13]

Mercifully, Caldwell's training in New Zealand, though staid and plodding, had done its work. In his logbook, next to his initial flight at Norwich, he penned 'no instruction', likely a reference to not requiring direction from his trainer.[14] He needed only one more flight before going solo. On that memorable day, he ascended to 500 feet and proceeded to complete three landings without any fuss. Two days later, he gained his flying 'ticket' before advancing to the Shorthorn. He completed all this without incident and within days was flying for nearly an hour and at an altitude of 5500 feet. This was real flying, and Caldwell found it splendid. However, for every airman who took easily to the air, there were many who found flight less agreeable.

Spragg nearly lost his life on two occasions. In the first incident, he was thrown from his seat while the aeroplane was scuttling along at a mere 15 feet off the ground. He was launched headfirst — a human bullet — towards the tail section of the machine and bounced off the tail-planes before tumbling to the blurring dirt and grass. The steel inside his flying helmet saved him from serious injury. The second incident was even more life-threatening.

While Spragg was approaching Norwich aerodrome with an observer, the aeroplane's engine seized; the pusher's propeller tore itself off and severed the rudder

controls as it cartwheeled away. Spragg wrestled the machine into a shallow, slow descent. Then, at 50 feet, the aeroplane stalled, the nose suddenly dipped and 'it dived straight to earth'. Just before impact, the two men 'jumped clear'. Spragg got the worst of it: one shoulder was injured and some of his teeth were knocked out.

Nonetheless, the leap saved their lives. Nearby lay scraps of timber, remnants of fabric and a smouldering and pinging engine, which, on impact, had torn its mounting bolts and busted its way forward through the cockpit like a freight train. As Spragg wrote to his father, had they remained in their seats 'they would almost certainly have been crushed to death in the debris'.[15]

Spragg was dispatched to hospital and would reappear in Egypt as an equipment officer and then an instructor at the local School of Aerial Gunnery. Caldwell farewelled many other men in East Anglia through injury. Some, lacking both aerial aptitude and the requisite character qualities for an RFC officer, were sent packing before they could kill themselves. Others lacked even the necessary initiative or ability for non-flying duties.

Disturbingly, pilots unfit for an active frontline squadron might be recommended for instructing in Britain. One officer, 'of delicate health and . . . on "light duty"' was not allowed to fly above 200 feet and was not even considered 'capable' of working with equipment. He was, however, considered 'a safe, though not very bold pilot, and I think there is not more work in the Royal Flying Corps more suited to him than elementary instruction in flying'.[16]

On 3 June 1916, Caldwell was posted to 45 Squadron, Sedgeford, for his final advanced training. Callender arrived three days later.[17] Caldwell's new unit was gearing up for deployment to the Western Front. Unlike Norwich, with its large, well-established hangars and commodious buildings, Sedgeford was more a collection of hastily assembled huts and tents in open countryside. He was met by the unit's commanding officer, Major William Read. While his squadron was working up to reconnaissance duties in France, he also oversaw the training of men like Caldwell, who was one of 20 crammed into the limited accommodation with the unit's personnel. In all, 55 officers and aircrew in training passed through the squadron before it was deployed across the Channel.[18]

The son of a prominent West Auckland businessman, Wesley Spragg's hopes of becoming a Royal Flying Corps pilot were undone by a series of life threatening accidents.

The most intriguing character to train Caldwell at Sedgeford was the Honourable Eric Fox Pitt Lubbock. Born into a wealthy family — his mother, Alice, was the widow of the 1st Baron of Avebury — the angelic-faced and kind-hearted Lubbock had entered the war in 1914 as a private in the infantry. This was almost unheard of: upper-class men usually became officers. He was an incongruous member of a motor transport section populated by men with working-class backgrounds, manners and language. Initially the non-commissioned officers (NCOs) took delight in ordering him around and assigning him the most demanding and filthy tasks, but he took it in his stride and won them over. Whenever friends from Eton and Oxford visited him they were shocked to find him knee-deep in the mud and muck, wrestling with a stranded lorry alongside his mates.[19]

The intervention of none other than the commander-in-chief of the British Army in France, Sir John French, and the war minister, Lord Kitchener, eventually got Lubbock transferred to the more gentlemanly, but considerably more dangerous, RFC. In 1915 he served as an observer on the Western Front and after shooting down a German machine was awarded the Military Cross before beginning training as a pilot. By the time Caldwell arrived at Sedgeford, Lubbock was a captain and had just acquired his pilot's wings with 45 Squadron.

During Caldwell's training, the squadron hosted a diverse range of aeroplanes, including the Avro 504, Bristol Scout C and D, Martinsyde S.1 and Royal Aircraft Factory BE12.[20] Caldwell's time was largely spent with the Royal Aircraft Factory BE2c, 10 of which had recently arrived. These were a revelation after rickety Longhorns and Shorthorns, and certainly nothing like the home-built aircraft of the Walsh brothers. Both the BE2c and its predecessor, the BE2b, were weapons of war, their robust silhouette familiar to many Kiwis, thanks to the exploits of two pilots with a New Zealand connection.

Born in Yorkshire and of Māori descent through his mother, William Rhodes-Moorehouse was a motorcycle and car enthusiast, an aviation pioneer and a some-time pre-war visitor to New Zealand. He was also an early entrant into the fledgling RFC.[21] On 26 April 1915, he went on a lone sortie in a BE2b against the railway junction at Kortrijk in Belgium. After releasing his 100-pound bomb in a low sweeping attack, Rhodes-Moorehouse plunged into a heavy barrage of small arms and machine-gun fire coming from the local church's belfry and was struck in the thigh. Bleeding

Eric Fox Pitt Lubbock was an undergraduate at Oxford when Britain declared war. Awarded a Military Cross as an air observer, he returned to Britain to train as a pilot in 1916.

profusely, he crossed enemy lines on his homeward flight, only to be struck twice more by enemy fire.

He only just made it home, and though badly wounded refused to be taken to hospital, insisting that he give his report first. He died the following day. The newspapers in New Zealand saw him as one of their own: 'On the outbreak of the war he put his luck and daring at the disposal of Kitchener and Co. and this time had the worst of the gamble, though the Reaper's hook couldn't get him until he made all Flanders sit up and take notice,' wrote the Christchurch *Star*.[22]

Rhodes-Moorehouse, who was awarded a Victoria Cross (VC), the first given to an airman, became an empire-wide hero for his exploits. Local politicians used him to drum up enthusiasm for the war, especially among athletic young men like Caldwell. In October 1915, the New Zealand president of the War League asked sportsmen to follow the lead of a quartet of their famed countrymen in uniform: four-time Wimbledon champion Anthony Wilding, swimmer Bernard Freyberg, rugby player William Hardham and motoring enthusiast William Rhodes-Moorehouse.[23]

In 1916, New Zealander Alfred de Bathe Brandon, a lawyer, was instrumental in destroying a huge German Zeppelin airship, *L15*, which attacked London on the night of 31 March that year.[24] After a long chase, he attacked the behemoth head-on and from above, flying over its 536-foot length as it directed machine gun fire at him. Brandon then dropped explosive darts. Despite the crew's attempts to lighten the load by throwing everything possible overboard, the Zeppelin, already damaged by anti-aircraft fire, plummeted into the sea off the Kent coast. Like Rhodes-Moorehouse, Brandon became a hero in Britain and at home.[25]

It was with some excitement, then, that Caldwell strode out to fly a BE2c. He undertook five short familiarisation flights under dual control, the last under Lubbock's tutelage, before a trouble-free solo on 9 June 1916.[26] Others were less fortunate. Although the BE2c was an inherently stable machine, which made it ideal for training purposes, engine failures, indifferent construction and pilot error were ever-present dangers. A single error of judgement could bring low even the most accomplished airman. One 'expert' pilot, who had allegedly looped a BE2c, came badly unstuck when he attempted to show off to a group of expectant trainees. 'Against the wind the machine arose at once and began to climb steeply, the pilot waved farewell as he passed us by, about fifty feet up.'

The students continued watching, then on the breeze came the sound of an engine spluttering as the BE2c dropped its nose. If the pilot had landed in a field, he would probably only have damaged the undercarriage and wounded his pride. Instead, he made a novice mistake: he turned towards the aerodrome. He lost air speed and altitude rapidly, missing a shed by inches. The aeroplane vanished behind a building with a huge crash. It lay prone on the ground, a tangle of wreckage.

The pilot and passenger were slumped forward, motionless. As the mechanics tried to extricate them, 'there was a flicker of flame from beneath the fuselage [and] with a roar a great flame shot up from the burst petrol tank. It swept back over the passenger; when it reached the pilot he moved uneasily, seemed to shake himself, fumbled with his safety belt, then jumped out just in time, his clothing on fire.' Unholy cries for an extinguisher pierced the air as men appeared with axes to hack through the burning wreckage and free the passenger. It was impossible. The passenger could not be saved. Thirty gallons of burning fuel beat back the rescuers; 'before our very eyes he was burnt to death, roasted. It took a long time; it was ghastly . . .' The next day the commanding officer was brutal and unsympathetic in his assessment: 'A pilot must never turn down wind at a low altitude when faced with the possibility of a forced landing.'[27]

It was remarkable that no one was killed during Caldwell's training at Sedgeford. Some men, however, were seriously injured. Aeroplanes were regularly 'stood on their noses' and undercarriages crushed by inexperienced pilots, and two airmen were forced out of training through injury. One spun his machine out of control on landing, bending it like a pretzel; the other survived a near-fatal crash. Both were hospitalised, and only one would belatedly return to flight training. As Caldwell's mother, from London, told readers of the *Waikato Independent*, 'there are more killed learning to fly than in the war, partly the learner's fault, but largely from the faulty machines . . . Nearly all the aerodromes are short of machines, and the men practise on old ones, some of which are very faulty.'[28]

C aldwell's only real difficulties were a couple of wayward cross-country flights over East Anglia. The ability to fly via maps and local landmarks was an important skill for any airman who hoped to progress to France. On a 'very misty' 10 June, he took off for an extended flight, only to lose his way. He made a forced landing, then asked some locals for directions back to Sedgeford.

In the second week of July, Caldwell once again went astray. After collecting a new Royal Aircraft Factory aeroplane from Thetford aerodrome, he found the monotonous East Anglian countryside disorienting and was forced to land near the small village of Laxfield. A bemused Caldwell discovered he had been heading south-west rather than north. After purchasing fuel, he leapfrogged north-east to Sedgeford via a stopover at Norwich. A simple one-hour flight had taken three hours.[29]

Caldwell discovered, as did other antipodeans, that the locals were sympathetic and helpful. 'On my first day up at Newcastle,' wrote a compatriot, 'I got lost in the mist, so landed in a big field, inquired the way home, swung my own propeller, and ran round and jumped into my seat while about a dozen villagers hung on to the wings and tail of the machine for me.' When he got lost again and landed near a substantial country manor, he 'got a great reception. They couldn't do enough for me, especially when they learnt I was a New Zealander. It is quite amusing the way people at Home look upon the colonies as something wonderful for fighting for the Mother Country.'[30]

Caldwell also learnt something of the duties he might be asked to carry out in France: aerial combat, bombing, artillery observation and photography.[31] The training was rudimentary and not much more than an introduction. 'From the trainees' point of view, instruction in Higher Aviation was a matter of passing a written and practical examination and flying as many trips as he could, during which, if he did not kill or injure himself, he would learn from his own mistakes.'[32] Caldwell collected his 'wings', his rank confirmed on 17 July.

As Caldwell's posting to the Western Front drew near, an intimate gathering convened at his mother's London hotel suite. Mary, Vida and Keith were joined by a smattering of Wanganui Collegiate and King's College old boys, including Geoff Callender. Mary Caldwell and her daughter had been part of a guild making bandages for hospitals, which had been warned to expect large numbers of casualties and were working overtime. The guild was in the thick of preparing parcels for prisoners of war: 'bread, butter, or margarine, cheese, jam, oxo, tea, cocoa, sugar, etc.' As Mary Caldwell explained, 'You chose a prisoner to whom you became a godmother, undertaking to supply him with a parcel every week.' There were 'terrible tales of starvation of our soldiers, while committees actually exist in London to supply luxuries and flowers for our German prisoners'.[33] The two Caldwell women also sent parcels to family friends on the Western Front.

Mary and Vida Caldwell had great stories of their summer adventures at the seaside resort of Broadstairs, Kent. On their first night, they had just gone to bed when they heard guns, and 'the unmistakable noise of some monster in the air . . . Everyone in the hotel collected downstairs at the front door, and presently the searchlights got right on to the monster and we had a splendid view of it, just like a great silver cigar. Then the anti-aircraft guns began to speak, and for a few minutes it was very thrilling.' The pair watched as bombs tumbled from the Zeppelin. The airship began to swerve and dodge as if the British guns were 'getting too near to be comfortable'. Near Ramsgate the Zeppelin quickly ascended and receded from view.

Over the following evening, a blackout was strictly enforced. One night, when Vida 'struck a match to get our bearings in our rooms', a soldier bellowed: 'Put out that light you damn fools.' From above their room a female resident added: 'They're damn fools whoever they are.' The Caldwells snuffed out the match and lay low while the soldier and the woman at the window engaged in loud conversation. Soon an officer was rapping on their hotel door and Mary and Vida explained to the amused gentleman what had in fact happened. 'Alright, I'll tell the Johnny outside that no harm was meant.' Mary discovered that the woman 'who had used such bad language was in ordinary times one of your highly proper, polished ladies of the true English type, which made it all the funnier'.

During the day, women, children and not a few soldiers, many convalescing, thronged the beach. Music wafted from a military band on the pier. As Mary reported, 'A little distance out to sea are numbers of patrol boats, and every now and then a destroyer dashes past kicking up a tremendous spray. Overhead seaplanes are flying out to sea on scouting expeditions, and most afternoons we watch them returning to an aerodrome at Westgate.'[34]

Also at the hotel reunion was Harold Beamish, the son of a Hawke's Bay farmer and a former Collegiate pupil. He had bypassed the Walsh brothers' flying school in favour of direct entry into the RNAS. Established in 1912 alongside the RFC, the RNAS was formed to protect and control Britain's coastal regions and vital sea lanes. Seaplanes and airships were harnessed to work with the Royal Navy, but the greater part of the war's RNAS formations were deployed on the Western Front in reconnaissance, bombing and combat duties. A letter furnished by his uncle, a former Royal Navy doctor, to an admiral swiftly propelled Beamish into RNAS training at Cranwell, which he began just as Caldwell completed his advanced training.[35]

In the latest dog-eared copy of the school magazine, the boys read that James Allen had attended the December prize-giving, at which their names were mentioned. Caldwell and Beamish were two of the 350 old boys now serving 'under the flag'; that was more than 50 per cent of the graduates aged between 20 and 30 years of age. Of these, 32 had died, 'seven are wounded and missing, in many cases with but faint hope of their survival.'[36] There were rumours that James Dennistoun, who had received the Polar Medal for his efforts in supporting Scott's Antarctic expedition, had been brought low in aerial combat on the Western Front.[37]

Later it was revealed that he and his pilot had been shot down on the enemy side of the lines. After numerous operations by German surgeons, he died of his gunshot wounds. Allen, whose son had been killed at Gallipoli, was sympathetic to the school's losses but had a grimly realistic message: 'Many more will have to go, and the roll of honour will be a longer one than is in the School today.'[38]

The war was close now. All too soon Caldwell's orders arrived. He packed his kit, kissed his mother goodbye and abandoned London for France.

CHAPTER SIX

Flaming Onions

C aldwell arrived at Candas in northern France in the third week of July 1916. The once sleepy French provincial village had, like the whole north-west of France, been transformed by the arrival of the British.[1] The Royal Flying Corps' No. 2 Aircraft Depot was a substantial logistics and supply hub. Fields to the north-east of the town were overrun by tents, buildings, hangars and a long sweeping aerodrome.[2] Newly arrived machines were lined up for dispersal along the British sector; others were crawled over by mechanics, riggers and carpenters. Overhead the sky was criss-crossed by arriving and departing aeroplanes. It was a shock to men like Caldwell who had trained in the tranquil English countryside. As one new arrival wrote:

> Not a man to be seen. Women, boys and old men are doing all the work in the towns and the fields. All the carts are driven by women, and nine-tenths of the women are in black. I certainly never realised there was a war on in England. No one does. You can't help it out here. Everything is khaki or blue. Every town is full of British soldiers either resting or doing work behind the lines. Hospital cars, transport and staff cars crowd the dusty roads.[3]

Now an airman with wings on his jacket and a pilot's logbook tucked in a pocket, Caldwell was about to put his character and skill to their sternest test.

The Allied plans for 1916 called for a major French attack, with British support, in Picardy, northern France, near the upper reaches of the Somme river. Although previous offensives had demonstrated that the entrenchments, barbed wire, machine guns and artillery barrages delivered horrendous numbers of corpses and mutilated men for little territorial gain, it was still hoped that, given sufficient force and effort, the impasse between the Central Powers and the Allies could be broken. The assault was to be launched in July, but in February a surprise German attack at Verdun forced the French to withdraw the divisions it had selected for its offensive, leaving the British as the principal force on the Somme.

Given the depleted forces at his disposal, British Expeditionary Force (BEF) commander General Douglas Haig was compelled to limit the objectives of the battle to relieving pressure on the French at Verdun and inflicting as many enemy casualties as possible. To do so, the British funnelled vast numbers of men, materiel and air power into their northern quarter of the Western Front.

Brigadier Hugh Trenchard oversaw the RFC's accumulation of resources. When the BEF had left for France in 1914, it was with only four air squadrons and little more than 1000 officers and men. By the time Trenchard's build-up was completed in 1916, the RFC had 64 operational and 33 reserve squadrons and over 46,000 personnel.

The main tactical unit at Trenchard's disposal was the squadron. By 1916, an 18-machine-strong squadron was populated by between 100 and 200 aircrew and supporting personnel. Pilots, observers, mechanics, fitters, riggers, carpenters, cooks, orderlies and clerks all played a part in its efficient functioning. Several squadrons were organised into wings, and a pair of wings into a brigade. Each of the five armies of the BEF was allotted a single brigade, consisting of a Corps Wing and an Army Wing. The Corps Wing squadrons undertook support work with the ground forces, including reconnaissance, contact patrols, artillery cooperation and localised bombing operations, while the Army Wing squadrons carried out offensive patrols and protected the corps units as required.[4]

In preparation for the assault, Trenchard gave his corps units six tasks in descending order of priority: aerial reconnaissance, aerial photography, observation and direction of artillery, tactical bombing, contact patrols and offensive sorties against German intruders. His 167 machines on the Somme outnumbered the Germans' 129 and, significantly, included more fighters.

On 1 July 1916, after seven days of artillery bombardment during which over a million shells were lobbed at the Germans, the British infantry left their trenches and advanced on the German line. Far from incapacitating the enemy, the artillery had forewarned the Germans, who hastily reinforced their position. As the British advanced, the enemy emerged from the safety of their deep trenches. The result was the most costly day in British military history — over 60,000 casualties. In total the combined losses would be one million over the next four months.

On 29 July, as news of the early heavy losses reached Candas, Caldwell was posted to a frontline BE2 artillery cooperation and bombing unit, 8 Squadron, at Bellevue. With other officers, he was loaded into a weathered and dust-caked RFC lorry for a long and bumpy drive that unceremoniously dumped bone-sore men at their units along the way. Unlike bustling Candas, Bellevue was an intimate aerodrome occupied by a single squadron. Caldwell was initially housed in the village. For many airmen, the living conditions in provincial France could be challenging. New Zealand pilot Clive Collett was billeted in a farmhouse near his aerodrome. 'The people are very kindhearted but don't know what a bath is and all seem to live in one room. Perhaps this is owing to the way they are crowded with refugees from the districts occupied by the enemy, but still it does not explain why donkeys and fowls should be allowed to share the same roof,' he wrote in a letter to his brother.[5]

Airmen looked forward to moving onto the aerodrome, even if this meant, as it did for Caldwell, relocating to a tent pitched beneath the swaying branches of a local farmer's orchard. It was an idyllic setting and the '1916 summer was a lovely one'.[6] It was difficult to believe that he was only 6 miles from the Somme.

Caldwell stowed his kit, placed his few possessions next to his bed and met his batman. Most batmen acted as orderlies or butlers, polishing boots, making beds, procuring cups of tea and packets of cigarettes. Many were elderly men, who enjoyed their plum positions away from the squalor and terror of the trenches. The tents contained a collection of English, Welsh, Scottish and Irish officers with the odd colonial like Caldwell thrown into the mix. He was surprised to find that his tent brushed shoulders with that of one of the RFC's most recognised celebrities, the pioneering fighter pilot Albert Ball.

I n 1916 aerial combat was still in its infancy, but Ball was one of its leading exponents. The role of aviation in reconnaissance and bombing was well appreciated, but not until the war was serious thought given to defending or even attacking other machines in air-to-air combat. Early practitioners had taken rifles up with them, while some wishful theorists advocated flying above an airborne enemy machine and dropping bombs on it. Neither idea proved practical in the unstable, light biplanes.

By 1915 more powerful engines meant aeroplanes could carry machine guns. An observer in a two-seat machine could now swing the weapon around on an enemy and open fire. Then, in mid-1915, the Germans introduced the Fokker Eindecker, a monoplane fitted with a synchronised machine gun that fired through the arch of its spinning propeller, making it the first true point-and-shoot fighter. In skilled hands, the Eindecker was a terrifying wunder flugzeug, a wonder plane.

Ball, who was part of the fight back against the Fokkers, arrived on the Western Front at the same time as newer Allied machines, including the French-designed Nieuport 11. This fighter — or scout, as such British armed light single-seat aeroplanes were routinely called — had a machine gun mounted on the upper wing that fired over the top of the propeller. In his former unit, 11 Squadron, the Englishman had achieved six victories over enemy machines, including a Fokker Eindecker.

It was heady stuff, made more fascinating by the fact that Ball had been 'demoted' to a corps cooperation squadron. 'We understood that "Bum and Eye Glass" Higgins had sent him to us to quieten him down,' Caldwell later explained, as 'he had been getting a bit difficult.'[7] (General John Higgins, commander of III Brigade, had been shot in the backside in South Africa and wore a monocle.) Higgins also probably realised Ball was depressed and fatigued from his extended work in aerial combat. He was certainly downcast about leaving his enemy-hunting unit and his famous vegetable garden. An avid gardener, he regularly wrote home for more seeds and plants.[8] At Savy he had built a greenhouse and cultivated the land behind his homemade hut.

Soon after joining 8 Squadron, Ball volunteered to deliver a spy behind enemy lines. The day before Caldwell arrived, Ball had been joined in his BE2 by the undercover agent simply known as 'Monsieur Victor'. They took off into the gathering mist over Bellevue at 8.15 p.m.

Ball had evaded three German fighters and anti-aircraft fire as he flew deep into enemy territory. A few seconds later, three Fokkers appeared. As Ball noted, 'We had no guns, for the machine could not carry his luggage etc and guns, so we had to dodge the beasts. At last it was so dark they could not see us, so they went down. The "Archie" guns started, also rockets were sent up to try and set us on fire. Oh it was nice! I really did think the end had come.'[9] Ball located a desolate field and landed, but when a timorous 'Victor' refused to disembark, he was forced to find another

Until his death in 1917, Albert Ball was the Royal Flying Corps' highest-scoring ace. He was Keith Caldwell's inspiration and neighbour during his brief sojourn with 8 Squadron.

more solitary landing spot more suited to his passenger's liking, but it was no use. After several further failures, Ball returned to Bellevue, where he landed at 10 p.m. Despite the spy's unwillingness to cooperate, Ball was praised by Higgins and Hugh Trenchard.[10]

On other occasions, Caldwell noted Ball's aeroplane being loaded with baskets of pigeons and writing paraphernalia and cases of automatic pistols and ammunition — supplies for agents already engaged in espionage.[11] Little wonder that, in Caldwell's words, Ball 'was a hero to us'. During Ball's brief stay with the squadron, Caldwell spent many evenings sitting with others outside his tent, listening to Ball's stories and music from his gramophone.

C aldwell's commanding officer was Major Patrick 'Pip' Playfair, one of the RFC's founders. A sharp-featured, steely-eyed Scotsman, in 1912 Playfair had gone on his first joyride with aviation pioneer Geoffrey de Havilland.[12] He attributed his decision to attach himself to the fledgling air service to his propensity for hard work and fiscal frugality — the RFC demanded more in peacetime than the artillery and paid more.[13] A scar near his left eye was a souvenir of a close call during flight training, when his machine had gone into a vertical dive and embedded itself in a field. At 27, he was considered an old hand with strong connections to all the senior RFC officers. The Bellevue unit was his first operational command.[14]

The squadron was divided into three flights, A, B and C, each with six machines. Caldwell was in the flight of Captain Percy Ross-Hume, who had been with the squadron since February. The New Zealander found him a 'rather severe lean serious man and I think he regarded me as the "wild colonial boy"'.[15] Ross-Hume had scraped through 8 Squadron's heavy losses earlier in the year and was determined to give his charges the best possible introduction to war. Caldwell had a lot to learn, and his flight commander set about informing him of the squadron's responsibilities and the role he would play.[16]

Initially, 8 Squadron had concentrated on reconnaissance operations, photographic sorties and contact patrols, which involved staying in visual contact with the advancing (or retreating) British infantry and reporting back to the local

The greatest threat to Allied airmen in 1916 was the point-and-shoot Fokker Eindecker. Its synchronisation gear allowed the pilot to fire through the arch of the propeller — a revolution in air-to-air combat. With its arrival, the 'Fokker scourge' commenced.

headquarters.[17] In this way, senior commanders were continually aware of the ebb and flow of a battle. As Playfair explained, aeroplanes with distinctive markings would

> fly low making the signal 'where are you?' Mostly by means of repeating a succession of A's on a klaxon horn. The Infantry's reply was to light flares, and some of them carried metal mirrors, the flash of which it was hoped would resemble a heliograph. Battalion and Brigade Headquarters had special signalling lamps and cumbersome panels, often consisting of six or eight laths which could be used to spell out messages (they were painted white on one side) being moved by means of tapes. It was said that these messages could be read as high up as six thousand feet.[18]

It could be dangerous work. 'For some reason or other,' in a preparatory operation, 'the red flares, which were to have guided us failed to materialise, which meant that our aircraft had to fly very low to identify our troops by the colour of their uniforms' — the Tommies in khaki and the Germans in field grey. Fortunately, the rifle and machine-gun fire was wide of the mark, but one machine ran into a balloon, hitting and sliding down its tethered cable like a bow on the strings of a violin.[19] The men miraculously emerged unscathed.

As part of the British Third Army's III Brigade, 13 Wing, 8 Squadron was on the left flank of the main July assault. Its early contact work was soon overtaken by bombing sorties and artillery cooperation, accomplished in the BE2c and its newer sibling, the BE2d. (Other than dual control and a modified fuel system, the BE2d was almost indistinguishable in appearance and capabilities from its predecessor.)

These aircraft were slow, ideal as trainers or, at a pinch, for home defence duties, but were now outmatched by almost all the enemy's aeroplanes in France. Still, the BE2 was stable and reliable and airmen found it generally forgiving in flight.[20] On artillery cooperation sorties, Caldwell flew with an observer, but on bombing missions he flew solo, since his machine could not carry both bombs *and* an observer.

On 1 August, there was an early morning test flight at Bellevue and by mid-morning men were engaged in artillery work. At lunch, Caldwell watched Ross-Hume take off at the head of a bombing mission and he counted the five-strong flight in when they returned two hours later. By 7 p.m., the squadron had flown just over 30 sorties, more than half of them operational.[21]

Percy Ross-Hume decided that the relative calm of the early evening was perfect for sending Caldwell up on his first limited flight over France — 30 minutes with two practice landings.[22] It was a familiarisation jaunt, enabling Caldwell to renew his acquaintance with the BE2 and get his bearings on the aerodrome and its environs, so different from East Anglia. It was a glorious sight, the sun setting over the French coast, the farm, tents, huts and hangars clustered near the orchard and the landing-ground pointing east over rolling fields to the smoke and thunder of the trenches.

With this and two more aerodrome flights — a 10-minute excursion and a 35-minute bomb sighting and map-reading exercise — under his belt, Caldwell, who had fewer than 30 flying hours in his logbook, was told he would be part of a bombing raid on 4 August.[23] As one incredulous airman scrawled at the bottom of his logbook that showed only 22 hours' flying time: 'Am now supposed to be a *pilot*.'[24] Such low pre-combat flying hours were a significant factor in the high mortality rate among airmen.

Caldwell's arrival on the Western Front coincided with the appearance of growing numbers of French Nieuports as well as the Airco DH2 and Royal Aircraft Factory FE2 pusher biplanes. These machines, operating with III Brigade's Army Corps squadrons, would provide defensive cover for many of Caldwell's subsequent operations. As he explained to his family, 'Generally, five bombing machines, accompanied by three protectors or flying scouts [fighters] took part.'[25] This meant that, though the Fokkers were still a real danger to a single unprotected BE2, the threat was diminished.

The greatest danger to Caldwell lay in enemy anti-aircraft fire. The enemy called it 'flak' after the German word fliegerabwehrkanone, meaning aircraft defence cannon, but most British aircrew simply knew it as Archie, a slang abbreviation from a comic song, 'Archibald! Certainly Not', made famous by George Robey.

German flak came in various guises but most commonly as shrapnel or high explosives with fuses set for various altitudes. 'The shrapnel bullets each left a thin line of smoke,' wrote future Victoria Cross recipient James McCudden, 'so that as each shell burst the shrapnel came from each burst in the shape of a fan. These shrapnel shells did not burst very loudly but they had a most effective radius.'[26] They were seldom terminal to an aeroplane — the timber and fabric biplanes could sustain multiple punctures and tears — but could seriously injure the crew.

High-explosive shells were of a completely different order. The violence of a direct or near-direct explosion could reduce an aeroplane and its crew to a dirty smear across the sky. The sudden release of energy at supersonic speed from such a shell meant that even an explosion in the vicinity could displace a tremendous amount of air, tossing a biplane and its startled aircrew about.

Other anti-aircraft guns made up for their smaller calibre ammunition by firing in bursts, sometimes accompanied by bright tracer fire designed to help the gunner find the target, which to all the world looked like a string of flaming onions. The fabric skin of the biplane, covered with highly flammable nitrocellulose dope, was particularly susceptible. Being set alight at altitude was the greatest of all fears. Empire airmen were not issued with parachutes, and to avoid slow incineration, which could be fatal or cause severe burns, they could only shoot themselves or jump to their deaths.

Playfair recorded the fate of a pilot named Watkins, who was 'very badly burned indeed' when his plane went down in flames. 'He told me that the machine had flared up and that the fabric had been burnt off one wing and part of the tail plane and the fire had gone out. The machine went down out of control and crashed in No-Man's Land, whence Lieut. Watkins was rescued by the infantry.'[27] To avoid such a fate, Caldwell was told to zigzag and quickly change his altitude when under fire, to thwart the German strategy of using bracketing shots below and above an aeroplane in order to place the fatal middle shot. Such advice did not prevent flak accounting for nearly a quarter of all RFC losses in 1916.[28]

The assault on 4 August was a combined operation. Caldwell's five-strong flight would be accompanied by a formation from a neighbouring squadron, protected by an escort. Their target: German positions at Croisilles, 8 miles south of Arras.[29] In the afternoon, Caldwell strode out onto the aerodrome to inspect his machine. He walked the aeroplane, running his hands along the wires, checking them for tension and condition, all the while hunting for faults in the tightly stretched fabric. Mechanics made their final touches to the machine, armourers attached the two 112-pound bombs beneath the wings, and Caldwell — arrayed in his flying boots, long leather overcoat, goggles and gauntlets — lowered himself into the cockpit. He strapped himself into his harness and began the BE2 starting procedure.

His eyes flicked over the instruments as he opened the fuel cock, partially opened the throttle for choking and confirmed the ignition was off. He told the starter mechanic that he was ready.[30] Both men acknowledged that the ignition was off, and Caldwell opened the choke ring as the mechanic pulled the propeller around. They heard the wet sucking sound of fuel reaching the carburettor.

Keith Caldwell joined 8 Squadron as a freshly trained 21-year-old at a time when the life expectancy of a novice Royal Flying Corps was often counted in days.

All was primed and ready. The mechanic called 'Throttle set' and then 'Contact'. Caldwell adjusted the throttle to a quarter of an inch, turned the ignition on and called 'Contact'. The mechanic swung the propeller and the Royal Aircraft Factory 1a V8 engine came alive — a handful of cylinders bursting into life and the rest following in quick succession. The wake from the spinning four-bladed propeller bathed Caldwell in thick smoke as the excess fuel was burnt off. The tappets standing proud of the engine cowling jumped lazily. He let the engine run, finding its temperature, before waving off the chocks.

The ground crew stepped back, and Caldwell gently opened the throttle, mindful of the load he placed on the gears driving the camshaft. The aerodrome was hard, and the aeroplane's wooden tail-skid ran easily over the dry grass as he taxied into position. He took off into the wind at maximum throttle, the tappets now bouncing rapidly, flicking up oil. The machine climbed slowly upwards. It was 4.50 p.m. and he was the trailing aeroplane in the loose formation.

The pasture and crops of Bellevue gave way to a lattice of rear trenches, forward British positions, then no man's land and then, finally, the German lines slipped beneath the BE2d. The outward flight was surprisingly uneventful but laden with apprehension. 'There are times in life,' wrote one airman of his first 1916 sortie, 'when the faculties seem to be keyed to superhuman tension.'

> You are not necessarily doing anything; but you are in a state of awareness, of tremendous alertness, ready to act instantaneously should the need arise. Outwardly, that day I was calm . . . but inside my heart was pounding and my nerves straining, waiting for something, I did not know what, to happen. It was my first job. I was under fire for the first time. Would Archies get the range? Would the dreaded Fokker appear? Would the engine give out? It was the fear of the unforeseen, the inescapable, the imminent death which might, from moment to moment, be ruthlessly laid upon me.[31]

Caldwell arrived over the target at a height of 7000 feet, and, in unison with the flock of BE2s, dropped his bombs. Fires broke out in Croisilles below them as the pilots dipped their wings and turned for home.[32]

Returning from an objective was often the most challenging phase of an operation: the flight struck a strong headwind and the struggling BE2s were tempting targets. The Germans opened up with anti-aircraft fire. 'Many of the shots coming in very close and it was rather upsetting,' Caldwell later told his mother.[33]

Eventually, the white puffs of gunfire receded and after his inaugural two-hour mission he circled Bellevue.

Caldwell throttled back the engine, the tappets slowed and the aeroplane shed altitude. It floated above the grass, then touched down, bouncing gently along the aerodrome. He taxied in. The mechanics assessed the rhythm of the engine and skimmed their eyes over the airframe as the BE2d came to a halt. Caldwell set the throttle to idle and switched the ignition off. He pushed up his oil-splattered goggles and, drained but elated, sat for a few minutes in the cockpit.

By the second week of the month, Caldwell was happily ensconced in the squadron and had been on several bombing expeditions, including a strike on Boyelles railway station and a munitions dump with Albert Ball and several others.[34] Then, on 13 August, Caldwell reported that he took part in a 'most exciting' operation against a secret and 'important objective', the Douai aerodrome, 20 miles behind the German lines, to which the enemy was transferring increasing numbers of aeroplanes.

The low clouds that had been hindering operations from Bellevue lifted in the late afternoon. Ross-Hume was guiding the flight of seven to the target. Two earlier forays by 11 and 23 squadrons had preceded 8 Squadron's assault, and he knew that they would be met by fully alert German spotters and anti-aircraft fire. The preceding efforts had delivered light 20-pound bombs but now, in the late afternoon, Caldwell and his co-workers were loaded with 112-pound bombs. The BE2s appeared over Douai at 6.40 p.m.

'The Huns must have known we were coming, as they put up a tremendous fire on us all over the place,' Caldwell wrote later. 'The place was alive with "Archies" and flaming "Onions" . . . tearing round in the middle and all round us in great style. I don't know how they missed getting some of us. They put up a tremendous barrage of fire on the home side of the objective. However, we all got back safely, and I think we were darned lucky.'[35]

On the edge of the formation on the return flight, Caldwell was awash with adrenaline and in the mood to celebrate. He and the Rhodesian pilot flying just off his wing did a 'couple of loops' over the enemy lines to show the Germans in the trenches there were no 'ill-feelings'. Doubtless, the air and ground crew at Douai were less convinced. The aerodrome was pockmarked with holes. Some bombs had fallen alarmingly close to the hangars and personnel were still recovering from the terror of being bombed three times in a single day.[36]

CHAPTER SEVEN

Maniacs

In the First World War, artillery was the king of the battlefield. With the capacity to churn up large amounts of ground and wound and kill people over great distances, the opposing big guns often dictated the planning, course and execution of campaigns. Caldwell's work was dominated by artillery patrols or 'artillery shoots', directing the oversized guns onto targets that were out of sight for the crews operating them. It was a two-man job, and on these operations Caldwell flew with a number of different squadron observers.

The task was demanding and repetitive for both pilot and observer, requiring considerable concentration and technical aptitude in a cockpit stuffed full of maps, binoculars and a small one-way wireless for Morse code. With these tools, the two-man BE2 crews were responsible for ranging their own artillery in on enemy trenches, fortifications and, increasingly, German artillery.

For the most part, the patrols did not cross the enemy lines, making interception by German fighters unlikely, but if the Fokkers did appear, Caldwell had a modicum of defensive firepower. On artillery patrols, the BE2 observer sat forward of the pilot, wedged between the upper and lower wings in a forest of spars and rigging, limiting the use of the Lewis machine gun. Firing forward would shred the propeller, and careless rear-directed fire risked damaging the tail section.[1] (Later two-seat machines placed the observer behind the pilot, giving the Lewis a much-improved arc of fire.) Some

BE2s were fitted with a second machine gun for the pilot to operate.[2] Flak remained a constant menace, as did British artillery shells bound for enemy positions.

Much of the artillery consisted of standard large-calibre guns augmented by heavy howitzers. The guns were manoeuvred around the battlefield by horses, but the howitzers often had to be dismantled before being relocated by a traction engine. The standard British field gun, the 18-pounder, fired its shell in a flat arch over 3 miles, but the 15-inch British howitzer lobbed its massive 1450-pound shell tennis-style over 6 miles. Launched at great speed, over 1100 feet per second, the howitzer shell slowed as it reached the apex of its flight, then hovered momentarily before falling on its target.[3] Airmen who strayed into the path of shells risked being thrown about wildly.[4]

During August, Caldwell flew on 29 occasions, half of which were 'arty' patrols. These flights, including testing and practice jaunts, were punctuated by days of heavy demand. On 16 August, for example, he flew five times: a one-hour 26-minute artillery patrol, a 55-minute artillery patrol and three infantry cooperation and signalling practice flights encompassing 32 minutes.[5] By the end of August, he had added nearly 50 hours to his logbook. In one month, he acquired nearly twice as many flying hours as in the previous nine months. Increasingly, the artillery cooperation sorties began to dominate the squadron's activities.

Some men loved the artillery cooperation operations. 'It was wonderfully exciting and interesting,' wrote one pilot. 'Nothing can give a more solid feeling of satisfaction than when, after seeing the shells from the battery you are directing fall closer and closer to the target, you finally see a great explosion in a German gunpit and with a clear conscience can signal, "OK!"'[6] Others, including Caldwell, thought them repetitive and grim. The monotonous long oval loops stretching from the British guns to distant targets could last a mind-numbing three hours. 'You have to pilot the machine, watch the target for bursts and work the wireless, all at the same time while "Archie" is probably at work also.'[7]

There were, however, considerable consolations to being in the RFC. The Somme push of July and the subsequent smaller battles — Delville Wood, Longueval, Trônes Wood, Ovillers, High Wood and Pozières — had gained the initial lines of enemy trenches but were always met by German reinforcement and counter-assaults. Blasted earth, defoliated and splintered trees and fouled waterways were fertilised by the corpses of Allied soldiers. In the heat of summer, the stench from bloated bodies was unimaginable.[8]

The squalor and terror of the Somme convinced many army officers — without any first-hand knowledge of the dangers the airmen faced but looking enviously at what seemed to be their oases of peace and civility, safely tucked behind the rearmost trenches — to apply for the RFC. By 1916 it was the most oversubscribed service in the British military. One infantryman, facing filthy trenches and an infestation of lice, 'used to look up with great envy at these aircraft flying round about, [and so] immediately put in an application to join the Royal Flying Corps'.[9]

The aerodromes certainly offered welcome respite from the relentless sorties that frayed the nerves of even the staunchest of airmen. On a hot day, 8 Squadron aircrew relaxed under canvas and only when the wind blew the wrong way did the sound of distant guns compete with their gramophones.[10] Bellevue was not perfect, however. 'Terribly hot here, much worse than Auckland,' Caldwell wrote to his family, 'but nights are cooler. We have an absolute gift in Lieutenant [David] Burt, who used to play the violin in Madame Melba's Company. He plays rippingly everything under the sun. The Squadron had a cricket match yesterday against the men, and we play an infantry team tomorrow. Wish I was in Cambridge [New Zealand] for a "rest" cure.'[11]

To break the tedium on quiet days there was always Amiens, barely 25 miles from Bellevue.[12] On Wednesdays, operations permitting, the men stripped off and washed in an open-air bath — a luxury item uplifted from an unguarded hotel. Mid-afternoon, they jammed into a Crossley Tender, the light truck used by the RFC to carry personnel, and bounced their way along dusty roads hemmed with red poppies and yellow mustard flowers.[13] They routinely booked a bistro table for dinner before dispersing across the city to see the sights and shop for themselves and the mess. They could stroll along the canal and the Somme river; even skirted with wartime sandbags, the cathedral was an imposing guardian.

Despite the host of refugees and uniformed men, 'you could buy almost anything you wanted in this town,' wrote Robin Rowell, from the unit. 'Where some of the things came from, heaven only knew. You might easily have forgotten that France was at war, and within twenty miles at that.'[14] Tobacco, clothing, toiletries and boots could be purchased from the pretty little stores. Madame Carpentier and her daughter ran one of the bookshops that supplied the airmen with pencils with which to scrawl in their logbooks and diaries, postcards and writing paper and perhaps the latest edition of the mildly risqué weekly *La Vie Parisienne*, with its pictures of scantily clad women.[15]

Many officers frequented the often-crowded Hôtel de Rheims, where the food was good but 'so was the bill for the proprietor'. Aviators like Caldwell searched out hidden gastronomical treasures. One of these was Aux Huîtres, a diminutive fish and oyster shop with a spiral staircase at the back that led to an 18-person restaurant frequented by locals and French officers. 'Once seated it was a matter of getting on with the job. Everything is done double-quick time by [the proprietor] Jeanne, who talks nineteen to the dozen.' The food was cheap and delicious. Their favourite dessert was a crêpe, dusted with powdered sugar, doused with rum, then set alight.[16]

After one particularly tedious sortie of repetitive artillery circuits, Caldwell peppered the German trenches with a drum or two from the observer's Lewis machine gun.[17] On 16 August, as he and observer Wilfred Corbishley were returning from an artillery patrol, Caldwell decided to loop his machine. The Englishman was a 'loop virgin' and Caldwell had never attempted it with a passenger. At 4000 feet over Doullens, west of Bellevue, he pushed the controls forward to gain speed, then pulled the joystick back towards his belly. The BE2's nose lifted, but not as well as Caldwell anticipated — his heavy observer was too much for the 90 horsepower engine — and they stalled, upside down. They looked down at the orange tiles of Doullens' houses and shops, and the great spike of the town's distinctive belfry, awaiting their impalement. At that moment the Lewis gun slipped its mounting and smashed into a wing, ripping the fabric. It was wedged precariously between the wing's broken ribs.

Caldwell regained control of the machine low over Doullens before striking for home. 'I tried to get Corbishley to climb out to retrieve the gun but he was large and a bit windy and would not budge,' recalled Caldwell. 'When we landed, I taxied to the furthest hangar from ours, got the flight sergeant to come down and fix the repairs, and thus my commander, Ross-Hume, of whom I was scared, never got to know.' Strangely enough, Corbishley 'was not perturbed by the loop (he thought it was quite normal)'.[18]

Caldwell also tried his hand at the dangerous business of balloon busting. To assist aircraft in artillery observation work, both the Allied and Central Powers used tethered balloons connected to artillery batteries by long telephone cables. Filled with hydrogen gas, the balloons and their two-man crews made tempting but difficult targets, given that they were surrounded by palisades of anti-aircraft guns and small arms. If an enemy machine threatened to attack a balloon, the crew would parachute from the basket while strong winches hauled the balloon down as it was defended by a withering storm of bursting shells and bullets.[19] Many RFC pilots reckoned the balloons were more dangerous than the Fokkers. Only Albert Ball could claim to have shot one down and that was with his old unit, when flying a nimble single-seat fighter.

In the third week of August, as they were returning from a two-hour bombing sortie, Caldwell's observer, Charles Clayton, spotted a lone balloon and Caldwell turned towards the target. Clayton cocked the Lewis machine gun as the BE2 began its dive.[20] It was an abortive attack: the Germans were too quick and the balloon was pulled to earth before he could do any damage. In that same week he had his first significant encounter with the enemy in the air. This was a relatively rare event, given the Germans' reluctance to engage in direct combat. As Caldwell observed in a letter home, 'We have complete command of the air, and are continually flying over the German lines, while not a single machine of theirs ever ventures near our lines.'[21]

The Germans, cautious in the extreme, attacked only when the odds were strongly in their favour, behind their own lines and against lone and valuable intruders. On 24 August, while on a routine artillery patrol, Caldwell and observer Norman Harris were flying at 7000 feet, 8 miles behind the German lines, when a trio of Fokkers spotted their BE2 and moved in.[22] Harris turned the Lewis on the German monoplanes, spraying machine-gun bullets while Caldwell manoeuvred the BE2 around to present a smaller silhouette. Harris let off a string of rounds and the enemy retreated, turning away at speed.[23] It was the New Zealander's first attack on an enemy machine.

E arly in the evening of 18 September, Caldwell went up on a joy ride, spotting artillery flashes with one of his favourite observers, Patrick Welchman MC, whom Caldwell described as 'a keen chap' who 'wanted to win the war, even in a BE2c'.[24] Caldwell's only reservation was that Welchman was *too* keen, undertaking low-level flights that attracted disconcerting and prolific small-arms fire. The New Zealander believed 'there was no future' in allowing frustrated German infantry to pelt away at them for very little gain. He did, however, favour another crack at balloon busting or locating an enemy machine to 'have a scrap'.[25]

One and a half hours into the sortie they broke for the enemy lines and a spot of troublemaking, but there were no balloons and no German aircraft in the darkening sky. Eight miles over enemy-held territory, Caldwell pushed the rudder over to return to Bellevue, when the sound of a 'machine gun firing like the blazes' cut through the

German observation balloons were extremely dangerous targets for Allied airmen. A small number of pilots revelled in taking them down, but most dreaded the intense fire from defensive anti-aircraft guns and small arms.

noise of the engine. They had been jumped by a pair of German two-seater fighters. The LFG Roland CII, nicknamed the Walfisch (whale) for its shape, was a formidable opponent and, by Albert Ball's estimation, the best German machine of 1916.

There was no outrunning the Walfisch and so, with his heart racing, Caldwell turned and closed to 100 yards, right into the teeth of the Roland's fire. Welchman fired the Lewis, but had only got 10 shots off when the 'gun jammed and stopped firing'. Suddenly the second Roland opened up on the trapped RFC machine, its gunfire bright in the descending gloom.

Desperate, Caldwell used one of the few advantages at his disposal — the excellent turning capabilities of the BE2 — and put the machine into a vertical turn, 'trying to minimise us as a target and make the turn as tight as possible'. He and Welchman were now horizontal, parallel with the earth 4000 feet below; the observer, tethered to the cockpit by his security belt, hung on for dear life. As the first Roland climbed about 100 feet above the BE2 and came down on it from behind, Welchman 'quickly got the Lewis off its front lug, undid his belt, put it on the inter-seat lug, knelt on his seat and then started popping off above my head at the Hun behind us. Dusk was starting to set in and Welchman was a dark chap, and all I can remember was seeing his rows of teeth and the determined strain lines down his neck as he was shooting.'[26]

The two machines were now only 30 yards apart, the set jawlines of the German airmen visible beneath their goggles. Welchman let off 40 bullets, the tracer fire a luminous trail arching towards the enemy. The rounds were banging into the German aeroplane and Welchman's drum was almost spent when he let out a shout of joy. The Walfisch had been harpooned and entered a vertical dive, thick ribbons of smoke marking its death plunge towards a village below.

As Caldwell and Welchman 'cheered like maniacs' and started to follow 'to make sure that he crashed properly', the other fighter 'crashed past us firing all the time, and we turned after him, firing with our front gun again. We fired 20 shots, and then he cleared out, and we never saw him again.' After losing their way, following 'the scrap', they took an hour to get back to Bellevue. 'They "Archied" us like anything, and sent up flaming rockets to set us alight, but we kept clear of these.'[27]

Caldwell and Welchman were euphoric and their commanding officer was thrilled: it was the squadron's first aerial combat victory.[28] But despite this success the

Flying his BE2c, Keith Caldwell and his observer Patrick Welchman shot down their first enemy machine in September 1916 — 8 Squadron's first victory in aerial combat.

BE2s of Caldwell's squadron were quickly slipping into obsolescence and he found it difficult to replicate his initial triumph, even against the more staid machines still lingering in the German inventory.

Among the artillery and reconnaissance sorties of September, October and early November he had the odd engagement with the enemy that emphasised the changing fortunes and increasing frustrations of the British airmen. On 26 September, Caldwell and Welchman were 6000 feet over German-held territory when they spotted what they thought was a pair of two-seater British machines. German bullets whizzing through the centre-section struts of the BE2 soon told them they were wrong. Welchman's attempts at reprisals were thwarted by a series of machine-gun jams.

Fortunately, it was a hit-and-run strike and the Germans fled east. When a trio of German reconnaissance biplanes appeared below them, they dived, only to have the Lewis jam again almost immediately, probably due to variability of ammunition, with only three-quarters of a drum expended. Caldwell's attempts to use a lumbering, ill-equipped BE2 against the German reconnaissance machines were admirable but ultimately futile.[29]

As the Somme Offensive wound down and winter advanced, the frequency of operations fell away. Caldwell's logbook became increasingly filled with mundane, short test flights and he hungered for a transfer out of the Corps Wing and into an Army Wing single-seat fighter. He had paid his dues with 8 Squadron, having flown on nearly 100 occasions over three months, two-thirds of them operational sorties, and racking up 125 hours of flying time with over half a dozen different observers.[30]

He pestered Playfair, who had been elevated to leading 13 Wing, and the squadron's new commander, Major Ernest Gossage, for a transfer.[31] Caldwell had set his heart on following Ball — who, posted to Home Establishment in England, was agitating on his behalf — to find a place in one of the few squadrons equipped with fighters capable of mixing it with the new German aeroplanes, including the fearsome Albatros models. Eventually his superiors acquiesced, 'to have some peace probably'.[32] In the second week of November Caldwell left for No. 1 Aircraft Depot at St Omer, south-east of Calais, for intensive instruction on how 'to fly scouts'.[33] His series of flights in single-seat Bristol Scouts and Morane-Saulnier parasols and biplane fighters were, however, soon interrupted by the news of his posting to 60 Squadron.

By the end of 1916, although the British and French had made their greatest advance on the enemy since the Battle of the Marne in 1914, the 6-mile territorial gain seemed a dismal return on the loss of over a million Allied and Central Power men. That several of Haig's objectives remained in German hands further weakened claims of British success. Despite this, the RFC had come of age above the Somme valley. Air power was now a vital instrument of war: reconnaissance sorties furnished generals with valuable intelligence; photographic missions produced images of unparalleled battlefield detail; contact flights informed headquarters of the infantry's progress; artillery cooperation guided shells to their targets; bombers struck railways and aerodromes; and offensive patrols harassed enemy machines. But it could not last. For the RFC and Caldwell, the balance of the air war was about to change.

Within 24 hours of Caldwell's first success back in September, another airman had secured his first official victory: the arrival of the Prussian pilot Manfred von Richthofen announced a slow alteration in the fortunes of the Allied airmen and a supplanting of the earlier German aces and their Fokker Eindeckers by a new breed of pilot and the next iteration of German aeroplanes. Men like von Richthofen, Ernest Udet, Josef Jacobs and Werner Voss all arrived on the Western Front in 1916, and after September they increasingly had the benefit of new, markedly superior flying machines.[34]

Fitted with powerful 220 horsepower engines, many of the new German two-seaters could fly above the British fighters unmolested, while an excellent power–weight ratio gave them a distinct performance advantage. Foremost among the fighters was a handful of new Albatros models, the DI and DII. With pointed snouts and sleek fuselages sweeping back to large tail fins, they were shark-like predators. Their twin forward-firing machine guns and speed made them deadly foes: the RFC lost 80 airmen in August 1916 and 142 in September.[35]

The decline in the intensity of operations in October and November hid the true extent of the swing towards the Germans, but Trenchard, the astute commander of the RFC, was under no illusions and communicated his concerns to Haig, who in turn wrote bluntly to the Army Council on 30 September. After 'extraordinary efforts to increase the number and develop the speed and power of his fighting machines, [the enemy] has unfortunately succeeded . . . Within the last few days [he] has brought into action on the Somme front a considerable number of fighting machines that are

Overleaf: **Despite its rotund appearance and nickname 'whale fish', the LFG Roland CII was one of the best German aeroplanes of 1916. Sitting above the upper wing, the pilot and observer had an unrivalled field of view and the revolutionary semi-monocoque design prefigured the Albatros machines to come.**

faster, handier, and capable of attaining a greater height than any at the moment at my disposal,' he wrote.[36]

The Germans were also reorganising the structure of their air service. The establishment of the Deutsche Luftstreitkräfte (German Air Force) in the first week of October brought the observer, flak and aeroplane forces together into one organisation.[37] The Germans further specialised their flying formations into discrete reconnaissance, bomber and fighter units. The single-seat fighter units, Jagdstaffeln (hunting squadrons), were known simply as Jasta. Fighters previously regarded only as protection machines for reconnaissance or bombing aeroplanes were now operating with a greater degree of autonomy in seek-and-destroy missions. Observers on the ground spotted and tracked incoming intruders, then telephoned through to the Jagdstaffeln, which were immediately scrambled to intercept.[38]

The first of these hunting squadrons was Jasta 2, commanded by the great Oswald Boelcke, whose famous *Dicta Boelcke* became the first air-combat manual. It was a systematic and clinical guide to aerial combat; in other words, how best to kill enemy airmen without being killed yourself: keep the sun behind you; fire only at close range; attack from behind; never forget your own line of retreat; and work as a team. It would be two years before the British had a similar manual. Von Richthofen had dispatched his first victim while flying one of the new Albatros designs under the tutelage of Boelcke in Jasta 2. It was a dangerous confluence: 86 per cent of casualties during October were at the hands of the fighters.[39] Caldwell's new posting was about to thrust him into the centre of the storm.

CHAPTER EIGHT

Fire Eaters

On 18 November 1916, Caldwell arrived at 60 Squadron, which was operating from an old French aerodrome at Savy-Berlette, some 15 miles north of Bellevue. On elevated land above the straggling line of farmhouses that made up the diminutive Savy village, the aerodrome was generous, leading one airman to dub it an 'almost infinite landing-ground'. The Scarpe river, which meandered east to Arras and then on to the front lines, gave airmen a shining silver thread to guide their outward and return journeys.

There were seven canvas-covered, wooden-framed Bessonneau hangars, each capable of housing four machines, and a collection of huts. Two of the hangars and several of the buildings had been left behind by the French, along with an extraordinary collection of trench maps, pasted from floor to ceiling on the walls of the commanding officer's sanctum.[1] Also based at the aerodrome was Albert Ball's old squadron, now equipped with Royal Aircraft Factory FE2b bombers.[2]

As part of III Brigade's 13 Wing, 60 Squadron was a battle-scarred survivor of the Somme Offensive. At the centre of the attack, it had incurred the full wrath of the German air service. After the squadron lost its commanding officer and two flight commanders, Trenchard was compelled to pull it from active duties for a short period.[3] With the arrival of Albert Ball in the third week of August and the gradual conversion of its aircraft to French Nieuports, the squadron had clawed its way back from the brink. The use of Nieuports reflected French ascendancy in Allied single-seat fighter design in 1916 and the limitations of British machines such as the Vickers 'Gunbus' pusher biplane. France had entered the war as the most advanced aviation nation in the world and its engines and aircraft were still widely used even by the powerful British aviation industry.[4]

Central to the reconfiguring of machines and men into specialist squadrons, 60 Squadron was one of the first exclusively single-seat fighter units engaged in offensive patrols and in escorting other units, like Caldwell's old 8 Squadron, on bombing raids. The unit quickly gained reflected glory from Ball's continuing success — an astonishing 20 victories in six weeks — and recognition for its extensive espionage work and pioneering use of rockets in combat.

Although the squadron was famed for its deployment of the revolutionary air-to-air rockets, the airmen were under no illusions about the difficulties and dangers of the Le Prieur incendiary weapons. Fired electronically from tubes attached to the Nieuports' outer struts — four either side — they were famously inaccurate, and airmen had to fly to within 360 feet of their targets to have any chance of hitting them. The squadron had already dispatched one balloon with Le Prieurs, when, on the morning of the big 15 September assault on the Somme, during which tanks were to be deployed for the first time, Trenchard asked for volunteers to shoot down a trio of German observer balloons. Their destruction would prevent the enemy seeing the lumbering tanks as they entered the field of battle. When the squadron's volunteers were waylaid by enemy aircraft, one pilot fired his rockets at a German two-seater. The machine was hit, caught fire and crashed — and the squadron claimed the first air-to-air missile victory in the history of aerial combat.[5]

C aldwell's new squadron commander, Major Robert Smith-Barry, was a strong-willed Irishman who also possessed a good deal of personal charm. While on operations during the retreat from Mons in 1914, his two-seater had suffered engine failure and he had crash-landed, killing his observer and breaking both legs.[6] Despite his lingering injuries, he was an excellent pilot who 'could do anything with an aeroplane and delighted in frightening his friends with incredible aerial antics'.[7] As a squadron commander he could be severe. On one occasion, when he borrowed a flight commander's machine, he was livid when he discovered, neatly tucked away in the cockpit, an emergency package — silk pyjamas, a razor, a toothbrush and 500 cigarettes — should the pilot ever fall into the hands of the enemy.[8] But he was also generous and loyal to his men and misdemeanours were soon forgotten. Caldwell recalled his first encounter with Smith-Barry.

> My second morning, when I went down to breakfast in the large farmhouse he had requisitioned, he looked very hard at me and said 'you will find one at Avesnes (nearby).' I asked my Flight Commander later, what did he think Smith-Barry meant? . . . [He] replied, 'Try getting your hair cut in Avesnes, it is rather long.' I did so and that evening in the mess, received a quick nod and smile from the C.O. . . . He took some getting used to, but as time went by, I met him many times later in the war and found him a delightful chap.[9]

Smith-Barry's disregard for the top brass and paperwork became legendary. On one occasion, soon after he was asked for well-overdue squadron reports and returns, the squadron office was burnt to the ground in the dead of night. 'We in the squadron all took it for granted that this had been Smith-Barry's way of dealing with the backlog,' said one amused pilot.[10] In the view of one of his successors, Smith-Barry did not give a damn for anyone with more gold braid than sense and was a fine 'original commander, almost too original, in fact even for the RFC, where, if anywhere in the fighting services, originality was encouraged'.[11]

Smith-Barry inserted Caldwell into C Flight, where his flight commander was Captain Eustace Grenfell, a dark-haired, Essex-born airman who had been one of the RFC's first fighter pilots.[12] Flying a Morane Bullet in early 1916, he had secured a quadruple aerial victory in a single day, three of them against the dreaded Fokker Eindeckers. Grenfell was awarded an MC and sent home to Britain as an instructor, but was recalled to the Western Front during the Somme Offensive.

So that C Flight might more quickly scramble to intercept intruders, Smith-Barry had placed the six-man unit at the edge of the aerodrome, up against the Bessonneau hangars. This location became their private little world, with its own mess and living quarters housed in two Nissen huts. 'We were,' observed one airman, 'very much apart from the rest of the squadron, even the CO rarely interfered with us.'[13] The other two flights, their staff officers, and the squadron's NCOs and mechanics, were billeted in Savy.

With Caldwell's arrival, C Flight was evenly divided between Englishmen and colonials. Grenfell's countrymen were Harry 'Reggie' Smart and William 'Willy' Fry. Smart entered the RFC by way of the Royal Engineers, and Fry was a feisty Middlesex-born pilot who had gone to war in 1914 as a private in the London Rifle Brigade.

After being sent home because he had lied about his age, Fry returned to the war as a commissioned infantry officer before finding his calling with the RFC. Caldwell's fellow colonials were two South Africans: Henry 'Duke' Meintjes and D'Urban Armstrong. Caldwell and Meintjes were immediate friends.[14] Armstrong, a Natal native, was the youngest of the group at only 19 years of age.

The flight commander, 26-year-old Grenfell, was the 'old man'. He commanded in the air and the men followed his lead, but he could also join in their roughhousing and high spirits. 'The pilots of the flight were a happy, wild lot,' wrote Fry, 'and one sensed this immediately on entering the little Mess.' Going to bed to avoid the mayhem was futile. One evening, tired, Fry sought an early night while the others partied. The darkness and calm of the bedroom fled when they piled themselves on top of Fry, 'making a frightful racket and refusing to go away'.

Fry, 'rather desperate', grabbed his oil lamp and hit Grenfell over the head with it, though he 'hardly noticed the blow'. It was only when Fry 'felt something warm dripping' onto his hand that he realised someone was bleeding badly. 'It took several minutes to make them understand that something really was wrong.'

> We sorted ourselves out, someone fetched a torch and we discovered that Grenfell was bleeding from a deep cut on his head and forehead where I had broken the glass lamp on him. Someone went in search of the medical orderly and a doctor and Eustace was stitched up and kept in sick quarters for the night. He appeared the next day wrapped in bandages. I had visions of trouble for striking my senior officer, but all was smiles, right up to the CO. I think I had established myself by standing up for myself in the rowdy C Flight.[15]

In the hangars near the mess, Caldwell found his heart's desire: four single-seat Nieuports arranged herringbone fashion. As he knew from Ball, the speed of these 'priceless little buses [gave] you a great chance of getting a Hun'.[16] They were certainly a vast improvement over the BE2, which was 27 feet long from propeller to tail and had a 37-foot wingspan, while the Nieuport was only 19 feet long, with a 26-foot wingspan. The French-designed aeroplane also had a much more muscular 110 horsepower Le Rhône engine, which gave it a top speed of 110 miles per hour and a climb rate that carried the fighter to nearly 10,000 feet in a mere 12 minutes. The squadron had both Nieuport 16s and 17s, the latter slightly longer and wider, which improved its aerodynamics and manoeuvrability.

The Nieuport was not, however, without its dangers. After only one night with

Above: **Pilots of C Flight, from left: Arthur Whitehead, Lindsey Weedon, Henry Meintjes, Keith Caldwell, Andrew Binnie and William Fry.**

Right: **Middlesex-born William Fry was one of Keith Caldwell's 60 Squadron colleagues and a fast friend. The two men shared accommodation and a victory with the squadron. In the 1970s they corresponded often and at length, discussing their shared wartime experiences and the doings of their respective families.**

C Flight, Grenfell dispatched his newest pilot on a test flight with his usual casual aside: 'And I hope you break your bloody neck' — his way of reminding his men of the serious business at hand.[17] Caldwell squeezed into the narrow, low-slung cockpit, with his head just proud of the fuselage. If the instrumentation panel in the BE2 was poor, the Nieuport did not even have one. Anything added was simply secured to the various steel and timber elements that lined the front of the cockpit. In the French escadrilles (squadrons) it was not uncommon for pilots to add their own instrumentation to their machines, which they would prise from the wreckage and recycle if they crashed.[18] At the two RFC depots, however, the newly arrived machines were fitted with a handful of British instruments.

The rotary engine demanded careful and systematic attention just to get a successful start. The mechanics checked and topped up the fuel and oil tanks, then oiled each of the cylinder's pushrod rocker, valves and springs, before priming them with petrol from a large brass syringe. Caldwell flicked on the ignition, set the air lever, and the ground crew swung the propeller. When the cylinders caught, Caldwell increased the fuel lever to keep the engine running.

With careful coordination of the air and fuel levers, it was possible to run the engine between cruise and full speed, but anything below that generally required the pilot to 'blip' or 'buzz' the ignition, that is, turn it on and off. Blipping was needed for taxiing and landing. The resulting sudden surges and decreases of power made the aircraft sound, to a layperson, as if it were misfiring or suffering some malfunction. It was a visceral and unnerving experience for the uninitiated, the machine rocking along its length like a dog shaking off water and thick black smoke pluming in the process. Caldwell's old BE2 engine had been a 'refined gentleman'; this was a feisty Parisian street-brawler eager for a stoush.[19]

Caldwell continued to fine-tune the air and fuel mixture, assessing the correct combination by the sound of the engine and the amount and colour of the exhaust smoke produced. As another Nieuport pilot noted, 'A rich engine sounds soft and a bit fluffy, the smoke is black and thick. A lean engine sounds sharp and reedy and will backfire, smoke is reduced and light. The correct mixture sounds strong and the smoke is grey.'[20] It was a dark art to which successful pilots quickly accommodated themselves, but it also highlighted the symbiotic relationship between the airman and his machine. It was not just technical knowledge but the airman's ability to measure and feel such subtle variations that made flight possible.

As the Nieuport spluttered out onto the airfield, Caldwell was mindful that the rotary engine had one final trap for the unwary. Unlike the radial engines of the BE2, in which the pistons rotated the crankshaft, which in turn spun the propeller, in the Nieuport the entire engine rotated, along with the propeller. Although this ensured a good power-to-weight ratio, it did produce gyroscopic forces that took some getting used to, especially during takeoff and landing. Caldwell later confessed that he initially found the Nieuport difficult to fly:

> It was only a very small aeroplane, with a very small wingspan and a big radial 110-hp Le Rhone, which generated a tremendous amount of torque and it pulled to one side when taking off. You had to use full rudder until you got about half your speed up, then slowly decrease rudder and centralise it, and pull back and you would be in the air; it had a very good rate of climb.[21]

This takeoff was trouble free, but as he climbed to 4000 feet Caldwell saw puffs of smoke bursting over the aerodrome: the anti-aircraft crews had spotted an intruder. It was an enemy two-seater 'well over our side of the lines'. When, pulse quickening, he turned the nose of the aeroplane, the response to his hand on the stick and feet on the rudder pedals was immediate. The Nieuport was like nothing else he had flown. He pulled in the German aeroplane with ease. 'I attacked at close range, got into a spin, then chased him the whole way down to the enemy trenches, firing all my three Lewis drums on the way. I believe the observer was hit, as he disappeared from view, but the A/C [aircraft] was last seen still flying low, so imagine he got back.'[22]

Bitterly disappointed, Caldwell returned to the aerodrome to complete some practice landings, on the last of which the rotary engine nearly got the better of him. 'Found it hard to land,' he noted in his logbook that night, 'didn't taxi too well (bent wing tip).'[23] As he later recalled, 'During landing, you operated a thumb switch that kept cutting the ignition but you had to get bursts of air on your rudder to keep the aeroplane straight, otherwise, it would go round and do what you called a ground loop — the engine pulled you round. But you got the hang of it.'[24] Despite his disappointment, the flight had been a remarkable 20-minute initiation to the Nieuport, which, he concluded, was 'very nice in the air'.

The last two weeks of the month were uneventful: the occasional test flight, a flying visit to his old colleagues at Bellevue, escorting bombing operations and undertaking offensive patrols. The enemy appeared to have abandoned the field. The ground underfoot was wet, the canvas heavy and mud was being tracked everywhere.

The low-lying cloud hindered extensive operations on both sides of the trenches. It was, however, possible to escape the increasing winter gloom in the Nieuport, and airmen like Caldwell regularly pierced the clouds to inhabit, if only temporarily, a sky that, in the words of British airman Cecil Lewis, was 'a level plain of radiant whiteness, sparkling in the sun. The light seemed not to come from a single source, but to pervade and permeate every atom of air — a dazzling, perfect, empty basin of blue. A hundred miles, north, south, east, west. Thirty thousand square miles of unbroken cloud plains!'[25]

In the inactivity of late November, Smith-Barry had sent C Flight — minus William Fry, who was on leave in England — for some much-needed gunnery instruction. Caldwell was keen. Despite his strong flying abilities and fearless attitude, he was not a good shot, as the near miss on his first flight with the squadron had shown: 'Here was, indeed, evidence of poor shooting and I was disgusted.'[26] Caldwell and the others flew their Nieuports to Berck-sur-Mer, overlooking the English Channel.

The single Lewis machine gun on the upper wing would fire just above the spinning propeller tips, and was fixed at an upward angle of 10 degrees to the line of horizontal flight. If you were attacking a target from behind and below this was an advantage, but it eroded accuracy for airmen who were poor at deflection shooting. Moreover, the Nieuport had to dive steeply to get a line on ground targets, followed by a hasty pull-out that put undue stress on the airframe.

Then there was changing out the drums by using the machine gun's Foster mounting. The quadrant-shaped I-beam rail allowed the gun to be slid back and down in a single smooth action; the pilot could then change out the drum without having to stand up. Ingenious pilots, particularly Albert Ball, also discovered that from this lowered position they could fire obliquely forwards and upwards. Though vastly improved, drum changing remained challenging, especially for the less robust pilots. 'I found them heavy to handle while flying,' confessed Fry. Even the stronger pilots did not relish changing a drum out, especially when under attack, as enemy airmen were particularly aggressive when they saw the Lewis had been pulled down.[27]

The air-to-ground gunnery lessons were against non-retaliatory, passive targets, but even so the course was hardly a rip-roaring success. The weather had turned particularly cold and nasty and Caldwell was only able to fly on two days. The first flight, on 2 December, was a complete washout as Caldwell flew around for 45 minutes, attempting to locate the ground targets: three 'Fokkers' marinating in the mud of a local lagoon. Two days later he found the dummy Fokkers and made a series of strafing runs, expending three drums' worth of ammunition in the process. 'Rest of the time weather dud,' Caldwell wrote. He spent the time 'clay pigeon shooting [and] revolver shooting miniature range moving targets'.[28]

As the temperature plummeted and the men nearly froze in their small hut, someone had the bright idea of lighting the gas stove for heat. It worked after a fashion, but as the pilots slept carbon monoxide gathered in the unventilated room and then in their lungs and red blood cells — they were slowly being poisoned. Caldwell was shaken awake in the early morning by a batman who had found the others nearly unconscious. 'They would soon have been dead if not discovered,' recalled William Fry.[29] Mercifully the men were left only with dull headaches, lingering nausea and temporary dizziness.

After days of weather-induced inactivity, Patrick Playfair, 13 Wing's commander, ordered a series of offensive patrols for 11 December. Flights of six machines each from 60 Squadron would carry out a morning and midday offensive patrol.[30] Smith-Barry chose C Flight for the morning patrol and Grenfell gathered his men for a foray over the front lines.

When Caldwell entered the mess, he found a reconfigured set of pilots. Smart and Armstrong, who had returned to England, had been replaced by Etonian Arthur 'Tiny' Whitehead and Lindsey Weedon from South Africa. Fry was still on leave so his spot was occupied by Londoner Albert Daly. With clear instructions to follow Grenfell's lead and stay in formation, C Flight filed out onto the frosty airfield. The Nieuports shook off their three-day slumber, barking into life before they taxied out. The pickings had been thin in the previous weeks, and little was expected in the way of prey over the trenches.

They climbed above the aerodrome, the air temperature falling some 5 degrees for every 1000 feet of altitude. It was bitterly cold when the flight levelled out at 10,000 feet. Far below, the trenches stretched as far as the eye could see. The great opposing armies were hunkered down for the winter; only airmen ventured out for battle. The formation flew along the line, scanning the skies for intruders.

Just before they crossed the Allied trenches near Dainville, Meintjes saw puffs of smoke from anti-aircraft batteries. Grenfell fired a red flare, signalling attack, and dived; the pack followed. Caldwell spotted the quarry at 5000 feet: one of the latest Albatros C-series, general-purpose two-seaters. As the six Nieuports closed in on the German aircraft, the enemy observer swung his Parabellum machine gun on the assailants, firing off short bursts.

The Nieuports crashed through, Lewis guns firing. Meintjes unloaded half a drum at close range, Weedon and Whitehead made a series of attacks and Caldwell 'dived down, firing over [the enemy's] tail'.[31] He got in close on two occasions. The first time his gun stopped after about eight rounds. As he closed in he got off about 20 rounds from around 25 yards behind and above the Albatros.

The German machine lost speed and altitude even as its pilot attempted desperate evasive manoeuvres. The predators followed their cornered game down. In the frenzy, Grenfell's bullets hit home, striking the enemy pilot in the foot and peppering the Albatros.[32] Wounded and exhausted, the pilot signalled his surrender. Grenfell followed him down until the Albatros landed in a ploughed field. Caldwell watched from above as the pilot and observer, in their long leather coats, piled out of the machine.

Grenfell was keen to make the most of this rare opportunity to secure valuable intelligence from the Germans, but he was in such a hurry to land that he stalled and crash-landed near the Albatros, damaging his machine and breaking his leg. When Meintjes saw that Grenfell was in danger of being trapped in his Nieuport, he landed in the next field, as did Weedon and Whitehead.

Caldwell, though, was in serious trouble. In the violent gyrations of the attack, his left-hand wing had turned in the socket that attached it to the fuselage. He felt the controls go slack and just managed to push the stick right over to the side of the cockpit and reduce his speed for an emergency landing.[33] He touched down and bumped over the ploughed field.

Concussed and with a bleeding gash on his forehead to go with his broken leg, Grenfell was gingerly freed from his bent Nieuport.[34] Lindsey Weedon assisted the injured German pilot, kneeling down and tugging off his boot to reveal the bullet wound and congealing blood.[35] When the observer set light to the Albatros, it exploded, wounding him; some British soldiers from nearby trenches were singed by the ball of flame. It was not the unit's finest hour.

The episode caused a tremendous row. The arrival of a brigadier general soon afterwards only heightened RFC embarrassment. The pilots, for their part, blamed the soldiers. Meintjes was blunt: 'I think if the infantry had been quicker coming up, the machine ought to have been saved. As it was, they stood around and watched the observer blow it up.'[36] For Caldwell, the sole saving grace was that he was credited with a victory, albeit a sixth share — his first as a scout pilot. His official career tally was now a magnificent two.

With Grenfell carted off to a casualty clearing station, Smith-Barry made Meintjes flight commander. Caldwell had as many victories, but the South African was much more experienced with the Nieuports and had been with the unit since its formation. Caldwell felt the choice was obvious.[37]

In the coming weeks, many of Caldwell's offensive patrols were with his flight commander and William Fry. Meintjes took the point of the tight V formation, with Caldwell behind to the left and Fry on the right. Although Meintjes led the operations, Fry and Caldwell were careful not to let Duke, as he was known, lose his head. Meintjes was by all accounts a bit of a 'fire eater', who needed gentle handling. At the tail end of a long patrol over the lines, when Caldwell and Fry felt they had tested their luck long enough, the pair would exchange looks behind Meintjes' back before firing a short round of Lewis bullets in front of their flight commander. Meintjes would snap his head around, searching for the enemy. If the sky was clear of Germans, he would turn an impish grin on Caldwell and Fry. Then, to make sure that authority was asserted, he would press on a little longer before turning for home.[38]

As weather allowed, Caldwell's final sorties for the year were offensive patrols and escort duties, two of which resulted in his submission of combat in air reports. On 16 December, during a noon patrol near Arras, he saw an intruder, an Albatros two-seater heading north-west at 13,000 feet. Caldwell began a long and determined climb from 5000 feet. It took him three-quarters of an hour to position his Nieuport within striking distance, cleverly between the Germans and their route home. The enemy pilot attempted to bust through, 'firing over his back gun'. Caldwell replied in kind, emptying a drum from the Lewis at a speculative 70 yards.

> While I was changing my drum the H.A. (Hostile Aircraft) came round on my tail and fired a few rounds then div[ed] away eastwards. I followed when the drum was on and fired the second drum at close range. The H.A. then turned round and climbed up steeply, trying to get on my tail again. I put a third drum on and followed the H.A. across the lines followed by two De Havillands. I could not gain much on the H.A. diving to fire the drum at about 80 yards range. It did not seem to take any effect as the German still kept on his dive.[39]

Four days later, in his last sortie for the year, Caldwell had the same frustratingly inconclusive results when escorting FE2s from Savy's other formation, 11 Squadron, on photographic duties. The two-man pushers and their Nieuport guardians were 15 miles over the lines when the enemy appeared.[40] There was a rolling scrap all the way back to the British lines. A German green-coloured two-seater, set upon by a gaggle of Nieuports, spun down past Caldwell, out of control, and he dived to follow.

To his surprise, the doomed machine righted itself at 7000 feet. It was a ruse. He got behind the aircraft and fired about 30 rounds. The German tumbled, but Caldwell's joy evaporated when the two-seater flattened out, once again, at 4000 feet, and disappeared to the east. Caldwell was still learning his trade. The encounters had demonstrated the futility of firing at extreme range and the cunning of German pilots with considerably more experience than his one month in combat.

The winter of 1916–17 was harsh, one of the coldest in memory, and unlike anything Caldwell had experienced. Routine operations were the first casualty. Low cloud cover and freezing temperatures limited visibility and untended engines became large metal ice blocks. 'Trouble with the engines was awful,' New Zealander William Shirtcliffe told his family, 'because the carburettor would freeze up just as you left the ground, probably meaning a landing in a field, where they would be thawed out with hot cloths.'[41] Once in the air things were even worse: one airman was 'so intensely cold and miserable, that I did not trouble to look round at all to see whether any Huns were behind me or not; in fact, I did not care whether I was shot down or not. I was so utterly frozen.'[42]

C Flight's huts kept the rain and wind at bay, but when the snow fell, the bone-rattling cold seeped past all defences. Even basic ablutions were a grinding struggle. Mindful of morale and the need to keep headstrong young men occupied, Smith-Barry placed Sergeant Major James Aspinall in charge of off-duty entertainments. It was a popular choice. Aspinall, with his scimitar moustache, was one of the squadron's disciplinarians but also a great humourist, 'though often unintentionally'. 'Jimmy' to his subordinates, to Caldwell and the commissioned officers he was the 'Great Man'.[43]

One of his offsiders, Sergeant Alfred Nicol, had famously organised a November rugby match in which one individual, 'apparently out of sheer devilment', had, in a scrum, stripped naked except for his boots and staggered off the pitch caked in mud, much to the merriment of the onlookers.[44] As Caldwell was to learn, NCOs like Aspinall, confidant to a series of 60 Squadron commanding officers, and Nicol, were the institutional glue that held squadrons together.[45]

Smith-Barry was a music lover, and he formed an orchestra that included two sergeants on violins, a pair of corporals on cornets and another on percussion, and Nicol on piano. Aspinall also took over C Flight's hangar for a boxing tournament, to which squadrons from neighbouring aerodromes sent contestants. It was a pugilist gala with the orchestra ringside on a stage adorned with multicoloured bunting.[46]

The grand event of December was Robert Smith-Barry's send-off on Christmas Eve. He had long been a vocal critic of RFC training. He blamed limited flying hours and poor instruction for the deaths of so many young men in their first few weeks at the front and advocated a complete overhaul of the current methods and system, including the establishment of a school for instructors. Trenchard was now sending Smith-Barry to Gosport, on England's south coast, where he would revolutionise military aviation training at the School of Special Flying. Trenchard, Higgins and Patrick Playfair joined the celebrations at Savy, rubbing shoulders with Caldwell and the other officers. It was a 'riotous and musical Christmas Eve celebration' and a rare opportunity for C Flight to spend time in the squadron's main mess, away from their own secluded building.[47]

During Christmas and the New Year, between concerts and sporting events and surrounded by the scattered detritus of Christmas parcels — crumbling bricks of fruit cake, tins of salty beef, sugary lollies and buttery shortbread — the men pored over letters and newspapers from home.

David Caldwell was in New Zealand — letters from home to his son told of wins on the golf course and bowling greens — but Mary and Vida Caldwell were as busy as ever in London, working at the New Zealand Soldiers' Club in Russell Square, which had opened in August 1916. As Mary wrote to her husband, in a letter that was reprinted in the *Waikato Independent*: 'You would be surprised at the number of our men who come straggling in at intervals all night for meals; hot things till 12, and then only boiled eggs and cold eatables and tea and coffee, etc., till 7 am. They like New Zealand women to attend them, and some are very pleased to have a little talk when there is a spare minute or two for it.' One night, during a lull around three o'clock, the nine women on duty, plus a young soldier acting as a porter, 'repaired to the kitchen and had a solid meal of bacon and eggs and chipped potatoes. Rather a comical scene; all seated round the table with our heliotrope overalls on, the night porter at one end of the table, the professional cook at the other end, and the paid char woman at the sink washing pots and pans.'

Every morning, about 2 a.m, 'a big burly policeman' came in for a meal. 'The soldiers are a fine lot and very cheery, and always polite and nice to the two waitresses — Vida and an English girl.' Mary Caldwell shared a common attitude towards German

Nieuports

CHRISTMAS 1916

"60" Squadron

prisoners of war. When an airship was brought down over London by the RFC, 'The commander of the captured Zeppelin was too full of enmity to eat the breakfast of bacon and eggs offered him. Fancy offering the Hun anything so good with eggs at three pence each, and our men starving in Germany.'[48]

Back in New Zealand, the Walsh Brothers' flying school was slowly releasing more men for war. In September 1916, four more men qualified for the Royal Aero Club certificate. On the day of their flight tests, 'The humming of seaplane engines was heard at frequent intervals all afternoon, and occasionally one would catch sight of a machine soaring up high in the air or volplaning down and sending up showers of spray as it struck the water,' wrote the *New Zealand Herald*.[49] Vivian and Leo Walsh were only too happy to remind the reporters of their two graduates already at war: Caldwell and Callender. Early in November, newspapers were reporting that a wounded Callender was in London.[50]

Callender had been posted to 20 Squadron at the beginning of the Somme Offensive, flying FE2s in reconnaissance, bombing and escort work.[51] On 20 October, he and his observer were on a reconnaissance sortie south of Lille when they were attacked by an enemy aeroplane. Their main tank was struck and Callender was hit. German bullets shredded sections of the wood-framed machine, driving splinters into his left check and arm. The observer fired the Lewis machine gun over the back of the FE2, compelling the German to flee, but the FE2's engine had stopped. As they glided towards the Allied lines, they managed to attack another German machine, sending it into a steep dive.[52]

After crossing the lines at 3000 feet, the badly damaged FE2 crash-landed. Both men survived. By late December, Callender was well on the road to recovery in England and Caldwell was relieved and delighted to hear that his old training mate had been awarded the Italian Silver Medal for valour.[53] But, while recovering in mid-1917, Callender was involved in a flying accident and deemed unfit for active duty.[54] He completed his war service as a flight instructor in Home Service duties.

Sixty Squadron's 1916 Christmas card highlights the long shadows cast by the Nieuports from a low-slung winter sun. Snow, low clouds and freezing temperatures impeded aerial operations.

CHAPTER NINE

Black Crosses

As 1916 turned to 1917, there were two changes at the squadron: a fresh commander and a new aerodrome. Robert Smith-Barry's replacement, Major Evelyn
Graves, was a somewhat severe individual. Thin and angular like his predecessor, he
walked with a limp. Early in 1915, he had broken an arm and a leg in a training accident
at Netheravon, in south-west England.[1] Frustrated by staff duties, he pestered his
superior officer, Higgins, to be restored to active operations, and carried out very
good work as a flight commander before his posting to 60 Squadron. Caldwell found
Graves, who had been born in India and partly educated in Germany, intriguing, and
'rather a serious sort of chap', but held him in high regard.[2]

Graves' first task was transferring the squadron a couple of miles south of Savy to
Filescamp Farm aerodrome, near the village of Izel-lès-Hameau, known as Le Hameau.
This would be Caldwell's home for most of 1917. Filescamp, which easily accommodated
three squadrons, bordered a spacious and largely flat landing ground. Within sight of
the village at the eastern parameter, clustered around the farmhouse and its buildings,
were 60 Squadron and the Airco DH2s pushers of 29 Squadron. The mess and quarters
were set in the farm's orchard. The squadron's hangars ran along the northern flank of
the large home occupied by Monsieur Tetus, his wife and two children.

Some of the farm dwellings were substantial fort-like structures, including a brick
tower overlooking a large quadrangle formed by the house, a cow shed, rabbit hutches,

pig pens and granaries.[3] At dusk, the animals were corralled into the quadrangle, part of which was a midden — a 6-foot pile of animal waste and straw, often populated by chickens, ducks, geese and pigeons scratching and pecking for insects and fly larvae. In winter, this fertiliser was spread across the fields. As William Fry noted, 'evidently that was the way of farm living [in France] and no one appeared to mind.'[4]

In the first few weeks, the extreme cold drove the men indoors. Whenever Caldwell ventured outside, hands plunged deep into the pockets of his British Warm, and walked through the snow to the hangars and maintenance buildings, he would see the silver-doped surfaces of the Nieuports glistening. While the airmen had their feet up, the air mechanics, affectionately dubbed 'Ack Emmas', were hard at work. Each machine had an assigned fitter, who maintained the engine, and a rigger, who looked after the wings and airframe, which kept the machine 'true' and taut. Standard in-line engines required an overall check every 300 hours, but the Le Rhône rotary was disassembled every 30 hours. As Caldwell had discovered only a month before, one weakness in the integrity of an airframe and an aeroplane could disassemble itself in mid-air. The wires and struts had to be correctly aligned for strength and predictable performance in the braced airframe.[5]

When flying was possible, the weather created challenges. The concrete-like frozen ground was particularly harsh on the wooden tail-skids, which frequently had to be replaced. The cold engines were notoriously recalcitrant. 'We had to burn lamps under our magnetos at night, in the hangars, to make engine starting easier in the morning,' recalled Caldwell.[6] And then there was the armament. Because the synchronised machine guns on the German single-seat fighters ran along the hot engines of their aeroplanes, they were operable in the coldest weather, but the Nieuports' wing-mounted Lewis guns were exposed to the Arctic-like conditions.

'There was only one Lewis gun on the top wing, which wasn't really enough, and in winter,' lamented Caldwell, 'when it got very cold, the oil would freeze up.'[7] Frequent bursts were required to keep it effective. Over the following weeks, machine-gun lubricant with higher tolerances was introduced to alleviate the problem.

In the vernacular of the airmen, 20 January was a 'dud' day for operations. Most of the squadron headed for Amiens, leaving behind a trio of officers who made a series of practice flights over the aerodrome. As they made their lazy circuits, an unexpected aircraft emerged from the mist. The black crosses were clear; it was a German two-seat Rumpler, occupied, unusually, by a lone airman.

The Nieuports frightened the enemy pilot down onto the airfield, and he immediately set his machine on fire. A motley collection of ground crew rustled up some guns to advance on the bonfire and the airman, who, when captured, gave the squadron commander, Evelyn Graves, a desultory salute. He and his observer had become completely lost on a sortie and had landed at another RFC aerodrome, where the observer had disembarked to ascertain their location. When he was captured, the Rumpler pilot had opened the throttle and taken off. Later that day the pair were reunited at Le Hameau, where the observer soundly berated his pilot for his poor navigational skills. The senior German officer then enjoyed tea with the squadron before being removed to a prison camp.[8]

Other, friendlier airmen lost their way in that misty, cloud-laden winter. Among them was a very cold and worried Leonard Rochford from 3 (Naval) Squadron RNAS. After two and half hours adrift, he had broken through the clouds at 500 feet. Below him stretched an aerodrome, but was it Allied or German?[9] He was relieved to spot the line of Nieuports outside the hangars. After dipping his wing and wheeling over the airfield, he landed and taxied his Sopwith Pup to the front door of a hangar, where a tall pilot with a mop of unruly black hair informed him he was at Filescamp Farm. 'Keith Caldwell was the first person to greet me,' Rochford later wrote. After he had met Graves and reported to his commanding officer, Major Redford Mulock, Rochford stayed overnight with 60 Squadron.

> Keith Caldwell, or 'Grid' as he was always called in the RFC, was a New Zealander and that day I had met him for the first and only time. I was immensely impressed by his personality and during the evening enjoyed a long and interesting conversation with him. Likewise, he seemed interested in me as I was the first pilot of a naval squadron he had met. He wanted to hear about the squadron and the Sopwith Pup and I discovered that he knew our 'Kiwi' Beamish, having gone to school with him in New Zealand.[10]

Nicknames like 'Grid' and 'Kiwi' were part of public schoolboy and RFC tradition; the argot of an exclusive yet informal club. Some were based on nationality. Many New Zealanders, like Harold Beamish, were called 'Kiwi' or even 'Maori', regardless of their heritage. (The boys at Wanganui Collegiate had called Beamish 'Blocky', but his new 'Kiwi' moniker was a fine fit for the effervescent New Zealander.) Others were given humorous and sometimes unkind names. Rank was no impediment, as 'Bum and Eye Glass' Higgins discovered. One corpulent officer was dubbed

'Pregnant Percy', and one poor haemorrhoids-afflicted soul simply 'Piles'.[11] Caldwell's nickname probably became attached to him over the winter of 1916–17. As William Fry explained, 'There have been several versions of how Caldwell became known as "Grid" throughout the RFC.'

> My version is that one day at Savy, soon after his arrival, we set off on an offensive patrol, Meintjes leading, and on the way to the line Caldwell fell behind and then turned back. The patrol carried on without him. When we walked back from our machines after returning, Caldwell was standing in the gap through to the hangar. Meintjes asked, 'What happened to you Caldwell?'
>
> 'My grid was lousy,' he replied, meaning his machine was not going well.
>
> Thereafter, in the flight and in the RFC he was known as 'Grid'. He told us that as boys in New Zealand they always called their bicycles 'grids'. The remark was typical of him, everything explained in slang without waste of words.[12]

Once applied, the name stuck. Grid and Kiwi were now two members of the newly created fighter units on the Western Front: specialist single-seat fighter squadrons. The RNAS squadrons were equipped with some of the best machines on offer in 1917, including Nieuports, Sopwith Pups and Triplanes, and they performed extremely well over the Western Front — a welcome boost to Hugh Trenchard's forces.

When regular sorties resumed in the third week of the year, Caldwell, through no fault of his own, almost immediately came unstuck. On 27 January, a very cold day, he was on patrol at 12,000 feet when an intruder was spied near Logeast Wood, south of Arras. Caldwell pushed the stick forward and dived on the enemy machine. He closed to 50 yards and fired. The Lewis was kicking and firing bullets when, inexplicably, the engine stopped and the Nieuport's nose began to drop. The German pulled away and escaped. At 5000 feet, Caldwell turned the Nieuport onto the line of the distant British trenches and furiously attempted to restart the engine.

He checked to see if the fuel cock had been bumped off, then cycled through the ignition, blipping it on and off. Was the fuel mixture out of kilter? When nothing worked, he resigned himself to the inevitable and checked his height, air speed, distance; making the Allied positions was going to be close. The small tin pinheads along the forward trenches coalesced into Tommy helmets. He was going to make it. Caldwell managed a jittery forced landing and the Nieuport came to halt 700 yards behind the British trenches. He scrambled free and bounded for cover.

Through Zeiss binoculars, the enemy had followed Caldwell's plunge east and now saw their chance for some competitive shooting. The abandoned aircraft was a bright silvery target. Caldwell heard the whistle and whine of shells crossing over the German emplacements, no man's land and finally British soldiers. The frozen earth cracked and splintered and the forlorn machine jumped, peppered with clods of earth. Caldwell watched as a cluster of direct hits atomised the Nieuport's frame and nudged the misshapen steel and aluminium engine around the battlefield like a football. The pummelling went on for a day and a night until there was nothing of the plane left to salvage.[13] Over lunch at the local battalion headquarters, field staff officers commiserated with Caldwell. It had been a close call.

The air war was about to take a colourful, yet deadlier, turn as the Germans consolidated their efforts around new machines, specialised fighter units and a clutch of new aggressive airmen along the front. In the vanguard of this was Manfred von Richthofen, a recent recipient of Germany's highest military award. The Pour le Mérite, or 'The Blue Max' as it was commonly known, was an acknowledgement of the Prussian's widely lauded accumulations, over the previous months, of 16 confirmed kills. Von Richthofen was a determined and calculating hunter, collecting trophies from machines he downed and sometimes taking pictures of his dead adversaries. 'I never get into an aircraft for fun,' he said. 'I aim first for the head of the pilot.'

In Jasta 11, he surrounded himself with up-and-coming luminaries, many learning their trade under his guidance. Now they were flying an even newer model of the formidable Albatros. The Albatros DIII had a higher climb rate than its predecessor and was the best machine on the Western Front in the first half of 1917. Richthofen's signature Rotes Flugzeug (red aeroplane) furnished him with his 'Red Baron' moniker, and was emulated by his colleagues and protégés, who painted their machines bright colours. It was the nucleus of what would become known as the Flying Circus.

Towards the end of January 1917, Filescamp was flooded with orders for patrols to 'stop hostile artillery machines from working and secondly to catch any that may persist'.[14] The headquarters of 13 Wing wanted all pilots, but especially those in the Nieuports, to gain sufficient height and catch the enemy by surprise. On the morning of 29 January, Meintjes, Caldwell and Fry were flying at a bone-rattlingly cold 14,000 feet. (Many of 60 Squadron had taken to plastering their faces with whale oil to ward

Manfred von Richthofen, the commander of Jasta 11, his fellow pilots and dog, Moritz. From left: Sebastian Festner, Karl Emil Schäfer, Manfred von Richthofen, Lothar von Richthofen and Kurt Wolff.

off frostbite.) Around them cumulus clouds piled up. The sky above was bright and blue and the countryside below a winter white, broken only by silvery rivers and the dark veins of the trenches.

Meintjes spotted movement and wiggled his wings. Caldwell and Fry gently rocked their Nieuports over and looked down. There, just a few hundred feet below, stark against the snowy backdrop, were eight colourful enemy machines. 'The black crosses on the wings were startlingly clear,' said Fry.[15] It was Jasta 11: yellow, black, green and blue-patterned Albatroses led by a blood-red machine.

Concealed by the clouds, the RFC trio manoeuvred, placing the sun directly behind them. Then Meintjes dived in, followed by the New Zealander and the Englishman. The startled Germans broke formation, two heading off south-east with Meintjes and Fry in hot pursuit, and the others going in multiple directions, with Caldwell latched onto one. Meintjes filled his gunsight with an enemy fighter at 25 yards, fired a burst and struck a fatal blow; the aeroplane began an ugly fall before crashing, a stain on the snow. Fry, on the tail of another, fired, but the target dived steeply, fleeing east. He was unable to pursue, as other Germans were upon him.

In the chaos, Caldwell found himself firing at one target and then another. The startled Nieuport's shoulders twitched in the violent cut and thrust. He expended a drum and pulled the Lewis down on the rail to change it out. After flinging the empty drum over the side, Caldwell inserted its replacement while holding the stick between his knees, all the while totally defenceless.[16] The Lewis reloaded, he began firing again and a German started to spin down.[17]

Then he spotted Meintjes firing on a diving aeroplane, but with two on his own tail. Caldwell set off in a steep spiral to help. The Nieuport was in full stride when there was a loud bang and petrol began to pour over his knees and feet. Explosive bullets had punched holes in the petrol and oil tanks. The First World War airman's greatest fear — being burnt alive — was now a horrifying possibility. Behind him was a persistent German pilot in a red aeroplane.[18] Caldwell fled. 'For a minute or two the sky seemed full of milling machines,' said Fry, 'then the fight was over as suddenly as it had started, and the sky was clear of enemy machines.'[19]

Caldwell limped west in search of the nearest RFC aerodrome. When he landed at Bellevue, his old unit, 8 Squadron, came out to see one of its long-lost sons: Keith

Albatros DIII fighters at Douai, France. The second-nearest, dark machine was one of several flown by Manfred von Richthofen. Keith Caldwell had numerous dogfights with the colourful machines of Jasta 11, including at least one battle with a deep-scarlet Albatros.

Caldwell, covered in oil and reeking of fuel. The Nieuport was riddled with holes and, in his opinion, 'probably a write-off'.[20] He watched it being dismantled and dumped on the back of a lorry.

The battle against the Albatros machines became the focus of many a conversation in the mess in the weeks and months that followed. Immediately after the encounter, though, the trio was unaware of who they had attacked. As Fry wrote years later,

> We had no idea at first that we were up against a specially organised and trained unit with a new type of machine, and it certainly was a bit of luck that we managed to survive. The speed and tempo of the fight was something none of us had experienced before and was a foretaste of what air fighting was going to be like in future . . . Compared to that fight, all that had gone before was preliminary sparring.[21]

Though for decades it proved impossible to confirm that von Richthofen was flying the scarlet Albatros, many were convinced. Whoever it was, Caldwell reckoned he was a 'pretty good pilot'.[22] It had been Caldwell's lucky day: it was remarkable that the incendiary rounds had not set him alight. Graves gave Caldwell, Fry and Meintjes the use of his Crossley car and a day off. They drove down to Bertangles aerodrome to see two friends, the Australian Stanley Goble and Canadian Raymond Collishaw, of 8 (Naval) Squadron RNAS. It was a gathering of aces in the making.

The revival of operations had revealed stresses in the squadron, especially for those who had been on the Western Front for a protracted period. Months of sorties, the ever-present prospect of death and the strain of almost continual work were slowly grinding Caldwell and the others down. Airmen could perform at their best only if they had extended breaks from the front line. Graves believed Caldwell needed some time away, and so on 10 February he requested that Caldwell and Meintjes be given four weeks of special leave, for the following reasons:

> 1. Both of these officers work together
> 2. They have displayed exceptional dash in their fighting on offensive patrols and an untiring keenness on every occasion
> 3. Their influence on the other pilots in the Squadron, most of who are very young and have just joined is most valuable

4. They are both keen indeed on staying with the Squadron and do not relish the prospect of instructing at home.[23]

Meintjes had been with the squadron since May the previous year and Caldwell had been in France since July 1916; both men were well overdue for rest and recuperation. Henry Meintjes and the long-serving William Fry were posted to Home Establishment, away from the front; Caldwell was granted a woefully inadequate nine-day respite from flying duties.[24]

His indefatigable efforts and considerable leadership abilities were not, however, going unnoticed. The commander of III Brigade recommended him for a Mention in Dispatches (MiD), official recognition of gallant or meritorious action in the face of the enemy, noting that Caldwell had 'done very good work both with an artillery and latterly with a scout squadron. His example to new pilots [had] been most excellent.'[25]

Caldwell's skills as a pilot were also acknowledged when he was sent to No. 1 Aircraft Depot at St Omer to undertake an evaluative test flight and complete a report on a new and potentially game-changing machine, the Sopwith Camel. Its lineage was readily apparent: it had the family looks of the Sopwith Pup, but the body was deeper and the gravitational central mass of the machine — the engine, weaponry, fuel tank and pilot — were all concertinaed forward.[26] Compact and snub-nosed, it had twice the power of the Pup and was highly manoeuvrable.

Thanks to his experience and proficiency with the Nieuport, Caldwell knew well that rotary engines, with their strong torque, could throw the imprudent. The 130 horsepower Clerget engine of the Camel propelled Caldwell to 120 miles per hour in his 30-minute flight on 2 March. He not only found the aeroplane 'very fast' and nimble, he was also impressed with the paired Vickers machine guns that gave the Camel its name. It was the first RFC scout to possess twin guns firing through the spinning arc of the propeller. What did concern Caldwell in his report, though, was the inability to clear stoppages in the starboard Vickers.[27] Both guns were right-hand fed, which meant that the mechanism of the starboard gun was hard against the airframe. This problem would not be solved until much later in the year.

With the departure of Meintjes to England, Caldwell was elevated to temporary captain and given command of C Flight. It was a significant promotion and acknowledgement of his high standing among the men. Flight commanders were the sinews that held the squadron and its airmen together. A weak or dithering squadron commander could be balanced by strong, resourceful flight commanders, but a good commander and his squadron could be completely undone by incompetent or inattentive flight commanders.

Not all squadron commanders were active participants in operations, but all flight commanders led their men into battle, setting the tone and conduct of aerial combat. As Caldwell knew, a firm but encouraging hand by its leader underpinned the confidence and likely success of a flight. His charges included Lindsey Weedon and Arthur Whitehead, Englishman Frank Bower and Australian Alan Binnie.

Throughout February and the first week of March, Caldwell flew nearly every day. Aside from a few odds and ends — test-flying the Camel and 'balloon strafing with rockets' — the greater part of his work involved offensive patrols, escort duties and, for the first time, photo reconnaissance sorties.[28] Higher command had decided that rather than send a clutch of Nieuports to escort a two-seater on photographic duties, it made more sense to dispatch a Nieuport fitted with a camera alongside other Nieuports in an offensive patrol.[29] Some of the medium-distance photography could be completed under the cloak of a routine patrol with a bevy of protecting single-seat scouts, and often more expeditiously. The Nieuports and other single-seat machines could provide important supplementary pictures to those already being produced by the two-seaters.

During 1917, the large, often hand-held or externally mounted cameras used between 1914 and 1916 were progressively superseded by smaller models that could be concealed inside the aircraft. In the Nieuport, the camera was suspended inside the fuselage just behind the pilot's seat. A small hole cut in the fabric gave the lens a bird's-eye view of the countryside. Getting the shot was an exacting business. At the designated location and height to which the camera had been calibrated, Caldwell flew at a set speed, exposing photographic plates at predetermined intervals by using a Bowden cable that released and reset the mechanism.

The intelligence provided by these flights was immense and highly detailed. A single print, taken from 6000 to 8000 feet, could capture 10 square miles of battlefield. When it was enlarged, it was possible to 'count railway trucks and engines in sidings [and] frequently tell whether they are empty and full'. You could distinguish between 'main line, temporary light railways, roads, cart tracks, and footpaths' and, with a magnifying glass, pick up the tracks of men marching across a field in single file. Hidden or camouflaged guns were visible. Not only could you see whether a trench was deep 'by the shadows or if it [had] water in it', but also by 'how may rows of barbed wire entanglements it [had] in front of it'.[30] In 1917, hundreds of thousands of prints were produced, many of them arriving on the desk of an officer at a local headquarters within 40 minutes of the photograph being taken.[31]

In this late-winter period, Caldwell carried out 21 flights, a third of which were photographic sorties, either photographing the front himself or providing escort duties to others.[32] His efforts were a small part of an intelligence-gathering exercise in preparation for the year's campaigning on the ground. But even with a wealth of individual photographs and the ability to make out the smallest of details, there remained the problem of interpretation. What did it all mean?

Despite their own heavy losses in 1916, the Allies believed that the Germans were increasingly vulnerable and that a decisive battle was just around the corner. After all, the Germans had suffered huge casualties at Verdun and on the Somme and were facing economic catastrophe, thanks to the British Naval Blockade and to a substantial division of resources to fund their two-front war. The newly appointed commander-in-chief of the French armies on the Western Front, General Robert Nivelle, a charismatic and strongly opinionated man, orchestrated an April offensive that would marshal vast amounts of troops and materiel in an attack along the Chemin des Dames ridge adjacent to the Aisne River.

This move would exploit the vulnerable German bulge in the front between the Scarpe and the Ancre rivers: the Noyon salient. To allow for the reallocation of French resources, the British Expeditionary Force would take over a French sector and shoulder diversionary operations. In return for supporting Nivelle's initiative, the French would support Haig's offensive later in the year to capture the coastal ports being used by the Germans for their submarine attacks on Allied merchant shipping.

The Germans, however, had other ideas. What the photographic reconnaissance flights revealed, but incompletely understood, was the creation of imposing defences, the Hindenburg Line, well behind their exposed salient. Even as Caldwell was flying on his photographic sorties, the enemy had already begun to leave its forward positions for this imposing bulwark of entrenchments, gun emplacements, forts and fields of barbed wire. This would derail Allied plans and allow the Germans to rationalise their resources along a much shorter and better fortified position. They were playing the long game.

With insufficient resources for an offensive on the Western Front, the Germans were preparing an energy-sapping defensive posture that had two purposes: defeating the Russians on the Eastern Front would allow the redistribution of German troops to the west, while giving the U-boats their best chance to diminish Britain's war-making capacity through unrestricted submarine attacks. If this plan did not win Germany the war in 1917, it would at least set it up for a crushing offensive the following year.

To prevent the Allies successfully monitoring the German abandonment of the salient, the Luftstreitkräfte deployed their Jastas on interception missions. On 6 March, 20-year-old Englishman Philip Joyce was to fly one of the camera-fitted Nieuports, with Caldwell, Lindsey Weedon and Frank Bower running interference.[33] The flight took off at 9.15 a.m. and set a course for the northern sector of the German salient. Caldwell led the sortie, his Nieuport's right-hand spar trailing the fluttering flight commander's ribbon. Over the German positions, Joyce began his photographic routine while his sentinels maintained a vigilant lookout. It was a trouble-free operation and the four Nieuports wheeled for home.

Once over the British lines and close to Filescamp, Caldwell, Weedon and Bower waved off Joyce and turned back to hunt down a pair of German aircraft they had seen in the distance. The Nieuports relocated their prey near Cambrai and dived on an Aviatik, which fled east. Caldwell and Weedon then attacked a green two-seater of unknown type. The observer fired explosive bullets at the RFC pair and entered a spiral descent before flattening out at 3000 feet to flee for home. When Caldwell's flight landed at Filescamp they were surprised to learn that Joyce had failed to return. Then, further disturbing news arrived: the commanding officer, Evelyn Graves, was dead.

Not long after Caldwell's quartet had taken off, Graves, leading A Flight, had embarked on a midday offensive patrol. Twenty minutes into the operation, they observed an FE2 being attacked by eight Albatros fighters. They sped to intervene but arrived only to see the cornered biplane fall to earth. The enemy set upon Graves, who was killed instantly by a bullet through the eye. His plummeting machine caught fire and crashed north of Rivière. 'Major Graves shot down in flames this side [of the lines] by Huns,' Caldwell wrote in his logbook that night.[34]

In the weeks that followed, neither Joyce nor his aeroplane was found. Only after the war was it revealed that Jasta 1 had claimed a victory over a Sopwith rotary machine on the return route to Filescamp. Joyce had probably been hit by the

Above: **From left: Keith Caldwell, Spencer Horn, Robert Chidlaw-Roberts and Frederick Selous in October 1917.**

Below: **Philip Joyce's Nieuport 17 lies in a muddy field. His body was recovered by German troops on 16 March 1917.**

Westphalian pilot Wilhelm Cymera, his second victim on the way to becoming an ace.[35] The two deaths, within hours of each other, were a blow to Caldwell. He judged Evelyn Graves 'one of the best COs I ever knew'.[36] Philip Joyce was the first man he had lost under his command.

These sobering tragedies, the unrelenting sorties and the pitiless cold of the previous months told on Caldwell. His skin broke out with eczema and scabies. He was physically and mentally run down and after eight months at war, in which he had flown on no fewer than 160 occasions, his overdue extended leave finally came through.[37] His last flight was the ill-fated photographic sortie with Joyce; on 12 March he was placed on Home Establishment and returned to England.[38]

In London, his condition failed to improve and 14 days later he was admitted to a fever and infectious diseases infirmary: Grove Military Hospital in Tooting Grove. He had suppurating boils on his lower limbs, and on 15 April he was operated on under chloroform and then confined to bed. After 10 days, he was well enough to transfer to north London and a temporary residence at The Berners Hotel, where his mother and sister plied him with food and ensured that he rested. On the last day of the month, he appeared before a medical board, his condition completely improved.

He had spent so much of his leave in hospital and convalescing that he was granted a further three weeks. During his recovery, letters from the front arrived with the daily copies of the London newspapers. They were full of disquieting rumours of a new offensive.

CHAPTER TEN

Hot Stuff

The Germans' planned withdrawal caught the Allies by surprise. The first sign was spiralling columns of black smoke as far as the eye could see: in their scorched-earth retreat, the Germans were burning everything in the salient. Sixty Squadron was sent up, as new arrival William 'Moley' Molesworth recalled:

> We crossed the lines and expected to get it pretty hot from Archie, but strangely enough, nothing happened. Heading towards Croisille, we came out of thick cloud and saw a most extraordinary sight. For miles around every village was a blazing mass with smoke columns, like great water-spouts, ascending upwards to the clouds. Along the roads one could see lines of retreating men making for the Hindenburg defences, which we could plainly distinguish owing to the amount of barbed wire entanglements round them.

On the days when flying was not possible, the airmen toured the newly vacated German positions. 'Having seized a tender, we pushed off after breakfast towards the line,' wrote Molesworth. 'No Man's Land was dotted about with shell holes. A few broken stumps of trees lined the road — war worn veterans that had stood the test of battle.'[1] The bleached skeletons of French infantry hung in the tangled barbed wire where they had been killed in 1915.

The desire for more air intelligence, and the German determination to deny it to the RFC, led to appalling losses. In the second half of March, C Flight was shorn of Arthur Whitehead and Frank Bower. Whitehead was caught in a carefully laid ambush. The decoy, a lone German two-seater, lured the Englishman in before he was jumped by a quadruplet from Jasta 2. Whitehead's attacker was Westphalian Werner Voss, whose bullets set the Nieuport on fire. Whitehead survived the flames and the crash but was badly burnt. He became a prisoner of war and Voss's fifteenth official victim.[2] The details of Bower's death made grim reading.

In the last week of March, a brace from C Flight was attacked by nine Albatroses, one flown by Kurt Wolff.[3] Struck in the back by an explosive round, Bower suffered horrific injuries. He made it back across the lines, holding his intestines in one hand and controlling the stick with the other. He landed, tumbled out of the aircraft and staggered about 40 yards before collapsing.[4] He died of his wounds the following day.

In Caldwell's absence, the flight's new commander, Alan Binnie, was now overseeing a very different force from the one his Anzac colleague had commanded only weeks before. To make matters worse, Caldwell was informed that the squadron had received a batch of structurally compromised Nieuports. Heavy losses in the last week of March had required new machines from the Nieuport factory in Paris, but some were so badly constructed they soon began to break up: one fell apart while diving on a hostile two-seater; another collapsed during practice flying; and, on a third, the wings folded upwards when the machine was pulling out of a dive. On another occasion, a 60 Squadron pilot had to apologise to his commanding officer: 'Sorry I left the patrol. My lower plane [wing] came off, so I thought I had better land.'[5]

The outcome could be fatal. Twenty-four-year-old Chaloner Caffyn, a goalkeeper for the British national field hockey team before the war, was shooting at stationary ground targets from 2500 feet during a training flight when his starboard wing detached itself from the machine. His death, on 28 March 1917, came within one week of his arrival at the unit. The cause of these accidents was the 'badly seasoned wood . . . being used by the French manufacturers, who also allowed a lot of little screws to be inserted in the main spars, thus weakening them considerably'.[6] RFC headquarters moved to remedy the situation, but it was too late for Caffyn.

April brought more shocking losses to the Allied air services and 60 Squadron as they supported the preparatory BEF operation at Arras and the opening days of the French Nivelle Offensive. Although the Luftstreitkräfte was outnumbered in the British sector, it had superior machines and a smart defensive posture. Trenchard's dogged offensive strategy was tested to breaking point by the Germans' astute tactical decision to fight on their own side of the lines with well-coordinated Jastas. 'Bloody April' had begun.

On 7 April, 60 Squadron lost three airmen, one of them falling to von Richthofen. When the Battle of Arras started two days later, the unit experienced its worst long weekend of the entire war. On Saturday, 14 April, there were four casualties, among them Alan Binnie, who had led an offensive patrol. Of his five-strong flight, he was the only one with anything resembling sufficient combat experience. All the others had only flown a single sortie; John Cock from Nelson, New Zealand, had flown none.

At 9.15 a.m., Binnie spotted a pair of German two-seaters and dived with his greenhorns in tow. Unfortunately, it was another carefully laid ambush. The RFC flight was set upon by six members of Jasta 11. It was a feeding frenzy. Kurt Wolff, Sebastian Festner and the two Richthofen brothers, Manfred and Lothar, each destroyed a machine. In attempting to protect his charges, Binnie was hit by Lothar von Richthofen: 'I got an explosive bullet through the left arm from somewhere underneath.' Blood spurted all over the cockpit. The wounded Australian put out a fire that had been ignited by the incendiary round, then fainted at 3000 feet. 'When I came to, I was on a stretcher with my wound bound up, lying beside my machine which was a total wreck and about 500 Huns around me.'[7] Binnie's arm was later removed by German surgeons. In all, three of the flight were captured and imprisoned. John Cock, whose wings had been sewn onto his uniform only 11 days earlier, was killed immediately.[8]

Sunday, 15 April was a poor day for flying but 60 Squadron went up even so and lost two machines and pilots. And then came a dispiriting Monday. C Flight spotted a British two-seater under attack and moved to relieve the beleaguered machine. Jasta 11 again took advantage of the situation. Four men were shot down; three were captured. The unit and RFC had entered a vicious cycle of fresh replacements followed by more losses. Graves' replacement, Alan Scott, who had taken up his post on 10 March, was forced to suspend operations for two days. During Bloody April, the squadron had a 100 per cent casualty rate, losing its entire complement of 18 airmen. The total casualties for the RFC and RNAS was 422 aircrew and 280 machines, over double the losses of the previous month and 20 times higher than that of April 1916.[9]

In May 1917, six more 60 Squadron pilots lost their lives. That month also saw the death of Albert Ball. The irrepressible Englishman, who flew with 56 Squadron and was credited with over 40 victories, was last seen chasing Lothar von Richthofen's red

Albatros when he flew into thick thundercloud. No one knew exactly what happened, but his loss was greatly mourned by Caldwell and all who had flown with Ball. He was only three months short of his twenty-first birthday when he died.

Caldwell, eager to get back to work, telegraphed Scott to say he was 'fit and ready to return'. Scott, in turn, wrote to his superiors: 'I hope very much that it will be found possible to re-post him to this Squadron.'[10] Although there was a suggestion that Caldwell might be sent to 56 Squadron to fly the new SE5 fighter from the Royal Aircraft Factory, the well-connected Scott — an Oxford-trained London barrister, with a range of famous and flamboyant friends, including Winston Churchill, the cigar-munching former First Lord of the Admiralty — got what he wanted: Caldwell received his posting back to the Nieuports and 60 Squadron.[11]

In the third week of May 1917, Caldwell found his squadron's little corner of the Western Front much changed. Freed from their winter lodgings, Filescamp Farm's animals were out grazing; the fields were rich in wheat, corn, barley and oats and the orchard was in full leaf. The warm French sun promised a hot summer.

Scott gave Caldwell an enthusiastic welcome. Scott had a deft touch with both his superiors and subordinates. One contemporary, William Sholto Douglas, described him as 'cheerful and imperturbable, and charming in his manner towards everyone', but a 'ham-fisted pilot'.[12] Scott relied on a pair of walking canes: injured in a training crash that had snapped both his legs, in order to complete his instruction he had to hobble out to his machine with a cane in each hand before being hoisted and levered into the cockpit by mechanics.[13] Scott was widely admired for his tenacity and recklessness in the air; on numerous occasions he returned from an exuberant sortie with his aeroplane 'riddled from end to end'.[14]

Prudence and official orders dictated that most squadron commanders led from the ground, but Scott led by example in the air. In this way, he acquired all his victories in aerial combat after his promotion, as his 1917 Military Cross citation made clear:

> He has on several occasions attacked and destroyed enemy aircraft and taken successful photographs under heavy fire. He has constantly shown the greatest courage in attacking numerous hostile machines single-handed, during which

Alan 'Jack' Scott was commanding officer for much of his time with 60 Squadron. Eccentric and strong-willed, he was one of several officers to have a significant influence on Keith Caldwell's career and leadership.

on two occasions his own machine was considerably damaged. His great coolness, dash, and resource have set an excellent example to his squadron.[15]

Scott also liked to venture abroad on lone patrols for a dust-up with the enemy or to keep a fatherly eye on a patrol he had dispatched. In the third week of May, on what he officially called a 'recreation' flight at 7000 feet over Monchy-le-Preux, he spotted eight red Albatros fighters. He proceeded to attack the mob, barely escaping with his life under the withering fire of the up-and-coming Karl Allmenröder of Jasta 11. Only a forced landing saved him.[16] Some pilots, particularly German airmen, accumulated trophies from aircraft they had shot up, but Scott happily adorned his walls with the detritus of his *own* maltreated machines. As Caldwell noted, Scott's office was full of Nieuport debris.

Scott was also notoriously casual. Soon after Caldwell's return to the unit, he flew on the dawn patrol unshaven and dressed only in pyjamas, a Burberry coat, bedroom slippers and snow boots.[17] Once airborne, Scott found more than he bargained for when he attacked a formation that turned out to be the Flying Circus. Outnumbered and outmatched, he made a forced landing near the front lines. His mind then turned to the morning's long-anticipated inspection of 60 Squadron by no less a figure than the Third Army commander, General Edmund Allenby. Frantically, Scott acquired a horse and was seen bouncing along in his pyjamas before transferring to a staff car and racing to the aerodrome.

As he later wrote, out of sight of the impatient top brass, and '[my] costume being hardly that prescribed for inspections, [I] dived into [my] ... hut, did the quickest shave on record, and timidly approached the glittering cortège.'[18] Allenby was bemused, the brigadier and wing commander less so. Scott, who had met Caldwell just before he went on leave, observed that the New Zealander was 'beloved by everyone'. Nonetheless, Caldwell was 'a curious instance of a fine and fearless fighter, but a bad shot' who did not then have 'many Huns'.[19] The remark reflected a six-month drought in victories for Caldwell.

As leader of B Flight, Caldwell shared his quarters with the commanders of A and C Flights: William Molesworth and William 'Bish' Bishop. Moley was a curly-

From left: Billy Bishop, William Molesworth and Australian pilot Graham Young horseplaying in front of their barracks, dubbed the 'Abode of Love'.

haired Irishman with a vivid imagination and a good eye for prose, Bish an effervescent Canadian with serious eyes but a ready smile. At 21, Caldwell was a year younger than his roommates but half a head taller and more robustly built. All three were exceptional airmen, but Bishop, whose uniform and current role could barely contain his self-confidence, was on the way to becoming a wartime celebrity. 'Hardly a day passed during April and May without Bishop destroying at least one Hun machine,' recalled Alan Scott years later.[20] While the squadron was sustaining heavy losses, Bishop achieved a remarkable 17 victories, making him one of the RFC's most prolific pilots. As Molesworth told his family, 'Our "stunt-merchant" is good at this game, and continues to add to his score, seldom coming back without firing his red light.'[21]

The trio shared a half-barrel-shaped corrugated-iron Nissen hut with the cubicle partitions removed and furnished with tables, comfortable chairs and rugs. A coal stove provided heat in winter, and petrol lamps gave excellent light for reading and writing.[22] It was a convivial space, with ample room for games of cards and other sociable activities not always feasible in the rowdy mess. 'But their move evoked mocking gestures from some other pilots, who began by painting "Salon Bar" on a filled-in window space, and followed this up with "Hôtel du Commerce" under the rounding edge of the corrugated-iron roof,' recalled one Filescamp Farm airman. 'Finally, some more gifted wag painted "Abode of Love" on the door, and the name stuck.'[23]

By mid-1917, RFC officers were often able to bring over 'practically every article of kit' they desired; infantry officers would have had to leave nine-tenths of it behind.[24] Among Caldwell's belongings was a prized gramophone and a small collection of records, reminders of his days with 8 Squadron when he and the other pilots reclined outside Albert Ball's tent listening to classical and wartime hits.[25]

Caldwell's immediate concern was his own flight of five men. William Gunner and William Jenkins were 'veterans' of March and April, but Roland Harris, Warren Gilchrist and Ralph Phalen had only arrived in May, the last two only three days before Caldwell's return. He had more time in the field than all five combined. And according to one of his former superiors, Gunner had a problematic background. His chief difficulty lay in 'working the rudder correctly' and he lacked 'experience and skill'. After proving 'totally incapable of flying two-seater Nieuports' and working as an observer, he was sent to No. 1 Aircraft Depot, St Omer,

> where he flew a Bristol for an hour and a half and did not smash it, so was returned here. He put up another disgusting exhibition and finally landed in

a colossal pancake from a height greater than the sheds. Luckily there was a strong wind blowing and he merely turned on to a wing tip. But I am fully convinced that he can't fly the two-seater and hope for your sake that he does better on the single. Anyhow he will merely do himself in if he does crash and that is not so bad.[26]

In the following weeks, under Caldwell's leadership, Gunner would become a well-regarded fighter pilot.

Like many good flight commanders, Caldwell was protective of his men, especially the new arrivals. After the war, Scott singled out Grid and a handful of others as having 'always played for the squadron, and not his own hand', taking 'endless pains to enter young pilots to the game, watching them on their first patrols as a good and patient huntsman watches over his young hounds'.[27] Caldwell attempted to keep them alive long enough to learn to fly in formation and follow his lead — not an easy task for a freshly posted pilot constantly adjusting his air speed and too often mesmerised by the immediate environment of cockpit, engine cowling, struts, spars and wires, all dominating his near vision. Added to this was the cold, the battering and clatter of the pistons and tappets and the wind whistling through the wires. All of this meant that formation flying, let alone looking out for potential threats, was initially challenging.

Caldwell had to instruct Harris, Gilchrist and Phalen in the rapidly developing observational arts of 1917, such as figure-eight scanning while gently corkscrewing the aeroplane to elevate blind spots and being prepared for a confrontation with a menacing Albatros intent on wiping them from the sky.[28] As one 60 Squadron airman wrote of his first flight: 'The way I clung to my companions that day reminded me of some child hanging to its mother's skirts, while crossing a crowded street.'[29] Novice airmen were regularly placed at the rear of the formation or tucked in the middle. Nonetheless, men with inadequate instruction and flying time were thrust into operations against well-organised and determined foes.

Some proved ill suited to the stresses of piloting a single-seat fighter. Caldwell was realistic about referring to Scott men who were a danger to themselves and others. Despite the shortage of airmen, Scott was forced to write to his superiors about a man who 'lost formation and on several occasions . . . he either failed to start with the patrol, being unable to start his engine (once), or, having started came back because he had lost his leader'. This airman got completely lost on one sortie and only reappeared 'by accident' about the same time as the patrol arrived over the aerodrome. He was recommended for two-seater reconnaissance work.

Another 60 Squadron pilot proved unresponsive to clear direction:

> I beg to report that the . . . named officer is not capable of performing the work of this squadron. I have given him a very extended trial of nearly two months, during which time he has had far more instruction given to him than the average pilot. He does not show the slightest improvement, though he does try. He can carry on all right at ordinary flying and makes fair landings, but war flying on a Nieuport Scout is too difficult for him. I have tried him as a last resort at photography, and his three efforts at this were quite hopeless, again in spite of a good deal of instruction . . . In the meantime, I have stopped him flying on offensive patrols.

When Scott was temporarily absent or on longer leave, it fell to Caldwell and Molesworth to organise any necessary transfers. In the last week of the following month, the New Zealander would be forced to write an assessment regarding one young man who, despite his keenness, was 'not naturally a scout pilot: he has difficulty in manoeuvring his machine during a fight'. But though he seemed to lack 'the requisite dash and initiative for a pilot of a single-seater machine . . . in a two-seater he would, I am sure, do quite well'.

Molesworth, too, feared what might become of this airman should he find 'himself in a tight corner'.[30] Never fully reconciled to Caldwell's assessment, the pilot later secured a posting to a frontline squadron of Sopwith Camels. Within two days of his arrival, he received a gunshot wound to the right arm.[31]

On his first day back, Caldwell was in the air for his first intoxicating flight in three months. After 15 minutes above the aerodrome at 2000 feet, he became fully reacquainted with his machine in a one-hour escorting sortie and a final warming-down jaunt. The following day ran a similar course. On both occasions, his patrols included Gunner and the novice Gilchrist. Then the fighting began.

On 25 May, Caldwell led his flight out on hostile aircraft duty, an aggressive offensive patrol seeking out enemy observation machines and tussling with the escorts. It was a heavy morning of dogfighting, in which some 20 Albatroses swirled and fired at the Nieuports and various other RFC machines, including a Bristol F2b Fighter and a clutch of Sopwith Triplanes from the local naval squadron. No sooner had Caldwell escaped the clutches of one Albatros than another was on his tail. 'I turned to follow this machine again, when I was attacked by one Scout from behind. I turned and got on the tail of this machine, which dived steeply after a few shots, and when following was again attacked from behind and the right by two scouts,' he wrote that night in his after-action report.[32]

It was Jasta 11, with Karl Allmenröder creating havoc. In the mêlée, the former Rhineland medical student and his wingmen separated Gilchrist from the RFC herd. The young man, badly wounded, force-landed on the wrong side of the lines and was captured. It was Caldwell's first loss in his new command. There were further scraps over the next two days. Then came one of the defining moments of his flying career.

Like Caldwell, German ace Werner Voss had begun his career in a bomber squadron before transferring to a fighter unit. Here he was befriended by Manfred von Richthofen, and the pair became collaborators and competitors in numerous assaults on the pride of the RFC. Voss was a curious mixture of brutality and gentlemanliness. He was known to strafe defenceless, downed adversaries, but also to visit the survivors of his attacks in hospital. On the airfield he was notoriously scruffy, often covered in grease and mucking in with the mechanics, but he always flew in his best officer's attire, including a silk shirt and scarf, in order, he said, to look his best for the girls of Paris should he suffer the indignity of being captured. By the time he was given temporary command of Jasta 5, the 20-year-old tanner's son, from Krefeld in North Rhine-Westphalia, had amassed 28 victories in his great rivalry with von Richthofen.

The great James McCudden and Mick Mannock, who flew with 56 and 40 squadrons respectively, had both been outshone by Voss. In late 1916, McCudden had spotted a lone Halberstadt fighter flying in languid circles through puffs of black anti-aircraft fire over a village well to the rear of the British lines. McCudden's commander led the flight in while the English flying ace positioned himself between the intruder and the German lines in the unlikely event that the latter survived the unequal battle and scampered for home. The RFC machines were filling the air with bullets, but the Halberstadt was unbelievably slippery and 'fought like anything'.

The German cheated his way free and darted past McCudden, who swung in on the enemy and began firing. 'He at once turned and put me off his tail. This went on until the Hun . . . turned at right angles, so that I got a very close view of the pilot at about 20 yards, I swear that he was grinning.' McCudden was awestruck: 'What he was doing over our lines I do not know, but he was a very cool and experienced hand, for I must admit he made us all look like fools.'[33]

McCudden and others were persuaded that the pilot of the Halberstadt was none other than Werner Voss showboating in the face of numerous foes.[34] By mid-1917, the German was flying an Albatros DIII that had a reddish-purple hue on the upper wings, an effect created by the fabric made up of alternating purple, green and dark brown lozenges. The fuselage was plain varnished plywood, decorated with good luck symbols, including a red heart and a Hindu swastika. Mannock recorded his own brush with the German aerial maestro: 'Ran into my old friend the "purple man" again a few weeks ago. No luck. He's a marvel. For ten minutes I was three hundred feet over him, and he manoeuvred so cleverly that I was unable to get my gun on him once. He got away in the end.'[35] It was Voss whom Caldwell is believed to have met on 28 May 1917.[36]

An hour before midday, Caldwell took off, leading Gunner, Jenkins and Phalen on an offensive patrol. Along the way, they picked up an RFC two-seat Bristol F2b Fighter. Scanning the sky, they spied two formations of scouts, 'nine in one and six in the other'.[37] In the pursuit, Gunner and Jenkins were beset by technical difficulties and the Bristol was also left behind. Caldwell and Phalen pressed on and were rewarded when, over the ruined town of Lens, they spied a pair of enemy two-seaters below. As Caldwell dropped the nose of the Nieuport onto one of the intruders, and the machine gun sent bullets in long arching streams, the German observer shouted at his pilot, who put his aeroplane into a spiralling dive. Caldwell fired off more rounds, but as he closed in for the kill, he heard the bark of twin Schwarzlose machine guns and turned his head to see three enemy fighters hot on his tail: Voss, plus Otto Konniecke and Kurt Schuhmann of Jasta 5. Caldwell faced them alone; Phalen was already dead, killed by Schuhmann.

Caldwell pried himself free from the Albatroses, but one, with fluttering streamers on his wing tips, hung on.[38] The Nieuport was thrown around the sky as Caldwell twisted and turned to avoid the well-directed 8mm machine guns. Caldwell's fuel tank was struck, and the engine began to falter. His heart hammered. This was no ordinary foe; this was the first time he had encountered a German aircraft the Nieuport could not outmanoeuvre.[39]

Desperate with fear, he tried every trick he knew, but to no avail; the 'flying wire, aileron control and strut and main spar were shot through'.[40] The Albatros was 20 miles per hour faster and, in the hands of one of Germany's best airmen, impossible to shake off.[41] Below, Allied soldiers watched the pair descend in broken steps from

Werner Voss was arguably the best pilot of the German war effort. Keith Caldwell survived a frightening encounter with Voss and later witnessed the Westphalian's fateful last dogfight in September 1917.

7000 to under 1000 feet above Lens. Then, some luck. Caldwell's motor came on in a last desperate climbing turn and he found the German machine banking ahead of him. 'I fired for the first time until about colliding point and then whipped on to his tail, missed hitting him and he quickly drew away.'[42] Only 200 feet above the ground, the Albatros set a course for the German lines. The two other scouts made 'half-hearted' attacks, but Caldwell was able to turn for home, leaking fuel and nursing the chewed-up Nieuport.

The ground crew gathered around in admiration at Caldwell's ability to bring the badly damaged grid home, if not entirely in one piece. Long hours lay ahead to get it airworthy again. Shaken, and with bullet holes through his clothes, Caldwell was unharmed and ecstatic to be alive.[43] 'When I returned . . . from patrol, an anti-aircraft battery west of Lens had phoned through, reporting this scrap and said they thought it had been Voss's machine.'[44] His logbook entry for day recorded his adversary as 'Vosserino' and 'hot stuff'.[45]

Billy Bishop's successes in aerial attacks were predominately accumulated on his well-known solo hunter–killer missions. 'He works by himself a lot now,' Molesworth noted, 'preferring to surprise the Hun by hiding rather than by trying to get him in a scrap'.[46] Not everyone was pleased with Alan Scott's endorsement of Bishop. William Fry had recently returned from leave to find himself 'running [Bishop's] Flight and leading nearly all the patrols as the Flight Commander was very much the lone hunter and off by himself . . . It is difficult to imagine whom amongst the previous COs, would have tolerated, or at least, not encouraged, the male equivalent of a "Prima Donna" in one of the Flights.'[47] But Scott, himself a practitioner of lone-wolf tactics, encouraged Bishop, aware that he was a rising star — he had 22 victories to his name by the end of May — who could win laurels for the RFC and 60 Squadron.

In early June, the Canadian ace proposed a surprise attack on an enemy aerodrome and invited his roommates to join in. Molesworth was on leave, replaced temporarily by the experienced William Fry. Burdened with the heavy demands of scheduled routine patrols and after a late night in the mess, both Caldwell and Fry declined the offer of an extra and highly speculative flight.[48]

Undeterred, at 3.57 a.m. on 2 June, Bishop took off in search of a sleepy German airfield. He crossed the enemy lines 15 minutes later and near Anneux found an abandoned aerodrome. Soon, though, he hit the jackpot: an airfield with buildings, hangars and a line-up of plump machines — Albatros fighters and a two-seater. As he recorded in his autobiography, Bishop opened fire, 'scattering the bullets all around the machines, and coming down to fifty feet in doing so, I do not know how many men I hit, or what damage was done, except that one man, at least, fell and several others ran to pick him up'. As he 'watched the fun', he 'heard the old familiar rattle of the quick firers'. Not daring to go too far away, 'as then I would not be able to catch the machines as they left the ground, so turning quickly and twisting about, I did my best to evade the fire from the ground. Looking at my plane's [wings], I saw that the guns were doing pretty good shooting. There were several holes in them already and this made me turn and twist all the more.'[49]

Bishop's concern was well founded: the taxiing machines were in the throes of taking off. He sat in behind one ascending from the field and 'as cool as can be' opened fire and brought it down. Another crashed into trees under his withering fire. A third was fatally struck in a turning low altitude dogfight and sent 'crashing to the ground'. Low on ammunition and fearful of the arrival of machines from alerted neighbouring aerodromes, he pushed off for home.

Over the still-sleeping huts of Filescamp Farm he fired off his signal lights frantically in celebration of his success. The ground crew rushed out to see Bishop crawl from the cockpit, and breathlessly replayed the sortie for the squadron's pilots.[50] Scott was thrilled and, as Bishop recorded, 'within three or four hours, I had received many congratulations upon this stunt, and what I had planned as merely a way of shooting down some more of the Huns, I found the authorities considered a very successful expedition.' Bypassing the usual RFC channels and using a well-positioned friend, Scott got word of Bishop's flight to Allenby.[51]

But Caldwell and Fry were uneasy about elements of the story. The next day, Fry went over to the flight hangar, where Bishop's machine was the centre of attention: 'I remember clearly seeing a group of about five bullet holes in the rear half of his tail-plane, the elevator, within a circle of not more than six inches diameter at the most. Whatever machine was on his tail must have been very close indeed to achieve this group.'[52]

To Fry this was not evidence of extensive ground fire, and the close circle of bullet holes was entirely inconsistent with the wide spread of holes created by an enemy pilot raking a Nieuport with deflection shooting. Some of the bullet holes appeared

Overleaf: **Two of 60 Squadron's 'stars': the light and manoeuvrable French-designed Nieuport and the lone-wolf hunter, Billy Bishop. The Canadian ace was a celebrated personality in the British air service but became a figure of considerable debate in the decades afterwards.**

to have black cordite around them, suggesting they were made by an unusually close machine gun.

Curiously, according to Fry, Bishop's Lewis machine gun was missing. The Canadian claimed it had jammed, and that when he was unable to get it back up into position he had thrown it over the side. Fry later speculated that Bishop may have landed and at close quarters fired his own machine gun at the Nieuport before throwing it way and taking off for Filescamp Farm. Fry found the 'maintenance crew of the aircraft . . . discussing their suspicions . . . which I discussed with them, but we took care to keep to ourselves'.[53] 'Every one of us, except Jack Scott, knew what was going on,' said Caldwell decades later, 'and there were moments when some of us nearly went to tell the CO what was happening, but we did not like to'.[54]

When Scott went on leave in the fourth week of June a phone call came through from 13 Wing headquarters asking for verifying details of the sortie. Caldwell was in a bind: it did not sit well with him to cast doubts on a fellow airman's claims, and he liked Bishop, who was popular, brave and exceptionally talented. Moreover, to do so would have contradicted Scott's unquestioning support. The result was the sparest of reports, a handful of words that evinced no enthusiasm for the task and reflected the paucity of real corroborating evidence. All that was known with any precision was Bishop's time of departure and return, and the damage done to his machine: '17 bullet holes. Trailing edge of lower plane shot away in two bays.'[55]

Bishop had recorded the time he 'arrived at the hostile aerodrome' as 4.25 a.m. but, because he could not be certain of its location, Caldwell wrote: 'Distance 30 miles. Aerodrome S. of Cambrai'. The report was based on 'personal evidence only'. There were no eyewitnesses and later research showed that the Germans had recorded no such attack on any airfield in that region on the day in question.[56]

Scott and others, however, were convinced, and within a few weeks Billy Bishop was awarded a VC for an action to which he was the sole witness. The strangeness of it all had the potential to cast doubt on Bishop's other aerial exploits, many of which were similarly unseen. While Scott was away from the third week of July to the first week of August, and Caldwell was overseeing the squadron, the Canadian's victory rate took a noticeable dip. Was this because Caldwell was more circumspect about accepting poorly supported claims or simply because, as Bishop's logbook recorded, the Canadian flew fewer sorties in this period? If the latter, did he undertake fewer flights because he knew he would find little sympathy from Caldwell?

The pair of combat in air reports submitted by Bishop during Caldwell's regime were ambiguous at best. On a 24 June claim, Caldwell wrote that 'Captain Bishop was out alone' and explained the lack of independent verification, but the claim was accepted without confirmation.[57] On 28 June, the Canadian reported attacking a single-seat fighter which 'then dived down, apparently to land'. Caldwell assessed the claim as 'indecisive' and noted that 'Captain Bishop was again by himself'.[58] At some point, however, the report was inexplicably upgraded to a 'German machine which fell out of control and broke in pieces before crashing'.[59]

All this confirmed William Fry's suspicions about Bishop's loose attitude to claims. On his very first outing with Bishop in early May, they had fired on an enemy two-seat machine at very long range with 'very little chance of hitting them'.

> On landing, Bishop came up to me and to my surprise said, 'we got him alright, did you see him go down and crash.' Now I had not seen a German machine go down . . . But such was Bishop's reputation in the Squadron that I thought he must have attacked and brought down another, closer machine, which I had not seen. I was certainly not going to contradict him. I was young and unsure of myself, feeling very much on trial under new management, and was not going to jeopardise my place in the Squadron . . .

But many years later, Fry could 'still recollect the sight of the German two-seater turning sharply away and it giving me perhaps the first suspicions as to my Flight Commander's credibility'.[60]

CHAPTER ELEVEN

Leading Lights

The losses of Bloody April and May 1917 were accompanied by very significant French setbacks in the Nivelle Offensive. Tactically the French secured several German emplacements west of the Hindenburg Line and the British advanced along the Scarpe River. Nonetheless, a decisive battle against the Germans remained elusive and, subjected to high losses and convinced of General Nivelle's cavalier and wasteful use of his men, French soldiers mutinied in May. Nivelle was replaced by General Philippe Pétain.

Meanwhile the weight of the Allied effort swung north to Flanders, where British offensives would relieve pressure on the beleaguered French and regain ground lost in 1914, including strategically important ridges south and east of Ypres; they would also clear the Belgian coast up to the Dutch border. These objectives, including Passchendaele, would consolidate the Allied position in the northern sector of the Western Front, preparing the ground for the impending arrival of large numbers of Americans the following year.

The preliminary effort was at Messines Ridge, south of Ypres, which afforded the Germans a commanding view across the British sector; for the Allies, its capture was vital. The assault on Messines was opened with one of the biggest series of explosions in the history of warfare, detonated in tunnels dug by British, New Zealand and Canadian troops over nearly two years.

At 3.10 a.m. on 7 June, the earth shook as upended German positions were pounded by a concentration of over 2200 artillery pieces. British troops, with bayonets fixed, swept across no man's land to overwhelm the dazed Germans. To blunt the British advance, German artillery desperately needed guidance from the Luftsteitkärte's reconnaissance machines, and two-seaters were in abundance over the battlefield the next day. As soldiers swarmed newly captured German positions, 60 Squadron was thrust into the action in increasingly important wireless interception patrols.

Caldwell was aloft with William Gunner and William Molesworth on a morning patrol when they encountered a string of German intruders. On five separate occasions over two hours, they attacked no fewer than six German two-seat machines. That afternoon, Caldwell took part in another two-hour patrol, firing on a two-seater accompanied by a fighter.[1] All of the attacks were inconclusive. The Germans wanted intelligence but were circumspect in the face of the Nieuports. It was part of a continuing game of cat-and-mouse with the German reconnaissance machines. When ground observers spotted an enemy two-seater, they phoned the squadron, a horn sounded and three waiting men would take off to intercept. Then, in Molesworth's words, the 'hide and seek begins'.

> We try if possible, to hide in the clouds and approach the Hun when he is off guard. He, on the other hand, departs hurriedly into Hunland when he spots us, and as soon as we go, he comes back to carry on his job. We then turn on him again, but he is off like a flash, and so it goes until another three machines relieve us. It is really quite amusing at times, and, although we do not often bring our man down, we give him such a devil of a time, that he hasn't much of it to spare for his companions on the ground.[2]

As Caldwell noted after another fruitless attack in the second week of June, 'My patrols are still finding great difficulty in getting to close quarters with these enemy artillery machines.'[3] The elusive two-seaters were often protected by the groups of prowling sharks spoiling for a fight, the Albatros DIIIs.

Despite having more combat entanglements with the enemy than any other airman in the squadron, by mid-1917 Caldwell still had only two victories to his name. A few claimed this 'defect' was due to his poor marksmanship, but it was also widely acknowledged that Caldwell was parsimonious and cautious about making claims on his own behalf. 'Remarks on Caldwell being such a bad shot I think wrong,' wrote William Fry, 'it was that he would never make a claim unless absolutely certain of the result.'[4] This was also the opinion of Caldwell's superiors. As 13 Wing's commander, Lieutenant Colonel G. F. Pretyman, said a month later, 'This low number of enemy machines to his credit is due to his extreme modesty, and I have no hesitation in saying that he must have destroyed a considerably greater number of machines.'[5]

Caldwell's official change in fortunes began on 14 June when, on a morning offensive patrol, he fell upon three Albatros DIII fighters. Caldwell selected a flamboyantly painted machine with green, black and white tipped wings and whose fuselage glowed in luminous yellow. At 50 yards, 'I fired 15 rounds . . . into the cockpit.' The machine 'turned over and fell out of control as far as I could watch him, but as I was attacked by two enemy scouts from behind, I did not see this machine hit the ground.'[6] Two of the flight, William Jenkins and 19-year-old John Collier, corroborated Caldwell's report but likewise failed to see the Albatros crash. Then, however, came a phone call from an Allied anti-aircraft crew, who had seen the Albatros 'going down out of control'.[7] The squadron's intelligence officer marked it down as a confirmed victory, Caldwell's third claim, and his first enemy fighter.

Over the next couple of days, Caldwell recorded another victory.[8] Above Vitry, he and Fry were leading an eight-strong patrol of two flights when five enemy fighters of Jasta 12 bounced them out of the sun. Fry's flight joined battle, driving the Albatros machines down out of Caldwell's formation.[9] Soon all the machines were in a dogfight, and the rattle of machine guns punctuated the air. One of Fry's flight was extricated from an Albatros only to once again fall under fire from another determined foe. The German closed to within feet of the Nieuport before they collided at 2000 feet. Torn fabric and splintered wood sprayed the sky; two wrecked machines and their helpless occupants plummeted to the ground.

Caldwell attacked one enemy ineffectively before diving and firing '20 rounds close range at [a] Hun scout who dived vertically'.[10] Fry and Collier made sure of the assault and shared the 'destroyed' victory with Caldwell. Silesian pilot Hermann Becker made landfall with this shot-up aeroplane but was badly wounded.

On 24 June, Caldwell was directing an evening patrol south-east of Douai when three Albatros fighters were spotted. Leading the diving charge, Caldwell fired '40 rounds at 50 yards range at the top of the enemy aircraft'. The German pilot wheeled around in the face of the withering fire and dived east. His prey gone, the New Zealander located another 10 enemy machines below. Higher, and able to catch the intruders unaware, the patrol forced the enemy down to barely 500 feet; Caldwell caught two machines in the cross-hairs of his gunsight. They 'seemed to go out of control', was his subsequent laconic summation of the impact of his weapons fire.[11] Thanks to numerous witnesses, and a burning carcass on Douai aerodrome, Caldwell was given a destroyed and shared in one 'out of control'.[12] In the space of 10 days, with the double victory carrying his total to eight, Caldwell was now a fighter ace.

Next month, two more victims fell to his guns. Both his after-action reports were perfunctory. While patrolling over Graincourt-lès-Havrincourt at 14,000 feet, on 3 July, he 'dived at 7 E.A. [enemy aircraft] about 1,000ft below. I got within 30 yards of one E.A. before firing and then fired 50 rounds. The E.A. turned first to the left then to the right and then dived vertically, side slipping at times on the way down. I followed this E.A.s movements for about three minutes until he was lost in the haze.'

Then, on 15 July, he shared another claim with two from his flight. The trio fired over three drums at ranges from 80 to 20 yards before the enemy machine was last seen 'vertical close to the ground'.[13] The recording officer noted that this was confirmed by anti-aircraft personnel. One squadron member, Gerald Parkes, fell to the enemy. The heavily decorated Bavarian Adolf Ritter von Tutschek, commander of Jasta 12, shot through the young Englishman's fuel tank and wounded him in the arm. Forced to land, Parkes attempted to set fire to his Nieuport, but Tutschek circled, firing his machine guns near Parkes until German soldiers arrived and took him prisoner.[14]

Official reports gave no indication of the claustrophobic and chaotic battles in which short bursts and violent manoeuvres were the only means of hitting and avoiding the enemy. In a letter to his parents, Molesworth played up the bravado and played down his proximity to death. He was over La Gravelle when he saw two German two-seaters heading south-east: '"Here we are, my son," I said to myself. "We'll just hop down and put the gust up one of these Huns." No sooner said than done, I pushed my nose down and, when within range, opened fire. The next thing I knew was a perfect hail of bullets pouring around me.' Molesworth described the next few minutes:

> Crackle! Crackle! Crackle! . . . There's a Hun on my tail . . . The blighter is making my grid into a sieve . . . Let's pull her up in a good climbing turn and have a look at him. Heavens! It's the Circus. I wonder if old Richthof is the leader. The dirty dog nearly caught me out this time . . . don't hold fire long or he'd have made me cold meat by now. Let's give him a dose and see how he likes it. Here he comes, straight at me, loosing off with both guns. I hope we aren't going to collide. Missed! Bon! Everything's A1. Wish I'd hit him though. I must pull her up round

quick or he'll be on my tail. Hang! I can't shoot for toffee, but he's pretty dud too, thank heavens. Once again boys, round with her. Let him have it hot. No good. Try again. Confound it, there's my beastly drum empty. I must spin and change it. Good enough. Now, where's the blighter?

As the enemy machine came down on Molesworth's right, 'Crack! Crack! Crack! Bang! Zip! Zip! There goes my petrol tank; now for the flames. Cheero! No luck this time, you old swine. Wait till I get you next show. I managed to pull the machine out, just scraping over the trenches. The engine was still running, although the petrol was pouring out all over my legs. A few minutes afterwards the engine conked out altogether, and I had to land in field.' He was immediately surrounded by a crowd of men, including some artillery officers, 'who took me off to their mess and offered me a "tot", which was thankfully received, while they sent off a message to the squadron'.[15]

When Molesworth's Nieuport finally arrived at the aerodrome, there were six bullet holes in the propeller; the cowling had been shot away; there were large holes in the bottom of the petrol tank and sides; the main spar on the right-hand top plane was broken; the rear right-hand undercarriage strut was badly damaged; and there were 28 holes in the fuselage, and 10 in the plane, 'two or three missing the pilot's head by less than an inch'.[16]

Caldwell's 15 July engagement was the catalyst for official recognition of his outstanding efforts. Scott was fulsome in this recommendation. He pointed out that Caldwell had been with the squadron since November of the previous year and had done 'most excellent work during the whole of this time, with the exception of two months when he was away sick. He has had 59 combats in the air, in every one of which he has displayed considerable gallantry and skill.'[17] Higgins agreed, stating that Caldwell had also 'shown an excellent example to the rest of his squadron'.[18]

The result was a Military Cross. As Molesworth said, 'every cloud has its silver lining. This time it is in the shape of an MC for one of our Flight Commanders who thoroughly deserves it. He hasn't managed to get a big bag yet, but there is lots of the "good stuff" in him.'[19]

The news of Caldwell's award was widely applauded in the squadron and with a boisterous gathering in the mess. Caldwell generously presented his prized

Adolf Ritter von Tutschek posing in front of a captured Royal Aircraft Factory SE5a. Highly decorated for his efforts on the Eastern Front as a professional soldier, he entered the German air service on the Western Front in 1917 and accumulated 27 victories before his death in the late spring of 1918.

gramophone to B Flight, which gave them 'countless hours of amusement'. It became a mainstay of festivities, playing many of Caldwell's favourite songs, including, 'Some Girl Has Got to Darn His Socks' and Al Jolson's 'Ev'ry Little While'.[20]

Commendations, birthdays and visiting dignitaries were all occasions for celebration in 60 Squadron's mess, with its bar, piano and well-used chairs. On the memorable night when RFC commander-in-chief General Hugh Trenchard was a guest, an extremely inebriated Billy Bishop performed an elaborate tap-dance on top of the piano, while belting out the famed RFC ballad, 'The Dying Airman':

> Oh, the bold aviator was dying
> And as 'neath the wreckage he lay, he lay,
> To the sobbing mechanics about him
> These parting words did he say:
>
> 'Two valves you'll find in my stomach
> Three sparkplugs are safe in my lung, my lung,
> The prop is in splinters inside me,
> To my fingers the joystick has clung.
>
> 'And get you six brandies and sodas
> And lay them all out in a row,
> And get you six other good airmen
> To drink to this pilot below.
>
> 'Take the cylinders out of my kidneys
> The connecting rod out of my brain, my brain,
> From the small of my back take the crankshaft
> And assemble the engine again.'

When the audience booed and a bemused Trenchard said, 'My boy, stick to flying', the Canadian complained the piano was 'dried out', then poured a quart of the squadron's prized champagne into the instrument. 'It was three in the morning before the celebrants made their way to bed for a few hours' sleep before the dawn patrol.'[21]

When news came through of Bishop's VC, and 'after much celebration, singing and dancing, the Very light experts took command. Thus armed they began to raid the neighbouring squadrons . . . the number of coloured lights that appeared in the sky, in the huts, going through one window and out the other on the opposite side, created pandemonium that startled even the rats,' recalled another airman. 'We thought the whole place was going up in flames. Many of us stood by with troops armed with fire extinguishers, while the "Great Man" whirled about like a piece of paper in a gale.'[22]

As a later Filescamp resident, Arthur Gould Lee, wrote, 'these dirge-like doggerels were a mock-heroic rejection of fear, a maudlin scoffing at mortality, a reduction of gory extinction to the level of nursery rhymes, yet they were sung lustily by veterans who had seen sudden death, and escaped with their lives by inches, as they were by novices from England, to whom a violent end by bullets was still entirely an abstraction.'[23] Lee and others also appreciated Filescamp's rural aspect and orchard.

> Here in the hot weather we could sit in the shade with the light breeze rustling through the branches, and all was peace except for the mosquitoes and the wasps. In theory the fruit was the property of Monsieur Tetus, but . . . there was seldom much of a crop for his workers to collect . . . To sit among the trees, their leaves filtering the sun as one took a nap after a bountiful lunch, was indeed the height of contentment. From our seats . . . we couldn't even see the hangars at the top of the slope. We were far, far away from all the ugliness of war, especially the war of the trenches.[24]

The squadron possessed its own small collection of horses, dogs, goats and even a young pig. Caldwell periodically went riding with Scott and enjoyed the companionship of the dogs, with the exception of Bishop's large port-black part-Airedale, which was, as its owner candidly admitted, 'quite the smelliest dog he ever knew'. The Canadian recalled that 'Grid tried sprinkling him with face powder, but this only produced an even more offensive odour, and the dog was ordered to find sleeping quarters elsewhere'.[25] The 'long suffering little porker was at different times painted with either a red, white and blue roundel or with German Maltese crosses on its back and ears, plus a streamer on its tail', much to the amusement of the men.[26]

Over the previous winter, Caldwell's rugby prowess had been on full display, but it was his gift for tennis that shone in summer. Under Aspinall's direction, the squadron had laid down a tennis court with fine red gravel from a local mine, and by June 1917 it was the pride and joy of the men. Caldwell headed the list of good players, alongside Molesworth, and brothers David and George 'Zulu' Lloyd, who came from what were then known as the British sub-Saharan possessions. Caldwell's habit of using slang and simply making up words infiltrated a squadron tennis tournament, as Molesworth explained: 'I expect you wonder where all these weird names come from. They are invented by one of our commanders, who is also a "coloured troop" and one of the leading lights of the squadron.'[27]

The bouts of tennis were highly competitive affairs. They were also sweat-inducing in the sweltering summer. As well as playing in pyjamas, in which they sometimes even flew, to keep cool, the airmen created individual outdoor baths and then a pool, described by one mechanic as a 'masterpiece'.[28] Molesworth elaborated:

> Some pilots each dug a hole, about a foot deep and three feet long, and covered
> it with a ground sheet, pegged down at the corners, making a single-seat bath
> in which they could lie with a cooling drink and a book, although they ran a
> risk of being bombarded with mud, stones and various other missiles . . . These
> single baths were such a success that a large pool, twenty feet square by three
> feet deep was dug.

When 'the whole population of the nearest village' turned up to watch, the airmen, who bathed naked, were rather disconcerted. 'Most of the chaps managed to rig up something in the way of a bathing dress by buying various articles of clothing in the neighbouring village, but I was forced to content myself with a type of female undergarment, which seemed to cause great amusement amongst the ack-emmas. The village maidens were highly delighted and thought it quite the thing, now that we were decently clad, to watch us at our aquatic sports.'[29]

When operations were 'washed out' or they were rewarded with a day off, the men visited the local village for items that included articles of furniture for the mess or the 'Hôtel du Commerce'. There were also excursions further afield. 'Four of us aviated over to Paris-Plage, near Étaples,' recalled Molesworth in July, 'and tested our grids by firing them into the sea'. The town was filled with British servicemen and the pilots landed opposite the Hotel Continental. Guards were posted on the machines. 'We wandered about the village for a bit and then started for home, stunting about to amuse the populace, which had collected on the front to see us off.'[30] Outings to Étaples, one of the BEF's most important bases in France, also had the advantage of accommodating visits to licensed brothels.

Fleeting sexual liaisons with prostitutes were common. Poet Robert Graves wrote of the Red Lamp, the army brothel in Béthune: 'I had seen the queue of a hundred and fifty men waiting outside the door; each to have his short turn with one of the three women in the house. My servant who stood in the queue told me that the charge was ten francs a man — about eight shillings at that time.'[31] As British pilot Robert Chidlaw-Roberts, who would be posted to 60 Squadron in August, recalled, 'They'd come out doing up their trousers and rejoin the group and go back in again.'[32]

Leave in Paris offered greater opportunities. Cecil Lewis noted that to many young airmen, this was not the 'beautiful city of elegance and gaiety, of palaces, fountains, and boulevards where you sat under the chestnuts, munched *fraises des bois* floating in cream and sipped a *vin rosé* [but] a gigantic brothel where women wore nothing but georgette underwear and extra-long silk stockings'.[33]

William Fry told Caldwell of one Parisian foray during which an airman awoke during the night to find the woman he had met at the theatre 'fully dressed, going through his pockets. He jumped out of bed and stood with his back to the door to prevent her escaping. Moving swiftly across to the opposite side of the room, she slipped out through a hidden door. Undeterred, he gave chase in his pyjamas and followed her downstairs into the street where he recovered his money and papers.'[34]

Other dangers lurked beneath the sheets and brought a chill to even the most hardened of airmen. In this pre-antibiotic age, venereal disease on the Western Front reached plague proportions.[35] The treatment — the intravenous administration of toxic arsenic or mercury, or a dreaded scraping of the urinary tract — was painful and potentially worse than the disease. Of course, to be sent home for a sexually transmitted disease was humiliating.[36] Many young airmen, though, took the risk, not wanting to go to their graves without having enjoyed the pleasures of the flesh in the towns of France.

July brought several significant changes for the squadron. Alan Scott was shoulder-tapped for the leadership of 13 Wing. Before being deskbound, he determined to get in as much flying as possible and on 10 July was seriously injured in combat, barely making it back to Filescamp. Covered in congealed blood, he had to be extricated from his extensively damaged Nieuport. He was replaced by the ever-smiling William Kennedy-Cochran-Patrick, one of the first RFC fighter pilots to accumulate 20 victories.[37] Unlike his predecessor, the Scotsman obeyed a directive that had been issued in February 1917 but routinely disregarded by Scott: 'When Squadron Commanders wish to lead a patrol or any duty involving flying over the lines, they will refer to the Wing Commander before doing so. It should be clearly understood that a Squadron Commander's principal duties are on the ground, and if sufficient attention is given to these there is little likelihood of time left for frequent flying.'[38]

The squadron also began phasing out its trustworthy and long-serving Nieuports in favour of one of the RFC's latest single-seat fighters, the Royal Aircraft Factory SE5, which, in addition to the two-seat Bristol F2b Fighter and the Sopwith Camel, would prove instrumental in turning the tables on the Germans in the second half of 1917. It would become the mainstay for 60 Squadron, and for Caldwell, until the end of the war.

The SE5 was slender but brutal, with a lean waist, a muscular upper body and a boxy nose. The squared-off wings were arrayed in a dihedral fashion, like two slightly raised eyebrows. Its eight-cylinder engine projected forward of the pilot, and the elongated exhausts running down past the cockpit accentuated its aggressive look. The SE5 sported twin machine guns: a Vickers firing through the propeller arc and a single Foster rail-mounted Lewis on the upper wing. With its sharp edges, it wasn't beautiful, but it was superbly functional and pilots adored it.

The love affair had a lot to do with its performance. It was stable, fast and able to operate at high altitudes. Though famed for its agility and ability to turn inside the enemy, the Camel was tricky to handle. In the hands of a good experienced pilot it was a wonder, but in the hands of an average newly trained individual it could be a death trap. It was said to offer airmen the choice between 'a wooden cross, the Red Cross, or a Victoria Cross'.[39] The SE5, by contrast, was easy to fly, nimble but sure footed. Its inherent stability meant a pilot could fly hands-free while changing out an ammunition drum, and even pilots with only rudimentary instruction could fly it capably. Its 150 horsepower Hispano-Suiza engine made it faster than the Camel, whose speed fell off markedly at higher altitudes.

As a result, Camels would increasingly be restricted to lower-level operations while the SE5s dominated the heights. The Royal Aircraft Factory machines also proved to be modifiable. Former mechanic James McCudden improved the speed and service ceiling of his SE5 by fitting high-compression pistons and tweaking the airframe. 'It was very fine to be in a machine that was faster than the Huns and to know that one could run away just as things got hot.'[40]

The Camel became the better known of the two machines in the post-war era — thanks in large measure to the popularity of W. E. Johns' fictional Camel-flying Biggles — but it was the SE5 that delivered the goods for the most successful airmen in the British air service. McCudden, Edward Mannock and Andrew Beauchamp-Proctor all acquired most of their many victories in the SE5, which became known as the 'mount of aces' and the 'Spitfire of the First World War'. These attributes, however, would only become evident with time, and the men of 60 Squadron were initially reluctant to exchange their reliable Nieuports for untried machines with inevitable teething problems. Many of the early SE5s, hand-me-downs from 56 Squadron, were plagued with engine difficulties and Kennedy-Cochran-Patrick was at first forced to prohibit his men from crossing the lines lest an errant engine led to capture or death.[41]

The moment the new machines arrived was captured by a film unit sent to the Western Front to record the activities of the RFC. In the rare footage, the 60 Squadron airmen were lined up before the camera. Bishop, the VC hero, was centre stage with the tall, dark-haired Caldwell and fidgety Molesworth at his side. Others included William Gunner, Spencer 'Nigger' Horn and Frank 'Mongoose' Soden, holding one of the unit's dogs. 'Charlie Chaplin isn't in it now with us!', wrote Molesworth.

> We were cinematographed the other day. Some of us stood in a row and tried to look pleasant and unconcerned, but this was rather difficult, as everyone was making rude remarks about us. We then bundled into our new grids, which we had just got, and started off on a stunt formation, nearly running down the old cinema man to put the wind up him. After we had done a circuit, my radiator began to boil, and I was forced to come down. Thank heavens it was a good landing, as the old man was still at it turning the [camera] handle. My part of the show was to be known as 'Pilot landing for more ammunition after fierce fight.'[42]

Caldwell was lively and humorous but looked rather solemn in many surviving photographs. When asked about this after the war, Chidlaw-Roberts replied, 'that may be so but they give the wrong impression. He had a marvellous sense of humour.' Caldwell's tendency to dip his head forward in photographs was part of his general inclination to stay out of the limelight. The film footage, however, revealed him as he was appreciated by his fellow airmen. 'Everyone loved "Grid" ... he was my best friend,' said Chidlaw-Roberts.[43]

On 13 July, Caldwell picked up an SE5 from St Omer and, between sorties in the Nieuports, made a series of positive familiarisation flights. During an offensive patrol in a Nieuport, however, the Le Rhône engine faltered, and Caldwell was forced to land in a field of corn.[44] The machine was unflyable and was transported to No. 2 Aircraft Depot for repair. The next day, with Kennedy-Cochran-Patrick's approval, he went up on one of the squadron's first operational sorties with the SE5.

On 29 July 1917, keen to get to grips with their new grids, Caldwell, Bishop and Gunner went on an early morning patrol. Gunner had improved beyond measure under Caldwell's guidance. Two months earlier no one had wanted him, but by summer Alan Scott was describing him as 'an indomitable fighter and good pilot'.[45] He now had more than a dozen combats and at least one German machine confirmed. In one big dust-up, Gunner had saved an inexperienced airman from certain death while being attacked by seven enemy machines. Wounded, and with blood pouring down his face, he shepherded the young pilot back to base before taking off again to resume his assault on the enemy 'in spite of the fact that his scalp wounds had hardly ceased bleeding'. By the summer of 1917, Gunner was one of the squadron's more experienced airmen and had a Military Cross for his efforts.

North of Vitry, a two-seater Aviatik crossed the path of the trio. Caldwell was suspicious: the lone reconnaissance machine looked like bait, a decoy with Albatros friends lurking nearby. He was right; four enemy aeroplanes from Jasta 12 fell out of the sun, Tutschek leading the assault. His attacking clutch of machines was augmented by the arrival of three more Albatros fighters.

Then, early in the fight, Gunner's engine failed. He tried to glide his way out of the mêlée, but Tutschek's bullets struck home and the SE5 caught fire. Unwitnessed by Caldwell and Bishop, Gunner went down, trailing orange flames and a ribbon of black smoke. The two experienced colonials, now a duo against seven, fell into a series of dogfights that tested the capabilities of the SE5s to their limits. Caldwell fired 50 rounds from one of his guns at 100 yards before the target spun out of the way. Caldwell chased it down, caught it as it came out of its spin and fired again.

Under determined fire, the enemy pilot wisely dropped into another spin. Caldwell was then attacked by a pair of bullet-spitting Albatroses. He managed to get behind one of them and pulled the trigger, but both his guns failed. As Bishop later wrote, Caldwell

> was so furious at this bad luck that for several minutes he stayed in the fight, just to bluff the Huns. Then one of them made it a little nasty for him, and it was necessary to escape. Back to the lines he went, making short dashes of 100 yards every now and then, two Huns following him all the way, and firing at him as he went, but owing to pure good flying and clever manoeuvring he was able to avoid even having his machine hit. Then . . . realising that I was alone in the middle of it he came back all that way, without either of his guns in working order . . . I still think it one of the bravest deeds I have ever heard of, as he had a hard time getting back to me, and then also in escaping a second time. He returned to the aerodrome, landed, had his guns fixed, and immediately hastened out again in the hope he would be able to help me.[46]

Caldwell had run a great risk of being killed, 'while absolutely helpless to defend himself in any way'. It was 'typical of him. He's always getting shot up helping others out of scrapes.'[47]

Despite the odds, neither Caldwell nor Bishop had sustained significant damage to their machines, and Bishop was enthusiastic about the new machine's speed and fire power.[48] Over the following days and weeks, the lingering problem with the engines would be rectified and the older SE5 machines were rotated out for the newer and more powerful SE5a.

In addition to the RFC roundels on the wings and rear fuselage, and the thin blue, white and red stripes on the tail rudders, many airmen personalised their machines in August. British propriety gave way to brightly painted noses with a colour-keyed diagonal sachet on the rear fuselage and wheels. Some brightened up their aeroplanes with blue or red, but Caldwell's sported glowing sunflower-yellow highlights and a small green fern leaf on a white-tipped tail section. This was an appropriate addition, given that, in 56 Squadron, the machine had been flown by former Rangiora, New Zealand sheep farmer Frederick Horrell.[49]

William Gunner had been one of the longer-serving 60 Squadron airmen. After six months of flying and fighting with his mates, he was gone. He was 26 years old. His loss was keenly felt by Caldwell and the men, a reminder that the busyness of operations, the games of tennis, the forays to the local towns and boozy nights merely stifled the reality that death crouched at the door, and that they might be next. All but one of his B Flight team from May had been lost: Warren Gilchrist, Ralph Phalen, Roland Harris and Gunner were all dead, as were many of their replacements.

And then there were the numerous accidents and the inexperience of new arrivals. Roland Harris had died when the right-hand wing of his machine collapsed in a dive on a practice flight, and headstrong novice Gerald Parkes had paid the price for disobeying Caldwell's explicit pre-flight instructions to stay in formation.

Caldwell had to live with losing men who had become his friends and for whom he was accountable, and there were times when his actions had resulted in a man's death. Guilt was a lifelong burden in such cases. On 3 July, Caldwell lost Alexander Adam, a 21-year-old from Elgin, Scotland.[50] Decades later, the memory lingered: 'When leading a Nieuport flight over the lines in a strong adverse wind, I dawdled too long, hoping for a quick shot at a Hun formation below us, left it too late, and we

lost a fellow named Adam, brought down by a "zooming" Albatros from below. I was naturally very upset at this bad judgement on my part. We had a job extricating the others from a bad situation, as I remember.'[51]

Caldwell was aware of Gunner's large family: his father, William, after whom he had been named, his mother, Louise, and three older sisters and five brothers. Moreover, Gunner was engaged.

At first, Gunner's final moments remained unresolved. If he had force-landed safely on the Allied side of the lines, it would have been reported. He could have come down in German-occupied territory and been captured. A telegram was dispatched to his family in Arundel, Surrey: 'Regret to inform you 2Lt W. H. Gunner MC General List and RFC 60 Squadron reported missing July twenty-ninth. This does not necessarily mean that he is wounded or killed.'[52] It was to this sliver of hope that his parents, siblings and fiancée clung. At the squadron, Gunner's clothing, toiletries and personal effects were gathered up and recorded.

When August and September passed with no news, a younger brother, Charles, wrote directly to the squadron commander, who promptly replied that they had 'heard nothing either of him or his machine', but that the Germans were likely to publish a list of machines and men downed on their side of lines in due course.[53] Then in early October, nine weeks after Gunner's disappearance, a letter arrived addressed to his father, reporting that, 'in the list of English Air losses for the month of July, published by the *Norddeutsche Allgemeine Zeitung* on 18 August' was this entry: 'SE One Seater, Motor Wolseley. [engine number:] 700/2233. Occupant burned.'

The machine had been identified as Gunner's. The information was 'considered to be probably correct, but will not be accepted officially until after the lapse of a rather longer period . . . [The] Secretary of State for War, [desired] to express his sincere sympathy with Mr. Gunner in his great trouble.' Five months after Gunner had gone missing in action, the authorities told the family that they were 'now regretfully constrained to conclude that he was killed in action on that date'. William's father replied three days later: 'We have been hoping there was a chance of his being a prisoner but fearing the worst we are moved in our grief, that he has given his life for our King and Country.'[54]

The confirmation was followed in due course with regular reminders of the family's loss: William's name in the official published casualty lists, the delivery of

William Henry Gunner became a highly valuable member of
60 Squadron under the tutelage of Keith Caldwell. His death was
felt keenly by his family, fiancée and brothers-in-arms.

his kit from the Western Front and the assessment of his gratuity — £22 17s 6d. His parents' sorrow was multiplied when William's brother Arthur was killed in action the following year.

Gunner's fiancée, however, was unconvinced by the official pronouncements and her mother contacted Kennedy-Cochran-Patrick in France, who confirmed the information already available. Her last despairing effort was a letter, again sent on behalf of her inconsolable daughter, to the Air Ministry on 7 December 1918: 'I believe his machine was burnt as the number of his engine was given . . . but this does not imply he was killed. My daughter is engaged to him and still feels there is hope (because someone we know had his machine burnt, he was reported "missing" and after a long time wrote to his people he was [a] prisoner.) His mother . . . believes him dead so I do not suppose they will make further enquiries or write to you.'[55]

In the wake of the demanding sorties and the deaths of his men, Caldwell was sent on a brief furlough to England between 4 and 18 August, which coincided with the arrival of his father from New Zealand. The family gathered at Bexhill-on-Sea, one of the many small south England seaside resorts favoured by Mary and Vida Caldwell.[56] Caldwell found time to write to his old school. 'I have been over a year in France now, flying, and have had the luck to so far exist. At the end of another month or so I am coming home to instruct for several months; this will be very welcome. Things have been fairly strenuous most of the time, and practically all my squadron have been killed.'[57]

It is impossible to know how Caldwell's mother felt about her son's physical and mental condition, but when his old training instructor from East Anglia, Eric Lubbock, was briefly sent home in 1917 from his flight commander duties with 45 Squadron, his mother, Lady Avebury, was shaken by his appearance: 'He is so thin and white and tired looking. I dread his going back now more than ever. One's whole life is a big dread these days . . . I would give anything to have him here for the night to see his darling face once more — to kiss him again. Oh, my God, how I love him and how frighted I am!' Lubbock returned to France and his mother wrote what would be her last angst-ridden letter.[58] The letter was returned unopened; her son was killed on the day she composed it.

The beaches of southern England were heavily frequented by airmen on leave. Keith Caldwell reads the newspaper with his mother Mary at his side in 1917.

CHAPTER TWELVE

Clever Caldwell

W hen Caldwell returned to the Western Front, the Allies' major offensive, the Third Battle of Ypres, which had begun on 31 July, was in full stride. Following the success at Messines, the Allies launched their main assault to gain control of the ridges south and west of Ypres. But the grand plan to clear the Belgian coast was abandoned in a progressively wet August, and would finally grind down in November in the mud of Passchendaele. Both sides poured increasing numbers of troops into an intractable battlefield in what was later described by a German general as 'the greatest martyrdom of the world war', with over half a million casualties for limited territorial gains.

The poor weather and the lingering difficulties with the SE5 engines impeded 60 Squadron's operations in August, but on 7 September the unit was transferred to 11 Wing under the command of the newly promoted Lieutenant Colonel Alan Scott. From their new base of operations, further north at Sainte-Marie-Cappel, they would be supporting the Second and Fifth armies. Leaving Filescamp Farm for the small airfield and ragged bell tents east of St Omer was an unwelcome shock. The only consolation was that they had ransacked everything not tied down to furnish their muddy new home; some of the pirated goods were flown to Sainte-Marie-Cappel strapped to their undercarriage struts.

The aerodrome was close to the front line and the busy local town of Cassel.

Scott described it as 'perched on a hill, [it] has a fine square, from which a beautiful church can be seen, and the square and streets are cobbled. The road which leads into the town from the east enters through a short tunnel, which emerges right into the square itself.' Huge howitzer batteries would arrive, hauled by caterpillar tractors, 'grunting and chugging from the tunnel into the town, and through it, making for some spot further to the rear'. The highest point of Cassel offered a 'wonderful view of the Western Front . . . puffs of smoke in the distance, captive sausage observation balloons, aeroplanes, and roads teeming with hundreds and hundreds of motor-lorries slowly crawling along.' Scott had also seen 'miserable-looking German prisoners' cleaning the streets, all looking 'white, pinched, and sickly'.[1]

A change in personnel accompanied the change of scene: Bish and Moley were sent on Home Establishment for a well-earned break. Their replacements — Robert Chidlaw-Roberts leading A Flight and Spencer Horn leading C Flight — fell in with Caldwell, now the senior flight commander.[2] Both British men were Sandhurst graduates who had transferred to the RFC from the army. Chidlaw-Roberts had met Caldwell 'on the train in Victoria Station . . . when he was [re]joining 60 Squadron. I said to him, "What squadron are you going to?" And he said, "60". I said, "So am I," and from that moment on we were friends.'[3]

In addition to defending the RFC's two-seat artillery cooperation machines and attacking those of the enemy, Caldwell and his co-workers were to carry out one of the more recent developments in the air war: low-level strafing sorties in support of the infantry. The fighters would be peppering the enemy positions, assembly points and aerodromes with bullets and bombs. Caldwell had already demonstrated an aptitude for this in August, when, on an offensive patrol, his flight had dived on ground targets at Biache-Saint-Vaast and other towns; the 'eight grids fired 200 rounds each . . . [on] places of importance'.

As the recording officer noted, 'This was quite Capt. Caldwell's own idea, as there were no E[nemy] A[ircraft] on the Army Front he occupied his time in the above manner.'[4] At Sainte-Marie-Cappel, all 18 SE5s — half of them the newer SE5a machines — were fitted with racks to deliver four 25-pound Cooper fragmentation anti-personnel bombs.[5]

At the height of an offensive, these operations were nerve-wracking affairs, placing the 60 Squadron pilots, flying in pairs, between howling shells lobbed across the battlefield and the violence of the ground war. Even for experienced airmen it could be a hellish task, as one recalled: 'Our job was to fly into that tunnel below the flight of field gun shells, look for any target we could see — any Germans in trenches,

enemy machine gun posts — anything at all — shoot it up, fly through the tunnel and come out at the other end. We were warned that we must not try to fly out sideways, if we did we would almost certainly meet our own shells in flight and be brought down . . . Once we entered the "tunnel" there was nothing for it but to . . . go through to the very end.' It was an inferno, the air 'boiling with turmoil of the shells flying through it. We were thrown about in the aircraft, rocking from side to side, being thrown up and down.'[6]

Diving on gun emplacements and trenches meant dropping very low. It was at the bottom of the dive that an exploding shell from your own artillery could toss a light fighter like a toy up to 600 feet, before it fell again to 200 feet, the pilot almost helpless in the wake of the blast's concussion. And there was always the possibility of being hit by ground fire. With so many men firing their rifles during the Passchendaele battle, almost a third of losses in strafing sorties were, according to one estimate, attributable to ground fire.

Despite the large deflection angle required to 'lead' the rapidly moving aeroplane into the bullet of a rifle, infantry did hit low-flying targets. Sholto Douglas saw one soldier raise his rifle, fire and fatally strike a German aircraft. He then leapt from his trench, chased down the fleeing pilot and tossed him to the ground in a flying rugby tackle.[7]

On a misty 12 September, Caldwell and Chidlaw-Roberts told their respective flights they would be undertaking a strafing sortie. Each machine would be fully laden with four high-explosive bombs. Caldwell's flight was the southern arm of the attack near the old fortress town of Le Quesnoy. Over no man's land, he flung his SE5a down and the flock followed. 'The fighters spat bullets, flicking up dirt as German soldiers sought cover in water-filled shell holes, terrified horses galloped away, dragging swaying wagons . . . [and] marching troops ran in confusion.'[8]

As the trenches quickly loomed, Caldwell tensed and released the bombs from their racks, the steel tail fins smoothing out their death flight before they struck the ground. Chased by the exploding bombs and persistent ground fire, the SE5s climbed away, only to be met by enemy fighters. Childlaw-Roberts lost one man, who was forced to land behind German lines and was captured.

This low-level strafing also exposed the SE5s to marauding fighters who had the upper ground and therefore the advantage in dogfights. Moreover, September saw

Robert Chidlaw-Roberts, top right, reads a letter from home while William Kennedy-Cochran-Patrick (wearing a cap) looks on. Keith Caldwell is reclining with his mates in profile.

the arrival of one of the most feared machines of the war, the German Fokker DrI Triplane or 'Tripe', as RFC airmen dubbed it. Though not particularly fast in a straight line or a dive, this rotary-powered triplane had impressive manoeuvrability, far better than any Allied machine. The Flying Circus and some of Germany's most ruthless airmen were rapidly abandoning their older Albatros D-series machines for the DrI.

Seven days later, as the fighting continued on the ground, Caldwell witnessed one of the most famous aerial battles of the war. Late on the afternoon of 23 September, he was leading a combined offensive patrol near Ypres, with Chidlaw-Roberts and Harold Hamersley bringing up the rear. Hamersley, an Australian Gallipoli veteran, saw a Nieuport scout being attacked by a red-nosed Albatros. He dived to rescue the Nieuport only to belatedly realise that it was in fact a Fokker DrI. 'I put my nose down and opened fire', said Hamersley.

> The 'Tripe' passed under me, and as I zoomed and turned, the Hun was above me and heading straight at me, firing from about thirty degrees off the bow. There was a puff of smoke from my engine and holes appeared along the engine cowling in front of me and in the wings. Realizing I could do nothing further in the matter, I threw my machine into a spin. The triplane followed me down, diving at me, while I was spinning, and I had to do an inverted dive to get away.[9]

Chidlaw-Roberts tried to intervene, firing off a few rounds with both guns at close range at the dark-coloured Fokker. 'In seconds, he was on my tail and had shot my rudder bar about. I retired from the fray.' He knew he had encountered 'somebody I couldn't handle and the sooner I got home the better'.[10] Who was this extraordinary pilot flying an extraordinary machine?

The first Caldwell knew of the fracas was 'seeing an SE going down in a hurry towards Ypres with a blue-grey triplane close in attendance'. The RFC machine looked doomed, but Caldwell set off to rescue it, only to be beaten to the battle by a flight of 56 Squadron SE5s, headed by James McCudden. The Fokker should have had no chance, but, as McCudden later wrote, 'its handling was wonderful to behold'.

Trench strafing often required flying below the lobbed shells of the great artillery guns into a thicket of small arms fire and was not for the faint hearted. Here, in a popular postcard from the war, a Sopwith Camel and Royal Aircraft Factory SE5a attack enemy trenches.

The pilot seemed to be firing at all of us simultaneously, and although I got behind him a second time, I could hardly stay there for a second. He movements were so quick and uncertain that none of us could hold him in sight for any decisive time . . . I now got a good opportunity as he was coming towards me nose on, and slightly underneath, and had apparently not seen me. I dropped my nose and pressed both triggers. As soon as I fired up came his nose at me, and I heard clack-clack-clack-clack-clack, as his bullets passed close to me and through my wings. I distinctly noticed the red-yellow flashes from his parallel Spandau guns.[11]

As the Fokker whipped past, McCudden looked into the cockpit and saw the pilot was flying without headgear, his hair as black as night.

Early in the fight, the German removed two SE5s from the fray. The first sustained a punctured radiator, the second was shot through the main spars, its longerons were punctured, a tail-plane rib smashed and there were bullet holes in the wings, fuselage, radiator and propeller. The German pilot had 'whipped round in an extraordinary way, using no bank at all, but just throwing his tail behind him'.[12] The airman nursed his SE5a home, where it was written off.

'It was really 56's affair and we watched from above and we felt six to one was pretty good odds,' said Caldwell. 'We were more or less spectators in my opinion, as there was little room for us to join in.' As to the identity of the lone German, 'My guess at the time was that it must have been Voss, having seen him in action and having been on the receiving end at least once. One recognised the magnificent, aggressive flying display.'[13] As another witness observed, Voss 'was in and out and round our scouts, zigzagging like forked lightning through the sky. None of our men could get him.'[14]

At one point, English ace Arthur Rhys Davids found the pointed tip of his propeller nearly on top of the German's tail. He fired, and for the first time Voss dived and flew in a straight line. 'He made no attempt to turn until I was so close to him I was certain we would collide, he passed my right wing by inches and went down.' When Rhys Davids next saw the enemy, he seemed to be gliding west, his engine off. Rhys Davids dived again, fired, then reloaded 'and kept in the dive, I got another good burst and the triplane did a slight right-hand turn still going down. I now overshot him (this was

James McCudden, who had a background in mechanics, joined the Royal Flying Corps as an observer before training as a pilot in 1916. In the famed 56 Squadron he became one of the war's exceptional airmen, was awarded a Victoria Cross and was dubbed the 'Young Lionheart of the Air'.

at 1,000 feet) zoomed, and never saw him again.'[15] The triplane's movements were very erratic just before McCudden saw it hit the ground and Voss was killed.

Caldwell was too high to see through the gathering gloom and mists below but felt that Voss could have escaped by spinning down earlier in the fight and for some reason had chosen not to. That evening in the mess Rhys Davids was congratulated for his success, mostly by those who had not been there, and the officers speculated about the German's identity. But, as one of the pilots involved later confided, 'Our elation was not nearly as great as you might have imagined. It was an amazing show on the part of Voss. I remember at the time feeling rather sorry that it had to end the way it did. Rhys Davids, I think, was genuinely upset.'[16]

The battle lingered long in the minds of those who had participated in it or were spectators. 'As long as I shall live, I shall never forget my admiration for the German pilot, who single handed fought seven of us for ten minutes and also put bullets through all our machines,' wrote McCudden in 1918. 'His flying was wonderful, his courage magnificent, and in my opinion, he is the bravest German airman who it has been my privilege to see fight.'[17] 'We all agreed that he was first class,' recalled Chidlaw-Roberts, 'the best in the German Air Service, magnificent chap.'[18] Although in the popular mind von Richthofen was the war's leading fighter pilot, many Luftstreitkräfte and RFC airmen considered Voss to be the greatest of the German pilots. 'He was a terrific chap and rated easily No. 1.,' said Caldwell after the war.[19]

Confirmation of Voss's identity came quickly, and the 20-year-old ace, with 48 victories to his name, was buried without a coffin or military honours near the front lines. Five weeks later, 20-year-old Rhys Davids was killed 5 miles from Voss's grave. The young Etonian always flew with a volume of William Blake's poetry. As Rhys Davids' biographer, Alex Revell, wrote, it was almost as if Blake had written their epitaphs:

> And thou, Mercurius, that with winged brow
> Does mount aloft into the yielding sky,
> And thro' Heav'n's hall thy airy flight dost throw,
> Entering with holy feet to where on high
> Jove weights the counsel of futurity;
> Then, laden with eternal fate, dost go
> Down, like a falling star. From autumn sky,
> And o'er the surface of the silent deep dost fly.[20]

The graves of both men were lost to the mud of Passchendaele.

The air war rolled on, with intensive operations in the 20–25 September Battle of the Menin Road. Caldwell was just one of hundreds of airmen in 26 squadrons supporting an 8-mile-long effort on the ground. On 25 September alone, there were 12 reconnaissance sorties, 63 photographic flights and 42 contact patrols. In 12 bombing raids, 70 enemy batteries were engaged, thanks to aeroplane and balloon observation. Several fighter squadrons were caught in aerial combat up and down the lines.[21]

Among these was a 60 Squadron offensive patrol led by Caldwell. It was a clear day for operations and at 6000 feet the SE5s observed seven Aviatik and Albatros two-seaters pushing west. Caldwell wiggled his wings and dived, with his men in pursuit. The enemy spotted them early, wheeling their machines around and retreating east.

Caldwell rallied the flight into a patrolling formation and waited. 'Ten minutes later these EA returned and were again attacked. I dived steeply at one, the rearmost ... painted green.'[22] He poured 100 rounds into the machine and it turned over, falling vertically, the black crosses on the wings a smudged blur. This was Caldwell's final victory with 60 Squadron; his last tussle, on 4 October, against an Aviatik two-seater, was inconclusive.

Caldwell did not record this last combat in his logbook; in fact the period 11 September–10 October contained only a single entry, for his 25 September victory. The squadron's recording officer, however, was conscientiously completing combat reports for 11 Wing: Caldwell flew 37 sorties over this month, more than one a day.[23] Enemy machines were spotted on most days and often engaged. The empty pages in his logbook might be explained by the last sentence in a 6 October 1917 letter from Kennedy-Cochran-Patrick.

After setting out Caldwell's dates of service, he noted that the New Zealander had been flying for 13 months, with very limited leave. 'All the time he has been with No. 60 Squadron he had shown great dash and offensive spirit and has proved an admirable Flight Commander. He is now however beginning to feel the strain of active service flying and I consider that a spell of work on Home Establishment is necessary.'[24]

From the end of his previous leave until his last offensive patrol with 60 Squadron, Caldwell had flown no fewer than 110 operations, over a third resulting in an engagement with the enemy. It was a heavy workload when combined with his responsibilities as flight commander and the unrelenting list of friends and subordinates wounded, killed or taken prisoner.

From 10 October to 10 November 1917, Caldwell joined his family in England for a well-earned break.[25] His father was still in England for part of this time. London, which had been under attack since May 1915, was very much a wartime city — army khaki and navy whites, sandbags and wardens, searchlights and anti-aircraft batteries and, here and there, the blackened bricks and shattered timber left by German air raids. In 1917, the Zeppelins that Mary and Vida Caldwell had already experienced were largely replaced by aeroplanes such as twin-engine German Gotha IVs, the first large aircraft to be mass produced during the war and capable of delivering over 880 pounds of bombs.

On the moonlit night of 4 September, 11 people were killed and 62 injured in a raid that was extensively reported in the newspapers.[26] During David Caldwell's stay in London, the bombers attacked the capital on many occasions; one raid struck a building opposite the family's hotel.[27]

Despite a general shortage of staff and imported goods, Macky, Logan and Caldwell had been flourishing. Its five factories in Auckland were producing large volumes of their popular Cambridge brand of suits and shirts for the domestic market and thousands of overalls for the NZEF. But no one remained untouched by the war. At the March 1917 meeting of the Cambridge Golf Club, of which David Caldwell was president, the committee had decided to send a message of congratulations to the newly promoted Flight Commander Keith Caldwell and letters of condolence to the relatives of two young members, brothers who had been killed.

The New Zealand newspapers had kept tabs on Keith Caldwell's progress, including the curious fact of his name being drawn in a ballot for military service. Although young New Zealand men had volunteered in their droves in 1914–15, this had slowed in the following year and in 1916 the government had introduced conscription. As the *Waikato Independent* noted, 'Flight Commander Caldwell has been on active service for some considerable time past, and a short time ago was awarded the Military Cross for gallantry. It is to be regretted that more care is not taken with the list of men balloted as ridiculous mistakes like this could easily be avoided.'[28]

His decoration had, of course, been reported at home. The first mention came in a *New Zealand Herald* report on the opening of a pupils' recreation hut at the Kohimarama flying school on 3 October. In speaking proudly of star ex-pupils who had joined the RFC, Leo Walsh referred to Caldwell's MC.[29] By 24 November, the *Herald* could publish the details, under the headline, 'Reward for Gallantry — Auckland Airman Decorated'. The award had been made for conspicuous gallantry and devotion to duty when leading offensive patrols.

Under the headline 'Clever Caldwell', the *Feilding Star* reported a few days later: 'On one occasion he led a patrol of five machines against twelve hostile aircraft, all of which he drove down out of control. Flight Commander Caldwell has personally destroyed five hostile machines, and has had over 50 contests in the air, in all of which he has displayed splendid skill and fearlessness and set an example to his squadron.'[30]

Excerpts from Caldwell's letters made sporadic appearances in the *Wanganui Collegian*: 'I have seen "Blocky Beamish", J. A. Carr and D. Gray. The latter had a bad smash, and broke both legs. [Trevor] Bloomfield came across Jack Smith, who was wounded flying in France, but all right, and doing light work at Home.'[31] Though not mentioned by Caldwell, another notable pupil was former missionary turned aviator Cuthbert Maclean who, by the war's end, would be New Zealand's highest-ranked airman. On the ground other old boys were also making their mark. Leslie Andrew was awarded a Victoria Cross after an attack at Passchendaele on two machine-gun posts, during which he demonstrated 'cool daring, intuitive and fine leadership, and his magnificent example was a great stimulant to his comrades'.[32]

And Harold Gillies would become the war's most famous plastic surgeon for his pioneering work in reconstructing the faces of badly disfigured men. Caldwell would have had no illusions about the grim nature of the wounds Gillies was dealing with, but the boys at the school got a very brief and sanitised version. 'The main principle of the work is the building up with actual flesh and bone those parts of the face which have been blown away.'[33]

The school was also doing its bit to help the war effort in other ways. Money ordinarily spent on the annual school river picnic was diverted to greatly appreciated cricket gear for men on the Western Front — 'Many, many thanks for so glorious a gift' — and a special outing for recovering patients arranged by a school contact living near a hospital in England. 'My wife and I have taken a special interest in cases of those men whose faces have been maimed and disfigured by wounds, and so we took out fourteen and gave them a whole day on the Thames at Shepperton. I only wish the school could have witnessed the joy of these poor chaps, in spite of all they have been through.'[34]

Over the winter of 1917–18, Caldwell had a trio of postings in Britain. In November, he spent two weeks at the School of Special Flying at Gosport near Portsmouth, where many of the instructors were former 60 Squadron members, requisitioned by Robert Smith-Barry. Caldwell's mentor was his old squadron commander Euan Gilchrist.[35] Flight training had changed so much that, despite their extensive experience, large numbers of airmen like Caldwell were attending the course. Each intake had its share of colonels, majors and captains and a liberal sprinkling of DSOs and MCs. As one of the instructors noted, many incoming officers asked: '"Why should a pilot like me come here to be taught to fly? I have been flying for over a year. I have been to France and have shot down six German planes." But one and all left amazed that they had lived so long, astounded at what they learnt, enthusiastic to spread the need back to their own aerodromes.' Some of the RFC's best airmen considered they learnt more at Gosport in two or three weeks than in the previous two or three years.[36]

The school was a revelation for Caldwell, who had been trained under the old regime. Smith-Barry had thrown out the old instruction methods, blaming them for the heavy losses in France. During the Battle of the Somme in 1916, he had refused to send newly arrived novices over the lines, on one occasion telling Trenchard, 'They've only seven hours' flying sir, and it's bloody murder.'[37] Smith-Barry showered Trenchard and his staff with ideas and wrote papers for a reformation of flight training until he was allowed to establish the Gosport school.

Rather than being protected from hazardous situations, the students were introduced to dangerous manoeuvres in a controlled environment using dual-instruction aeroplanes in which the pupil and teacher could communicate via voice tubes in their helmets. The old Maurice Farman Longhorns and Shorthorns were replaced by the venerable and solid Avro 504, and frontline machines were also inserted into the training schedule to ensure that no pilots ever arrived in France without having flown the machine they were expected to fight in.

'The scene at the [Gosport] airfield, to anyone used to the normal rules of procedure, was extraordinary, even alarming', recalled one experienced instructor-turned-pupil. 'Aircraft took off and landed in all directions — up, down and across wind — and the sky was filled with Avros stalling, spinning, looping, apparently missing one another by inches.' But he found the experience 'extremely stimulating — even electrifying. I believed that I knew something about flying before I went to Gosport, but the course certainly opened my eyes, and made me realise what I had to learn.'[38]

One frontline captain walked out onto the aerodrome to see 'Smith-Barry with four pupils flying in formation on him in Avros. On a signal from him all span simultaneously and came out together a few hundred feet from the ground level. This was part of his gospel, that aerobatics, and the dash and confidence, were not only safe, but were essential for mastery in air combat.'[39] Dubbed the Gosport System, Smith-Barry's revolutionary methods, which also lowered casualty rates on the training aerodromes of England,[40] spread to France and the United States; as Trenchard liked to say, Smith-Barry 'taught the air forces of the world how to fly'.[41]

After completing his course, Caldwell was sent from south England to Scotland, where, according to the *Wanganui Collegian*, he was 'playing golf in Ayrshire'.[42] He was in fact at the School of Aerial Fighting at Ayr in south-east Scotland; there he joined several very accomplished pilots in teaching the rudiments of aerial combat to novice airmen. His students in 'A Squadron' were entering the final phase of their training before deployment to France. 'The course was simple,' wrote one of the participants, 'the instructor showed the pupil what to do and what not to do during an air fight. Besides practising fighting, trainees were encouraged to throw their aircraft around with abandon, in order to gain the maximum confidence in the machines. It was an excellent course. Its teachings saved my life more than once in actual combat.'[43]

Caldwell's logbook entries for his own early training were rather tame compared with the stunting 'half-rolls, stalled climbing turns, Immelmanns and spin turns' recorded by the airmen under his instruction in late 1917.[44]

Ayr was home to a range of machines, and Caldwell's squadron was furnished with Bristol F2b Fighters and Sopwith Camels. Flying the latter extensively in Scotland gave him a new appreciation of its ability to turn on a penny in a mock dogfight with an SE5a. 'I have been aviating "Camels" a lot lately and am getting rather fond of them,' he wrote his mother. He believed the Camel could out-fly almost anything and its manoeuvrability undoubtedly saved many lives.

> The weather has been wonderful lately, blue sky all day and we had machines in the air all day — I've been . . . [flying] Bristol Fighters once or twice, trying to get use[d] to them after scouts. They are very easy to fly but too heavy on controls for pleasure. We have great fights in the air between the three different groups, Bristol Fighters, Camels and SE5s. Yesterday 3 of us on Camels chased a poor SE with [Gerald] Maxwell from 56 Squadron from 5000 ft down to 50 ft.

In between instructing he did indeed play golf, kicked a football around and enjoyed Scottish hospitality. 'The dance went off very well the other night pushing at

Overleaf: Third row from top, fourth from left, Keith Caldwell sits among attendees of the School of Aerial Fighting, Ayr, Scotland.

4.30 [a.m.]. We didn't undress but just lay down till 7.30 & then aviated.' On Christmas Eve, the airmen had a 'blind in the mess worse than usual'; the following day was a 'half-holiday for officers and men so all the hangars are shut up with the grids inside'.[45]

After a short leave with Mary and Vida Caldwell, he embarked on his final Home Establishment stint, as a flight commander at the Central Flying School at Upavon in Wiltshire, under the command of Alan Scott. The school was, in Caldwell's words, 'a very big show' with large red-brick buildings, crowds of huts, a golf course, swimming baths, tennis courts and a picture show every night with accompanying orchestra. He travelled to numerous venues and events in Scott's 'lovely limousine'.[46] Caldwell and the other instructors made the most of the school's proximity to London.

> Apart from the rather intensive long hours instructing, which I never cared for, much, it was a most happy time; so many good friends were there. Sometimes at a weekend, we would fly SEs or Pups up to Hounslow with suitcases strapped on the side and spend a very bright evening at a 'Show' then supper at the 'Piccadilly Mansions' plus the Gaiety theatre chorus, catered for by the Savoy Hotel. Then limp back in the early am to Upavon. Sometimes it would be foggy & then we would have to follow the roads at 50 [feet], I don't think we ever failed to get to London, the incentive was so attractive . . . Some of the girls were well born and later married the odd peer.[47]

The Gaiety Girls were an extremely popular chorus troupe appearing in Edwardian musical comedies and later musical burlesques. On one occasion 'the entire chorus joined us at the Piccadilly Mansion for late supper after their Show and believe me or not it was all very circumspect'.[48]

Much of Caldwell's initial work involved rudimentary and mundane lessons for the novices at the school. Despite vastly improved instruction methods, there was still danger. One his students was killed in a crash and another 'two pupils collided and were also killed'.[49] Caldwell also familiarised himself with two of the most recent technological developments in military aviation: the deflection teacher and the camera gun. The former involved training on the ground with a target on a trolley that changed position rapidly, while the trainee 25 yards away had to follow with his gunsight. In this way it became second nature for airmen to track a quickly manoeuvring enemy. The camera gun resembled a Lewis gun 'with a large box for breech [containing] a roll of film which registered the destination of each "bullet" when the trigger was pulled.

One roll of film per man per gun each day was the aim. The film would be developed within the hour and results posted in the mess "in order to foster a competitive spirit among the pupils", as the [training] manual put it.'[50] For Caldwell and the other Western Front veterans, 'Quite a bit of use of camera gun in mock dogfights with other instructors at Central Flying School . . . showed up faults in deflection shooting.'[51]

On 25 January 1918, Caldwell wrote to his mother. 'Things mildly strenuous here lately for me. Not in the flying line but chiefly office work. I have been give[n] C squadron and have been a budding Major for 3 days now. I was gazetted as Major on the 15th January and it has only come through just now. There is an awful lot of work in running a squadron here and you get no time at all for exercise. 8 am till 7.30 pm.'[52]

CHAPTER THIRTEEN

Dentist's Chair

The 1917 October Revolution had knocked Russia from the conflict, freeing Germany to concentrate its forces against the French and British armies in the west. In the spring of 1918, before the weight of American ground forces could make themselves felt in France, the German High Command hoped to settle the war in its favour with an offensive bolstered by nearly 50 divisions — 1 million men — freed from the Eastern Front and newly developed stormtrooper units. The first and main assault of the Spring Offensive, planned for the third week of March, was Operation Michael, which was designed to burst through the Allied lines, dissecting the British and French sectors along the Somme river before plunging north to outflank the BEF and drive it into the sea.

The United States' entry into the war also affected the Luftstreitkräfte. Fearful of the potential American industrial production of airframes and aviation engines, the Germans launched their Amerika Programme, which aimed to double the number of Jasta they could field on the Western Front to 80. Despite shortages in men and materiel, they were generally successful. For example, German output of aeroplanes leapt from 8100 in 1916 to 19,400 in 1917, with the greater part of the increase towards the end of that year.[1] For Operation Michael, the Germans assembled a 730-strong armada, including over 320 single-seat fighters. The British machines were more widely dispersed, and at the point of the German main effort against the British

Third and Fifth armies numbered only 580 machines, just over 260 of them single-seat fighters. 'For the first time, the German air concentration for the battle on the Western Front was greater than that of the Royal Flying Corps.'[2]

The SE5a, Sopwith Camel and Bristol F2b Fighter edged out the prevailing German Albatros DV and Pfalz DIII in performance, but the Germans' numerical advantage, coupled with the dangers posed by the Fokker DrI, meant the British would be sorely tested in the weeks that followed — and even more formidable German machines were only weeks away from entering the fray.

In 1917, South African General Jan Smuts was asked to report on the state of the air war and the reforms needed for British military aviation. Greatly influenced by the German bombing campaign against Britain, which suggested that future aerial warfare could potentially wreak 'devastation of enemy lands and the destruction of industrial and populous areas on a vast scale', he made a strong case for an amalgamation of the RFC and RNAS into a single independent service.[3]

Several leading lights, including Hugh Trenchard, resisted the move, fearing that it would weaken cooperation with the army. Nonetheless, the case for removing the unhealthy competition for resources between the RFC and RNAS and for preparing a force to meet the likely developments in military aviation was strong, and the Royal Air Force (RAF), the world's first independent air service, was established on 1 April 1918. Meantime, the British were continually strengthening their position on the Western Front with more machines, trained airmen and the newly formed frontline units.

In the second week of March, Major Keith Caldwell assumed leadership of an SE5a-equipped squadron, mobilising for war at the Hertfordshire village of London Colney. Initially a training unit, 74 Squadron was to be converted to a frontline formation, with deployment in the early spring of 1918.[4] It was Caldwell's first command of a large formation. Just two years earlier, his direct responsibilities had lain with himself and his observer; a year later he was accountable for a six-man flight; now, at the age of 22, he was faced with an 18-strong squadron of commissioned and non-commissioned officers plus mechanics, riggers, carpenters, electricians, sailmakers, armourers, storemen, orderlies, batmen, cooks and even a blacksmith.

In France, his purview would extend to accommodation, workshops and hangars, and in addition to the aeroplanes he was accountable for a Crossley touring car, five Crossley light tenders, seven Leyland heavy tenders, a Leyland workshop lorry and eight Phelon & Moore motorcycles and their drivers and riders.[5] In all, he oversaw some 200 personnel and a fighting force that had an establishment cost of £60,000 and a monthly maintenance bill of nearly £19,000.[6]

In preparation for war, the greater part of the squadron had been sent to the School of Aerial Fighting in Ayr. When they returned, they found that their old commander had been replaced by 'a most striking figure', a New Zealand major with an MC and 'a reputation as a determined fighter'. He was 'tall, well built, with black hair and a chin which could not deny his strong character. The great Alan Scott, whose opinion of air fighters was respected throughout the flying corps, estimated that Caldwell (or "Grid", as he was known) had engaged in "more fights for the number of times he had been in the air than any other pilot".'[7]

Caldwell was blessed with a trio of outstanding flight commanders: captains Edward 'Mick' Mannock (A Flight), Wilfred 'Youngski' Young (B Flight) and William Cairnes (C Flight). Both Young and Cairnes were arrivals from 19 Squadron. Before the war, Young, born in Dorsetshire, had been a rubber planter and member of the Malay States Volunteer Rifles, but when he heard of the German invasion of Belgium and France he left to 'join His Majesty's military forces in England'. In mid-1916 German machine-gun fire had wounded him in both legs, perforating his left calf and a toe.[8] Cairnes, who was born in Ireland, had attended Rugby School and the University of Cambridge before becoming an officer with the Leinster Regiment. In 19 Squadron, the pair had acquired three confirmed victories apiece, flying the well-regarded French-designed Spad single-seat fighter.

Mick Mannock was an altogether different species of airman. Caldwell had once met the restless and mercurial Irishman when he was in 40 Squadron and had been 'impressed with his dedicated keenness to get as many Huns as possible . . . He was a tall, thin man, about 6 feet, with reddish-brown hair and a ruddy complexion. He spoke rather quickly and sounded nervous in a way. He didn't sound Irish as had been mentioned in various books. Not exactly public school, but a pleasant mid-English. He was a striking figure [who] always carried a cane.'[9]

A complex and thoughtful child, Mannock preferred his own company, playing the violin, reading and studying English flora and fauna. His father, a former soldier, suffered from debt, drink and depression and eventually abandoned his wife and five children. Forced to leave his studies in his early teens, Mannock found work

Edward Mannock was Keith Caldwell's senior flight commander in 74 Squadron. Mannock complemented Caldwell's emphasis on teamwork and provided invaluable experience, gleaned in vicious combat in the preceding months. His four months with the 'Tigers' were the most productive of his exceptional career.

first with a local greengrocer, then as a barber's assistant, before turning his hand to clerical duties and then becoming a telegraph linesman in 1911. He was a collection of contradictions: a good cricketer and staunch supporter of the British Empire who agitated for Irish Home Rule and vociferously advocated socialist politics at any opportunity. He had no time for inherited status and privilege.

In 1914, he took up employment in Turkey at the Ottoman Telephone Exchange, but after war broke out found himself interned as an enemy alien. He suffered under a cruel regime of inadequate food, ill-treatment and the wasting effects of malaria and dysentery. When the Red Cross secured his release, he was a scarecrow, covered with scabs and suppurating sores. It was a slow and painful journey home to England via Bulgaria, Syria and Greece.[10]

Barely recovered, Mannock entered service with the Royal Army Medical Corps but loathed their middle-class attitudes and had no desire to tend injured Germans in the field; he would rather kill them. Mannock applied for the Royal Engineers where, as he told his mother, 'I'm going to be a tunnelling officer and blow the bastards up, the higher they go and the more pieces that came down, the better!'[11] Eventually he settled on the Royal Flying Corps. To make up for a weakness in one eye, he allegedly sneaked into the medical hut to memorise the chart before his examination, which he duly passed. In training he learnt from James McCudden how to recover from a spin at low attitude and proved to be an adequate pilot but a difficult officer, his political views and informality at odds with many of the public schoolboys populating the RFC.

When he arrived in France on the anniversary of his release from his Turkish prison, 1 April 1917, he was posted to 40 Squadron, flying Nieuport 17s. He immediately made a bad impression by sitting in the chair of a recently killed squadron favourite and offering his inexperienced advice on how to fight the Germans. He survived Bloody April, but only just. On one occasion his plane's lower left wing completely detached itself and he was forced to crash-land. Sholto Douglas summed him up well:

> It was the vehemence of Mick Mannock, and his forthrightness of expression, that left us in no doubt about the intensity of the patriotism that drove him on, and that was coupled with his very real hatred of the Germans. And yet, because of the slowness of his start, there was at first a doubt in the minds of those with whom he flew about his ability and even his desire to fight. Being an older, more articulate, and more experienced man of the world, Mannock did not hesitate to voice his opinions, even if he had not yet proved himself;

but his self-assurance, while not being in the least arrogant, was resented by some of those who thought, because they happened to be scoring, that they knew better.[12]

Mannock's good 40 Squadron friend William MacLanachan acknowledged that the Irishman's first two months with the unit were nerve-racking as the Luftstreitkräfte Albatros machines cut a swath through the RFC.

> I have seen Mannock in his early days, burying his head in his hands and trembling from head to foot, after he had spent ten minutes of adrenal energy in keeping clear of the hail of lead that was being fired at him from four or five machines simultaneously. He, like all brave men, was the first to admit that his one and only desire was to save his life — so, if the 'King of Air Fighters' could show such terrific mental and physical upheaval, what would have been the effect on an inexperienced pilot who had lacked even a little of Mannock's will and spirit?[13]

That Mannock survived the carnage was testament to his slowly mounting abilities. Avoiding the enemy and simply staying alive hardened him to the necessity of ruthlessness in the air and made him protective towards freshly arrived subordinates. He was a sluggish starter in aerial victories, but in the summer of 1917 he made good on his promise as a fighter pilot, accruing 15 officially accepted claims, earning promotion to flight commander and achieving an MC and bar. Caldwell was 'delighted to find that Mannock was the senior flight commander' and felt that, with him in the ranks, 'we might spin when we went overseas and got up against the enemy'.[14] The two became inseparable friends.

The remaining pilots were a diverse bunch, almost evenly divided between British airmen and colonials from South Africa, Canada, Rhodesia and New Zealand. Their ages clustered around 19 to 26; the youngest was 17, the oldest a 34-year-old with a wife and family. Caldwell was younger than nearly half of his charges. Most were freshly graduated trainees, with a sprinkling of men with modest experience in a frontline squadron. For the majority, this was their first posting to active air duty.

Caldwell soon laid out his expectations and hopes for the squadron:

Overleaf: London Colney, March 1918. From left: Edward Mannock, Keith Caldwell, Benjamin Roxburgh-Smith, Jarrard (adjutant), Andrew Kiddie, Wilfred Young. These stellar pilots would accrue over 120 victories in aerial combat with 74 Squadron.

You are being equipped with the finest fighting aircraft in the world and are particularly fortunate in having three experienced flight commanders. I'm sure we will be a very happy family. When we go to war, you must all fight like hell. It must never be said, however, that a pilot of 74 ever failed to go to the aid of a comrade, even if he is in a position to knock down a dozen Huns. Any man failing to assist another in trouble will get the pleasure of my boot up his backside. I need not point out, gentlemen, that I have big feet.[15]

In the days that followed, Caldwell's flight commanders added weight to his words. 'Mick says that he [Caldwell] is the bravest man in the Air Force, and that he will frighten hell out of us when he is leading patrols. This, coming from Mick, makes us wonder what we are in for,' wrote Welshman Ira Jones years later.[16] Caldwell then began preparing his airmen as quickly as possible. With so many inexperienced pilots, he immediately ordered daily flying sessions with the SE5s and set Mannock to giving regular lectures on a range of topics.

According to one witness, Mannock's manner was authoritative and compelling. The seminars were 'delicious dishes of offensive spirit . . . After listening to him for a few minutes, the poorest, most inoffensive pilot was convinced he could knock hell out of Richthofen or any other Hun'. After watching the newbies using all the stunting tricks they had recently acquired, Mannock praised their enthusiasm but injected a jolt of realism: 'They will be no damned use to you when you get a Hun on your tail.' Stunting was good for gaining confidence but dangerous in combat, depriving the pilot of speed and altitude. He warned them against such antics when put to the test by the best machines the Germans could offer.

When we get to the war . . . don't ever attempt to dogfight a triplane on anything like equal terms in altitude. He'll get on your tail and stay there until he shoots you down. Take my advice. If you ever get into such an unfortunate position, put your aircraft into a vertical bank, hold the stick tight into your belly, keep your engine full on — and pray hard. When the Hun has got tired of trying to shoot you down from one position, he'll try another. Here's your chance, and you'll have to snap into it with alacrity. As soon as your opponent starts to manoeuvre for the next position, put on full bottom rudder, do one and [a] half turns of a spin and then run like hell for home, kicking your rudder hard from side to side, so as to make the shooting more difficult for the enemy. And keep praying!

Mannock's first lecture began and ended with his oft-repeated axiom for air combat: 'Gentleman, remember. Always above, seldom on the same level, never beneath.'[17]

As well as giving lectures himself and leading flights, Caldwell was coming to grips with the wider squadron and its personnel. In this task he was aided by his three principal ground officers. Harry Coverdale, a former English rugby international fly-half, was his gunnery and armaments officer; Clifford Mansfield, of Surrey, his equipment officer; and William Joseph Julius Everard Mount Everard who, in addition to his excessively long name, was apparently fluent in French, Spanish and Arabic. He was Caldwell's recording officer.[18] With these men and the experienced NCOs, Caldwell organised the unit's departure for France on 22 March, barely two weeks away. It was a tight schedule made more difficult by the high volume of machine and personnel transfers and a long list of logistical considerations. He found he had a surfeit of pilots.

As Canadian airman Leonard 'Spearmint' Richardson wrote in his diary, 'He wonders why in hell so many pilots were sent to him since he has all the pilots he needs except one spare.' When Caldwell asked Richardson what experience he had with the SE5a, the reply was 'lots . . . But I think he knew I was lying . . . [and] he told me to take a machine and get a little extra flying practice.' In the end, he was taken as a spare, 'because if nothing else I know how to shake a cocktail!'[19]

Added to all this were the usual minor issues involved in running a squadron. Men were admonished not to use the telephone for private purposes or smoke outside the hangars, and no 'passenger flights of the "joy-ride" type' were permitted.[20] Because of the 'unnecessary loss and damage caused to the public by flying at low altitudes over roads frequented by horse traffic, and over animals grazing', this practice 'must cease immediately'.[21] The nationwide shortage of leather to make boots meant 'brown shoes may be worn by officers when employed in offices or off duty'. Discipline became more of a problem as departure neared. Several men, mostly mechanics and armourers, decided to spend more time than allowed off base seeing family or drinking at local pubs. Such absent without leave cases were summarily dealt with by docking pay.[22]

The supporting staff and ground crew would leave first for France and establish a beachhead; the pilots would then fly the SE5s across the Channel. But the first wave of departure coincided with the launch of the German Spring Offensive on 21 March. In the early morning, Winston Churchill, as minister of munitions, was inspecting forces on the Western Front when, in his words, 'there rose in less than one minute the most tremendous cannonade I shall ever hear . . . It swept around us in a wide curve of red leaping flame stretching to the north far along the front of the Third Army, as well as of the Fifth Army in the south, and quite unending in either direction . . . The weight and intensity of the bombardment surpassed anything which anyone had ever known before.[23] In the next five hours, more than 3,500,000 shells fell over 150 square miles; then Germans swarmed forward out of the persistent morning mist, low fog and smoke.

The next day, 74 Squadron was on the move, 'men of all ranks, riggers, fitters, cooks etc and all flying officers' baggage, under the command of Young', heading to Southampton from London Colney. The 150-odd men and their crates, trunks and bags arrived at Le Havre on 24 March. But four days later, they were ordered to re-embark for Southampton. As Richardson noted sardonically, 'my career in France has been short and decisive'.[24] The party headed for London, only to be rerouted to Dover and then to France again.

Back at London Colney, Caldwell was hosting one of the founding fathers of the RFC, General Charles Longcroft, who had come 'to say farewell, good luck, "God Bless"'. The visitor unwittingly raised an embarrassing issue.

> [He] took me aside for a small pep talk; telling me amongst other things to impress on my chaps the importance of getting close before firing, mentioning unfortunately, that they should have Bishop as their model! You can imagine my predicament. I could not rat on Bish too much of course, so I think I said that I served alongside B [Flight] for some months in 60 [Squadron] and that I could not recall his firing at particularly close range; not more so than many others. I told him not to bother too much about us, that we were well prepared, had good Flight Commanders, including Mannock with about 20 Huns to his credit. He felt a bit flat with his pep talk I think, and no doubt thought I was a cocky young colonial.[25]

Caldwell was not about to criticise Bishop, but nor was he going to allow the general to elevate an individual who did not wholly represent what he was seeking to establish: a close-knit community of airmen who put the well-being of their fellow pilots above personal glory. 'Wish I had a tape recording of that episode,' wrote Caldwell in a post-war letter. 'I would probably be ashamed of my brashness, telling a chair-born old boy how to win the war, if he hadn't mentioned Bish, I would probably have let him wander on.'[26]

Continuing problems with Young's advance expedition and the general chaos on the Western Front delayed the pilots' departure. The squadron was forced to cool its heels at a coastal airfield, protecting Britain from high-flying German bombers. 'We are doing Home Defence at present waiting for any Gothas that may come over during the day,' Caldwell informed his mother. 'As soon as things get more settled in France and they have an aerodrome for us we shall track over, I hope. We've been a fortnight, nearly three weeks now without a change of clothing. You had better not send any clothes or parcels to France yet as we may be here a week or two.'[27]

In the end, Caldwell and his airmen arrived at St Omer in France at the same time as the ground crew, on 30 March 1918.[28] On the flight, squadron diarist Ira Jones was responsible for the squadron's mascot, a small black puppy named Contact.

> Since we were crossing the 'Ditch' at 10,000 feet, I had no worries about engine trouble and was able to concentrate on the fascination of my first flight over the sea. The white-flecked expanse of water, dotted everywhere with miniature ships, looked like a child's table model, and was wholly delightful. It was not difficult to follow the canal from Calais to St Omer. By noon, we had all landed at the aerodrome. But not all intact. As usual, I had turned up-side down, and my friend Giles had followed suit. 'Contact' threw up.[29]

The sprawling airfield at No. 1 Aircraft Depot, just south-west of St Omer, was awash with men and machines. The larger sister of No. 2 Aircraft Depot Candas, No. 1 Depot had swelled to immense proportions since its early days as a small waypoint in 1914. Some 4300 technical personnel — nearly 10 per cent of the entire RFC establishment in France — were maintaining, repairing, modifying and salvaging pranged or war-damaged machines.[30] Also there were pilots awaiting deployment or war-wearied men on their way back to Blighty, plus hundreds of administrative staff. 'It is an ugly sprawling place,' noted one man, 'with scores of Bessonneau canvas hangars, and workshops, and rows and rows of Nissen huts for living quarters.'[31]

St Omer was a short ride away. From the top of a nearby hill, the town, with its cathedral and old buildings, looked to one airman like an 'old Dutch landscape painting'.[32] Upon closer inspection it was more Bosch than Vermeer, but it was not without its delights. The streets were overrun with uniforms and motorcycle dispatch riders, and staff cars, some scarred with bullet holes, bounced and coughed along the cobbled streets, swerving to avoid black-clad women, children and horse-drawn wagons. The men of the squadron kept a close eye on where they placed their feet:

'the people have a habit of throwing refuse out into the streets to be taken away.'[33]

On their first evening, Caldwell's men stayed overnight at the famed Hôtel du Commerce; some were disappointed.[34] 'I must say, I think France is a bit of a hole,' lamented one pilot. 'We are now at the best hotel in town but except for the food and a comfortable bed, it isn't in with a comfortable inn at home. It is purely an eating house, nasty and untidy. Kitchen chairs and tables lie about in a mucky looking room with funny looking wash basins in the corner.'[35] Some airmen were billeted in a backstreet café, where they ate 'at a long family table presided over by the stout, hairy patron in shirtsleeves, and food served by his pretty daughter, the room delicately odoriferous from the urinal against the wall outside'.

The new arrivals also noticed 'the long queues of British and Imperial troops waiting impatiently outside the licensed brothels . . . [and] a more refined officers' place, with a waiting room complete with out-of-date copies of *La Vie Parisienne*, right in the shadow of the Cathedral, which, as it was Sunday, was packed to the doors'.[36]

Two days later, the squadron was sent to an RNAS aerodrome near Dunkirk. The move coincided with the long-awaited amalgamation of the army and naval air services into the RAF. The naval units were renumbered from 200, so that 15 Squadron RNAS became 215 Squadron RAF, but the former RFC units retained their original numbers. Caldwell and his men also kept their ranks. Uniforms stayed the same; some men still wore the double-breasted 'maternity' style, but the ordinary buttoned officer's jacket, with RFC wings still prominent, became more common. Because of past friction between the RFC and the RNAS, Ira Jones 'was quite prepared . . . to put up with some unpleasantness as the guest of the RNAS squadron. To my astonishment, our hosts could not do enough for us. With the exception of one hasty remark by a non-combatant officer, we met with nothing but the utmost friendliness.'[37]

What was now the world's largest independent air force had more than 20,000 aeroplanes and 300,000 personnel. In the transition, Hugh Trenchard was succeeded by Major General John Salmond as general officer commanding the RAF in the field.

On 2 April, Caldwell was ordered to gather his forces at Dunkirk's Teteghem

Above: **Seventy-four Squadron awaits departure to France. Standing, from left: Lewis, Benjamin Roxburgh-Smith, Henry Hamer, Philip Stuart-Smith, Henry Dolan, Harris Clements, Ronald Bright, Charles Skedden, Harry Coverdale, Ira Jones. Middle, from left: William Cairnes, Wilfred Young, Keith Caldwell holding Contact the dog, Jarrard (adjutant), Edward Mannock. Front, from left: Percy Howe, John Piggott, Gerald Savage, Wilfred Giles.**

Below: **B Flight mechanics, 74 Squadron.**

aerodrome. It would be a brief period on the coast, mostly to find replacement vehicles and get his ducks in a row. 'All our transports, lorries and things were bagged by Headquarters as soon as they got to France and used in the great war on all sorts of jobs. My car is practically smoked out already and the springs are awful.'[38] A windfall of mess equipment arrived but, Caldwell lamented, 'About six valises belonging to the officers are gone astray somewhere, one of mine included, with Capt. Chidlaw-Roberts's name on it.'[39] Without cutlery, the pilots were reduced to eating with their pocket knives until the ground crew took pity on them and lent them some utensils. 'But we don't care,' wrote Jones, 'we're in France, which is the main thing.' But they did care about the lack of action.

> This is bad for us. Too much like sitting in a dentist's chair. To while away the time we have all been practising shooting at a target in the sea. It is a good idea, as we can see by splashing of the bullets if we are aiming straight. Of course, the target is stationary, so it is not much of a test of our ability. When we aim at the Hun he will not be so obliging unless he is fool enough to dive away from us instead of turning.[40]

Caldwell's squadron was at the fringe of the battle raging to the south, but his daily telephone calls asking for permission to start offensive patrols were routinely turned down.[41]

With help from Harry Coverdale, the pilots got their guns sighted. In lieu of sorties, Caldwell set the men to familiarisation and formation flying, some straying close to the trenches for a temporary adrenaline rush. A bored Cairnes ventured across enemy lines with a 'practice flight', during which his men received their first introduction to 'Archie'. Ira Jones's machine leapt around as anti-aircraft shells burst around him. He was a little shaken but fine, more concerned for Contact, who was tucked away in the cubbyhole in the SE5's fuselage known as 'the locker'. Jones spotted a hole in the locker cover: had the dog been hit or fallen out?

Only at the end of the one-and-a-half-hour flight did the full extent of the Archie-inflicted damage become clear when the fuselage snapped in two. 'Out jumped Contact, as fit as a flea, much to my joy. My machine was the first causality in the squadron, and I am proud of the fact. I am a firm believer in the motto, "Start badly, end well."'[42]

Caldwell was determined to build cohesiveness and esprit de corps. During one restaurant meal, two teetotallers — Jones and one of a small clutch of Americans in the squadron, Charles Skedden — were uncovered drinking wine-like beverages, notably a non-alcoholic French drink called grenadine. When some of the men began pressuring them to take wine, Jones noted that Caldwell deftly stepped in, saying that it 'was a good show that we don't [drink]; which is typical of him. He is a great leader of men. I would do anything or go anywhere for him, and I am sure that all the others would follow suit.' After the squadron moved to yet another temporary aerodrome, La Lovie, Jones overheard an airman with a resident squadron comment that although 74 Squadron's commanding officer was 'a cracker', the unit was nothing more than a 'ragtime crowd, [with] no discipline'.

Jones vehemently disagreed.

> [T]hey're talking tripe. One word from Grid, and the thing is as good as done. Certainly we cut out as much as possible the empty but deceptive type of discipline — 'Yes, sir,' 'No, sir.' 'Three bags full, sir.' We're a fighting squadron. We've come out to fight, and by our achievements as fighters we want to be judged, not by whether we wear breeches and puttees or slacks.[43]

On 11 April, Caldwell at last led his pilots to their final aerodrome — and it was one of the worst in France: Clairmarais North.[44] 'It is one damned rotten hole,' declared Richardson.[45] The aerodrome north-east of St Omer, on the slope of a hill, was small and L-shaped. Since it was barely 300 by 159 yards and had a 10-foot boundary hedge with tall trees on one side, the pilots ran a sweepstake on who would prang first. And 74 Squadron was not alone; they shared the modest aerodrome with a Camel formation, 54 Squadron, led by the tall, lean, slightly stooped Major Reginald Maxwell.[46] The officers of both units would have plenty of time to get acquainted in the next few weeks, and the Camels would be a nice complement to the SE5s of 74 Squadron in subsequent operations.

A mile away was Clairmarais North's southern twin, Clairmarais South, soon to be occupied by 1 Squadron's SE5s. All three squadrons were part of II Brigade's 11 Wing under Hesperus Andrias (Pierre) van Ryneveld.[47] The more than 150 machines under the South African's command were the core fighting force operating in support of the northernmost British army.

Unnecessarily, the ground crew had been sent to Clairmarais via Poperinge, just west of Ypres, worryingly close to the new German advance. After Operation Michael, the Germans had launched Operation Georgette on 9 April against the British Second and Third armies in the north. Operation Michael had drawn in the British forces around Amiens, leaving the route to the Channel ports vulnerable, and if Boulogne, Calais and Dunkirk could be isolated, General Erich Ludendorff would have his victory. Operation Georgette focused on the sector of Hazebrouck, where the British were relieving one of the two Portuguese divisions; the remaining division was annihilated by the Germans.

The next day, the British position collapsed, the defenders of Armentières fell back to avoid encirclement and the strategic Messines Ridge was captured. The British were barely holding on at the Lys canal, and the French would arrive too late to prevent the German push to the coast, just 15 miles away.

As one of only two Belgian towns not under German occupation, Poperinge had an overwhelmed casualty clearing station, a harrowing sight for those newly arrived in France. Long lines of men blinded by poison gas, one hand on the shoulder of another, shuffled through the town. 'The Hun is stirring Hell,' wrote Richardson, 'shelling Poperinge and starting to drive on Ypres Road and Messines Ridge . . . [we] go into Pop[eringe] to eat at Officers' Club, but the shelling got too hot for us, so we leave . . . We think it awful but perhaps the lads in the trenches would be willing to exchange with us.'[48] After midnight, unsettled by the rocking and shaking of the exploding shells, they were finally ordered to join the pilots at Clairmarais. That same day, 11 April, the Germans exploited more fractured and thinly defended positions. Merville fell, Nieppe was overrun and Messines was occupied by the enemy. The squadron was about to get out of the dentist's chair.

T he rapidity of the German onslaught caught the RAF by surprise. Nine squadrons were forced to abandon forward aerodromes to avoid being overrun — ground crews and equipment were hastily loaded into tenders and driven west; machines were flown out of the danger zone. Pilots looking over their shoulders saw a smoking front below them, flashing gun muzzles and German soldiers advancing on withdrawing Allied forces. One squadron was less fortunate. At La Gorgue aerodrome, barely 3 miles behind the original front, the fog was so thick that takeoff was impossible.[49] With the aerodrome being periodically bombed and rumours of enemy forces closing in, the men were ordered to herd their Sopwith Camels into a tight circle. Then they

The squadron's poet, Canadian Leonard Richardson, was also one of its diarists. He ensured his inclusion in 74 Squadron's roster for France by lying about his proficiency with the SE5a and through his prowess for mixing a fine cocktail. Keith Caldwell dubbed him the 'cocktail king'.

stepped forward and set fire to the machines. When the Germans arrived, they found a smouldering funeral pyre of twisted metal, burnt wood and blackened engines.

On the precipice of disaster, on 11 April Haig issued a special order '[t]o all ranks of the British army in France and Flanders', which Caldwell read to the men. He stressed that, despite the enemy's 'terrific attack', involving 106 divisions, he had 'as yet, made little progress towards his goals'. Then came the famous words:

> We owe this to the determined fighting and self-sacrifice of our troops. Words fail me to express the admiration which I feel for the splendid resistance offered by all ranks of our Army under the most trying of circumstances . . . There is no other course open to us but to fight it out. Every position must be held to the last man; there must be no retirement. With our backs to the wall, and believing in the justice of our cause, each one of us must fight on to the end. The safety of our homes and the freedom of mankind depend alike upon the conduct of each of us at this moment.[50]

Orders came through from van Ryneveld at 11 Wing headquarters: 74 Squadron was finally going to be thrown into the onslaught. The men were elated, if nervous; everyone wanted to have the first crack at the enemy.

Caldwell ran a draw and Cairnes' C Flight was given the honours. 'Mick is fed up to the teeth that he has not won the toss,' wrote an excited Jones.[51] Caldwell took the officers into St Omer for dinner at a well-known restaurant nicknamed 'George Robey's', after the famous British comedian. Richardson had a fine time: 'The food is good but Mick and Caldwell are better, which makes a delightful evening and gives promise of real companionship for the squadron.'[52]

Absent from the festivities were some of C Flight — eager pilots wanting to be at the top of their game in the morning. 'A wide-awake pilot will always crack a sleepy one,' reasoned Jones.[53] Dawn and the Luftstreitkräfte awaited.

CHAPTER FOURTEEN

Day of Days

As Caldwell walked out onto the aerodrome on 12 April 1918, the sky above was clear and inviting.[1] The men of C Flight, having downed a cup of tea and munched a handful of biscuits, were listening as Cairnes gave the pre-flight briefing: they would cross the lines near Merville and work up towards Ypres over the growing German salient. Mannock and Coverdale stood next to Caldwell, watching the men protectively. Despite the gravity of the situation, the pilots were keen, 'each thinking of the Hun he was going to down and no one of the possibility of death or, worse, a breakfast of black bread and sausages in the enemy's lines'.[2]

Caldwell offered words of encouragement and Mannock light-heartedly asked them 'not to disturb the Huns', lest there be none when his turn came. The New Zealander counted them out, pleased that it was a punctual 6 a.m. departure, but mindful of what lay ahead.

C Flight encountered flak at 6000 feet as they crossed the lines; the SE5s were bouncing all over the place, in a slightly drunk V formation. In the distance, a large fleet of machines was spotted 2000 feet above and 2 miles away, but closing fast. Jones was at the rear:

> Were they Huns? I couldn't make up my mind. But as they came on fast, the
> black Maltese Crosses on their wings soon settled the question. It was months

since I had seen any. How pretty they looked! And what pretty machines! They were all colours. Black, red, bright blue, grey, yellow — all the colours of the rainbow. It never struck me that they were aeroplanes flown by men, possibly crack pilots of the German air force. Men whom I knew as Huns; death-dealing gentlemen, possibly smothered in Iron Crosses and Orders *pour la Merite* [Pour le Mérite]. They looked more like a rather beautiful flock of birds. But I was soon awakened from my reverie.[3]

A riot of bullets and tracer fire preceded the arrival of the enemy machines. Cairnes took evasive action, swinging the formation away sharply, but Jones was separated from the rest. The leading German in a triplane latched onto the Welshman, while the others prevented the intervention of the rest of C Flight and waited to cut Jones off, should he attempt to run for it. Jones followed Mannock's advice and held the stick to his belly with the throttle wide open, and prayed very hard. He was in a vertical bank with strings of bullets falling behind him in the steep turn. Other German machines attempted brief forays against him but to little effect. Seconds seemed like years.

Ira Jones was repeating to himself, 'Keep cool, Van Ira, he can't hit you. His bullets are going behind', all the while shouting obscenities at the top of his lungs at the grinning German with the pug nose and shock of black hair.[4] When the triplane manoeuvred to get a better position, Jones took his chance and fell into a spin and then into a counter-spin, barging through a dozen German machines 'as I had done through a rugger scrum when cornered'.[5]

He scampered west with the enemy in hot pursuit, kicking his rudder left and right. Bullets whizzed past, but none struck home. The SE5's superior speed came into play and the furious noise of the Spandau machine guns faded. Jones chanced a look over his shoulder: the enemy were falling behind. Having slipped the net, he rejoined the waiting C Flight. As adrenaline seeped from his bloodstream, his bravado momentarily wavered. Was he a coward? Would he be able to face the enemy again? 'I was simply terrified of another flight over the lines.'

In a few minutes, however, flying in formation, he regained his emotional equilibrium. Caldwell was waiting at the aerodrome to count the formation in. As the men dismounted, he patted them on the back, offering words of encouragement.

Above: **A staged photograph of three pilots of 1 Squadron studying maps before a sortie, Clairmarais South, France.**

Below: **B Flight, 74 Squadron. Standing, from left: Wilfred Young, Clive Glynn, Andrew Kiddie, Philip Stuart-Smith. Kneeling: Gerald Savage, Robert Piggott.**

Jones told him that, despite no success, he now had confidence in the machine and his own ability to handle the Germans. 'Of course, you're better than those sods, the Hunnerinoes,' said Caldwell, 'but don't get overconfident. It's the first month, not day, that counts, Taffy.'[6]

Mannock, pleased that Cairnes' flight had failed to bag an enemy machine, took off at 8.25 a.m. His men found the air was still full of hostiles. Positioning A Flight between a flock of glistening silver Albatros fighters and their base, Mannock led a blistering attack at 13,000 feet.[7] Henry 'Bilo' Dolan fired two bursts from above and behind as he closed to within 50 yards. The Albatros turned over and plummeted down, out of control. When the dogfight was over, there were two crumpled enemy machines on the ground: both Mannock and Dolan had secured a victory.

Back at the aerodrome, they began firing off Very lights of all colours. It had been a good operation, drawing first blood for the squadron.[8] The men were fizzing as they climbed out of their SE5s. A grinning Mannock greeted the onlookers with his catchphrase: 'Always above, seldom on the same level, never beneath.' For Dolan, a former Royal Field Artillery officer with an MC, this was his first victory.

Caldwell, eager to enter the fray, slotted himself into Young's B Flight. It was the last operation of the morning and would be the New Zealander's first sortie since leaving 60 Squadron the previous year. The SE5a was now a familiar mount with its more powerful — and, thankfully, reliable — engine. As Jones had just discovered, the advanced 200 horsepower Wolseley Viper V8 — a British-built derivative of the well-regarded Spanish Hispano Suiza engine — offered superior speed and altitude: 138 miles per hour and 19,500 feet. Caldwell walked the pre-flight inspection, looking over the wood and cloth airframe and wings, running his fingers along the flying wires before checking the fuel tank and engine. He grabbed a centre strut on the port side of the machine, placed his left foot on the lower wing and swung himself into the cockpit.

Like most airmen in 1918, he had discarded his long flying jacket for a newly issued one-piece garment, known as the Sidcot suit. This forerunner of the aviator's jumpsuit was made of tan-coloured waterproofed cotton, with a rubberised cotton interlining and fur lining. A large button-down flap crossed over the chest. The wrists and ankles were snugly sealed with further buttons. Maps and small items could be stuffed into the large open pockets on the knees. It offered better warmth and less bulk in the confines of the tight airframe.[9] Caldwell's shoulders kissed the sides of the cockpit as he lowered himself into the seat.

The Aldis gunsight ran along the nose, with the Vickers machine gun close by its side. Above him was the wing-mounted Lewis machine gun. Caldwell was indifferent to both. As he said, many pilots disregarded the gunsight, preferring to 'watch their tracers and so avoid being denied any side vision. Personally, I, and many others, would have preferred an open ring sight.'[10] The Lewis was still prone to jamming and reloading was dangerous in a dogfight; Caldwell would rather have discarded it altogether. But these were minor niggles. The SE5 was a wonder to fly and, even when he was firing only the Vickers, more than a match for the current crop of German machines.

The khaki-coloured SE5s taxied out herring-bone style, turning side to side, criss-crossing over the path of the leading machine for better visibility past the long-nosed engine. They were like large predatory cats, shoulder blades climbing and falling as they made for the end of the small aerodrome. Caldwell opened the throttle and took off, the controls marvellously light and responsive in his hands. In the air, the flight gathered around Caldwell and Young and made for the British lines. No man's land stretched before them as they entered the field of battle.

The flight was at 17,000 feet south-east of Deûlémont, at the confluence of the Deûle and Lys rivers, when Caldwell spotted a lone Albatros DV fighter sporting a 'yellow fuselage, green wings with red and yellow checks'.[11] He pushed the stick forward, dropping the nose; the altimeter fell as the rev-counter rose. At 14,000 feet, he swooped on the Albatros, its chequered wings filling his vision before he fired a burst of five rounds right into the cockpit. The tracers, like bright meteors, stabbed holes in the fuselage. It was quick and decisive: the German machine stumbled and fell.

Caldwell followed, firing at intervals to ensure the enemy was not faking his death plunge. At 1000 feet, he pulled away as the Albatros struck the ground near a large balloon. The dark ploughed earth enveloped the bright and twisted bird. It was Caldwell's tenth victim and the first as commanding officer. The swiftness and the clinical nature of the dispatch was testament to the training and honing of his skills over the winter in Britain. This was a different Caldwell.

It was a bruising first day of operations for the squadron and the RAF. It was also the most important day of the offensive; Caldwell's men were just one element in the vast assault on the enemy. 'The result was that more hours were flown, more bombs dropped, and more photographs taken than on any day since the war began.'[12] Contact patrols provided the most accurate pictures yet of the German advance, and artillery cooperation flights ranged the big guns on the surging enemy lines. Most of the effort, though, was against the ground forces by low-flying RAF machines dropping bombs and peppering the German troops moving forward.

Over a 24-hour period, more than 4600 bombs were dropped, 3300 photographs taken and 110,000 rounds fired.[13] Caldwell's II Brigade comrades concentrated on blunting the Hazebrouck threat. It was a brutal and frenzied assault on massed infantry, communications centres, headquarters, clogged roads and railway junctions. The air fighting was unremitting; German formations of 15 to 20 machines roamed the blue arena in search of RAF machines. In the afternoon, Caldwell's flights went out on six more patrols.

In the last operation of the day, Mannock nabbed another, though he insisted that the other members of the flight 'should share in the credit of this enemy aircraft'.[14] For Benjamin Roxburgh-Smith, Percy Howe and Harris Clements it was their first aerial combat triumph. The squadron's five official victories were spread over six individuals.

It was a 'day of days' for 74 Squadron and one seldom equalled in the British air service of the First World War.[15] That all the men survived the baptism was even more gratifying to Caldwell. Many were exhausted and chose an early night. When Jones told Mannock about his sudden physiological distress that morning, Mannock replied, 'Most pilots have this reaction at some time or other. It is just a question of fighting resolutely against the desire to give in. This is the test of a MAN — whether he be a fighter or a coward.'[16] Caldwell led the celebration that evening in the mess, encouraging his men, in a brief speech, to remain undeterred in their duty to defeat the enemy at all costs: it was the Allies or the Germans.[17]

The achievements of Caldwell's men did not go unnoticed. The next day, when the weather turned against aerial operations, the squadron was visited by van Ryneveld, who was well known for his participation in the Second Anglo–Boer War as a boy.[18] He was immensely popular. He had a knack for getting alongside the men with an encouraging word or two and was renowned for flying his own Camel over the lines to assess for himself the situation in the sky. During a particularly testing time later in the year, Mannock confessed to Jones that 'If it were not for Van Ryneveld and Grid, I would ask for a month's rest. My nerves are beginning to fray.'[19]

The South African praised Caldwell and the squadron for their achievements under such demanding conditions. As a later historian noted, the unit was well on its way to becoming 'famous for its fighting prowess'.[20]

On 13 April, Caldwell summarised the events of the past two days in a letter to Mary Caldwell:

My Dear Mother,

Just a scribble to let you know everything is OK. Yesterday the squadron did its first day's work on its new front where the activity is great and did very well indeed. We crashed 5 Huns during the day, many of them being on this side of the lines and lost no one although several pilots had their grids hit. Cpt. Mannock got one and Bilo another in the first scrap. I got one with C Flight which crashed the other side. A Flight got another scout between the lot of them in the afternoon which crashed the other side and Capt. Young B Flight brought one down this side in the evening. The Wing Commander was very bucked [up] and came down to see us last night.

The war is very strenuous still and all sorts of movements are taking place, we will probably make another move very soon. The place we are at now is pretty awful, but some squadrons are worse off than we are I believe.

The weather is completely dud at present, and we are taking advantage of it by getting as much sleep as possible. Each pilot had three patrols yesterday. Last night the Hun dropped bombs quite close by . . .

Cheery 'oh
Your loving son
Keith

The following days were beset by mist, fog, low cloud and periodic rain. The ferocious battle on the ground continued, but the air component was kept on the sidelines. The men used the opportunity to settle into their new accommodation — a series of wooden huts, each home to two officers. The mess was a fair-sized wooden building and there were eight large, corrugated iron-roofed hangars. As temperatures fell, Caldwell directed the men to stay active. Both he and Maxwell saw the usefulness of sports to maintain fitness and burn off tension. A series of rugby games was arranged with their neighbouring 54 Squadron.[21] Of course, 74 Squadron was blessed in such tussles with its former English international and a Wanganui Collegiate star. 'These games were played in the spirit that the game demands — very hard, almost fierce, but absolutely clean,' wrote Jones in his diary.

Overleaf: **Keith Caldwell's first victim at the helm of 74 Squadron was an Albatros DV. This example was flown by Richard Flashar of Jasta 5 and has lost part of a lower wing.**

On our side, Coverdale and Caldwell were irresistible, and played with scintillating brilliance. These games were the first of eighteen victories which the Squadron won during its period in France. No match was lost. Thirteen out of twenty-one officers played these games. The spirit of determination and teamwork which is so essential for success in Rugby is the same spirit necessary in a squadron of successful air fighters. Mannock played rugby with the same determination and almost with the same fierceness as he fought in the air! The next best thing to shooting down a Hun, he contended, was 'a low, hard, flying tackle!'[22]

In the evening, the men played cards and read books and eagerly awaited mail.[23] When Jones's birthday arrived, Caldwell encouraged an evening of entertainment. Richardson mixed the cocktails. Caldwell dubbed one beverage the official drink of the squadron, nicknaming it the '#74 Viper', or simply 'the Viper'. The mess rang with rowdy renditions of 'I Can Dance with Everyone but My Wife' by the married Philip Stuart-Smith and Richardson's poor attempt at 'The Cobbler's Song' from the popular London show *Chu Chin Chow*. For his rotten exhibition Caldwell briefly called Richardson 'the Bootmaker'.[24]

But the war was on everyone's minds. On the evening of their first outing, RAF machines fleeing abandoned airfields attempted to land at Clairmarais. Some crashed and others had to be diverted because the aerodrome was simply too small to accommodate them. Day and night, reinforcing French troops passed by on their way to the front. And then there was the odd inaccurate bombing of the aerodrome by German machines and the earth-shaking sound of shells being lobbed by giant guns. At night, the eastern horizon glowed.

Five days later, as he told his mother, Caldwell had an 'exciting fight over Hunland at about 600 feet' but was fearful about the fate of one his men: 'Dolan and I went over together and got thoroughly lost, crashing all over the place trying to get back. My grid was shot through . . . badly, but no sign of Dolan yet, he's been out 5 hours now and it looks rather bad. I hope he is OK as he is one of our best fellows.' Dolan turned up late in the evening — his machine's engine had been shot through.

The next day, more top brass appeared. General John Salmond complimented Caldwell and his charges, reiterating that the five machines on the first day was a 'record'. The only downside to all this attention was that 11 Wing discovered Caldwell was a regular participant in operations and told him that he was 'doing too much flying'. 'This is rather bitter,' Caldwell told his mother, 'as the Huns at this point are pretty dud and quite easy to kill.' He would fly as often as he thought he could get away with.

On 21 April, the weather cleared sufficiently for more regular operations. The Germans had made important gains in Flanders, recovering territory lost in the previous autumn. It seemed impossible, but Passchendaele was about to be lost to the Germans. In the same pattern used nine days earlier, each flight would endure three patrols a piece. Under a heavy workload, Dolan, who was fast becoming an accomplished airman, accounted for a Fokker DrI. Cairnes' flight flew the last operation of the day, when the sky 'was lousy with Huns'.

In the first attack, Cairnes and Charles Skedden sent down a machine. The flight, which included the Londoner Sydney Begbie, soon spotted four lone Albatros fighters. While they were tackling these, another 10 arrived. It was six against 14, the squadron's first big dogfight, with only a brief time in which to fire and scoot away. 'We were waltzing around one another in a vicious circle,' wrote Jones, 'with machine guns spitting fire for all they were worth.'

> Suddenly there was a blaze in the sky nearby. I looked. It was Begbie's SE. A sudden feeling of sickness, of vomiting, overcame me. Poor old Begbie, I thought. How terrible! The kak-kak-kak of a machine gun a few yards behind me warned me of my own danger . . . I had another peep at him as I flew near. A Hun was still at him, pouring bullets into his machine. He was making sure of him, the dirty dog. While he pursued his victim, an SE — it was [Wilfred 'Twist'] Giles — dived on his tail. There was a kak-kak-kak! and the Hun dived away, not to be seen again. I hope he was killed, too. One by one the Huns left the fight. Giles and I flew towards Begbie's machine, which was floating enveloped in flames. It was a terrible sight.[25]

The flight returned with news of the victories but one man short. 'We had our first casualty the day before yesterday. Lt Begbie, down in flames,' wrote Caldwell.[26] The badly burnt 21-year-old died the following day in a German hospital.

Horrific though Begbie's loss had been, Caldwell could not allow the men to dwell on it. The squadron would not be brought to a halt; pausing meant endangering further lives. Maxwell in 54 Squadron was dealing with the same situation: he had just lost two pilots.[27] Caldwell invited the men of 54 over for a lively dinner. To keep their spirits up, the men were encouraged to play games, including the dangerous hi-cockalorum, a mess rugby game that involved two teams jumping on each other and pulling people off as the scrum nosily crabbed its way around the room, thumping against the walls, knocking over chairs and tables. When a few stood back, slightly shocked, Caldwell stopped the mêlée. 'The death of anyone amongst us must never be allowed to affect our morale. We will have a "full out" guest night whenever anyone is killed; that's an order.'[28] Then Mannock stepped forward into the centre of the assembly: 'Gentlemen, raise your glasses to Lieutenant Begbie and to Baron von Richthofen . . . in the hope that the bastard also went down in flames.' The Red Baron had indeed also been killed that day.

> Mannock smashed his glass to the ground and then turned to Lieutenant 'Swazi' Howe, who was the smallest man in the Squadron. Taking the small South African by the shoulder, he smiled. 'Now my fine young fella, it appears that we have lost our ball during this brief break in the play. I take pleasure in announcing that you are now "it."' Picking up the protesting Howe, Mannock threw him into the waiting crowd and then jumped on top of the men himself to send them all crashing to the floor.[29]

When Caldwell wrote to Sydney Begbie's family, he did not say how he died.

The death of von Richthofen, the greatest German ace, at the hands of a Camel pilot or Australian ground fire, was greeted with mixed emotions. Caldwell told his mother as an afterthought: 'P.S. Von Richthofen down this side, killed day before yesterday.'[30] The leader of the Flying Circus, with 80 official combat victories to his name, was admired as much as he was feared. As one pilot put it, 'A feeling of happiness as regards the fact that the Circus was broken, but it wasn't a feeling of hate. It was a feeling that a very good man had gone. That was true — he was a good fighter, a clever fighter. He used every move that he was taught and more. He was instinctive. To be a good pilot you have to become part of the aeroplane that you're flying.'[31] Many of the airmen in 74 Squadron were 'secretly sorry that he was dead'. Mannock, though, was having none of it: 'I hope he roasted all the way down.'[32]

Being wreathed in flames in a falling aeroplane was the deepest fear of all airmen. A wooden-framed machine with its engine and fuel tank encased in doped fabric was a potential flying torch. It was the stuff of nightmares for those who had witnessed a man thrashing around in fire. Others saw men jump from their machines to escape, twisting and turning as they fell thousands of feet to their death.

Mannock bluntly stated that he hoped Begbie had blown his brains out rather than suffer the hell of a fiery death. Mannock and many men flew with a service revolver for this very purpose. Richardson once heard a pilot ask Caldwell why they carried the bulky Webley revolver, to which Grid suggested he use his 'bloody imagination'. The Canadian elaborated in his diary: 'Since we don't have parachutes and perhaps it would be quite hot coming down in flame, we have the revolver to shoot ourselves in case we can't stand the heat.'[33]

Ira Jones asked why they had no parachutes.[34] After all, balloonists had been using them since before the war. The answer was none too clear. Some argued that providing a means of escape would have diminished fighting spirit and encouraged men to evacuate machines that might otherwise have been saved in a forced landing. This, however, was never confirmed, nor any individual held culpable for such a calculating and cruel assessment. The RFC had undertaken test flights with parachutes in 1917, but these had involved bulky tethered devices tucked under the fuselage of a machine rather than being worn by the pilot.[35] The weight and size of parachutes were certainly determining factors, but their absence remained a galling mystery to RAF airmen, who saw small numbers of German pilots escaping the flames in 1918.

Under such circumstances, grim humour prevailed. Caldwell and Mannock 'pulled one another's leg unmercifully; occasionally . . . Mick would faithfully volunteer to describe Grid's descent in flames to his mother, not sparing any detail.' Caldwell bet Mannock that he would be the first to 'sizzle' and gave an animated demonstration of 'the noises that would emanate from Mannock's machine as it floated a burning mass to earth!'[36]

T he German tide was still coming in, rolling slowly towards Amiens, as evidenced by regular visits by the Luftstreitkräfte bombers. 'The last ten nights the Huns have been very active bombing,' Caldwell told his mother. 'The French house I am sleeping in nearly falls down every time a bomb drops, and the [five] ladies of the house get awfully excited. Mick Mannock always dashes out and tries to calm them with "Restez-tranquil" or something of that sort . . . what they don't know about flying and the RFC isn't worth knowing. Mannock tells them they are spies which always rouses their wrath.'[37]

Despite these raids, the squadron settled into a rhythm of operations: three two-hour patrols of two flights each per day. Typically, A and B flights patrolled in the early morning, A and C at noon and B and C in the late afternoon. Occasionally, Caldwell would do a final full squadron 'show' in the evening.[38]

On 25 April, Kemmel Hill became the focal point for the enemy. It offered the Germans a significant vantage point and weakened the British hold on Ypres. Orders for 74 Squadron came from van Ryneveld.

> Machines will be employed in attacking detraining points, debussing centres, transports on roads, and troops being brought forward to press home the attack. It will be more important to do this a mile, or two miles behind the front line, than it would be to attack the enemy in the front line itself, because aeroplanes should be employed with a view to preventing the enemy pressing home the full weight of his attack by delaying the advance of his reinforcements, and not with a view to stopping the initial rush.[39]

Caldwell's men would combine with their Clairmarais North roommates, the Camels of 54 Squadron and the SE5s of 1 Squadron at Clairmarais South. The SE5s of 74 Squadron were newly fitted with bomb racks. Among the newbies in these strafing sorties was Richardson, who was replacing Begbie. Caldwell had ensured that the Canadian was given ample time with the SE5a, but nothing could prepare him for his first low-level sortie a few days later. As he explained to his mother, when he was 'over the lines on another fellow's machine on a bombing stunt . . . we got lost indirectly and got about 20 miles over the lines and on our way back I got my first taste of "Archie" anti-aircraft gun'.

> We were only 4,000 feet and Archie is very effective at so low a height. We immediately dropped our bombs and started split-arsing about for all we were worth, banks, dives, climbs and all sorts of stunts; that's the way we dodge Archie. Then we got machine gun bullets; tracers and field pieces have at us. Believe me I sure had [the] 'wind up' but we got through alright. Flying low, bombing and strafing is a rotten game . . . Well, I'm getting used to the game, but believe me, I sure didn't feel at home the first few times.[40]

The aerial operations were insufficient to stem the tide, and by noon the hill was surrounded and the British position at Ypres was on a knife edge.[41] Over the next three days, the weather prohibited further aerial operations but on 29 April the air battle was renewed with vigour and there was a changing of the guard at Clairmarais North.

Maxwell's 54 Squadron was withdrawn from frontline duties; the unit was bruised and fatigued, having sustained considerable losses since the beginning of the Spring

Offensive.[42] Caldwell was disappointed to see his friend go but found 54's replacement, 4 Squadron Australian Flying Corps (AFC), 'a very decent crowd'.[43] Australia was the only dominion to create its own independent flying force. The first of the AFC's four squadrons saw action in the Middle East, while the remainder flew over the Western Front. The Australians at Clairmarais were flying Camels under the command of a 'good straight chap, Wilfred McCloughry'.[44] The unit's slow start was remedied by a visit from Mannock and some handy instruction. As a result, the Australians became veritable 'Camel merchants', acquiring many scalps in the following months. Among their ranks was Arthur Cobby, a Prahran Victorian who, over less than a year of active service, would become Australia's greatest ace of the war.

On the day of their arrival, Caldwell invited 4 Squadron over for dinner and drinks. 'If they can fight as well as they can knock back cocktails,' wrote Ira Jones, 'the Hun is in for a fine time. Richardson, Toronto's cocktail wizard, mixes up what Grid has named the "74 Viper". By all accounts it's the goods. A couple are guaranteed to blow your head off. These Aussies make them appear to be made of milk and water.'[45]

In low-level bombing and aerial combat, A and C flights dropped 30 bombs and 74 Squadron's total air combat victories rose to 15.[46] After a two-seater was downed 2 miles on their side of the lines, Caldwell dispatched a crew to 'bring it back for souvenir purposes'. The squadron was slowly accumulating both trophies and a reputation with the enemy.[47]

In the last week of April the German attack on Flanders reached its height; the British lines held and the assault ground to a halt. But it had come at a high cost. Since 9 April, the British had suffered terrible losses: 330,000 casualties, including 80,000 prisoners of war caught in the German tide. The RFC had lost 1032 machines and 200 men had been killed.[48] The German fighter squadrons accounted for nearly half of these. That Caldwell had lost only a single airman was a minor miracle. As one of his officers noted, 'This is good arithmetic!'[49] It could not last.

The first sign that 8 May might turn nasty was when the dawn patrol came back without a machine: 19-year-old Englishman John Piggott was missing. As the early sun chased away the morning mists, the second offensive patrol prepared to take off. It was Cairnes' C Flight of Giles, Richardson, Andrew Kiddie, Ronald Bright and Philip Stuart-Smith. Engine problems on the ground, however, forced Cairnes, Giles and Richardson out of the sortie and Young stepped in to lead a reduced, four-strong formation. At 8.30 a.m., 40 miles east of Clairmarais, they encountered 10 triplanes over Zillebeke. It was to be a bloodbath. Young made the fatal mistake of attacking head on and from below. Richardson described what happened.

> Kiddie gets 3 Huns on his tail and after shaking them arrives at the drome with his bus looking like a sieve. Young gets his motor shot up and manages to land at Marie Capelle, our side of the lines. Stuart-Smith goes west; down in smoke and then flames. Bright follows him the same way . . . Skedden flies over the drome preparatory to landing, we are all watching when suddenly his wings let go and he dives into the drome and goes up in flames. We rush out with fire extinguishers, but they are not worth a damn. Such a terrible sight. We pick up his remains in a bushel basket . . . He was . . . a damn swell boy.[50]

It was a grim morning. As Mannock loudly berated Young for attacking from below, the latter replied that he had been a captain in 'the British Army and wasn't going to run away from any Huns'. As Richardson noted, 'no one would accuse Young of not having guts, just bad judgment'. It was a costly and powerful lesson. Caldwell asked his men to 'liven up . . . [their] comrades who were gone would not wish for them to mope, but go and knock hell out of the sods, the Hunnerinoes'.[51]

Ira Jones took Caldwell's injunction to heart, and after packing up his roommate Skedden's effects, took off for a late-afternoon sortie. He found his consolation, a lone German two-seater.

> I got up to point-blank range before firing. Then I let him have it. Almost at once he commenced smoking. There was a faint glow. Then a lovely bonfire as he went earthwards. I followed him down to the ground firing all my bullets at him. I then flew round him as he burned fiercely on the ground near Nieppe. I knew the enemy in the vicinity were firing hard at me. I didn't care. My soul was satisfied. It was a grand sight to see that Hun burning. I had had my revenge. Flying over our trenches, I could see our troops waving frantically. I waved back joyfully. They were not half as happy as I. I had destroyed my first Hun, in revenge for my pals, and it was a great feeling.[52]

After the Welshman landed, he passed the tender in which Skedden's body lay. 'I peeped in. All I could see was an old army blanket, but it was enough for me.' In accordance with Caldwell's orders, the squadron had a big evening, with some of the Australians as guests. Caldwell offered a toast to the 'four empty chairs and to their future'. He told his mother only that there had been 'quite a lot of war lately . . . we had a rather long day'.[53]

Piggott, though, was alive. He had become lost in the morning mist and crash-landed close to the enemy trenches. German artillery ranged in on the wounded SE5a, but Piggott set fire to the machine and crawled to safety. His nerves shattered, the young man was sent back to England on Home Establishment in early July.[54]

The casualties continued. On 12 May, orders came through for a squadron-strength evening patrol. With Caldwell away, Mannock led the sortie. After spotting a 10-strong intruder formation north of Armentières, he wheeled the squadron south and east and gained height for an interception. With a good 1000-foot height advantage, they struck. Mannock 'closed on the rearmost machine, firing at right angles to it. The German panicked and ploughed into a neighbouring aeroplane. Mannock then pounced on a Pfalz, loosing bullets from both his Lewis and Vickers in turn.'[55]

Mannock's three victories were supplemented by a host of claims from Young, Giles and the old man of the squadron, Roxburgh-Smith. It was his fourth victory. It was one of the squadron's most successful days, but it did not feel like it. Caldwell returned to find that 22-year-old Bilo Dolan was missing and Mannock grief-stricken.[56] The two men were close. Before departing for France, Mannock had flown on at least two occasions with Dolan to his hometown of Wellingborough, where the pair had entranced the locals with aerobatics.[57]

Over the Western Front, Mannock had nurtured his young charge in the ways of aggressive fighter pilots, with startling results. 'Dolan is developing into a corker,' recorded one airman. 'He has no fear. He goes, like Grid, bald-headed for every Hun he sees. If he doesn't meet with any bad luck, he will soon be one of our aces.'[58] By the second week of May, Dolan had six victories to his credit. The sudden death of his friend momentarily undid Mannock and he retired to his hut. His sobbing could be heard by those close by. When Caldwell called the men together for the obligatory post-loss festivities, Mannock managed to join in.[59]

Ira Jones's new roommate, 'Twist' Giles, formally of the Somerset Light Infantry, acknowledged the harsh reality of the situation.

> We had a job to do and we did it. We had no time to think about the human consequences, about the fact that it was another man probably with a wife and family back home in Germany that you were pursuing. The moment you held back on compassionate grounds it was odds-on that you were the one that

would be spinning to your death. There was really no room for the chivalry of the air concept that is talked so much about, except on occasions when we were on our side of the lines and there was no chance of the enemy escaping. Kill or be killed is a stark and clinical statement of truth when applied to the Western Front in 1918.

He acknowledged that the pilot's attitude could smack 'of callousness, of revelling in the horror of war when you consider the pranks we used to get up to, the way we collected "trophies" and so on. But if you didn't look after your own skin and if you didn't treat the whole affair in a decidedly eccentric way then you were heading for trouble.'[60]

Mannock's obsession with shooting down Germans continued unabated. Nearly two weeks before Dolan's death, as Caldwell recalled, he and Mannock had been flying together on the British side of the lines just outside Ypres.

> They spotted a Hun two-seater beetling back towards the lines, and got down just in time to prevent this. The Hun crashed, but not badly, and most people would have been content with this — but not Mick Mannock, who dived half a dozen times at the machine, spraying bullets at the pilot and the observer, who were still showing signs of life. I witnessed this business, and flew alongside of Mick, yelling at the top of my voice (which was rather useless), and warning him to stop. On being questioned as to his wild behaviour after we had landed, he heatedly replied, 'The swines are better dead — no prisoners for me!'[61]

'The loss of Dolan is a severe blow to us,' wrote Jones.

> He was a very full-out guy, and very popular. . . He was a bosom pal of Grid and Mick, so I expect to see some Hun feathers flying about to-morrow, if they can find any. This fight was the most successful the Squadron has had so far. Mick bagged three; Young, Giles and Roxburgh[-Smith] one each. This is Giles's first victory. He is very bucked about it. When we were getting ready for the patrol, he told me that he was feeling a little bloodthirsty and wanted to avenge Skedden. There is no doubt that the spirit of revenge should be cultivated

The loss of the likable Henry Dolan hit 74 Squadron hard. 'Got 7 Huns in 3 Weeks' Keith Caldwell wrote next to this image of Dolan in his photo album.

during a war. It helps the fighter to put a little more ginger into his fighting. 'Kill or be killed' is a good motto. I hate half-measures . . .'[62]

Losses meant the need for replacements. Eighteen-year-old Leigh Nixon, who joined the squadron on 1 May, was desperate to acquit himself in the air.[63] Caldwell set the Englishman daily non-operational flights so that he could familiarise himself with his machine and with the surrounding countryside. On the ground, Nixon observed and learnt from men returning from patrols. It was 74 Squadron's standard 'working up' procedure. In the mess, the men continually emphasised the lessons absorbed from Caldwell and Mannock and their own daily dances with death, particularly that, though it might feel natural, a pilot should never dive away from an enemy machine when under attack. The trick was to immediately set the SE5a into a steep turn and jockey for a better position — or, in Nixon's case, wait for help to arrive.

On 17 May, William Cairnes slotted Nixon into an 8.30 a.m. patrol and volunteered Jones as chaperon. The latter reiterated to Nixon the lessons of the past fortnight, but 'promised to try to get the Hun away from him'.[64] Forty-five minutes later, they encountered enemy fighters. Jones picked out an isolated light-green machine, a perfect introduction for Nixon. Jones attacked and expected to find his wingman following, but he was nowhere to be seen. He had become separated from Jones who, to his horror, watched Nixon diving away from a German who was pumping lead into him. The SE5a caught fire and became a swirling torch.

Nixon's first and last action was detailed in the magazine of the St Paul's Cathedral choir, in which he had sung as a boy: 'He was one of a patrol of eight and fell in with an enemy patrol of 10. He singled out his particular enemy, and followed him down far out of the fight, and was just going to finish him off, when two other Hun machines dropped on his tail, and he was seen to fall to the ground in flames.' Caldwell wrote to Nixon's family: 'Although he was with us such a very short time, I never saw a keener or more ambitious officer, and the whole squadron deeply regret his loss.'[65]

It was the first of two such letters Caldwell wrote that day. Nineteen-year-old Lambert Francis Barton was killed when his machine was struck by anti-aircraft fire at 7000 feet.[66] The freakish direct hit undid the machine, and both the flaming wreckage and Barton tumbled from the sky. He and Nixon had arrived with 74 Squadron on the same day and both were killed on 17 May.[67]

That evening, Canadian Sydney Russell, a former army officer who had also recently

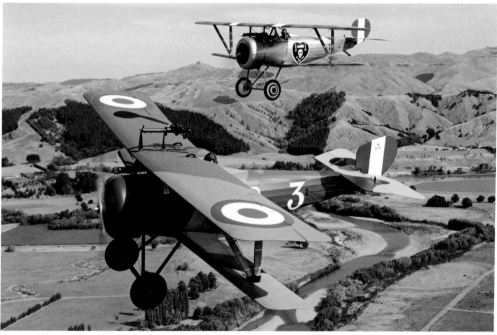

Above: **Pilots Tim Sullivan and Andrew Vincent fly an Albatros DVa and a Royal Aircraft Factory SE5a over the Wairarapa plains. All machines are from The Vintage Aviator Limited (TVAL) collection.**

Below: **The Nieuport 24 was a direct descendant of the Nieuport 17 that Keith Caldwell flew with 60 Squadron. These two examples are flown by Tim Sullivan (nearest) and John Lanham.**

Keith Caldwell's 74 'Tiger' Squadron was equipped with the legendary Royal Aircraft Factory SE5a. Framed by clouds above and a patchwork of fields below, Keith Skilling flies this TVAL example.

Above: **Scott McKenzie** flying a Fokker DrI triplane In the colour scheme of Werner Steinhäuser of Jasta 11 in 1918.

Below: The Fokker DVII was the premier mass-produced German fighter of the war. This example is flown by Jerry Chisum.

joined the unit, was hospitalised after he was badly injured when he crash-landed.[68]

These were not Caldwell's only losses. Hidden among the turnover of pilots were others who never even made it into operations. When they saw limping shrapnel- and bullet-riddled machines returning from battle, and the all too common near-death accidents, some novice airmen succumbed to the cold embrace of fear and refused to fly. At 74 Squadron, Mannock's tactic of regaling newcomers with stories of burning machines and fiery deaths did not help. The men who daily suppressed their fears in the face of imminent death were often disdainful of the timorous.

'Sometime today,' wrote Jones, 'one of the new members, who has been with the squadron only three days, turned yellow. He has been sent back to England. Why he wasn't sent to the trenches or shot I don't know. He went sobbing to Grid that he couldn't do the job. That he had nerves. And he has not even been over the lines! He'll now become an instructor or a staff officer and get promoted, I suppose.'[69]

Mannock had the man's wings ripped off. 'Many couldn't cope with the situation,' recalled Giles. 'You could understand the reasons why, but somehow we were scornful of their mental state. There was no place for the pilot who couldn't do what he had to do, because you would never be able to trust him.' Every month, a handful of men appeared on the list of fresh arrivals to the squadron who only days later were struck off its inventory, having seen little or no action at all.[70] To Caldwell's mind, it was a harsh necessity that served to lengthen the lives of those who remained *and* those who departed.

CHAPTER FIFTEEN

Bravest of
the Brave

As the squadron's losses mounted, the late spring of 1918 brought warmer weather. 'The countryside is getting to be beautiful,' wrote Richardson, 'fruit trees in bloom, trees all have leaves and crops are progressing. I don't believe I ever noticed the beauties of nature as I do now. It's just as pretty as home.'[1] But despite the improving weather and a pause in the German ground offensive, the air war continued apace. On 19 May, Caldwell was instructed to attack balloons spying on the British positions. With too many volunteers for the two available slots, he drew lots, and Jones and the South African Andrew 'Dixie' Kiddie were the 'lucky' winners. A Kimberley baker and confectioner before the war, Kiddie, at 27, was one of the 'old men' of the squadron. He was enjoying the better weather; before being shipped out to France, he had sought a posting to somewhere warmer, such as Egypt. As a medical examiner had noted, 'He . . . cannot stand the cold and damp of this climate which will probably bring on a return of malaria and melaena. Otherwise there is no organic trouble and he appears to be quite healthy.'[2]

Fortunately for Caldwell, but unfortunately for the Germans, Kiddie's request was denied and his baptism in balloon busting was the beginning of a very successful period in aerial combat for an officer whom many of the squadron considered rather 'staid and unruffled'.[3] Neither Jones nor Kiddie were under any misapprehension about the difficulties involved in attacking balloons; 'it's a hell of a game,' Jones wrote.

> The balloons are usually two or three miles back and as we have to go in low — today I was down to 2,000 feet — there is little hope of getting back safely if the engine gets hit or goes phut. The chance of being wounded or killed is great. Hell is usually let loose as we go zigzagging — terrified — back to our lines. Every Fritz, even staff officers, I believe, has a go at us with some missile or other. The relief one feels on reaching our lines is worth it, though. You feel you've achieved something. You've shown the Huns that you don't give a damn for them.[4]

Caldwell oversaw the allocation of Buckingham incendiary rounds, a special and dangerous ammunition, which were loaded into Kiddie and Jones's wing-mounted Lewis guns. These phosphorus bullets could be deployed against Zeppelins and observational balloons, but the 1868 St Petersburg Declaration forbade their use against enemy personnel in air-to-air combat. When using the rounds, pilots were generally required to carry written orders, but such niceties were often forgotten or ignored in the heat of battle.

When the flight spotted balloons near Armentières, Jones peeled away first and feigned being fatally hit by a nearby bursting anti-aircraft shell. The SE5a tumbled down, seemingly out of control, only for Jones to pull out a mere half-mile from the target. The Lewis gun was barking before the Germans awoke to the ruse. From 400 to only 40 yards, he closed on the inflated 'sausage', firing all the way, spirals of blue smoke trailing the spinning bullets.[5] The balloonists abandoned ship, parachuting down as Jones swung away. He lined up the Germans floating down under their canopies of silk.

Then the ground fire locked onto the Welshman. 'A flaming-battery got going from the ground, and I was soon in a maze of hate. The balloon was going down in flames and a huge volume of smoke rose to signify the importance of the occasion,' he wrote later. He 'hit the carpet', dancing left and right just above the dirt of no man's land for the British lines.[6] Five minutes later, Kiddie closed to within 30 yards, hitting his balloon by firing along its length. He estimated that at least 50 incendiaries found their mark.[7] The South African's assault was followed by a cacophony of ground fire, anti-aircraft and small arms, that chased him from the carnage. 'Smothered in corruption', he pointed the SE5a west and raced helter-skelter to the lines. Both balloons collapsed in an inferno of fire and black smoke, and Taffy Jones and Dixie Kiddie rejoined their flight overhead. Back at Clairmarais, the pair were the 'belles of the ball' and van Ryneveld's congratulations only inflated their delight. Jones promptly asked Grid for another go the next morning, but Caldwell was having none of it. Orders to attack balloons were one thing but freelance balloon busting by a pilot intoxicated with his most recent success was another. 'Perhaps it was just as well,' admitted Jones.[8]

That night, however, the Germans attacked the aerodrome, in one of an increasing number of nocturnal raids on St Omer's adjacent military camps and airfields. The evening before, German bombers had struck the large ammunition dump at Arques. On this night, however, not only was Armentières set alight by German bombers, but a bomb also fell on 74 Squadron's home. 'The Huns bombed with great vigour the night before last and started a few fires nearby,' Caldwell told his mother.[9]

He took precautionary action, emptying the hangars and dispersing the SE5s around the aerodrome, hidden in hedges. Men gathered their camp kit and were transported up the road to Lederzeele for the night. Such arrangements became all too common as the Germans attempted to disrupt RAF operations. Richardson knocked out a poem capturing the events of the past two days.

> The nights were bright and sultry,
> When the Hun came from the east,
> So we made our way to Lettezele [sic],
> Where we could sleep in peace.
> The big twin-engined Gothas,
> Were out to nightly roam,
> And when they dropped their pellets,
> They did not spare our drome.
>
> The night they first came over,
> A starry night in May,
> We had not yet retired
> To end a perfect day.
> With the 'Ack' shells whining,
> We heard the bombing thuds,
> And scattered to the ditches
> To dodge the 'Archie' duds.

There must have been a dozen,
From the searchlight on the planes,
Who dropped their pellets on the dump,
When Arque[s] went up in flames.
Of course we all felt happy,
Felt quite at ease — no doubt,
But yet, the following evening
We started sleeping out.

At Lettezele, beneath the trees,
There with our camp kit beds,
We slept in solid comfort,
While the Hun passed overhead
Then back by day to do our show,
We hope we did it well,
Yet early every morning,
We wished the Huns in Hell.[10]

Even so, the squadron continued to remove a significant number of Germans from the sky. The last 10 days of May boosted the tallies of many of Caldwell's crew. Kiddie, Cairnes and Young became aces and men like Wilfred Giles, Harris Clements, Reginald Birch and Percy Howe picked up one or two credits. Thirty-three-year-old Roxburgh-Smith — nicknamed Dad — was also elevated to an ace, a remarkable achievement in the eyes of many, given he was husband to Daisy, back home in Bromley, Kent, and father to three-year-old David and an infant daughter, Joy. Ira Jones later wrote:

Roxburgh got a two-seater in flames over Dickebusch Lake this morning . . . Old 'Dad' is proving himself a rare old sticker. Often, married men show a tendency to support the motto, 'Safety First.' But not 'Dad.' That the strain of combat affects his nerves is obvious from a cursory study of his actions and speech after landing. Although he laughs and is apparently full of the elation of the fight, it is obvious that inwardly he is suffering acutely from reaction. A married man with a family who fights without flinching, although afraid, is to me the bravest of the brave. 'Dad' is such a one.[11]

This was high praise from Jones, who was well on the way to becoming one of the war's leading pilots. The Welshman accumulated an astonishing 15 victories in May, only five shy of Mannock. As for Mannock, he was approaching the apogee of his career; on one noteworthy day, he destroyed four machines.[12] He rushed into the mess, shouting: "'All tickets, please! Please pass right down the car. Flamerinoes — four! Sizzle-sizzle wonk!'" He then turned on a youngster, who had been flying alongside him. 'Come on — toast this warrior. The bloodthirsty young devil shot down a Hun.'[13]

When a German pilot was captured, he enquired whether 'McCudden was with us', wrote Caldwell. 'I expect they must have got to know something about Mick M. by now and think he's McCudden.'[14] McCudden, however, was in England awaiting his return to frontline duties, while Mannock was accumulating victories and accolades.

Many promising fighter pilots' rate of victories fell when they were elevated to squadron command and were overrun with routine administrative work, but not Caldwell. He still flew almost daily, often leading the patrols. As Jones noted, 'I feel I must hand the palm to Grid for individual valour. It is prodigious, and impossible adequately to describe. All our squadron patrols which he leads are nightmares. He frightens us as much as we frighten the Huns . . . "The sods, the Hunnerinoes — crack them at all costs!" is his motto.' But though attracted by 'Grid's spirit', Jones could not 'help feeling that Mick is working on the right lines'.

> After all, we are here to kill without being killed, if we want to win the war. Yet the spirit of adventure which is inherent in me demands the thrill of a fight when and where the opportunity presents itself. 'To hell with tactics,' it thunders. Then the faint spirit of caution whispers: 'Don't be a fool. Go steady. A dead man is no good to his country.' I'm very puzzled and a little worried over this matter. I cannot make up my mind which path to take — Grid's or Mick's. Perhaps a little stroll each way will be my best policy for the moment. We'll see . . .[15]

One thing was certain: Caldwell was knocking out more than his share of enemy machines and was on track to becoming one of the war's highest-scoring commanders.

On 21 May, he was leading one of his traditional late-evening patrols when, below

Keith Caldwell's old schoolmate Trevor Bloomfield was a graduate of the New Zealand Flying School and in April 1918 joined 43 Squadron, flying Sopwith Camels.

him, he saw German fighters from Jasta 7 harassing Allied observation balloons west of Ypres.[16] He fell upon these, only to find himself under assault from an all-black Pfalz DIII at 4000 feet. Superficially, the rotund Pfalz resembled the recent Albatros models but by mid-1918 it was generally considered their inferior. Caldwell endured a handful of angry flurries before gaining the ascendancy in height and position, at which point the German exploited one of the Pfalz's acknowledged strengths, its ability in a dive away. The SE5a, however, would not be outpaced and Caldwell caught the Pfalz over Ypres, whereupon the black aeroplane dropped again in a dash east.

Barely 50 feet above the Allied trenches, the Viper engine at full throttle and the Vickers and Lewis machine guns running hot, Caldwell ran down the German aeroplane. 'I followed behind him . . . and finally after firing 250 rounds at him he dived into the ground and caught fire.'[17]

Caldwell celebrated his victory and the unit's considerable success that day alone: thanks to the fear of German bombers, he was the sole officer on the aerodrome. When the men returned in the morning, 'Grid . . . pulled all our legs unmercifully. He alleged that he had never had a more solid and delightful sleep.'[18] As Caldwell wrote to London, 'The weather is still simply gorgeous and this morning when I was up at 17,000 ft, I could see England quite easily. Some of us are going to fly down the coast for a swim as soon as we can get away, it is priceless weather for bathing.'[19]

Caldwell also hosted numerous airmen from his recent past, including Wanganui Collegiate old boys and pilots from 60 Squadron. 'Trevor Bloomfield perched here yesterday on a Camel and stayed to lunch; he is still going strong but has not had a chance to wage cunning warfare yet.' William Fry was now a flight commander with a unit specialising in low-level ground-attack operations. 'He is out with 79 Sqd on [Sopwith] Dolphins, but says that they have only got one Hun in 2½ months. He wants to get to another squadron,' he told his mother in a letter on 22 May.[20]

Seven days later, Caldwell and Mannock were leading a couple of flights when the New Zealander located the enemy. He wiggled his wings and pointed down — four Pfalz fighters, decked out with silver and black wings and red tails and cowlings. Caldwell signalled his men to follow as he pushed the stick forward. He fell upon the rearmost machine, only for it to evade his embrace, but fought the next target down from 9000 to 6000 feet. At close range, he fired the Vickers and Lewis guns and the Pfalz flipped on its back, then spun out of control and fell.[21] In the fighting, Giles was cornered. While concentrating on the destruction of another machine, he had 'carelessly allowed a black Albatros to pounce on him'.

Caldwell intervened: as Jones put it, 'The C.O. saved Giles's skin tonight.'[22] Caldwell and Mannock's teams were then set upon by a 'phalanx of Huns . . . from nowhere'. They fought their way back again, getting clear thanks to the sheer speed of the SE5. 'The wires were screeching with fear, the engines roaring with bursting energy,' wrote Jones. 'The pilots' nerves were taut. The speedometers registered nearly 200 miles per hour. Oh boys! What a game!' That night, a laidback Caldwell scrawled in his logbook: 'Chased home by 15 Pfalz.'[23]

Caldwell closed out the month with another credit to his name. On 31 May he was flying what he dubbed a 'special mission' — a speculative sortie spoiling for a fight with the Germans. Even at high altitudes the weather was warm, and Caldwell and his men had abandoned their Sidcot suits. Caldwell met up with Mannock and at 7.50 p.m., a mile west of Ploegsteert Wood and at 11,000 feet, they attacked nine Pfalz and Albatros fighters.

Caldwell pushed home his attack on the Pfalz to the brink of his own destruction, firing 120 rounds as he homed in, 'until practically touching'.[24] He barely avoided ploughing his SE5a into the enemy machine, which went down vertically and hit the ground.

'In the eve, the Major, Mick and Taffy each get a Hun,' wrote Richardson that night, 'They sure are Hun-getters.'[25] May proved to be Caldwell's best month of war so far; his four victories pushed the squadron's total for the month to an impressive 66, one of the best monthly bags of any squadron in the entire war. As Jones wrote in his diary, in recognition of their successes and fighting spirit, 'We've been nicknamed the Tiger Squadron!'[26]

On 26 May, many of Caldwell's men gathered for their first organised church service in France. For the squadron, as for thousands of others in the Allied forces, Christianity provided comfort and spiritual guidance. When Mick Mannock first met Ira Jones at London Colney, he had asked the Welshman about the medals he had won before joining 74 Squadron.

'What did you get those for?'

'I'm told for so-called bravery,' Jones said. 'It's stamped on the Military Medal.'

'Good answer. But what makes you fight so hard?'

Overleaf: **The front nacelle of a Royal Aircraft Factory FE2b light bomber serves as a pulpit for a chaplain on the Western Front.**

'I fight for my King and country, of course. I'm religious too, so I personally fight for Christian principles.'

'By Christian principles, do you mean you're fighting for freedom?'

'Yes, I believe in liberty of thought, free speech and kindness to those who need it.'

'Well done, Taffy. I also fight for liberty, particularly the liberty of the Emerald Isle. The world must never be held in bondage by the Kaiser and all he stands for. And I would readily die for such a cause.'[27]

The interminable sorties, the proximity to death and the outlandish carousing meant some, like Leonard Richardson, who was Catholic, wrestled with their religious convictions.

... it isn't easy for a fellow to stick to religious principles here because we don't have church and all the other religious environment to help us and after a day of nerve wracking over the lines one seeks light amusement for relaxation and of course I join in. Here a fellow has nothing but his own thoughts to help him and I often wonder if I am right or wrong, but I pray for strength. When I know what is expected of me, as a Christian, I can't help but think I fall down on the job, because as you know, up to a certain point I am full of fun, life and devilry.[28]

Many in the squadron were spiritually refreshed by the makeshift church service, which transcended denominational and class divides. 'Our Padre is fine and the service was held in a hangar on benches, boxes,' Richardson told his mother.

We had a piano to sing to and although we didn't have the pomp, splendour, etc. of a real church, it was one of the best services I ever attended. The Padre, (who has been wounded), knew just what he was praying for when he prayed for the soldiers and the wounded. He preached for a little in John 3. Oh! It was good to attend a church service though it was C[hurch] of E[ngland]. All of these men who went didn't know if they would see another service or not. Let me tell you, when you don't get a chance to 'dress up' and go to church every Sunday and then go and have a service in any old building, some men all greasy, muddy, dressed any old how, you realize just what religion means to some people. I never knew before. Out here we don't know creeds or anything else. It's just having God to fall back on and to know whether we win our scrap or go under that it's just what He wanted. We can't remember that all the time; it seems there are times when we forget it. But we always know.[29]

For those who had faith, death represented a transition from this life to the next. Those in the squadron who lost their lives were solemnly farewelled and given a Christian burial, as Richardson described in the poem he wrote in memory of Charles Skedden:

The Padre man and his comrades.
In their service Khaki dressed,
Offered a prayer, their last respect,
Then lay him to rest.
Wrapped in the flag he served,
He waits that short reprieve,
Side by side with a hundred more,
He sleeps, and yet we grieve.[30]

On a less serious note, the men enjoyed a newly installed and greatly appreciated swimming pool, sporting events and occasional larrikinism. The pranking of new airmen was a long-standing initiation rite. After a particularly rowdy night out, Caldwell and Mannock would creep into the hut of a sleeping comrade.

Caldwell would be carrying a jug of water; once inside Mick would pretend that he had dined and wined too well (in fact, he was a very moderate drinker), and would make gurgling noises as if he were going to be sick; as each 'retching' noise was made, Caldwell would splash an appropriate amount of water on the wooden floor. The poor lad asleep would suddenly wake up and jump out of bed to the accompaniment of roars of laughter, as his legs would be splashed with the remaining water.[31]

On days when patrols weren't possible, Caldwell and Mannock organised 'bombing raids' on friendly aerodromes; most famously, 1 Squadron at Clairmarais South. On one occasion Caldwell ordered the mechanics to get the grids out and load them with over 200 oranges. The raid was a stunning success. When the 'enemy' heard the roar of Viper-powered machines overhead, they looked up to see a shower of brightly coloured fruit descending, banging on the tin huts and the roof of the mess. One unfortunate pilot was struck and 'momentarily stunned'.

The upstart 'squadron of the moment' had successfully raided a venerable unit whose heritage went back to 1878 as 1 Balloon Company. It was a slight that could not be ignored, and within the hour overripe banana missiles fell on 74's aerodrome. As Jones recalled, 'Declaration of peace between the two squadrons resulted in a memorable evening at the popular "George Robey" café in St. Omer. What days! What memories!'[32]

Further celebrations were in order when Jones and Mannock received more awards. For his recent spate of victories, the former was awarded an MC, a fitting companion to his Military Medal for rescuing two wounded gunners under artillery fire on the Somme in 1916. Mannock was awarded a DSO and bar. Ranked just below a VC, the DSO was given for meritorious or distinguished service in combat; a second in the space of a month was almost unheard of. The achievement warranted a surprise visit to the squadron by the immensely popular Second Army commander, General Sir Herbert Plumer. As Jones wrote,

> It must have been a surprise to him, too. He is a funny little man to look at, but very nice to speak to. He is about 5 feet 8 inches tall, inclined to be rotund, has a podgy, red face, white hair and moustache, a twinkle in his eye, wears a monocle, and stands like the grand soldier he is — very stiff and erect. Though he flattered us on our fighting efforts, I have a suspicion that he did not approve of either the cleanliness or the mode of our dress. Mick, in particular, 'shone' in this direction. With no hat or collar, no Sam Browne, long hair, and muffled, he looked a typical bushranger.
>
> When we all rolled up (there is no other word), Plumer said to Grid: 'Which is Mannock?' Our D'Artagnan was duly pointed out to him. I really thought Plumer was going to pass right out. However, with a masterly effort he pulled himself together and staggered up to Mick with arm outstretched. Mick's dirty paw clutched his gloved hand and squeezed it in his usual hearty manner. Plumer's face twitched; for a second, I thought he was going to give a yell.

Plumer congratulated Mannock, but his face 'wore a puzzled look . . . I have an idea he went away wondering what sort of fellow this Mannock could be. I don't blame him.'[33]

Airmen from several squadrons descended on the mess that evening. Richardson worked overtime, 'concocting the "vipers"'.[34] Even Jones 'had a sip to see what it tasted like — it burned my throat and stopped my breathing. That was only the result of a sip. What a mouthful must be like, God only knows.'[35]

Ludendorff's Spring Offensive entered its third phase on 27 May: a massive surprise attack codenamed Blücher-Yorck. The focal point was the French front at Aisne, intended to draw French defenders from the British sector, leaving the latter vulnerable for the final push. A lengthy bombardment, supplemented by poisonous gas, was followed by 17 German divisions of Sturmtruppen advancing between Soissons and Reims.

It was a stunning success: the German soldiers took Aisne within six hours and pushed the Allies back to the Vesle river. Within three days, 50,000 Allied soldiers had been captured. On 3 June, the Germans lunged for the French capital, only 35 miles away, as the Allies threw in divisions to plug the gap. Over the following three days, heavy German casualties and lack of reserves combined with Allied counter-operations, including the arrival of the first American troops, stalled the advance.

To the north, in 74 Squadron's sector of the front, the first two weeks of June were marked by successes and losses as the weather swung between bursts of sunshine and bouts of rain. On the morning of 1 June, Wilfred Young claimed a brace and Ira Jones a single, and in the afternoon, Mick Mannock dispatched a trio. But affable flight commander William Cairnes was lost.[36] He was leading C Flight on an offensive patrol north-east of Estaires when he had the misfortune of tangling with Lieutenant Paul Billik of Jasta 52. A leading Luftstreitkräfte pilot, and future winner of a Knight's Cross with Swords, the Silesian was a master at extracting the best from the aging Pfalz. Jones witnessed Billik's clinical attack on Cairnes:

> A determined Pfalz got to within 25 yards of him and gave him the gun. His right wing was suddenly seen to break up, the nose of his SE dipped viciously, then downwards spun at a terrific rate. I watched him for a short while, sickness overcoming me. It is a terrible thing to see a pal going to his death. Then I saw red, and went for everything in sight, but my aim was bad. I got nothing in revenge . . . Cairn[e]s was a great gentleman, and we are all very cut up . . . [37]

Engine problems had stymied Leonard Richardson's involvement in the sortie, but he was devastated. 'My Flight Commander goes west. I'm glad I wasn't on that show. I like him so much I wouldn't care to see him get it. He was a peach of a man. Hell,' he wrote in his logbook.[38]

That day, Caldwell led a late-afternoon special mission 2 miles east of Dickebusch. With men in tow, he dived from 14,000 feet like a bird on a storm. Firing from 100 yards, he singled out one of four silver-coloured Pfalz fighters for special attention. Alerted, the enemy pilot swung away in a left-hand climbing turn but Caldwell cut him off; bullets punctured the Pfalz and the German machine entered a fatal spin.[39]

That evening the men gathered in the mess to toast Cairnes' memory and their successes in battle, including Caldwell's last-minute retaliatory victory. Caldwell 'didn't give a hoot about tactics,' wrote Jones, 'so long as the Germans were in the air "Grid" was happy.' Many of his colleagues and friends considered him the RAF's 'Marshal Ney', in other words 'le Brave des Braves'. (Ney gained this appellation from Napoleon for his remarkable rear-guard command during the retreat from Moscow in the ill-fated 1812 invasion of Russia.) But, as newcomers soon realised, Caldwell's approach could be nightmarish; sometimes his squadron's new pilots were as 'frightened as the enemy'. With the slowing of the German effort and several days in which adverse weather hindered operations, Caldwell, as Jones remembered, felt the need to seek out the enemy in his own backyard.

On one particular patrol in June, 19 machines had set off, but no enemy fighters were to be seen. 'All could visualise Grid cursing in his cockpit.' But then he 'showed his contempt for the enemy' by leading the patrol to Roulers and circling the German aerodrome at only 8000 feet — 'a direct challenge for them to come up and settle the business'. And, indeed, 'Dozens of planes with Black crosses shot up into the blue [but] in the air they showed no desire to fight. The nearest they got to us was 400 yards.'

After this 'rather Gilbertian nonsense' had gone on for about half an hour, the men of 74 returned home. Although Caldwell 'laughed uproariously' after landing, he was soon 'cursing the Germans, in the best colonial fashion, because, although superior in numbers, they refused to fight'.[40]

On 19 June, Caldwell was again looking for a reluctant enemy when, over Hazebrouck, he signalled with his wings and dropped the SE5's nose, diving 'like hell towards the ruined town'.[41] His men followed, and saw black puffs of Archie. Two German machines were attacking a British observer balloon, circling it as it went down in a pall of smoke. Then one of the Pfalz pilots went for another balloon. 'Cheeky devil,' Jones said to himself. 'You're asking for trouble, my lad.'

And he got it. It was really a sad sight, for as far as I could see he was spotted by all the pilots in the area simultaneously . . . His pal saw our approach. He wisely scampered homewards as fast as he could go. But 'Little Willie' was blind, either optically or alcoholically. He made no effort to leave for home until he heard Grid's guns barking behind him and his bullets tickling . . . It was then too late.[42]

Watching the drama unfold on the ground was a New Zealander with the Australian Engineers, Cyril Lawrence. 'Gee you should have seen that Hun jump. He tried every trick that he knew but our boy hung on . . . In less time than it takes to tell they were diving from everywhere. Just marvellous, every square foot of the sky delivered up a plane.'[43] When a unit of Camels joined in, Lawrence counted no fewer than 37 machines swirling and diving on the hapless German, who was turning and firing wildly.

The greatest danger for Caldwell and his men was being hit by, or colliding with, a friendly machine. Bullets from SE5s and Camels 'whistled at hair's-breath distances past our ears. It was screamingly funny, yet terrifying,' said Jones, who decided it was 'too damn dangerous' when 'a couple of Camels zoomed up within a few feet of my port and starboard wings simultaneously, and an SE, in its haste flashed downwards past the top of my propeller'. He climbed away to safety.

It was great to watch those SE5s and Camels zooming, diving, turning steeply and quickly, spitting fire at every possible opportunity at the erratic little flying wasp in the centre of the fray, who obviously had not a hope in Hell. It was only a question of time, I knew. Really, I felt sorry for this Hun as I watched his vain but heroic efforts to get back to his own lines and his agonising movements when he found every avenue of escape blocked.[44]

After a torrent of bullets from Harry Cobby, the Pfalz spun down into Nieppe Forest, where it became lodged in a tree.[45] Some then used the suspended machine, its pilot still inside, as target practice — diving, firing and pulling away. Later that day souvenirs were collected from the Pfalz, and the 'shot about' body of Unteroffizier Max Mertens of Jasta 7 was laid out in one of the Clairmarais hangars for the night.[46]

Like the other airmen, Cobby was struck by his unusual attire. Mertens was 'dressed in a swallow-tailed Beaufort coat, very much worn, breeches in a very bad state of repair and very dirty, and was without collar or tie. He had not shaved for some days and looked as though he had come off a "bender".'[47] Jones thought the German must have been 'blotto', which was not an unreasonable assessment given Jasta 7's well-known proclivity for wild fancy dress parties.[48]

Arthur Cobby, who flew Sopwith Camels with 4 Squadron, Australian Flying Corps, became one of his country's finest pilots. The Australian squadron shared an airfield at Clairmarais North with 74 Squadron, and in combined operations its Camels were a perfect complement to Caldwell's SE5s.

CHAPTER SIXTEEN

Immolation

The RAF aerodromes in northern France were military islands surrounded by productive French farmland. In addition to dairy, pork and poultry, northern France was blessed with vast rolling expanses of green and gold barley and wheat — vital fodder for the French effort. By mid-June 1918, crops were almost ready for harvest and Caldwell was instructed to remind the air and ground crew of the 'difficulties' faced by the older French men and the women and children cultivating land in the shadow of war. His men were forbidden to ride or drive horses or vehicles through crops or sown fields, or to play games on adjacent land. Horses were not free to go anywhere 'unless arrangements have been made with the farmer to whom the fields belong'.[1]

Much of this was successfully navigated, but mistakes were sometimes made. 'The other day while firing at a pond which we use for practice ... two perfectly good cows standing near were wounded and the excitement raised by the French was intense,' lamented Caldwell.[2]

While driving to St Omer for rest and recreation and taking lorries to No. 1 Aircraft Depot RAF for equipment and supplies, Caldwell's men would come upon the bedraggled human flotsam and jetsam of the advancing Spring Offensive. In a fit of compassion, headquarters had previously granted officers in charge of convoys discretion to pick up refugees, but due to the slowing of the German effort and the difficulties created by such largesse, this was now rescinded. Civilians were no longer 'allowed to enter or travel on any War Department vehicle unless in possession of a written permit, signed by a Commanding or Staff Officer, which will be issued only in very exceptional causes'.[3]

On 19 June, Hesperus van Ryneveld arrived to personally give Caldwell news he had been dreading: Mick Mannock had been promoted and when he returned from leave it would be to command 85 Squadron.[4] Mannock was more than the squadron's highest-scoring airman; he was also Caldwell's confidant, his most able supporter. Mannock was not just a tactical genius, but a commander whose pastoral care had produced several successful airmen and prevented the early death of many more. Giving men guidance in aerial combat tactics before flights, helping pilots to achieve their first victories on sorties and offering debriefings after operations were all part of Mannock's extraordinary leadership. Caldwell calculated Mannock 'let at least four or five claims go in favour of others in his flight'.

> It may be difficult for someone who wasn't there to appreciate the effect this could have on an unblooded pilot. To have even one German machine on his record instilled a great deal of confidence. He would not hand these out piecemeal; he had to feel that the pilot was worth the encouragement. The main thing about Mannock was that his successes were won in front of his followers; they could see how it was done. His tuition and example were of great value to the flight and the Squadron as a whole.[5]

Mannock pleaded to stay with the Tigers, but it was out of Caldwell's hands.[6] Van Ryneveld was determined that Mannock should take over from Billy Bishop who, though his unit had performed moderately well, was unwilling to give up his lone-wolf escapades. As Caldwell said, a 'C.O. who went off alone claiming victories was no use to the Squadron'.[7] Before going to his new command at St Omer, Mannock visited Clairmarais North, where he wept as he made an emotional farewell.

The loss of Mannock coincided with the arrival of a debilitating illness as Caldwell's men were struck down by headaches, vomiting and respiratory problems. The Spanish Flu had arrived on the Western Front with the incoming American soldiers. Something was clearly amiss when, on the night of 23 June, men retired early after a shared dinner with neighbouring 1 Squadron. Some woke with laryngitis-like symptoms coupled with nausea and lack of appetite, and others quickly succumbed to the highly contagious disease. Three days later Caldwell fell ill.[8]

Although this first wave of influenza was far less deadly than that which would follow in August, it nonetheless incapacitated large numbers of men. Military operations were curtailed as three-quarters of the French and half of the British soldiers fell to the virus. On the other side of the trenches, nearly a million Germans were suffering.[9] Aerial units were similarly afflicted: by 30 June, Caldwell was down to six able-bodied pilots out of 18.[10] According to one squadron diarist, the most severely afflicted were 'Grid, Birch, Richardson and Roxburgh', who would not be 'fit to fly for at least a fortnight'.[11]

Caldwell had 'nearly four days in bed with it and in that time could eat very little — temp 103'. Head and body still aching, Caldwell oversaw much depleted operations.[12] Fit airmen were forced to fly three or four patrols a day. Eventually Caldwell and some of the men were dispatched to the Duchess of Westminster's Hospital, on the coast at Le Touquet, 'to secure health'.[13]

Despite all the setbacks, a total of 33 victories helped to make up 74 Squadron's century in the third week of June.[14] One hundred victories in three months was a distinction that, as Jones wrote, 'no other British squadron can claim'. Richardson agreed: 'A record for the RFC in France.'[15]

The friendly rivalry that Caldwell subsequently established between his crew and Mannock's, based at St Omer, 'made the Huns patrol nearer Berlin than ever,' noted Jones. 'Often, on the last patrol of the day, they would join forces and sweep the sky from Ypres to Lens ... [l]ater congregating at George Robey's, where the "night would be made merry".'[16] In July, Caldwell signed off combat victories from long-standing members: Jones, Giles, Kiddie and Roxburgh-Smith. Newcomers also entered the ledger books: Sydney Carlin, George 'Bill' Hicks, Robert Harold Gray and Harold 'Doc' Shoemaker. Among these British, colonial and North American airmen, squat, rough-hewn Carlin was the wildcard.

At Ypres, in the second year of the war, Carlin had been awarded a Distinguished Conduct Medal (DCM), when, despite being injured, 'he refused to leave the firing line and kept the troop together in a very exposed position, with the trenches demolished on both sides, after all his seniors [officers] had been killed'. In 1916, he had received an MC on the Somme when 'under continuous shell fire he laid out a

Keith Caldwell and Edward Mannock set up a friendly rivalry when Mannock was given command of 85 Squadron. Based at St Omer aerodrome, the squadron performed extremely well under his leadership.

fire trench, and with his men held it against a counter-attack'.[17] In this action he was so severely wounded that his left leg had to be amputated below the knee. Deemed unfit for further action in the land war, Carlin promptly applied for the RFC. He was, understandably, rejected. Having already paid for a wooden leg, he took private flying lessons and eventually argued his way into the air service. During his training he was well regarded by Alan Scott and 'Zulu' Lloyd and affectionally dubbed 'Timbertoes'.[18] Carlin and Hicks, formerly of the Coldstream Guards, were to prove fruitful additions to the squadron.

Robert Gray was just one of three New Zealanders brought in to replace recent losses. His compatriots were Frederick 'Freddy' Gordon and Sydney Thomas Stidolph. Gray and Gordon were graduates of Caldwell's aviation alma mater, the New Zealand Flying School at Kohimarama, where they had cut their pilot's teeth on the school's slowly expanding collection of seaplanes. Gordon was also a Wanganui Collegiate old boy. Stidolph was a Gallipoli veteran invalided to Malta with enteric fever and medically discharged.[19] Like Carlin, he was determined to get back into the war and saw his chance with the flying service.

The rising number of colonials led to the unit being dubbed the 'Coloured Troops Squadron'.[20] Caldwell was actively angling to add more to the roster.[21] 'Gray, the NZer I spoke of has arrived,' he told his mother. 'I am going to show him the line, and later on we can carry out NZ offensive patrols.'[22]

The Americans in the squadron came from the fledgling United States Air Service (USAS). An independent but temporary branch of the US War Department, the USAS had a handful of squadrons in France, but its airmen also found homes in RAF units. Richardson noted that the squadron now had 'four Yanks', including Shoemaker, who was from Bridgeton, New Jersey.[23] He was delighted to be dispatched to 74 Squadron with its SE5s. 'I am to go over on the style [of aeroplane] that I have always liked and have been flying,' he wrote to his father upon receiving news of his posting.[24] The other 'Yanks' were Frederick Luff from Cleveland, Ohio; Conrad Matthiessen, from Chicago, Illinois; and Archibald Roberts, latterly from Havana, Cuba.[25]

With the departure of Mannock, Caldwell elevated Jones to commander of A Flight, where he readily took up the mantle of his mentor, with whom he remained in contact via phone calls and meals in St Omer. Wilfred Young, recently awarded a Distinguished Flying Cross (DFC) — the RAF's highest award for extraordinary aerial achievement and valour — for his determined leadership and 10 victories, retained command of B Flight and Clive Glynn from Liverpool was given C Flight.[26]

The newcomers were about to receive a frightening baptism that coincided with the final German offensive, an assault on the Marne. A massed attack on French positions around Reims continued the push towards Paris as Ludendorff hoped to draw more Allied troops away from Belgium and the northern end of the line. The early morning bombardment of 15 July awoke Parisians 100 miles to the west. Forewarned, the French Fourth Army escaped the brunt of the shells in strong defensive positions behind their forward line, and the well-directed French artillery shook the confidence of the advancing German troops.

To the north, Caldwell, fresh from hospital the day before, was bristling for action and, in Jones's words, 'celebrated his return by leading a typical . . . squadron patrol at breakfast hour'.

> As usual, he totally disregarded tactics. Crossing the line at Ypres at 12,000 feet, he made straight for Roulers Aerodrome. Here he circled around until a large formation of Huns arrived from above to accept his challenge. Then an unholy dog fight started. About forty machines dived and fired like madmen at one another; zoomed, turned, twisted, dived, and fired again and again. Machine guns spat their venom quicker than a gossiping old duchess: I saw an SE go spinning down with a cloud of Fokkers on his tail. It was poor old Grey [sic].

Jones spun around to follow a Fokker, which saw him coming. 'Round and round, faster and faster we went, neither able to get a shot at the other. Another Hun got on my tail, Roberts joined on to his, and another Hun swung in behind him. And so it went on, until the whole affair developed into a mad merry-go-round, with death the price of faltering.'

> Grid closed to within a few yards of a Hun's tail, pouring lead at him, even a Fokker could not stand that. He got windy, got out of his turn, and dived away. It was fatal. Soon everyone was flying all out to miss the floating pieces and one another. If the others felt like me, they gasped and felt sick at the bare fuselage, now turned coffin, [as it] dived vertically to destruction. Grey was avenged . . .[27]

Gray, miraculously, was still alive, albeit a prisoner of war. The New Zealander was not the only casualty: South African Percy 'Swazi' Howe was missing. It was later discovered that he had been wounded and crashed.

He gamely attempted to return to the squadron, but a blood loss-induced collapse delivered him to a field hospital near Hazebrouck. He was duly 'whisked off to Blighty'.[28]

On 19 July, the squadron was escorting Bristol F2b Fighters bombing Roulers when they were set upon by a large collection of German machines. Richardson, in the thick of a swirling mass of aeroplanes, was so intent on watching the fall of a German machine he had hit that he forgot his own tail and was 'very much surprised to receive a cockpit full of bullets ... His first burst got me through the shoulder, shot my main petrol tank, one of my magnetos and instruments. I remembered Grid's advice in such a situation — joystick full forward, engine full on, dive like hell and get away.' Richardson managed this and did get across the lines, but a 'peculiar thing' occurred:

> when I was hit and starting to dive away, I changed the angle of my tail plane for diving, which we could do from a control on the left side. I did this after I was shot through the left shoulder. Now I was crossing the lines and losing altitude, looking for a place to land, I wanted to change the tail plane again, for climbing and I couldn't because of my shoulder — so I dove into the ground at much speed.

His machine turned over and broke up but Richardson's only additional injury was skinned knuckles. He had crashed near the camp of the 105 US Machine Gun Battalion, who extricated him from the wreckage and took him to their medical tent. When Roxburgh-Smith and others arrived, Richardson learnt that Roberts was missing. 'Roxburgh had me sign a report because I was so confident that the Hun was proper shot down.'[29]

The following morning, Richardson's wound was dressed and he was wedged into an overloaded ambulance train. 'What a hellish ride. The train was full of the seriously wounded soldiers groaning and crying and yelling as we bumped along, stopped and bumped again until we arrived at Boulogne.' The hospital, though, was a revelation.

'It seemed like heaven to me,' he wrote in his diary. It was 'unbelievable to have a good-looking nurse make a fuss over me, whom I suppose is the umpteenth wounded man she has cared for. She even told me she heard of my "pukkah" fight, which of course is a lot of "Bull" but I loved it.'[30] Roberts was less fortunate. While shooting down an enemy machine, he was set upon by a Fokker triplane and biplane and was last seen over Menin, fighting for his life. He survived and was captured.

As the Allies launched a counter-attack on the Marne, the German advance was halted only 8 miles from its jumping-off point and French troops, supported by American, British and Italian forces and augmented by 350 tanks, reclaimed territory acquired by the enemy over the preceding months. Paris was secured and Ludendorff's forces and reserves were exhausted. It was the turning point of 1918; the momentum of the war had shifted.

On 26 July, the Western Front was swept by frequent rainstorms.[31] Few airmen were flying, but not all were resting. A few miles north of Caldwell, Mannock was determined to get another of his young understudies in 85 Squadron a confidence-boosting victory that did not involve a dangerous massed dogfight.

Like Caldwell, Mannock had received a handful of New Zealanders, including Donald 'Kiwi' Inglis, a Gallipoli veteran and DCM recipient, who was inexperienced as an airman and having trouble scoring his first victory.[32] His flight commander, the adventurous, 6-foot 3-inch fellow New Zealander Malcolm 'Mac' McGregor, had attempted to get Inglis 'blooded', but to no avail. (McGregor had survived a horrific crash in 1917 in which his face was smashed into his machine gun: he lost his teeth and fractured his upper jaw.) Inglis's keenness was obvious and Mannock stepped in.[33] 'Never mind Kiwi. I'll show you how it's done in the morning. Now see to your machine and your guns so that we can get off the ground . . .'

Before dawn, when Inglis stepped into the mess, Mannock was waiting. 'I hope we'll be able to find an early flying two-seater coming over,' he said. As they walked over the dew-covered grass to their machines, Mannock laid out his plan: 'Follow me closely and you'll get him in your sights, take careful aim and get as close as you can before you fire.'[34] The pair circled the airfield before flying east. Periodically, Mannock wiggled his wings and Inglis opened the throttle to close the gap, his eyes fixed on his commander's tail. Then, at 5.30 a.m., as the two men were flying close to the 'carpet', Mannock, without warning, started climbing 'full out'. As Inglis said later, 'I knew from this he must have spotted a Hun.'

The target was a two-seater and Mannock pounced, firing furiously. Suddenly he swung away, and the damaged victim was right in Inglis's gunsight. He fired a good burst into the machine, which caught fire and plunged earthward.[35] Then, inexplicably, Mannock pushed the stick forward and pursued the stricken machine, 'circling round and round the falling torch'. Only when the ground fire became too intense did he turn aside, weaving his machine evasively. Just then, the SE5a dropped its nose and Inglis saw an evil orange flame spout from the fuselage. Man and machine fell lazily into a downward right-hand turn. The left wing lifted suddenly,

and aeroplane dropped straight down, engulfed in black smoke and flames.

Inglis wanted to stay but heavy fire was shredding his machine. As he struggled with the controls, a well-aimed bullet punctured his fuel line and he was drenched in the flammable liquid. He made Allied lines and force-landed. An infantryman rushed up to the aeroplane to find Inglis bent over the controls, crying, 'Poor old Mick. The bloody bastards have shot my Major down in flames.'[36]

A telephone call to 85 Squadron from an anti-aircraft battery, which had recognised Mannock's machine, broke the news to the unit. Over in 74 Squadron, Caldwell and Jones took to the air in search of the wreckage in the Calonne–Lestrem area. 'It was really rather hopeless and useless,' said Caldwell. 'We couldn't hang about long as the firing was intense.' Mannock's body was never recovered.[37]

His men were devastated. 'We have lost our squadron commander,' wrote McGregor, 'went down in flames after getting over 70 Huns, and so the Royal Air Force has lost the best leader of patrols, and the best Hun getter it has had. In a month he would have had over 100. However, unlike other stars, he left behind all the knowledge he had, so it is up to the fellows he taught to carry on.'[38] 'Lots of airmen turned up at No. 85 to cheer up the lads,' wrote Jones. Luminaries like Arthur 'Mary' Coningham and Raymond Collishaw arrived, but at the forefront were Caldwell and 74 Squadron.[39]

'It was a difficult business. The thought of Mick's charred body not many miles away haunted us and dampened our spirits. There was more drinking than usual on these occasions; the Decca [record player] worked overtime; we tried to sing, but it was painfully obvious that it was forced, as there was a noticeable discord. It was damned hard,' wrote Taffy Jones years later. Caldwell delivered an after-dinner speech, assuring the men that Mannock would not have wanted them to mope. It was a valiant attempt, but Caldwell was visibly 'cut-up'.[40]

The loss of the best pilot in the RAF did nothing to settle the nerves of others still caught in the continuous heavy fighting. Men flying up to four times a day were plagued by nightmares and premonitions of death. By the time of Mannock's death, many men in 85 Squadron were showing the ill-effects of stress. Some confessed to being too nervous to hold a pen straight. Shaking hands and nervous twitches were

Malcolm — Mac — McGregor, a graduate of the New Zealand Flying School, was one of 85 Squadron's leading airmen. After the war he became a pioneering aviator in his homeland.

commonplace. 'I'm alright in the air, as calm as a cucumber, but on the ground I'm a wreck and I get panicky. Nobody in the squadron can get a glass to his mouth with one hand after one of the decoy patrols,' wrote one of McGregor's pilots. 'Some nights . . . Mac has to get up and find his teeth and quiet us.'[41]

The same symptoms were regularly observed in 74 Squadron. One airman who barely escaped death in the squadron's early deployment was tormented by the event. 'At the moment he is asleep. His body twitching in a dream. No doubt he is fighting the battle over again, as I do every night,' said Jones, who was himself afflicted.

> Had a terrible nightmare last night. Jumped out of bed eleven times even though I tried to stop myself by tying my pyjama strings to the bed. Each time I jumped out, there was a devil of a row. Poor old Giles got fed up to the teeth, as I kept waking him up. It was the usual old business, chiefly, of being shot down in flames and jumping out of my plane. One of the nightmares took a new line. I was forced down and crashed on top of a wood. As I wasn't hurt, I slid down a tree and ran to hide in a bush; but the Hun kept on chasing me and shooting me up, wounding me every time. At last, he landed in a clearing and chased me with a revolver until he caught and killed me. Lovely dream![42]

Nonetheless the squadron's routine of patrols continued unabated and novices needed careful introduction to the rigours of battle. A handful of line patrols in mid-July should have been a moderately safe start for Shoemaker, but on the third sortie, his engine's connecting rod broke and a cylinder punched a crater in the manifold. The propeller slowed its spin and stopped. Desperate to lighten the load and gain Allied lines, Shoemaker threw everything out of the SE5a, including the machine guns. He made friendly territory but misjudged the landing, hitting a road, before bouncing into a 4-foot-high sea of barley, where he flipped over.

Caldwell was advised of the mishap by the other flight members who had witnessed the escape. Shoemaker was unharmed and elated by his close call. 'It is all very interesting and amusing,' he told his father. 'I would not miss all this for millions of dollars, as it will never occur again in my lifetime.'[43]

At midday on 30 July, Caldwell sent him over the German side of the lines on an offensive patrol in the safe hands of Jones and a recent addition to the squadron, the

The dreaded Fokker DVIIs at rest at a German aerodrome. Keith Caldwell flew a captured DVII after the war and considered them a superior machine to the SE5a.

Canadian barrister George Gauld. The trio spotted enemy machines at 15,000 feet between Cassel and Ypres, and singled one out. As Shoemaker recalled,

> Our leader and observer opened fire on him and then we half-rolled to get a good position and I succeeded in getting under his machine. Our leader took another shot at him just as he half-rolled. The Hun was driving fast with me after him, giving him several good bursts of bullets from my machine guns. I followed him down to about 2000 feet, then one of my guns jammed and I broke away. I came down so fast I could not observe the location of my companions so started west for our lines as rapidly as possible, flipping about and darting to prevent the 'Archies' or Boche guns getting a good shot at me.

When he landed, Shoemaker, who was uncertain of the fruits of his labour, was immediately congratulated by Jones: 'You bagged the Boche machine, as I saw it dive headfirst, crashing into the ground, then bursting into a lively bonfire.' Shoemaker proudly declared: 'Downed my first aeroplane today.'[44]

It was just one victory on the squadron's most successful day in July. During the same lunchtime patrol, Jones and Kiddie both took down an enemy machine, while Caldwell, prowling west of Armentières, encountered five Fokker biplanes. He latched onto one and chased it down from 11,000 to 7000 feet before it filled his sights, then did a 'spin turn and came out on his tail', firing 60 rounds at only 50 yards. It was Caldwell's third for the month. His total now sat at 18.[45]

Jones picked up another mid-afternoon victory and final scalp in a late-afternoon patrol led by Caldwell, during which Carlin was successful against a Fokker. After the final machine returned to Clairmarais, an elated Shoemaker wrote: 'The Major with two others from our fliers also bagged one, totalling seven Hun machines for one day. Quite a day too, for new men in a strange land. It is now bedtime and another raid, possibly both.'[46] For the month of July, Caldwell's unit accrued at least 27 victories against the enemy, a tie with neighbouring 85 Squadron.[47] Despite the absence of Mannock, under Caldwell's sure direction, the unit had lost none of its potency or momentum.

August brought a string of changes for Caldwell. Notably, in the first week, Wilfred Young was posted to command 1 Squadron, and Caldwell was dispatched on well-deserved leave.[48] The latter coincided with the announcement that

Jones had been awarded a bar to his DFC. 'Bit silly when Grids got nothing. Feel very awkward about it and told Grid so. He just laughed and told me not to be so damned wet. "It's the honour of the squadron that matters, my lad," he said. "I'm going on leave today. Look after yourself. And keep on cracking the sods."'[49]

Mary and Vida were there to greet Caldwell in London, grateful that he was alive, although warworn. Many other former Wanganui Collegiate old boys had not been so fortunate; the April edition of the school magazine included a long list of names, in a small, condensed typeface, followed by obituaries of the recently fallen.[50]

After his accident-prone training in East Anglia, Neal Spragg had eventually been sent to Egypt as an instructor in the School of Aerial Gunnery. He still, though, managed to get airborne as a passenger on numerous joy rides over and around Cairo. After attending the 1918 New Year's Eve concert at the Aotea Convalescent Home at Heliopolis, he and his pilot took off for their home base. On the ground, the matron of the hospital tracked the flight and waved at the two young men; Spragg waved back. 'While we were watching the two happy boys fly past, "something" went wrong with the wing of the machine. It crumpled up and down came the aeroplane!'

The Maurice Farman Shorthorn crashed to the ground, pinning the pilot under the wreckage. Twelve men were required to lift the wreckage to extricate him. Spragg was thrown clear but sustained severe head injuries and died in front of the gathering crowd.[51] He was buried with full honours at Old Cairo Cemetery. Caldwell later learnt that Spragg was to be remembered in his home city of Auckland in a park bequeathed by his father on a hill near Huia, overlooking the entrance to Manukau Harbour.[52]

During the war, thousands of uniformed men and woman from all parts of the empire spent their leave in London. How much sightseeing Caldwell did is not known, but many of his fellow New Zealanders visited such famous places as the city's zoo, Buckingham Palace, the Houses of Parliament, Kew, the Tower of London, Madame Tussauds and, commanding the skyline, St Paul's. 'Words cannot express adequately its imposing grandeur,' wrote one New Zealand pilot, 'the beauty of the walls and roof with its patterns inlaid with gold, the size and immense proportions of the pillars, or the huge dome towering 400 feet above one's head . . . Standing at the entrance to the nave of the church, it seemed to me as though the floor space could be measured in acres; while the music from the organ echoed and reechoed till it died away in the distance.'[53]

Overleaf: **King George V inspecting members of 74 Squadron.**
From right: Sydney Carlin, Ira Jones, Benjamin Roxburgh-Smith.

In the north transept hung Holman Hunt's celebrated allegorical painting, *The Light of the World*, based on Revelation 3:20: 'Behold, I stand at the door and knock; if any man hears My voice, and opens the door, I will come in to him, and will sup with him. And he with Me.' Between 1906 and 1907 the painting had traversed the English-speaking world, including New Zealand, where it was met with widespread acclaim. Less sacred but devouring more military pay were silent movies and live theatre. Some films incorporated the war. In Cecil B. DeMille's *The Little American* (1917), for example, Mary Pickford played a nurse on the Western Front, caught up in an American–French–German love triangle. A favourite pin-up girl of the war, Pickford starred in no fewer than six films in 1918.

The stage was no less alluring in the final year of the war, when Shakespeare's *Henry V*, Puccini's *Madama Butterfly* and Verdi's *Il trovatore* competed with less-refined fare in the West End. Some stage productions echoed nationalist and propagandist themes, but most were musical hall productions or escapist plays — *Maid of the Mountains*, *A Little Bit of Fluff*, *The Case of Lady Camber* — staged at such theatres as Daly's, the Savoy and the Adelphi. The box-office monster of the war was the lavishly staged *Chu Chin Chow*, in which chickens, snakes and a camel appeared with a vast cast of actors, including a scantily clad harem that was, said the *Tatler*, 'very suitable to the sultry climate of old Bagdad'.[54]

Despite the distance, Caldwell's mind was never far from his men, some of whom, even with a morale-boosting visit from the king, were struggling under the unyielding pressure of operations. On 6 August, George V inspected 74 Squadron, with Roxburgh-Smith, Carlin, Glynn and Jones all standing straight-backed for the Tigers. 'Pity Grid is away and Mannock dead,' lamented Jones. The 'King will miss seeing two of his finest officers'.[55] It may have been a proud day, but the Welshman was near breaking point. 'Sleeping very badly. Found myself out of bed four times. Can't understand it happening every night. Damn silly.' After five months of service, and 37 victories in aerial combat, Jones was hospitalised and would not return to the squadron for three months.[56]

When the German Spring Offensive had finally ground to a halt in July, Ferdinand Foch, the Allied supreme commander, wanted to prevent the Germans from digging into their newly acquired territory. With a refreshed and greatly bolstered force at his disposal, he would plan and direct the onslaught. The recent victory on the Marne had raised French morale, and the BEF had received a large infusion of men from the Sinai and Palestine campaign, the Italian front and Britain. Also available was General John Pershing's well-equipped American Expeditionary Force.

General Haig's initial targets for the BEF, in what was later dubbed the Hundred Days Offensive, were vulnerable German positions near Amiens and then the Somme itself. To avoid alerting the Germans to the scale of the operation, the Allied assault would not be heralded by a large artillery barrage, but rather spearheaded by massed tanks with air support. At dawn on 8 August, bombers escorted by fighters would attack enemy airfields. The RAF would then launch powerful offensive patrols over German-controlled territory and, late in the afternoon, attack railway junctions to hinder German reinforcement efforts.

Just before his departure for France, Caldwell was recognised in London by a fellow Wanganui Collegiate old boy, Aucklander Howard Coverdale, who had completed his training in seaplanes at Kohimarama before leaving for the RAF in June. He was preparing to enter the School of Aeronautics, when he spotted a familiar face.[57]

I had great luck today — saw Keith Caldwell in the street. Did not recognise him at first on account of his moustache, but soon made sure by his slouch and the MC etc. He was going back to France the next day, being now in command of the 74th Scouting Squadron. He was looking very well, and rather taller and broader. He says they have a ripping time in France, and when not flying, stroll about in pyjamas and play tennis etc. Freddie [sic] Gordon is in Caldwell's squadron, and brought down his first Hun the other day.[58]

CHAPTER SEVENTEEN

Great Escape

O n 19 August 1918, 11 days after the commencement of the Allied assault, Caldwell found his squadron, which now resided at Clairmarais South, much revived and in high spirits. A 7-mile advance on the first day of the Battle of Amiens had proved decisive. German officers eating their breakfast had been surprised to find Allied soldiers pointing rifles at them, and large numbers of them were captured. Erich Ludendorff described it as 'the black day of the German army'. More territory followed and the Allied prisoner of war camps swelled with thousands of new arrivals. Within days, intelligence was indicating that the Germans were retreating, abandoning the hard-won territory acquired during the Spring Offensive.

'On our side the army seems buoyed by the enormous hope of getting on with this business quickly,' wrote one war correspondent. 'There is a change also in the enemy's mind. They no longer have even a dim hope of victory on this western front. All they hope for now is to defend themselves long enough to gain peace by negotiation.'[1] Within days of the offensive, Haig was brimming with confidence: 'A vigorous offensive against the sectors where the enemy is weak will cause hostile strong points to fall and in due course our whole army will be able to continue its advance,' he declared.[2]

Twenty-four hours after his return, Caldwell surprised the pilots with a set of false beards, black, white and ginger, which he had purchased in London. With a smile, he stated that he wanted everyone to wear one on the patrol so that 'the Huns would think the British were using "old timers" and take us for "easy meat"'. They patrolled for nearly two hours at 17,000 feet, waiting to shock the enemy, but the Germans were elsewhere. 'This was all slightly mad,' recalled Harris Clements, 'but it was things like this that kept us going and produced the wonderful spirit which one found in 74.' It also confirmed for the airmen that 'Grid had a great sense of humour and was a grand Commanding Officer'.[3]

It was a light-hearted beginning to a busy period in support of the offensive. The squadron flew regular patrols, intercepted high-flying photographic and reconnaissance machines and carried out wireless interruption work. When German aircraft were found to be adroitly directing their artillery by wireless communication onto Allied ground positions, the RAF used ground-based wireless compass stations to locate these machines.[4] Once a machine's course was charted by its Morse-coded transmissions, a phone call went to 11 Wing headquarters, which promptly dispatched Caldwell and his men to intercept. At regular intervals, too, 74 Squadron was asked to detach two pilots from its offensive patrols to sally forth and 'attack hostile kite balloons with flat-nosed Buckingham Ammunition'.[5]

There were usually three operations a day of various sizes. For example, on 23 August, Caldwell was ordered to run a two-flight offensive patrol at 9.15 a.m., a one-flight offensive patrol at 2.15 p.m. and a whole squadron patrol at 6.30 p.m. The morning and early afternoon patrols were slated for 75 minutes each; the evening patrol should be 'as late as possible'.[6]

For the last sortie, Caldwell waved to the ground crew and took off with the full squadron in tow, then headed east towards Passchendaele. To the south, flashes of gunfire and plumes of smoke indicated the heart of the Battle of Bapaume, where the British Third Army was advancing with the New Zealand Division in the vanguard, fighting its way to the war-scarred medieval town and castle.

Caldwell found an enemy formation of six of the latest-and-greatest German machines: Fokker DVIIs. He and Roxburgh-Smith were in the thick of it. As they dived, Caldwell singled out the enemy leader for special attention, Vickers and Lewis guns announcing his pugilistic intent. The German pushed the nose of his Fokker down into a thin layer of cloud. Roxburgh-Smith depressed his trigger, but both of his guns failed and he pulled away. Caldwell had better luck and at close range his bullets

Overleaf: **Keith Caldwell appears to be on leave when this photograph of 74 Squadron was taken in the summer of 1918.**

found their mark. The German inverted his wounded machine and dived north-west to escape.

'I followed,' Caldwell later reported, 'and at about 4500 again engaged EA at 50 yards firing until the Lewis drum ran out.'[7] The German machine failed to pull out of the plunge and crashed just east of Houthulst Forest at 7.25 p.m. Roxburgh-Smith unjammed his guns and picked off a couple of machines, sending them to the ground. The squadron's tally for the month numbered some 22 victories, a good effort, if somewhat down on previous months due to Caldwell's 14-day absence and the departure of Jones.[8]

September proved to be the best of times for Caldwell and his men but the worst of times for the RAF. The tide may have turned in the ground war, but there were still considerable challenges in the air. At the beginning of the Hundred Days Offensive, the RAF had nearly 800 machines on hand around Amiens, against a German force of nearly 370, with a similar number of Luftstreitkräfte reinforcements ready for deployment.[9] Moreover, with a large French air presence of 1100 machines to deal with, and the USAS beginning to find its feet, the Germans were facing daunting odds.

The Luftstreitkräfte, however, remained a credible threat given its defensive advantage — meeting Allied machines at a time and place, and in numbers, of its choosing. The marauding Jagdgeschwader (fighter wings), which numbered close to 70 machines, were lethal against smaller RAF formations. For example, on the second day of the month, Jagdgeschwader III (JGIII), under the command of the bull-faced ace Bruno Loerzer, claimed 26 enemy machines — the single largest daily haul in the history of the war.[10]

Increasingly, these formations were populated by the fearsome Fokker DVIIs, many of which sported a new powerful 185 horsepower BMW engine, capable of propelling the aircraft to 125 miles per hour and with a climb rate almost without equal in the war.[11] This engine upgrade almost made it a new model and ensured the competitiveness of the German air service right up until the armistice. (After flying a captured machine in the months after the war ended, Caldwell confirmed that the SE5a was 'not a match for a well flown Fokker DVII'.)[12] In September 1918, German

After sustaining an injury as an airman in the First World War, Clayton Knight turned his hand to aviation art. Here he recreated Keith Caldwell's final moments before his famous leap from his aeroplane.

airmen like Josef Jacobs, Franz Büchner, Paul Bäumer, Georg von Hantelmann and Carl Degelow were at their lethal best. The air war was entering its final deadly phase.

Caldwell and his men would demonstrate, however, that the SE5a was still a force to be reckoned with and a well-organised squadron something to be greatly feared. The unit opened its September campaign with three victories on the fourth day of the month. Before departing for the morning patrol, Carlin and Gordon were issued with incendiary rounds to fire on the German observation balloons. Caldwell once again led the patrol and at 14,000 feet found enemy intruders, and former agricultural student Frederick Hunt attacked.

The Englishman fired first a short burst, which sent the German machine spinning downwards, only to flatten out. A long burst sent it out of control. Caldwell noted in his report that it would have been Hunt's first confirmed aeroplane victim if members of the patrol had witnessed the final crash.[13] Caldwell had engaged four enemy machines from underneath, destroying a Fokker DVII. The squadron drove off the remaining machines.

Having cleared the area, Caldwell then sent Gordon and Carlin to attack the designated balloons. Two were sent down in flames, one observer escaping safely while the other fell to his death when his parachute collapsed. It was Carlin's fifth balloon victory, making him the squadron's unofficial 'balloon busting' expert.[14] Elsewhere the RAF was less fortunate, including a 12-strong formation of Camels that was hammered by JGIII: only four Allied machines survived. The next day Caldwell was nearly killed by one of his own pilots.

The story, which opens this book, of his 5 September collision with Carlin, his efforts to regain mastery of the damaged SE5a and his leap just before his machine crashed in front of Tommy soldiers was retold in the years and decades that followed. Although the details often varied with the retelling, all agreed that it was one of the great escapades of the air war and it ensured Grid's legendary status. After the wild night of celebrating the miracle, 'he brushed it all off as nothing out of the ordinary'. In England, Jones was not surprised.

> The next day Caldwell led a Squadron patrol with greater determination than ever. When higher authority heard of this, he was ordered not to fly over the lines again without permission. He was allowed to fly on our side of the lines, however, and in this way he was able to have as much fighting as before, because he used to wander far over the enemy's lines and shoot down Huns which he never reported! He was indeed a great leader of men. Such men as he are rare.[15]

Rain and clouds precluded extensive operations over the following 10 days, but Caldwell was kept busy with the arrival of new men, including more from North America. Canadian Richmond Mayson, who had been a bank clerk before the war, was overjoyed to be posted to one of the celebrated squadrons on the Western Front, blessed with a commander who was a 'wonderful pilot . . . [with] many Huns to his credit'. Mayson painted a vivid picture of his welcome. After meeting Caldwell and 'about 15 pilots of the squadron . . . I began to feel rather embarrassed and wonder if I was some crack pilot or a new commander-in-chief'. But then came 'the intricacies of a social evening':

> Anyone wishing to be rude might say it sounded like a house of hooligans, or sound as though the war was over. But really, it was not so. Our pianist would sit down before the piano or be forced there very quickly by half-a-dozen big and honourable men of the Royal Air Force . . . Then would begin a most wonderful assortment of song, starting off with 'There's an Old-Fashioned House' and going on to 'Me and My Gal', then 'Dixie' and back again to . . . sentimental songs like 'Perfect Day'. Everyone would stand around singing or shouting at the top of their voices, trying to make more row than the next one. At first, I did think they were a bit mad, but soon I joined in, trying to make a much noise as any. I think I succeeded too.

Sometimes, sticks and tin cans were used to make 'a noise of the rowdiest kind, [and] every now and again one wishing to imitate a drum would give a hard kick against the piano or wooden wall, and all but send his feet through it'.

On the days when they could not fly, Mayson recalled, they might eat and sleep, unless 'some energetic person suggest[ed] a game of football. The officers play the men one day, and the next day the men play the officers.' Or there might be a visit to the nearest town, 'probably for their monthly bath, whether they needed it or not, or perhaps for a haircut'. And the 'little pups we had were always a source of merriment to us. Put them on the floor together and they would be sure to start fighting, only in a playful mood.' One would pretend to be dead, 'then jump and spring on his opponent. Every little incident like this was good for us. It helped to divert our minds from our work, which was both trying and dangerous.'[16]

Overleaf: **Tiger Squadron on full display. Keith Caldwell occupies the cockpit of the SE5a at far right.**

As Mayson noted, many men enjoyed seeing the 'sights of war from the ground', but this was not without its perils. Thirty-two-year-old Rea Isaiah Hagenbuch from Bloomsburg, Pennsylvania, who joined the squadron on 1 September, was madly in love with English nurse Annie 'Winnie' Jones, who had cared for him while he was in hospital before his posting to the Tigers. 'Yesterday was rotten again,' he wrote to her on 11 September, so a group of squadron men went off to 'see an Archie battery at work [though] what we were really after was souvenirs. We went to a rather famous part of the front and visited a number of towns or what had at one time been towns and then went up to the front lines.'

> We split up and went wandering around looking through old German dugouts ... although we could hear the sniping of rifle fire and guns firing etc. We all felt perfectly safe ... suddenly whizz-zz-zzzz and a most horrible feeling went up my spine as a shell exploded close to us. The first one might have been fired at random, but almost immediately another followed and then about a dozen more ... [we must] have looked like a Mohammaden [sic] in prayer. Ran a few steps then whiz z z z!!!! and down on our faces. The first time I fell flat I was ashamed until I saw everyone else had done the same, then I felt better. Don't think for minute that I acted thru. caution but a feeling that makes caution seem like a lullaby ... my hair would naturally rise, my legs grew weak, and down I would go.[17]

When the clouds and rain eventually withdrew, the 74 Squadron pilots flew sorties in support of the Third and Fourth armies. The BEF was undertaking preparatory work for an advance on Havrincourt and Épehy, itself a precursor to a much bigger general offensive on Flanders with, as its objective, the Hindenburg Line and the recovery of the Belgian coast.[18] As 11 Wing orders demanded, each patrolling aircraft was to carry bombs, 'which are to be dropped on trains and railways, both light and broad gauge, but preference should always be given to troops and transport if they can be attacked at low altitude'. Patrols were then to work down as far as Bac-Saint-Maur. 'All pilots will pay as much attention as possible to enemy movement, and large concentrations are to be attacked with machine gun fire from the air.'[19]

'We are due for some trench strafing soon and lots of it,' wrote Hagenbuch to his sweetheart, 'and believe me that is where it's some hot work.'[20] The SE5s were now fully loaded with four Cooper bombs. Caldwell reiterated to his men the importance of getting rid of these as soon as practicable to allow for greater manoeuvrability in subsequent strafing or dogfighting. In the multiple patrols over the next few days, Caldwell was in the thick of it all, attacking Germans and assisting his own men.

On 17 September, north-west of Courtrai, Caldwell led a late-afternoon full-squadron patrol. At 15,000 feet, he spotted seven enemy machines below and signalled five SE5s to follow him down, only to find, at 13,000 feet, that he and his pilots were heading into a well-laid German trap: six more Fokkers approaching with height. He prepared to abandon the venture, but spied, 2 miles further east, a lone SE5 in trouble: it was Hunt, surrounded by three Fokkers. Caldwell made a mad rush to rescue him.

The Germans did not see him coming and, firing at close range at 10,000 feet, he brought down the first Fokker, which crashed north of Courtrai. As Hunt and his remaining twin tormentors were swirling around each other at 7000 feet, Caldwell kicked the rudder and pushed his machine down. The uppermost German, surrounded by bullets bursting from Caldwell's machine guns, tumbled over sideways and dived down south-west. This Fokker 'was certainly hit, but I could not waste time to watch results as the remaining EA still had height on the SE (Lt. Hunt),' Caldwell later reported.[21] In the assault he lost his Lewis to a broken extractor, but struck the last of the German trio with the Vickers — at least until it suffered an untimely jam. The flagging German spun down low before flattening out and skulking away.

Caldwell fell in protectively behind a shaken Hunt as they set a course for home, only to find more determined Fokkers. As the enemy closed in west of Roulers, Caldwell made the decision to turn and engage the nearest machine. It was an outrageous feint from the weaponless commander, but completely in character — a repeat of his audacious defence of Billy Bishop the previous year. It worked, frightening off the enemy and delivering Hunt safely to Clairmarais. Caldwell had his twenty-first and twenty-second victories, only his second 'double' in a single day.[22] The June 1917 victories had precipitated his MC; this action and those of the recent weeks led to a recommendation for an 'immediate award' of a DFC.[23]

A s the fighting intensified and RAF losses mounted, Caldwell was able to take comfort in the Tigers' relatively minimal casualties. Only four days later, on 21 September, he found his formation of five SE5s heavily outnumbered by more than 20 Fokkers over Lille. In the ensuing dogfight, Clive Glynn and Hunt were able to destroy a DVII each, while Roxburgh-Smith and Caldwell sent a pair down out of control. In the maelstrom, Caldwell personally attacked seven machines, with only time for a sharp burst at each. His victory came after he half-rolled onto an enemy machine diving away. At barely 25 yards, rounds of bullets struck the engine and cockpit, sending the Fokker down vertically, the propeller frozen.[24] But, as Caldwell remembered vividly years later, 'when another E.A. formation came in from the north, 10 or 12 strong, we were in dire trouble!'

> I saw Carlin's SE going down with explosive ammunition hitting it, but I could not help as I was in the centre of several persistent Huns. We had to do just what we could to save ourselves. Carlin crashed . . . Glynn and Hunt (of our five) were forced down on our side of the line and only Roxburgh-Smith and I returned to the aerodrome at Clairmarais . . . It was a sad ending to what we had planned would be a successful venture.[25]

But the skilled and tenacious Timbertoes survived and was limping towards the British lines when he was rapidly overtaken by rifle-bearing Germans and was forced to endure the rest of the war as a POW. In under four months with the Tigers, he had accumulated five victories over enemy machines and destroyed five balloons.

On the morning of 24 September, Caldwell and the squadron extracted some satisfying revenge during a patrol 3 miles east of Armentières.[26] The weather was fair with a smattering of cloud, and at 12,000 feet Caldwell signalled three men to follow him down to intercept seven enemy machines. As they neared the intruders, the men did a double-take: the aeroplanes looked like muscular Nieuport 17s, albeit decorated with black crosses. This was a new and deadly German latecomer to the war: the Siemens-Schuckert DIV.

Although its prototype designs were closely based on the light French Nieuport, the Siemens-Schuckerts that arrived on the Western Front in 1918 were much more robust and powerful. The airframe and wings were compact, and the massive 11-cylinder rotary engine turned an oversized four-blade propeller. The 'flying beer barrel', as it was soon nicknamed, was faster and more manoeuvrable than even the feared Fokker DVII, but its real strength was in its unchallenged rate of climb: it could ascend to over 3000 feet in two minutes, 10,000 feet in six minutes and 20,000 feet in 15 minutes. The first batch of the interceptor-fighter arrived in August but the numbers were too small to make a significant impact. By the war's end, only 125 had been produced, of which barely half saw service in battle. This was small solace for the RAF airmen who had the misfortune to meet them in battle.

The opposing forces — four SE5s against seven Siemens-Schuckerts — turned into each other, attempting to gain a height advantage. Caldwell engaged the leading German machine at right angles, firing until 'nearly colliding', the blue, white and red roundels of the SE5a flashing within feet of the Black crosses. They both pushed their rudders over and circled as Caldwell calculated the capabilities of the SE5a against this new foe.

Remarkably, in a tight turn, he managed to outmanoeuvre the Siemens-Schuckert and latch on to its tail. The German pilot pulled back on the joystick to utilise his superior climb rate, but it was too late: Caldwell had acquired plenty of speed. 'I easily followed him, firing when very close up,' he wrote in his logbook. It was a near-vertical climb and the bullets hit their mark.

Caldwell watched the enemy machine stall, stand on its tail for a second, then fall over to the right, skimming past his wingtip in a cataclysmic fall. As the Siemens-Schuckert brushed close, gathering speed, Caldwell glanced into the cockpit, where 'the pilot was leaning to the left . . . with his head down on his chest'. In his logbook Caldwell scrawled that the new 'Huns very handy in a dogfight'.[27] In the fracas, Hicks downed another Siemens-Schuckert and shared in the dispatch of a two-seat Rumbler C with Roxburgh-Smith.

I n the third week of September, Caldwell was ordered to relocate the squadron 15 miles east to the Belgian aerodrome of La Lovie. Though a rotten little airfield bordered by dykes on either side to trip the careless, it was closer to the action and the final supreme effort: an assault on the feared and vaunted Hindenburg Line.[28] Caldwell's squadron was a small part of Marshal Foch's plan, which combined the efforts of the French, British, American and Belgian forces in a converging offensive. Van Ryneveld reorganised 11 Wing to focus on close cooperation with the advancing ground forces.

Other than taking extreme care to discriminate between 'our own . . . and enemy troops', the air units were encouraged to shoot up and bomb enemy targets on the ground.[29]

On 28 September, Richmond Mayson was shaken from sleep by a terrific pre-dawn din. 'I jumped out of bed, went outside and saw a wonderful spectacle. The big battle had begun and for miles in all directions the sky was lit by flashes from thousands of

Overleaf: **The Siemens-Schuckert DIV was without rival for its rapid rate of climb. This post-war picture of the 'flying beer barrel' shows its massive propeller awaiting destruction in accordance with armistice rules.**

guns, both large and small. The sky was also lighted up by red rockets sent up by the Germans — a signal for help.'

> At 5:30 a.m., the boys are to go over the top, but just before they do, the rain commences to come down in torrents. What a pity it should start just then. I learnt afterwards that the rain did not stop our infantry in any way whatever for they advanced eight miles in places before that day was finished. There was a great concentration of our aeroplanes in the morning. They did great havoc amongst the retreating foe, bombing and machine-gunning the enemy transports and infantrymen.[30]

John Garver, from Ohio, was among those Caldwell selected for the post-lunch low-level action. Though he was still finding his feet in the squadron's busy schedule, he was keen to try his hand at the dangerous work. Caldwell placed him under the sure and experienced hand of squadron veteran Giles. 'Well,' wrote the young American, 'I've done a little for the cause at last and gee . . . I'm glad. I had heard about shooting up automobiles and troops along the roads, but now I've been doing a bit myself.'

> This afternoon [we] . . . took [to] the air with 4 bombs and guns loaded to the brim. We climbed to 8000 feet and crossed the lines above the barrage. Then we dived down to 1000 feet and looked for something to shoot up or blow up. I spied 6 guns . . . drawn by 4 horses each. Huns (Germans) were sitting on the barrels. Heading my machine in the direction they were going and flying at 500 feet just above them, I pulled the handle 4 times and boom, boom, boom, boom, right on them. I did not observe the damage as Archie . . . got bad and my machine sorta jammed and I was kept busy for the time throwing my bus about to keep them from downing me.[31]

Then, with Giles, he 'began to look for more victims'. When his leader dived on about eight enemy aircraft, Garver followed suit. 'Down we went firing into them. We came on them, the fire and smoke from our tracers, going pell-mell into the horses and wagons. Huns jumped and ran and crawled for cover in the ditches by the roadside. We zoomed up again and I was met with machine gunfire and Archie from the ground, I didn't have time to observe [the] effect of my fire, but I saw the horses galloping along with no drivers.' Ready for more, Garver spotted, below him, two men on horseback at a crossroads. 'To make sure they were Huns, I went gliding down on them but didn't fire. It was [then] too late to shoot . . . so I zoomed up and over getting ready for the fatal dive. When [I] gained my position, I saw the horses trotting along the road riderless, the wily Huns had sought cover . . . No shooting poor dumb animals for me.'

After missing 'several good chances by taking too much time to make sure that they were Huns', Garver saw a car that *did* contain Germans: 'They huddled together and looked up at me. I could see their faces and I could see the fear expressed. Turning my machine around I began the dive firing about 60 rounds pointblank into them. The car turned into the ditch and the Huns leaped over the side, sprawling into the ditch and on the road.'

> Zooming up again I again met with terrible fire from the ground. Zunk, one
> went into my tail. Looking around I saw a Fokker . . . gliding toward the ground.
> Instinctively, I turned toward him for battle. God was with me, and I looked
> up above me only to see 7 Fokker Huns waiting for the prey. I turned west and
> joined my patrol which crossed the lines and we soon landed at our aerodrome.
> As a result of this, my machine will be in the hospital to undergo treatment for
> wounds received. Eight bullets went into the wings, 2 in the tail and 2 in the
> fuselage where the tail fin joins the main spar. Some day, believe me, and I'm
> aching for more.[32]

On only his third patrol with the squadron, Mayson was included in a high-octane 12-machine raid on the German positions. With each aeroplane carrying two bombs, they climbed to fly over Ypres and then continue east until they reached Courtrai.

> By then, we were about 12,000 feet high. Some trains were moving into the
> town as we arrived, so our leader flew over them and gave the signal to 'Drop
> bombs!' Down went my hand to a small lever on my right — a pull and down
> fell my 'two pills'. These 'pills' that we carry each weigh 25 pounds. They are
> not to be taken with water, so we administer them to the Germans in the only
> way they can be digested. From each machine, I can see two bombs dropped
> and go down, down. I cannot watch where they fall; the leader has turned so
> we have to pay our attention to the formation and keep our place . . . After flying
> for about 2 hours, looking for Huns and dodging Archie, we turn our machines
> west and in a long glide we go home. I feel quite pleased with myself having
> dropped two bombs.[33]

RAF losses in these sorties were high, partly because of heavy anti-aircraft and ground fire, but also because of the violent weather encountered in the mornings. 'The heavy rain caused us to lose a number of our machines,' recalled Mayson. 'Their propeller[s] got broken beating against the rain, so were forced to land in the German lines.'[34] Caldwell's pilots, however, came through relatively unscathed and alongside 11 Wing's other squadrons they disrupted German attempts to reinforce threatened portions of the front. As September ended, Caldwell was able to look over a scoresheet in which the Tigers claimed over 30 victories against aeroplanes and balloons; his own five triumphs gave him his best month of the war.[35]

Surprisingly, given his results, he decided to remove the wing-mounted Lewis machine gun from his SE5a, perhaps in response to its breakage on 17 September.[36] Years later in a letter to Collishaw, he reconsidered the wisdom of his decision: 'I did a silly thing in removing my top Lewis gun, never liked it up there, leaving only the Vickers; my idea was to have a better performance & rely on getting close, forgetting of course that I was a rotten shot. Looking back, one should have mounted another Lewis, not taking the only one away.'[37]

Any death stung, but in four weeks when over 700 airmen were killed — September was the RAF's worst month of the war — Caldwell had lost only a handful of men.

CHAPTER EIGHTEEN

Richthofen's Bed

By the evening of 1 October, the heart of the Hindenburg Line had been breached and the Germans were in full retreat. To the north, in Flanders, the Allied sector now ran from Dixmude to Staden and to the left bank of the Lys at Comines-Warneton. Large-scale ground operations were halted there to facilitate preparations for the final push in a fortnight's time. Caldwell marshalled his resources, but organising replacements for men recently struck down by illness, on leave or lost in battle was proving difficult. The first significant loss was that of the promising Rea 'Shorty' Hagenbuch, who displayed the ruddy 'keenness' Caldwell favoured and was liked by the other men. He and Garver particularly enjoyed each other's company.

On the last day of September, the pair had visited the badly damaged town of Poperinge. Garver noticed 'that every building had been hit directly or by flying pieces or they had been so shaken by the concussion that they barely stood'. At a local café, there was 'a great rejoicing at the lunch table when a telephone message came announcing the glad news that Bulgaria had laid down her arms. This has been a victorious week. Even I got in on it and cleaned up a few Huns. Bulgaria's collapse is the big beginning of Germany's end. Hurray!' But the day was 'one of extremes for my sorrow and my joy. But sorrow outweighs all, for my best friend, my pal, my comrade, my dear Shorty . . . failed to return from his morning patrol.'

He went down on an enemy balloon. I saw him diving on it with his usual daring and I would not want to have him lost in any other action. But I have not given up hopes of his loss because Capt. Roxburgh Smith saw him last, flying west towards our lines, I pray to God that he will return . . . I feel as if I am alone in the war. We had planned to fight together unto death for the cause. And I know of no one who can take his place. My hope is that he will yet return for, without him, life is indeed barren. We got up together, ate together, walked together and went to bed together. We were inseparable. I must cry. Tears for the loved. He was to me what few can ever be. I would have died for him. If he never returns, I will be stricken until the pangs of sorrow have been done away by struggle thru time.[1]

Within days it was revealed that Garver's prayers had been answered: Hagenbuch's life had been spared and he was a prisoner of war. But Toronto motor mechanic Albert Sanderson had been killed. By the second week of October, two more Tiger pilots, Frank Bond and William Bardgett, had also been captured.[2]

The high rate of casualties in September and preparations for the next major operation were leading to unacceptable complications in procuring pilots. As Caldwell informed van Ryneveld on 8 October, when collecting a new airman from the 'Pilot Pool' at St Omer, his men often found that they were 'not ready and packed' or 'not in camp'. On one occasion, despite phoning through well in advance, Caldwell's staff found that the bewildered lieutenant was unaware of his posting to 74 Squadron. It took two hours to resolve the problem and for the pilot to pack his kit.

Another two-hour delay occurred three weeks later when collecting a new officer, and, on the same day, another pilot could not be located and the tender was forced to return the following morning. Caldwell requested that the problem be brought to the attention of the officer in charge of the postings, 'in order to save time, trouble and petrol'.[3]

Paperwork was a never-ending curse. Leave for the squadron's regular soldiers in France now had to follow a regimented schedule of payments to ensure that daily living costs could be met. It was a sliding scale: accommodation in Paris at a hotel with breakfast and dinner was set at 12 francs, whereas a 'room only' at the picturesque

Keith Caldwell and Sydney Carlin in their officer finery. Both wear cuff link rank tunics; Caldwell with RFC badges and Carlin an 18th Royal Hussars cap and Royal Engineers collar, representing his previous service. Caldwell removed the stiffener from his cap to make it 'floppy', a style popular at the time.

fishing village of Trouville on the Normandy coast ran to a princely 40 francs and was therefore to be discouraged. Aerodromes, with their many men and machines, had to deal with accidents and when these involved combined RAF and army personnel, a joint court of inquiry would ascertain the facts, but it would not be under oath or 'express any opinion'. Caldwell also had to instruct his airmen that taking a batman with them when they attended a course in England would now be permitted only if they were attending the Senior Officers' School.[4]

A relative hiatus in operations and mounting administrative duties limited Caldwell's flying time. Between 25 September and 13 October, he added only 10 hours to his logbook, mostly flights to assess the state of the line and weather conditions.[5] Other flights were designed to bring recent postings up to speed. Newcomer Englishman Reginald Hobhouse was impressed with what he saw: 'Everybody was amazingly keen and the morale was as high as could be — it was like going back 4 years to the days of 1914.

'It was not difficult to see at once the reason. The personality of "Grid" Caldwell was outstanding and his desperate keenness coupled with the very efficient leadership of his flight commanders gave the whole squadron a superiority complex.'[6] One of the few flights undertaken by Caldwell in this period was with two recent arrivals, one of whom was Richmond Mayson.

> The CO was leading the way in his machine with red streamers flying, and we two were to follow him, flying about 30 yards behind, each a little to one side of him ... We first flew over Poperinge, a place where there was very little movement, its four churches showing up amongst all the other wreckage like haunted buildings. From here, we flew east to Ypres, keeping about 2,000 feet high and just on our side of the line. Ypres is a city of awful devastation. Its buildings are wrecked without exception, its streets are torn up, railways torn up and everything that can be destroyed has met that fate ... What makes it look more ghastly is the ground for miles in all directions being covered by millions of shell holes. The earth is terribly torn, hills blown away, leaving huge craters, every tree splintered and not a bit of green grass to relieve the monotony of miles of turned-up soil ... Every one of the millions of holes is filled with water ...

After turning north to Houthulst Forest, they flew back over Ypres, passing Zillebeke Lake on their left and Dickebusch Lake on the right, 'landmarks that have proved of great assistance to airmen in finding their way about this part of the country'.

Continuing south, they passed Kemmel Hill, 'a place of very much hard fighting', and Messines Ridge. Mayson was reminded of his service in these places when he was in the Canadian Expeditionary Force in 1915:

> Many buildings that I had known three years ago and which were all right are now nothing but a bundle of wrecked wood and bricks. Turning west, we fly to the Nieppe Forest — another favorable landmark of the airmen. Then towards Bailleul we point our machines and as we fly over it, I think again of 1915, when it was full of civilians, shops open and doing good business, many happy homes and not much to worry about. But now it is the worst wrecked city I've seen after Ypres. This is war; nothing but kill and destroy . . . As we land, some mechanics run out and guide our machines in. 'Have we seen any Huns?' they ask. No! We've just been having a look at the horrors caused by war.[7]

Then came welcome news for Caldwell: the squadron had been ordered to return to Clairmarais South on 3 October. Their arrival coincided with high winds and rain; on most days a handful of sorties could be flown but many were a complete washout. 'Rain all day and I passed it as I usually do,' recorded Garver on 11 October.

> Up at 7.30am and had a run . . . and said a prayer. Returning to my hut I shaved, washed and dressed, after which I partook of an enormous breakfast — porridge with cream and sugar, bacon and egg on fried bread, plenty of bread, marmalade and butter, with a couple of cups of hot coffee. Read papers a while. Then sighted my machine. Took a walk before lunch. The afternoon was spent writing letters. Then tea and after that a walk till dinner, which consisted of soup, fish, beef, potatoes, cauliflower, sugar, butter, and plenty of sauces. Collecting in the mess, two bunches played cards, another group sang, while the rest read and wrote letters. I read a few chapters of *Oliver Twist*. Now to write my diary, then get ready for bed. Will read a bit and pray before sleep. Such is a rainy day of an American pilot with the RAF in France in the war of nations 1918.[8]

There were widely touted rumours of German efforts to secure a negotiated peace and that Germany had asked the American president, Woodrow Wilson, for a conference at The Hague. Garver, writing on 7 October, was not convinced that the Allies were 'ready for peace terms unless the Huns will guarantee that the agreements will be kept only by disarmament. We cannot allow her to keep her army and navy . . . The agreement would be but a scrap of paper. Only by a league of nations with armament and means of enforcement can the future of a world peace be guaranteed. Anyway . . . the Hun is far from licked yet. More of this bloody business will have to proceed ere he realizes the folly of his barbarous ways.'[9] Garver's opinion and Caldwell's preparations were put to the test a few days later.

On 14 October, Belgian and British forces swept the enemy before them in a broad front stretching from Dixmude to Lys, offering a rich range of targets for 11 Wing's machines. The air was clear of clouds and the Luftstreitkräfte faced demanding odds. RAF machines ranged freely behind the fleeing horde, bombing and strafing rail lines and trains.[10] Caldwell's squadron was set a demanding schedule of sorties. Mayson was sent out on a 6.35 a.m. patrol to provide cover for other machines doing this arduous groundwork.

He was plagued by engine trouble and fell behind the formation. He concentrated on his two closest colleagues, attempting to keep them in view, but when they disappeared, 'to my surprise I saw two Huns diving towards me at a great speed. Before I noticed them, they had got within easy shooting distance. They got behind me too, the worst possible place I could have them.'

> I had to do something and do it very quickly. Almost before I had time to think, I gave a very quick turn and went down, engine full on, my speed well over 200 miles an hour . . . Often, I had planned what to do in a case like this, so I put my plan into execution. I dived down and under our other machines that were below . . . I expected these Huns to follow me. They did for a while, but then left me. They must have realized my intentions.

Mayson had only just returned to the formation behind the other machines when he saw, coming down vertically from above him, an enemy machine. 'He was the one that my two friends up above had dived on. He might have been wounded and fainted and come to later, or he may have done this to get away. However, he came down vertical for about 7,000 feet and then flattened out and flew east to his home.' Almost immediately, 10 more German aeroplanes appeared. 'A nice little scrap followed, but only one fell, to the credit of our Major. I couldn't even get a shot in this time.'[11] Caldwell's 'credit' was a Fokker DVII. At 18,000 feet, he had spotted the lone enemy biplane 3000 feet beneath him. He manoeuvred the SE5a to attack and fired 50 rounds as the enemy pilot banked the machine east to escape, but it was too late.[12]

In the day's second patrol, Caldwell's men dropped bombs on enemy positions in an uneventful operation, but the mid-afternoon patrol was very different. It had begun harmlessly enough, with a lone Fokker on the horizon, but as the SE5s swarmed in, the enemy pilot let off a red flare and seven more DVIIs arrived. As Mayson noted, 'the little trap they set for us was turned on themselves'.[13] The initial contact between the opposing sides was a limited skirmish over Menin, but Caldwell soon turned his machine and led his men directly into the enemy. 'I went straight at one taking fire for fire,' reported Garver. 'Smoke and fire appeared to issue from his machine. The yellow Hun sideslipped [away].'[14]

Two Fokkers now fell on him and he was unable to observe the result of his action. As the dogfight escalated, the Tigers got the better of the battle. Roxburgh-Smith bagged two and Caldwell's countryman Sydney Stidolph a single, with a further two driven down in the 20-minute mêlée.[15] Mayson noted later:

> During the day, we had done between five and six hours of flying, so by night we were dead tired, thoroughly worn out and ready for bed. This work is very nerve trying for the whole time you are up, your nerves are continually on edge. Looking for Huns and trying to avoid being surprised and, at the same time dodging 'Archie', I can now understand why an airman cannot last much more than 6 months out here.[16]

The squadron's successes were emulated by the rest of 11 Wing. Van Ryneveld's machines dropped over 1100 bombs and strafed with more than 1000 rounds retreating troops, confused columns of transport and railway junctions.[17]

The German position in Flanders was in tatters. Only the late autumn rain prevented the Allied forces from trapping the better part of the retreating German forces in the days that followed. As mist and rain stalled aerial operations, pilots spent time in the mess playing cards, writing letters and reading in front of the roaring fire — and celebrating Roxburgh-Smith's bar to his DFC. There was time, too, for tales of battles won and lost in the air over the past three years. As Garver recorded in his diary, 'Major K. L. Caldwell gave us an account of the death of Voss — the perfect pilot of the war and a German at that.'

This had the pilots sitting on the edge of their seats, but they were not impressed by 'One fellow [who] monopolized the time by telling how to attack and get away from Huns. He just came a few days ago. Such boobs or smart heads are quite familiar and very disgusting. They are intolerable. I've only been here a short time but I have enough sense to close my mouth and open my ears . . . I talk only when I'm doubtful on a flying subject or maneuver and corrected, thereby obtaining a viewpoint worth retaining,' Garver wrote in his diary.[18]

Then there were social visits to neighbouring units. 'Last night, Grid Caldwell blew in with his three flight commanders,' wrote a pilot in 'Mac' McGregor's squadron. 'Grid used to break up most of our furniture for us on guest night at 85 Squadron.'[19] Day trips and other evenings spent in Calais and St Omer were eventually interrupted by news that the squadron was to move back into Belgium. On 23 October, the squadron squeezed into George Robey's for one last knees-up, belatedly celebrating Caldwell's twenty-third birthday.

The following day, Caldwell led the Tigers to Mercke, a newly captured German aerodrome that had once been home to the Flying Circus. The new squadron office sat next to the twisted and ragged remnants of a crashed German aeroplane, and some of the walls and ceilings of the officers' quarters were pockmarked with bullet holes and punctured by bits of blackened shrapnel. In one building, a British shell had pierced a door and struck the floor at the base of the stairs and required urgent repair. 'Seems funny to occupy a Hun aerodrome which only a week ago harbored our adversaries,' wrote Garver.[20] The pilots were reminded of Mercke's proximity to enemy positions when German shells exploded around the aerodrome.

They were, though, as Wilfred Giles wrote, staying in a 'fine' local chateau, 'with plenty of furniture and . . . two grand pianos left behind by the Huns'.[21] Caldwell had the honour of sleeping in Richthofen's bed near Courtrai, so the caretakers told him. 'It was a nice big chateau, alongside the aerodrome, belonging to some Belgian count,' recalled Caldwell. 'From the accounts given by the Belgian caretakers, the young Hun pilots behaved just as we did. Held parties, were gay and carefree.'[22]

Lodgings secured, Caldwell set his men, including the officers, to mucking out the hangars, which were filled with straw and shells. Caution was needed as there

Welshman Ira Jones (seated) and the men of A Flight. An Edward 'Mick' Mannock protegé, 'Taffy' Jones ended the war with nearly 40 victories in aerial combat and went on to publish a series of books chronicling the exploits of himself, Mick Mannock, Keith Caldwell and the men of Tiger Squadron. New Zealander Freddy Gordon stands at far left. Caldwell married Freddy's sister, Dorothy, in 1923.

were reports of landmines catching the unwary elsewhere across the newly acquired territory. 'I was careful indeed,' noted Garver, but 'no "booby traps" were found'.[23] Caldwell's SE5s were soon occupying hangars that only days before had been full of Fokkers.

Caldwell and the men visited nearby Courtrai; the American pilots reckoned they were the first Yanks to do so. The Belgians were friendly and wanted buttons and insignia as souvenirs of their liberation. Girls welcomed the pilots with handfuls of sugar and the streets were festooned with flags. 'Down one avenue I saw men, women and children carrying away sacks and baskets of food,' said Garver. 'On inquiry I found the good Samaritans to be the America Belgium Relief Committee.'

The railway station showed extensive damage from raids 74 Squadron had made on it in August. The next day they visited Mercke, where the cathedral spire had had a great chunk bitten out of it by an Allied bomb, but the cemetery was an unstained peaceful oasis. 'English soldiers and Huns were buried side by side with the same markings and grass mounds. Arranged in tiers and surrounded by a brick wall with stone steps up the pathway and old trees with new ones here and there marked the resting place of our enemies' heroes with passive beauty for miles around.'[24]

The last days of the month were operationally demanding, with plenty of enemy targets on the ground and in the air, where the Luftstreitkräfte was working overtime to cover the departing German infantry. On 26 October, Caldwell ordered two offensive patrols. He instructed the ground crew to load the grids with bombs and the pilots to work a line confined to the Second Army front. They would be cooperating with the Sopwith Camels of 70 Squadron.[25] The early morning patrols often gave pilots a memorable perspective.

> Along the whole front of attack — which was about 20 miles — I saw a huge cloud of smoke, snowy white, as though it might have been a mist. It must have been two or three miles broad. This had been put forward to cover the attack of our troops. Nothing on the ground was to be seen but, here and there, the tops of trees showing above the smoke like many little islands scattered over a lake. From both sides of the smoke, one could see flashes of flame from the hundreds of guns hurling destruction to many. Shells could be seen exploding and a big black cloud would jump in the air. Though it was a pretty sight, it must have been ghastly down below. I was thankful I was not down amongst it.[26]

On the mid-afternoon patrol that day, the SE5s and Camels arrived over the battlefield near Cordes, Hainaut. Dixie Kiddie was leading the formation at 12,000 feet when he spied seven Fokkers west of the patrol. He and Frederick Hunt both scored a victory each and another two Fokkers were driven down out of control. For Caldwell, the real revelation was 25-year-old Bostonian and former Packard Motor Company employee Jules Ferrand. He dived on a single Fokker, hitting it with machine gun fire; it half-rolled and the propeller stopped — the engine was knocked out. The enemy then fell into a steep dive and Ferrand followed, firing in the descent, pulling up only 500 feet from the ground. The German machine broke the canopy of some trees before punching itself into a field.

Fifteen minutes later, the young American climbed westward when, at only 2000 feet, he was set upon by over half a dozen DVIIs. He had everything against him — height and surprise lay with the enemy — but he kept his nerve. 'I dived west firing into the EA about me,' he wrote in his after-action report. 'I saw the right upper wing of one EA crumple up, and the machine fell down. Another machine fell down completely out of control NE of Tournai.'[27] All of this was confirmed by other airmen and Caldwell happily signed off the paperwork. The squadron had five more victories but had lost a newcomer, Murdo MacLean.[28] The Scotsman was last seen in combat at 1500 feet over Cordes.

That evening, a farewell dinner was held for one of the squadron's popular flyers: John Garver was being transferred to an American squadron.

> They gave me the place of honor. After we had done justice to the repast, Capt. Glynn DFC rose and gave me a toast. Before I could reply, they all stood, sang 'For He's a Jolly Good Fellow' and toasted my good luck and happy landings. My reply was feeble — a terrible effort but under trying circumstances. Dinner and toasts over ... we played the piano and sang between numbers dancing like Chinamen and chorus girls yelling, singing, wrestling, with the gramophone going — the boys gave me a farewell such as I will never forget. Off to bed at about one, the Major, Kiddie and I had a talk after which I finished my packing and slept soundly in MacLean's bed. He did not return.[29]

The mystery of MacLean's fate was soon discovered: he had been captured, the fourth of Caldwell's pilots to become a POW that month.

The last days of October were incandescent with aerial combat, some of the heaviest of the war.

Mindful of the vulnerable bombing targets which the German retreat had opened to air attack, the German command concentrated its air fighting strength in a desperate attempt to prevent the British day bombers from reaching the more obvious objectives. The enemy fighters flew in large formations, sometimes fifty strong, and there were many bitter engagements . . . The German pilots, at great sacrifice, served their comrades on the ground well.[30]

To combat this, and support the Allied push, Caldwell's instructions for 27, 28 and 29 October were clear: the squadron would fly two full patrols each day.[31] During each of these operations, the maximum number of bombs would be directed at the German soldiers and then the fighters would range against the Fokkers. On the first day of fighting, Caldwell's men made five claims; on the second they accounted for a single balloon; and on the third, six enemy Fokkers.[32] It was a flurry of victories that gave the squadron a monthly total of 39 enemy machines. Caldwell's contribution to this total was secured on 28 October, when he flew a late-morning patrol.[33]

At 16,000 feet, north-east of Tournai, he surprised a black, white-tailed Fokker and let loose with the Vickers as he chased his enemy to 12,000 feet. Bullets raked the German machine, punching holes in the fuselage and wings. It was clear that Caldwell had also struck the pilot, because the machine lost all semblance of controlled flight and the BMW engine roared plaintively at full throttle all the way down before it was silenced.

Looking for more action, Caldwell located a formation of red-tailed enemy machines scrapping with Camels at lower altitude. They were from 70 Squadron, under the command of Londoner Gilbert Murlis Green. With service in three theatres — home defence, Salonika and the Western Front — he possessed one of the RAF's more eclectic resumés. His eight aerial victories included not only run-of-the-mill Albatros fighters, but also such exotica as the twin-engine Friedrichshafen G seaplane and a three-man Gotha GIV. The last victim was the first heavy bomber shot down at night over Britain. Caldwell closed in on the fight until it broke up at only 50 feet, the enemy fleeing east.

Caldwell pulled the SE5a into a climb, straining the Viper engine as he headed towards a German two-seater under assault by Murlis Green between Roubaix and Tourcoing.[34] A red and yellow flame was kindled in the pilot's cockpit. Caldwell sneaked in behind the smoking machine and fired, but got off only 10 rounds when the Vickers failed. Caldwell could see that the observer was dead, slumped down, hidden within the fuselage, his machine gun sticking uselessly up in the air. The pilot turned west to land in surrender behind the Allied lines, but, as soon as he realised Caldwell was powerless to intervene, retreated east. He barely cleared his own lines and was last seen gliding at a height of 10 feet, the propeller lazily turning over. Caldwell was unable to claim the stricken two-seater but the Fokker DVII entered his logbook as his final and twenty-sixth victory of the war.

On the evening of 30 October, Caldwell's men pounded the keys of the Chateau's twin pianos, and its parquet-floored halls were alive with rampaging pilots ready for a long night of carousing. But then came the sound of a pair of night bombers headed for the aerodrome: the Germans were attacking Mercke's runway and buildings. Floating flares cast a ghastly pall and the leafless trees made monstrous shadows as the chateau's bones trembled and the windows rattled to the kettledrum of bombs. 'They obviously knew the aerodrome well,' wrote recently returned Ira Jones.[35]

> Probably it had been their own temporary quarters. At any rate, their accuracy was uncanny. Two bombs fell on the hangars, completely destroying more than a dozen aircraft. Another landed on the transport section and wiped it out. A fourth dropped on some huts in which passing troops of the Middlesex Regiment were sheltering. There were about fifteen victims, most of them killed. The aerodrome itself was scored with craters. Fortunately, not a bomb fell on the chateau where the pilots were quartered; otherwise, the Tigers who had created so much havoc among the Huns would have been wiped out.[36]

The soldiers' deaths and the destruction of many machines were a whetstone to the squadron's sword. Replacement aeroplanes arrived more promptly than the personnel reinforcements earlier in the month, and Caldwell launched a withering patrol on 1 November. At 3.50 p.m. the squadron found a formation of six unfortunate Fokkers west of Audenarde. It was a slaughter: three German biplanes were destroyed, two in flames. One German managed to parachute out of his machine but was captured on the Allied side of the lines. Another Fokker was driven down out of control.[37] It was the squadron's last big show of the war.

With a damaged aerodrome and the possibility of further raids, Caldwell removed the squadron to Cuerne in West Flanders. All agreed that the billets were 'pretty rotten' and a poor substitute for Mercke's palatial chateau. Caldwell's days were filled with keeping the squadron active but avoiding any major mishap. In this task he was aided by the absence of the Luftstreitkräfte. The patrolling Tigers seldom met the enemy in the air as it relentlessly strafed ground targets. 'The retiring Hun army now almost broken and fighting a desperate rear-guard action,' said Jones.[38] Caldwell signed off his last combat report on the fourth day of the month: a Fokker dispatched by Dixie Kiddie.[39]

As the German front dissolved, the Ottoman Empire, then Austria-Hungary, joined the Bulgarians on the sidelines. When the French and Americans crossed the Scheldt river in three places on 3 November, the pilots realised the end was very near for the Germans.[40] On the days when bad weather curtailed operations, Caldwell got the officers playing football against the sergeants or sent them off to the local towns — Bruges was popular — or to see other squadrons. At Halluin, 41 Squadron proudly displayed a captured Fokker for the men to prod and clamber over.[41]

On 10 November, the weather was fine and Caldwell launched two deep patrols. They ranged 25 miles over the German lines 'without meeting opposition in the way of enemy aircraft,' as Wilfred Giles wrote in his diary. 'The air was absolutely swarming with British machines and at one time I counted sixty. No wonder there were no Hun machines about.'[42] Talk on the aerodrome was that the Kaiser was going to abdicate. Caldwell and some of his crew were breaking bread with Mick Mannock's old 85 Squadron at Escaufourt. After the appetizer, as Caldwell sat talking with Mac McGregor, an excited mechanic burst into the officers' mess. 'Oh Sir! News has just come through that they are signing the Armistice tomorrow, and there will be no more war.' His superiors pretended to throw a glass at the luckless ack-emma, shouting: 'Out of this, you blighter, and take your dismal news with you.'[43]

'Everyone went into a wild frenzy', wrote Giles.

> A wonderful fireworks display immediately took place, bells rang in neighbouring towns, factories hooted and the army trains whistled various tunes. On the aerodrome we started bonfires with petrol and paraffin and used up all our rockets. We got rid of 600 gallons of petrol. A wonderful night never to be forgotten. It is hard to believe that all the fighting is over.

The next day, heavy-headed airmen awoke to Caldwell ordering the grids out and announcing one last sortie: an early patrol with orders 'not to cross the lines on any pretext whatsoever'.[44] 'Still,' Jones recalled, 'we hoped that if there were any Huns in the air, they might be tempted to put up a final show by attacking us on our side of the line, but it was not to be.'[45] The Luftstreitkräfte had laid down its arms, destroying its fleet on the ground or piloting the remnants eastward. As Caldwell's men flew low over recently liberated villages, 'the inhabitants were all out in the streets waving Belgian flags to us and everywhere was a sense of excitement and joy.'[46]

W ith the war over, Caldwell's squadron was but one tiny unit in a massive war-making apparatus in the throes of dismantling itself. In 1914, the RFC had consisted of five squadrons with only 2000 personnel; by late 1918, it had swelled to some 150 squadrons with over 110,000 personnel. The shedding of nearly all these units and individuals was a monumental and often befuddling task. On 17 November, 74 Squadron was relocated south to Froidmont, a well-camouflaged former Gotha bomber aerodrome close to the Belgian frontier. The temperature dropped quickly as snow arrived, periodically forestalling sightseeing flights to banish the boredom. Caldwell searched for a chateau to replace their farmhouse billets but the great local houses proved too damaged. Rumours that they were destined to move up the Rhine to join the Army of Occupation proved false and on 30 November Caldwell led the men to Halluin, near Menin.[47]

The squadron was now part of 65 Wing, X Brigade. Two days later an order came through forbidding joy rides, except with the wing commander's permission, but Caldwell ignored it.[48] Keeping men accustomed to a heavy and lively work schedule out of mischief was difficult enough without denying them their principal source of enjoyment. The pilots were accustomed to visiting other squadrons in their SE5s and even flying to Clairmarais 'for butter and cream' when the occasion demanded it. He also lent his own staff car out to the men for jaunts to the theatre in Lille and Tourcoing.[49]

Caldwell was ordered to 'assume temporary command' of 65 Wing. He was overseeing five squadrons and the Wing headquarters' staff.[50] It was his highest, and briefest, posting. As winter settled in, Jones took over command of the Tigers and Caldwell went on 14 days' leave over Christmas. Upon his return on 29 December, he found Taffy and 24 men admitted to the hospital at Courtrai; influenza had once again descended upon the squadron.[51] And it was not only his men who were missing: a good deal of the squadron's equipment had been taken on the evening of Boxing Day. As Wilfred Giles recorded, 'my hangar was broken into and the watch taken out of my machine. Those Belgians!!! During the past few nights one complete motorcycle, four motor lorry lamps, two flying suits, petrol and fire extinguishers have been pinched . . . Motor cars are disappearing from all units, by the tens. Although hostilities have

ceased, some more ammunition will still be used one of these fine nights.'[52]

With little more than a skeleton crew on deck and decreasing amounts of materiel to oversee, Caldwell went to Brussels for a couple of days to see in the New Year, only to return and find two RAF touring cars missing and news that the squadron would be 'mobilised in the next fortnight'.[53] On Friday, 24 January 1919, pilots of 35 Squadron arrived to fly Caldwell's SE5s away. 'I felt awfully sorry to part with my old "bus", which served me so well in the latter stages of the war,' wrote Giles.[54] Within days, the men were reporting to the Pilot Pool at St Omer for postings to home duties or other squadrons. If Caldwell grieved the demise of his cherished Tigers, he had little opportunity to do so because he was given temporary command of 108 Squadron.[55]

The man best known for his fighter exploits had started the war with a two-man bomber reconnaissance unit and ended his career in France with a two-man Airco DH9 bomber squadron. It was a very short posting, from 10 January to 3 February 1919, which ended with Caldwell's departure from France with a newly awarded Belgian Croix de guerre sewn next to the ribbons for his MC and DFC and bar.[56]

His final weeks in the RAF were taken up with an assortment of duties, including a posting to the Central Flying School and then, in early April, to south-east London 'for disposal pending repatriation'.[57] During this period, Caldwell and others from the squadron periodically caught up with one other, including men who had been recently returned from German POW camps, such as Sydney Carlin, who was in the RAF hospital in Hampstead.[58] Among those awaiting their fate in London was Mac McGregor. Both he and Caldwell had expressed their desire to leave the RAF, the former citing the need to look after his father's farm and the latter to help in his father's business.

In the meantime, the pair established a base of operation with Caldwell's mother in a cottage at Shoreham, near Brighton. They bought two motorcycles to travel the countryside — immune to speeding tickets in their uniforms — and for trips further afield they 'borrowed' an Avro training aeroplane from the local school of instruction.[59]

As arrangements were concluded for the return to New Zealand, members of the squadron and old Wanganui Collegiate School schoolmates joined Caldwell's

Above: Keith Caldwell wrote 'At Shoreham after war' next to these images in a photograph album. In the immediate wake of the war, the seaside cottage in West Sussex became a gathering place for the 74 Squadron pilots and Wanganui Collegiate old boys. Caldwell is at right in his pyjamas, a newspaper across his knees.

Below: Keith Caldwell's mother, Mary Caldwell, and his sister, Vida Caldwell, stand behind guests and visitors at Shoreham.

family and Mac McGregor in walking the beach at Shoreham and frequenting the local drinking establishments. Caldwell's mother and sister travelled home before him. On 5 June 1919 he boarded the SS *Bremen*, taking with him a Nieuport propeller, his Sidcot suit, a German Spandau machine gun retrieved from a Fokker DVII and a gleaming solid silver model of an SE5a, presented to him by the men of his beloved 74 Squadron.

Keith Caldwell astride one of the motorcycles he and Malcolm McGregor purchased to explore southern England upon their return to the country at the end of the war.

CHAPTER NINETEEN

Tea for Two

An unscheduled stop in Sydney delayed Caldwell's arrival home in late 1919, but news of his imminent return had travelled. Newspapers ran lengthy articles under the headline 'Major Caldwell's Exploits' and dubbed him 'The New Zealand Ace'. His was a compelling tale of a local boy who had triumphed on the Western Front, and journalists detailed his decorations, the number of enemy machines he had shot down, his miraculous escape after colliding with 'Timbertoes' Carlin and his various aerial battles against 'overwhelming odds', including his tussle with Werner Voss.[1] It was generally an accurate appraisal of Caldwell's career, though the *New Zealand Herald*'s assertion that the German 'crack airman' Voss had been born in 'Australia' may have brought a wry smile to Caldwell's face.

Like many returned men, Caldwell had found the transition from war to peace difficult and he struggled to accustom himself to the staid and decidedly mundane life at home. As he confessed decades later, 'I had a terrible time settling down. I could not settle at all.'[2] Thrill-seeking and wild parties were not on the calendar of social activities in Cambridge, but at the family's Auckland home he met up with numerous other veterans to smoke, drink and tell tall tales of their exploits.[3]

After one lively evening of partying, Caldwell arrived at a golf tournament bleary-eyed and still wearing his formal dinner attire, and began to play. He was making a hash of it and the club was forced to phone David Caldwell to come to collect his son.[4]

Unlike others in his situation, Caldwell had caring and wealthy parents to help ease his entry into the post-war world. When the celebrated Caldwell finally appeared in Cambridge on 29 August, his stay was surprisingly short. In the third week of September 1919, after only three weeks in New Zealand, he was on the passenger ship RMS *Makura* with his father, bound for Vancouver. The four-month trip included a stopover in Hawai'i and accommodation in some of the best hotels on offer.

During the voyage, Caldwell and his father explored his prospects. Would he set his course with his father's business, revisit his brief pre-war foray into banking or explore other avenues? In the end, he chose farming. Like other returned airmen such as Freddy Gordon and Malcolm McGregor, he would 'assuage his unrest with hard work', far from the temptations of the big city.[5]

When the Caldwells returned home, Keith went to Northland to work on a farm owned by a well-known Dargaville family headed by Alfred and Nora Harding. There he thrived, acquiring the skills he would need for the decades that followed, while satisfying his appetite for speed by racing up and down Ninety Mile Beach in various cars and motorcycles and burning off excess energy in hard farm labouring and in the local rugby competition. In 1921, Caldwell played for North Wairoa, where his reputation from Wanganui Collegiate preceded him. 'The three-quarter-line is a good one, especially if the centre, Caldwell, is all the Northern Wairoa enthusiasts say he is,' reported the *Northern Advocate*.[6] Caldwell lived up to expectations in defence and attack, where he was a 'powerful asset to the side' in games against Kaipara and Whangārei. When required, too, he delivered after-match speeches in which he 'paid tribute to the sporting conditions, good refereeing and the clean way in which the match had been contested'.[7]

Caldwell caught the eye of the North Auckland Rugby Union's selectors and was chosen for the representative team to play an international match against New South Wales at Whangārei in August.[8] It was an important and much-anticipated event for the region and a new grandstand was constructed at Kensington Park ahead of the game; the mayor declared the afternoon of the game a holiday and the local shops and businesses shut their doors.

> This was the first time in rugby history that the Northland men had appeared as a province against any opponents of note, and also marked the first entry of any big sporting combination to the portals of the North at Whangarei. Consequently, enthusiasm throughout the whole of the province was great, and from the remotest recesses the population made connection with

Whangarei by road, rail and water to swell the attendance at Kensington Park, where the game was played, to a crowd of something like four thousand people, anxious that the stranger within their gates should be taken in and done for handsomely. The Northland officials and population overwhelmed the visitors with hospitality, as they later hoped to overwhelm them on the field.[9]

The game was a thriller, the maroon-clad North Auckland team holding the Waratahs to 17–8 at full time. It was a good result against a side containing 11 players who had only recently starred against the Springboks, and Caldwell was praised for his line kicking.[10]

After the war, Caldwell had followed the government's lacklustre advancement of military aviation. In the autumn of 1919, Lieutenant Colonel Arthur Vere Bettington from the British Air Ministry had arrived in New Zealand to assess the dominion's future air force needs. He saw an expansionist and rapidly industrialising Japan as the British Empire's greatest threat in the Pacific, and the League of Nations as too thin a reed on which to rely in the event of international conflict.[11] New Zealand was vulnerable to attack from aeroplanes launched from aircraft carriers, which had been used for the first time during the war. To thwart this threat and play its part in a widely advanced empire-wide aerial defence system, Bettington proposed the establishment of an independent air force, employing distinguished pilots like Caldwell and surplus military machines on offer from the British government.[12]

It was an expansive and expensive four-squadron plan that failed in the face of naval and army opposition and fiscal realities. As a sop to aviation enthusiasts, the government established an aviation board which, in 1921, recommended the creation of a skeleton air force that could be expanded in times of war, but this was rejected.

Instead, the government opted to encourage civilian aviation, which could, if necessary, be converted to military purposes, and subsidised refresher courses for the pilots at the New Zealand Flying School, still based at Kohimarama, and Henry Wigram's Canterbury Aviation Company, based near Christchurch. Most of the

Above: Keith Caldwell, third from left, with teammates after an Old Boys vs School XV rugby match held during Easter 1920 at Wanganui Collegiate School.

Below: A group of pilots from the first refresher course in front of a Bristol F2b Fighter. From left: Freddy Gordon, Malcolm McGregor, Maurice Sinclair, Keith Caldwell and John Seabrook.

33 machines — 20 Avro 504s, nine DH9s, two DH4s, and two Bristol Fighters — accepted from Britain were dispersed to private interests that hoped to use them for mail services and other commercial endeavours.

In the end, the flying schools' activities proved uneconomical: the government paid out the Walsh brothers for their wartime efforts and bought Wigram's operation.[13] His old Sockburn aerodrome was renamed after him in honour of his aviation efforts. It was a sad day for Caldwell when the Kohimarama school piled up its machines on an Auckland beach and set them alight. The bonfire, however, forced the government's hand and it finally moved to establish a fledgling air force.

The new organisation comprised a full-time New Zealand Permanent Air Force (PAF) and the part-time volunteer New Zealand Air Force (NZAF). The PAF was minuscule, with only four officers and seven other ranks. When Geoffrey Ellis, who had 10 years of experience in the British air service, enquired about entering the PAF at his old RAF rank of corporal, he was shocked to be told that the present establishment of seven corporals was filled and that it 'would take an act of parliament to get an increase'.[14]

> Seven corporals indeed, it was staggering to think that there could only be seven corporals in a whole Air Force and I began to wonder what this Air Force amounted to . . . it gradually dawned on me that the total New Zealand Air Force was not as large as one of the many squadrons in the RAF and I could well believe that seven corporals would be sufficient. They also told me that there were no quarters. Everyone lived at home. There was only accommodation for the Territorial pilots when they came in for their courses. In answer to a further query they said 'No, they did not have uniforms.'[15]

The NZAF involved some 100 volunteers, and Major Keith Caldwell was appointed its commanding officer in June 1923.[16] His main activities centred on annual Wigram refresher courses designed to preserve skills acquired during the war. For the few staff on site, the arrival of detachments of pilots provided welcome excitement.[17] Joining Caldwell and his close associates McGregor, Freddy Gordon and Donald Inglis were a number of airmen who had served in the war, including bomber pilot and ace Euan Dickson, reconnaissance and bomber pilot Leonard Isitt and fighter aces Ronald Bannerman and Herbert Drewitt. Notable among the civilians was George Bolt, one of the nation's pioneering aviation engineers at Kohimarama and a pilot who had established a string of New Zealand flying records.

The aeroplanes used on these early courses at Wigram included the British Avro
504s, DH4s and Bristol Fighters.[18] Dressed in civvies, the airmen flew this modest
collection of machines and spent a good deal of time drinking and reminiscing
about wartime exploits. In the years that followed, newer machines arrived and
the government established a land and seaplane base at Hobsonville, on the north-
western reaches of Auckland's Waitematā Harbour, but the number of attendees
declined precipitously as the cost of travel to Wigram and the time away from work
proved too much for many territorials.[19] To overcome this impediment, Caldwell
supported a more regional solution. In 1922, he and a group of prominent individuals,
which included the governor-general, the prime minister and the mayor of Auckland,
advocated for the establishment of an Auckland flying club. Among its objectives, the
New Zealand Herald explained, was 'the provision of refresher courses for qualified
service pilots and the initiating and training of suitable aspirants in all branches of
aviation'.

It would also place 'at the immediate call of the Government, in case of dominion
or Empire need, a complete and efficient aerial unit', also capable of 'transporting
Ministers or members of Parliament, and authorised officials in emergency, and
mails and valuable freights'. Overseas visitors could be taken 'to main points of
interest', and the public educated 'in aeronautics by means of lectures and practical
demonstrations'. It was prepared, too, 'to carry out aerial training in all its branches
in conjunction with the New Zealand Navy and local defence bodies, and to carry
out sight and photographic surveys for Government departments, photographing
of health and tourist resorts and centres of general interest for publication, and
aeronautical meteorological research'.[20]

Progress, however, was slow, as the committee sought a royal charter for affiliation
to the much larger Air League of Great Britain and considered where the club would
be based and what aeroplanes to acquire. It was another six years before Caldwell
was elected a founding member of the Auckland Aero Club and in the intervening
time his life and priorities changed dramatically. The catalyst for this was his former
squadron member and friend Freddy Gordon.

The Caldwell and Gordon families shared Scottish origins and breathed the same
rarefied air enjoyed by Auckland's business and professional elites. When Freddy
Gordon returned from the war, his father, one of the country's leading surgeons,
invited Caldwell to the family's Hillsborough home so the young men could elaborate

on their wartime experiences. There Keith Caldwell's eye fell on Freddy's attractive sister, Dorothy, who had recently come to the attention of flirtatious royalty.[21]

In April 1920, King George V's son, the youthful and suave Edward, Prince of Wales, arrived in New Zealand to thank the dominion for its contribution to the war effort. Seething masses of New Zealanders turned out to see the 'playboy' prince and his extravagant 'royal yacht', the battleship HMS *Renown*. In Auckland Governor-General Lord Liverpool and his wife held a ball for the royal visitor and a 'happy few' guests at Government House.[22] After fulfilling his dancing duties with the Countess of Liverpool, the prince turned to the young socialites who had been invited, and his first choice was Dorothy Gordon.

The brown-haired beauty with the 'lively eyes' was less than enthusiastic: she leant in to her father and asked, 'Do I have to dance with him?'[23] When told she did, she found herself in Prince Edward's arms, waltzing to the music of the *Renown*'s liveried band.[24] When Caldwell saw photographs of the event, Freddy Gordon elbowed him, saying, 'If you don't make a move now, someone else will snap her up.'[25]

On 15 May 1923, after a year-long engagement, 27-year-old Keith Caldwell married 22-year-old Dorothy Gordon at Remuera's St Mark's church, which had been 'tastefully decorated for the occasion by girlfriends of the bride'.[26] The marriage of course made the social pages of the *Auckland Star*, which described Gordon's 'charming simple bridal gown of cream satin made in the longer newer mode, and with a train from the shoulder of the same material, lined with georgette. A tulle veil and a wreath of orange blossoms completed a charming ensemble. A bouquet of pale cream chrysanthemums was carried by the bride.'[27] The couple was a study in contrasts — Keith the larger-than-life, gregarious, party-loving, charismatic, outspoken force of nature and Dorothy the petite, shy, unpretentious, quietly spoken rock of stability. It was a match that lasted a lifetime.

David's wedding present to the young couple was an 1800-acre dry stock farm at Glen Murray in northern Waikato. Its tortured ridges, steep hills and serpentine gullies were nothing like flat and fertile Cambridge. Much of the property, which also had swampy lowlands, was overgrown with mānuka, 6-foot-tall bracken and small islands of native bush populated with the attractive broadleaf tree after which the farm was named: Tawa.[28] It was demanding country. In winter the pasture soaked up water, and mud sent vehicles slithering sideways into ditches and sucked off

Keith Caldwell and his fiancée, Dorothy Gordon, share a hammock at Wenderholm Regional Park, north of Auckland.

gumboots, and in summer the green hills became brown and parched. There were no pumps capable of drawing water from the local Opuatia Stream and no wells, so to water stock the farm depended on rainwater captured and stored behind small dams that dotted the property.

Drawing on his time in Dargaville, Caldwell brought in hard-working Dalmatian labourers to dig a long drainage trench and added a number of stock-watering troughs. These improvements were only partly successful and the farm remained vulnerable to periodic droughts. Moreover, as with much New Zealand hill country, its fertility was fragile and rapidly depleted. Aerial topdressing was decades away and Caldwell and his seasonal workers delivered handfuls of phosphate to the soil from heavy shoulder-borne sacks.[29] In their early years on the farm, Dorothy, back at the large, rambling weatherboard homestead, was able to approximate her husband's location by the tendrils of smoke rising from newly burnt-off land.

The isolated property lacked electricity or a telephone, and when the rudimentary unsealed gravel tracks were waterlogged and impassable, access to Auckland was only possible via a steamer across the Waikato River from Glen Murray landing to Mercer, followed by a lengthy train journey.[30] Supplies came in and produce left the farm on shallow-bottomed boats navigating the Opuatia Stream and Waikato River. Daylight hours were spent in heavy work on the farm and the evenings together under candlelight, where Dorothy taught her husband to knit. The couple had four children: Mary, born in 1924, Peter in 1925, David in 1928 and Virginia in 1933. All but one were born in Auckland under the care of Dorothy's father.

David came early, while the rivers were in flood. Caldwell found Dorothy in labour and, to his dismay, discovered the child was breech. Using all his animal husbandry skills, he turned the baby, only for him to be born not breathing. Gently he wrapped his stillborn son in a blanket, then turned his attention to Dorothy, who was bleeding heavily.[31] Then two-year-old Peter, brandishing a candle, set fire to the nursery curtains. As flames raced up the fabric, Caldwell was torn between his young arsonist's efforts and his wife's perilous condition. Outdoing his feats on the Western Front, he extinguished the fire and saved Dorothy. Miraculously, in the chaos, David 'sparked to life' and cried out. Dorothy later said she was pleased her husband had 'lambed a few times'.[32] The fireman-cum-midwife went straight back out onto the farm, leaving Dorothy with their baby and the aroma of acrid smoke clinging to the house.

Above: **The newly married couple at St Mark's church, Auckland.**

Below: **The Glen Murray farm homestead.**

Caldwell's most prolonged test came with the Great Depression. The nation's exports plummeted by 45 per cent, its income by 40 per cent. Meat prices fell and wool dropped to nearly a third of its pre-Depression value. Farmers stopped spending; jobs and wages were slashed. The government scrambled to implement public works schemes that would soak up the surging numbers of unemployed people queuing at soup kitchens in the cities and tramping the rural roads.

At Glen Murray, the farm's modest returns were slashed and the bank account emptied. Daily meals became plainer and wholly dependent on the farm-killed meat and Dorothy's tireless work in the vegetable garden, which she watered with preciously conserved bathwater. She kept the children clean with homemade soap, baked her own bread, separated cream and salted mutton to keep it fresh.[33] Such was the beggarly state of the coffers that, for one Christmas, Mary received a solitary hair ribbon.

To make matters worse, Caldwell had been kicked by one of the farm's horses. The resulting injury was never fully rectified.[34] He found himself short-tempered with his family. Werner Voss had been an enemy he understood and was equipped to fight, but the daily economic and emotional crises of the Great Depression were an altogether different adversary. When Caldwell's curt words struck home the children would retreat to their rooms and Dorothy would stand by the living room window alone, looking out over the farm, weathering the storm.[35]

David Caldwell had retired in 1925, well before the Wall Street crash, and was considerably better off than most, yet he offered his son and daughter-in-law little in the way of financial assistance.[36] Instead he dispatched missives from his annual Queensland holidays that instructed his son to take belt-tightening measures, unaware that, at Tawa, Keith and Dorothy had already lost their belts. Even so, while many others, including Freddy Gordon and Malcolm McGregor, were forced to surrender their farms, the Caldwells survived.

Caldwell raised his children as he had been raised, with conservative values and strict rules that were augmented, later, by boarding school educations at Wanganui Collegiate School for the boys and Woodford House in Havelock North for the girls. Like his father, Keith could be impatient with his children but he also gave them lives filled with good memories, many of which were formed at Glen Murray and during holidays at his father-in-law's beachside property at Ōrere Point on the Firth of Thames. At Tawa, Mary recalled, 'we used to go exploring, tree climbing, bird nesting,

Three generations of Caldwells. At back, Keith Caldwell's parents, David and Mary Caldwell. Sitting, from left: Dorothy, holding Peter, Caldwell, holding Mary, and Caldwell's sister, Vida. The child at the front is not known.

riding and picnicking. After we got home from school, we did various jobs such as rounding up stock, feeding animals, collecting kindling wood and often caring for new lambs.'

While riding to and from school, the children loved to throw themselves off their ponies onto the soft, dense bracken. Social gatherings for singalongs around the piano at duck shooting time, various church events and fancy dress parties in woolsheds were all part of the local farming community calendar.[37] At Ōrere Point, during the long summer holidays, the children roamed among the red-flowering pōhutukawa and learnt to swim in the sheltered waters. In the evening, Keith would put a record on the gramophone, take Dorothy in his arms and they would dance in the light of flickering candles to 'Tea for Two'.

By the mid-1930s, the New Zealand economy was in recovery. Tawa benefitted from the First Labour Government's spending and reforms, plus a revived international market for meat and wool. As the farm's prosperity improved, it became a local centre for equestrian events. A rough polo field was laid out, and at the 1935 Glen Murray sports day there were prizes for 'tilting the ring', 'maiden hunter', 'novelty gallop', 'snatching the handkerchief' and a 'polo pony test'.[38] It became an annual event. In January 1937, an advertisement in the *New Zealand Herald* promised, along with 'hunting and novelty mounted events', a programme that featured a 'motor event, obstacle race on foot, ladies' nail-driving, chainstepping, sheep-guessing, children's races and ladies' race'. An evening dance at the Opuatia hall closed off the day's festivities.[39]

Though a competent horseman, Caldwell did not ride competitively, and now in his forties, he had handed in his rugby boots. But he was still a force to be reckoned with on the golf course. A skilled amateur, he held the record at the local Onewhero Golf Club, always figured prominently in the leader boards at Cambridge, and picked up several regional trophies.[40]

And he still cut a dashing figure on New Zealand's growing civil aviation scene. He had donated the Caldwell Trophy to the Auckland Aero Club for an annual aerobatic contest and was often called upon to judge various air pageants.[41] On occasion, at popular air shows up and down the country, Caldwell took to the sky. The 1933 North Island pageant at Māngere aerodrome involved 20 machines and was witnessed by a crowd of some 3500. There were flyovers by two air force machines from Hobsonville — a Cutty Sark flying boat and a Fairy IID seaplane — and the great aviator Charles

Kingsford Smith in his *Southern Cross* swooped over en route to Ninety Mile Beach and then Australia.

There were parachute tricks from only 1000 feet, in which daredevils somersaulted before pulling the ripcord and landing right in front of the hangar, and stunt flying by a yellow de Havilland Moth that included hedge-hopping and aerobatics. Caldwell led three Moths in what the *New Zealand Herald* called a 'suburb display of formation-flying'.

> Assembling at 2000 ft., the pilots started off with a Prince of Wales' feather, the leader looping and the outside pilots making right and left-hand climbing turns respectively. Flying back over the field in close arrowhead formation, they then took up a line-abreast position, with very little distance between the wingtips. After a spectacular dive and 'zoom' over the clubhouse, the pilots finished by landing in arrowhead formation.[42]

The bombing demonstration was a crowd favourite. Caldwell led a trio of machines in diving on men carrying umbrellas and pelting them with bags of flour. The crowd was caught between cheering the attackers on and sympathising with the cowering targets. Caldwell and his charges were 'deadly' accurate.

The most spectacular event of the day was a 'Thrilling Air Duel' between Caldwell, flying a Hawker Tomtit, and Flight Lieutenant David Allan, chief instructor of the Auckland Aero Club, in an orange and yellow Moth.

> The two pilots commenced the battle about 3000ft. above the heads of the spectators. After a few preliminary manoeuvres, they started to circle closer, each trying to gain a vulnerable position behind the tail of the other machine. With the more powerful aeroplane, Wing-Commander Caldwell was then able, not without difficulty, to place his opponent at a disadvantage. In the 'dog-fight' that followed, Flight-Lieutenant Allan was gradually forced lower, until the appearance of a dense stream of smoke, which was greeted by cries of astonishment at its realistic effect, indicated that he had been 'shot down in flames.'[43]

In addition to his work with the territorial air force and promoting aviation at air shows, Caldwell was head-hunted as a 'consulting specialist' for Dominion Airways Limited, the primogenitor of Tasman Empire Airways Limited (TEAL) and ultimately Air New Zealand. General prosperity and advances in aircraft technology had facilitated the establishment of New Zealand's first major airline company, which operated four de Havilland DH86 Express Airliners and seven Lockheed Model 10A Electras. The airline's service manager was McGregor, who, after surrendering his farm at Taupiri, Waikato, and spending some of the Depression as a drover, had risen to fame in barnstorming exhibitions, record-breaking flights and establishing regular air services between Christchurch and Dunedin.[44]

As well as looking forward to aviation's future in New Zealand, Caldwell remembered the exploits and sacrifices of the past with a reunion in 1935.[45] At this first gathering of wartime airmen, 'serious speech-making was not the order of the evening'. As Caldwell said, 'the object . . . is more to recapture some of the lighter spirit of the war days and good comradeship which they evoked'.[46] The dinner included a selection of First World War-themed drinks and dishes: 'Cocktails Guynemer', 'Canapes Ball', 'Roast Chicken Voss', 'Peaches Mannock' and 'Cheese Biscuits Richthofen'.[47] Many of the 30 attendees congratulated Caldwell on his recent King's Silver Medal for 'persons in the Crown services and prominent citizens throughout the Empire'.[48]

Others noted his recent pilot's A Licence, a concession to the increasingly regulated flying requirements, even for those with Caldwell's considerable experience and status. The photograph of the event in the *Herald* showed black-tie-clad former RFC, RNAS, AFC and RAF airmen whose waistlines had grown over the years as their hair had thinned. It was agreed that there should be an annual reunion.

Those who had not survived were never forgotten. In proposing a toast to absent friends, Caldwell said that 'all flying men had lost many highly cherished friends during the war. We have carried on in a hard-boiled way since the war, but we still remember those stout fellows who have gone. We all realise their great loss.'[49] The following year, at the reunion in July, it was very personal for Caldwell, when he had to offer a word and toast for Mac McGregor.[50] The pilot he had befriended in France and who had made a significant impact on dominion aviation in the post-war era had been killed on 20 February in a crash at Wellington's Rongotai aerodrome. Caldwell had helped to raise funds to provide for the education of McGregor's four young children and had been a pallbearer at the funeral.[51] In a moving tribute to one of the nation's leading aviators, 'a Union Airways air-liner, flying low so that all her gleaming paint-work was visible against the dark background of the storm clouds, dipped her wing in salute.'[52]

Caldwell's wartime exploits were revived in the public imagination in the 1930s in two books by the irrepressible Ira 'Taffy' Jones. In his 1934 biography of Mick Mannock, *King of Air Fighters*, 'Grid' stood front and centre with the VC winner and the author's own barnstorming efforts.[53] The book was a success in Britain and the Commonwealth. A friend in Britain sent Caldwell a double-page spread from the *News of the World*, which ran extracts flanked by two images of Caldwell: one of him standing in front of his SE5a and another of him leaning out of the aircraft after his collision with Sydney Carlin.[54] Never shy in its coverage, and under the large headline 'Marshal Ney of the Air', *N.Z. Truth* declared the book a 'striking tribute to [a] Great New Zealander'.

A handsome headshot of Caldwell stared out at readers as the newspaper elaborated on the success of the unit under Caldwell's leadership and recounted his miraculous escape after his mid-air collision with 'Timbertoes' Carlin.[55] Caldwell's daring leap from his doomed SE5a was repeated in Jones's *An Air Fighter's Scrapbook* (1938), which revisited the war and also considered the author's involvement in the Russian civil war and the story of post-war aviation.[56] Caldwell had mixed views about the publications: on the one hand he appreciated Mannock getting his due, but on the other hand he was cautious, not only because of his own reluctance to talk about his achievements, but also because Taffy was inclined to exaggerate.

These various successes were not replicated when it came to Wing Commander Caldwell's involvement in the air force. He oversaw a reconfigured territorial organisation nominally consisting of four squadrons. The First World War pilots and growing numbers of aero club members were 'expected to do a fortnight's refresher course each year at Wigram or Hobsonville and undertake an additional six hours' flying during the course of the year'. Frustratingly, the programme relied wholly on the poorly funded PAF for machines and ground staff.

It was little more than a 'paper air force', in which socialising outweighed flying time.[57] The casual nature of the 1930s refresher courses was captured by one attendee at a 'bombing' exercise at Lake Ellesmere, who observed the unloading of the lunch hampers and learnt that there was a keg of beer for the mechanics 'in the usual place under the haystack'.

> In due course the Squadron pilots arrived in the Wigram [Bristol F2b Fighters] which were [then] lined up for arming. Bombing was first on the list and the armorer . . . got busy clipping the 8½ lb stannic chloride bombs to the racks. As these exploded, a white plume of chloride was emitted and was used to indicate the position of the bomb on impact in relation to the target . . . I was amazed

how few bombs got near the target. But no one seemed concerned . . . This was warm work and Sam's keg was very popular. The bombing was all over by lunch time, with the target still intact, and we tucked into the hamper . . .[58]

None of this was a problem for Caldwell, who enjoyed the relaxed atmosphere of the refreshers, but, in 1937, as he settled into his middle years and with a demanding farm to attend to, he decided it was time to step aside. His departure was regretted.

His magnificent war record, and the personal qualities which enabled him to organise and lead one of the most famous fighting squadrons on the Western Front, place him amongst the great wartime leaders in aerial combat. His retirement is a heavy loss to the Service, but although he will no longer take an active part in the Territorial Air Force, his presence in New Zealand will remain a fine example to all those who are now undergoing training, and who may one day be faced with the difficulties which he so successfully overcame.[59]

But German nationalism and expansionism were once again evident in Europe, and a newly industrialised, militaristic and empire-seeking Japan was raising alarms in the Pacific region. Caldwell's retirement would be short-lived.

CHAPTER TWENTY

Mutiny

I n the wake of the German invasion of Poland on 1 September 1938, Britain's declaration of war pulled its allies into another European conflict, and Keith Caldwell answered the call to arms. The interwar territorial air force had been starved of support and machines, but the threat posed by Germany and Japan in the 1930s had led to a modest expansion of the PAF, and in 1937 it was established as an independent service and renamed the Royal New Zealand Air Force (RNZAF). Caldwell was welcomed back into uniform to play a significant role in funnelling New Zealanders into the RAF as part of the Empire Air Training Scheme (EATS) and enlarging the RNZAF's own operational capacity domestically and in the Pacific. His return to military life coincided with two significant personal events: the purchase of a new farm and the death of his father.

With their three eldest children in boarding school and the Glen Murray farm testing their endurance, Keith and Dorothy decided to move closer to Auckland. The 84-acre Puhinui Road property in Papatoetoe, named Forres, was substantially smaller, flatter and more fertile than Tawa.[1] The agricultural boom that followed the Depression allowed the Caldwells to buy the new property in late 1939 without having to sell Glen Murray, and when Caldwell was appointed to the RNZAF, he installed farm managers at both Glen Murray and Papatoetoe.

On 1 December that year, his elderly father died. It was a significant loss, which

Keith felt keenly. Although a strict and demanding father, David had equipped his son with a good education, paid for his entry into the Auckland flying school, funded a generous lifestyle for him in the RFC and RAF and made possible his post-war farming career. The wider community acknowledged the senior Caldwell's business acumen, the *New Zealand Herald* stating that his 'business activities are written deeply into the history of Auckland and the dominion as a whole'.[2]

Numerous charities were benefactors of his considerable estate. Over £7000 was shared by 16 organisations, including the Salvation Army, the New Zealand Institute for the Blind, the Knox Home for Incurables and orphanages run by the Presbyterian church in Auckland.[3] The greater part of the estate, valued at close to £95,000, less a hefty estate tax, went to Mary. Upon her death, a third of this would come to Keith and two-thirds to Vida, now married and living in Fiji.

Three months into the Second World War, Wing Commander Caldwell arrived in Blenheim, with Dorothy and their younger daughter, Virginia, to take command of No. 2 Flying Training School, RNZAF Station Woodbourne. It was an ideal posting. Caldwell, of course, had considerable experience in managing large numbers of officers and other ranks, and it was a logical progression from his interwar territorial command. The only niggling doubts lay with his health.

Both the war and Glen Murray had taken their toll on his body. Now aged 44, and due to stiffness in his hips, periodic sciatic pain down his right leg and bouts of dyspepsia, he routinely slept lightly and was easily disturbed.[4] Generally he remained active, playing golf and the odd game of squash or rugby, but he was prone to sporadic bouts of ill-health.

At the newly established base — the first batch of some 30 students noted the smell of fresh paint and polished floors — it was Caldwell's job to guide the men through their intermediate and advanced training.[5] He and chief instructor Squadron Leader Barry Nicholl oversaw lessons on the school's Vickers Vildebeest and Vincent biplane bombers and the modern single-engine North American Harvard monoplanes. These machines were larger and more robust than the diminutive Moths the pupils had flown in elementary training.

When not in the air, the men occupied newly installed classrooms to study the 'theoretical side of air navigation, bombing and air gunnery, meteorology, airmanship and air photography; in addition, they were taught something of the organisation and administration of the Air Force to . . . prepare them for their forthcoming role as non-commissioned officers and maybe officers'. Advanced training covered a two-month period and was devoted exclusively to flying.

Caldwell and Nicholl paired the students up for long navigation flights in which they alternated pilot and navigator roles. Fundamental skills were learnt and practised, including how to determine the speed and direction of the wind, undertake aerial photography, use the camera gun and carry out 'instrument only flying' with 'no sight of land, sea or sky'. Caldwell and his staff initiated men into the demands of formation flying, the large Vildebeests casting long shadows over the Wairau Plains.

They spent the final month at armament practice camp, 'going every day to the bombing and air firing range at nearby Lake Grassmere [where] they practised the exacting tasks of bombing, both "low-level" from a few hundred feet and "high-level" from several thousands of feet'. They also tested themselves on the machine gun.[6] In recognition of his efforts, Caldwell was bumped up in rank to group captain in April 1942 and in June was given command of the much larger RNZAF Station Wigram, Christchurch, a position he would hold for the next 17 months.

Caldwell's appointment at Wigram coincided with an extensive reorganisation of the RNZAF. It had to fulfil its quota of aircrew for the war in Europe via EATS, but it also needed to turn itself into a fully operational force at home and for duties in the Pacific. The 7 December 1941 Japanese attack on Pearl Harbor, and the expansion of the Japanese Empire into Southeast Asia and the western Pacific, highlighted New Zealand's vulnerability — the possibility of an invasion could not be entirely ruled out. In response, New Zealand accelerated its efforts to bolster its nation's aerial defences, and the Allies established a defensive 'chain of island bases, stretching from Northern Australia through New Caledonia, the New Hebrides, Fiji and Tonga to Samoa'. Once the Japanese advance was checked, these islands could act as supply and personnel hubs for launching counter-operations with the Australians and Americans against the enemy.

In general, the North Island stations were given over to operational squadrons and accommodation for the expected influx of American forces for subsequent Pacific offensives, while the South Island stations concentrated on training.[7] With over 2500 personnel at its height, including some 300 in the Woman's Auxiliary Air Force (WAAF), Wigram, with its four wings — headquarters, flying, maintenance and wireless — was the largest of the southern stations by a good margin.[8] By the time Caldwell appeared, a good deal of the building expansion was complete and he found

a much bigger establishment than he had known before the war.

More land had been acquired and workshop accommodation had increased by 70 per cent and storage facilities by 30 per cent.[9] The old wooden buildings and hangars were overshadowed by much larger concrete edifices as, in addition to an ever-expanding airstrip and accommodation blocks, the station now boasted a bomb construction hut, a radio mechanics' workshop, electrical and wireless school buildings and a rifle range. There was an exponential increase in ground staff: fire crew, butchers, cooks, coppersmiths and fabric and metal workers.[10]

Wigram's primary purpose, during Caldwell's tenure, was wireless and radar training and multi-engine flight instruction, predominantly on Airspeed Oxfords. Large numbers of electricians, radar operators and radio mechanics, wireless operators and wireless mechanics, and multi-engine pilots acquired their 'sparks' and 'wings' badges at Wigram before heading to Europe and the Pacific. Most of those arriving in Britain became aircrew in Bomber Command's large four-engine aircraft — Short Stirlings, Handley Page Halifaxes or Avro Lancasters — attacking German cities by night.[11] Smaller numbers were slotted into Coastal Command's very- long-range aircraft — Consolidated B-24 Liberators — protecting Allied convoys from the German Kriegsmarine (navy) U-boats. Even fewer airmen operated high-flying twin-engine machines — de Havilland Mosquitos — in reconnaissance and pathfinding operations.

Those ushered into the Pacific flew twin-engine Catalina flying boats and Lockheed Hudsons and Venturas. In Europe, most New Zealanders were allocated to mixed RAF squadrons containing men from all parts of the Commonwealth, but a small portion served in six so-called 'New Zealand Squadrons', with aircrew who were almost exclusively Kiwis.[12] In the Pacific, the RNZAF squadrons were composed entirely of New Zealand air and ground crew.

Caldwell's house at Wigram — with its large drawing room, spacious dining room, four bedrooms and a maid — was appropriate for entertaining dignitaries and blessed with grounds and flower beds that suited Dorothy's love of gardening. Like all of the properties in Sockburn, it was exposed to Canterbury's raging nor'westers — the original plantings around the house were uprooted and scattered by these winds. The nearby freezing works, abattoirs and fertiliser factory periodically produced clouds of flies that in summer were only just held at bay by screen doors.[13] Caldwell's

Keith Caldwell at his first command of the Second World War, Station Woodbourne, RNZAF, Blenheim, in 1941.

Jaguar sports car was his principal means of traversing the station, but was often requisitioned by Dorothy, in the company of Lady Clark-Hall, for weekly trips into Christchurch for supplies.

Lillias Clark-Hall's husband, Group Captain Sir Robert Clark-Hall, was officer commanding at the newly established RNZAF Harewood Station in north-west Christchurch. In 1943 he was promoted to air commodore and appointed air officer commanding Southern (Training) Group in the Cashmere hills. Effectively, he was Caldwell's immediate superior. More than a decade older than Caldwell, he possessed a wealth of experience and a resumé extending from the 1900 Boxer Rebellion in China to the First World War RNAS and the interwar RAF. As Clark-Hall and Caldwell collaborated in training men and women for the war, their wives tirelessly packed mountains of calico-encased parcels for the men overseas, served on 'endless committees caring for servicemen's welfare' and entertained their families at Wigram and Harewood, especially those who were strangers to Christchurch.[14]

C aldwell's work at Wigram station was unending and demanding. Matters of considerable import jostled with the mundane, from the implications of wearing 'New Zealand' shoulder badges overseas and at home to a proposal to issue individuals with their own crockery to reduce high levels of breakage at Wigram. He was against the wearing of the badge in New Zealand. 'We did not have it in the last war, and there is no need for it this time. Evidence of overseas service will no doubt be found in the awarding of appropriate medals when the war is over. I feel that if the NZ badge was intended to denote exposure to danger overseas, then the majority of the population of many cities in England should wear some emblem; and also the merchant service.'[15] As for the crockery, he scribbled a for-and-against list. The 'saving of costs to the country' would be offset by the 'nuisance of carrying cups and cutlery' to daily meals.[16]

Many families of those serving felt that Caldwell had little else to do but to solve problems faced by their sons and daughters in uniform overseas or at home. Some parents, including those of men who had already seen two tours in Europe with the RAF, he could help, but other issues proved intractable, including a comical dispute

Keith Caldwell inspecting members of the Woman's Auxiliary Air Force at Station Woodbourne, Blenheim, in 1941.

Overleaf: Keith Caldwell sits at front, eighth from the left, with sergeants in front of an Airspeed Oxford.

between a protective father and his wayward son, Harley.[17] 'This boy, our only son, has caused us considerable anxiety for some time past', wrote Sydney Cattell, a local doctor, 'as like so many lads of his age he is restless and unsettled.' Could Caldwell see his way to getting him into the wireless course? In this way the 18-year-old might calm down before being sent overseas. He attached a heartfelt letter from his son.

> I am neither unfit to fly nor am I a coward — it is only the so-called parental apron strings that are holding me back . . . I fully realise that I am your only son, but if I am fit to fly a plane or [at least serve] in a plane would it not be unpatriotic to withhold me when my country calls. It has been proven time and again that one man can turn a battle — who knows — I may be that man . . . Some of my relatives have expressed an opinion that they wonder if I will ever make good, and you too have said often, 'My god, I don't know what will become of you, I am damned if I do!' Well, they say that every person has his or her niche, and perhaps flying will be mine . . . It would be a hard blow Dad if after going through the medical and finding myself fit you still refuse your consent. They say it would mean waiting until I am 21, and the war won't be over by then — ask Winston [Churchill].[18]

Harley even invoked God and king, but Caldwell was unmoved. The young man concluded the war as a gunner in the New Zealand artillery.[19]

Sometimes Caldwell was called upon to rein in officious staff. For taking snapshots on the station, an overzealous officer charged the wife of a Wigram sergeant with breaching photographic regulations. News of the hefty £20 fine made it all the way to Wellington and, as a result, Caldwell received a letter from Air Commodore Victor Goddard, Chief of the Air Staff. He did not blame the local magistrate for his 'ferocity and zeal', but rather the Wigram security officer for 'failing to consult Caldwell as to the advisibility of making a criminal charge'.[20]

Caldwell agreed, reminding his staff that a degree of pragmatism was required in such matters, and, along with Goddard, made a financial contribution to paying the fine.[21] Less easily resolved were complaints from the public over what they saw as rowdy and inappropriate dinners and dances held by the RNZAF in the community.[22] In reply to such concerns, Caldwell trod a middle path:

I need to hardly mention that Wigram being a large place, there are many units and organisations wishing to hold their own functions from time to time for the purposes of relaxation and to foster a unit or team spirit. Provided the control of these dances or concerts is satisfactory, I believe it is all to the good, but the holding of many dances off Station may tend to give the Christchurch public rather a wrong impression. [23]

Clark-Hall gave approval for 21 dances a year, over half of which were devoted to the monthly graduation ceremonies of the senior flying course.

These were a highlight of Caldwell's work, reviving memories of his own First World War training. He used the presentations to reinforce the values he had learnt in the earlier conflict, though prudence perhaps demanded that he refrain from regaling the graduating cadets with stories of his own high-spirited partying on the Western Front or his sometimes relaxed leadership of 74 Squadron.

Remember that as pilots, you are not the only important person in your aircraft. The pilot certainly takes it off and puts it down but the navigator gets you there and brings you back and your air gunners deal with any enemy fighters which come within range. Remember to cultivate the team spirit all you can. That is, play for the side of the Squadron, not for self. Don't forget the ground crew who work long hours to give you a safe and sound aircraft to fly. Take an interest in them and let them feel that any successes you may have, are theirs too.

He reminded them, too, that they would not be asked to do anything they were not capable of doing. 'If your confidence is lacking a bit . . . [remember] those senior officers who have allotted you your task, have assessed your value and are quite sure.' And he recommended that they 'cultivate a high sense of self discipline. In other words, set yourself a high standard and don't let yourself down. New Zealanders have a reputation for being thorough, dependable and modest. Remember that one bad show can do a great deal of harm and good behaviour all the time is just what is expected of you.' He concluded with a mantra that had guided his own military career: 'Be brave in deed, modest in word'.[24]

Overleaf: **The Station Wigram over-30s rugby team.
Keith Caldwell is in front, holding the ball.**

The presence of significant numbers of women at Wigram generated several challenges for Caldwell. In January 1941, the RNZAF was the first service to accept women into its ranks. Many WAAFs were employed in traditional clerical, medical or domestic duties, but others excelled in specialist aircraft trades, as wireless operators or meteorological assistants. So popular was the auxiliary force that within two years WAAF's numbers peaked at nearly 3800 women. Hundreds of these women passed through Wigram, and Caldwell was at the forefront of establishing and administering regulations and procedures for their training and welfare. For example, early editions of the station's standing orders booklets required inserts to deal with the question of how WAAF personnel should be addressed and whether female officers should be saluted by airmen.

It was decided that WAAFs would be addressed by their civilian surnames, prefixed by Mrs or Miss, and that airmen were 'not required to salute WAAF personnel'.[25] With time this latter directive was reversed and airmen were required to salute WAAF officers 'on all occasions', though WAAFs saluting male officers was not made compulsory.[26]

More pressing was the type and availability of accommodation for women at Wigram. Despite the large and ongoing building programme, Caldwell's tenure, like that of his predecessor, was bedevilled by an unrelenting housing shortage, especially for WAAFs. One objected when told she would have to sleep in the recreation room and share laundry facilities with the men:

> I appeal as a woman, on the grounds of sensitiveness when dressing and undressing in the presence of others . . . I should point out that we are women and not boarding school children and every consideration should be given to the matter of having curtains or screens . . . There is also the question of laundering . . . it is not possible or permissible to have female undergarments hung outside on lines on any part of the Station, and at all times the drying room will have to be used for this purpose and the airmen would have access to the laundry in the collection of their personal washing . . . I presume this matter has never been considered from a woman's point of view.[27]

All of this came to a head in 1943, when normal barracks were deemed unsuitable for the women and allegations were made that Caldwell's headquarters had solved this problem with 'compulsory evictions' of families from the married quarters. It

Anglican Archbishop Campbell West-Watson and Keith Caldwell at Wigram in 1944.

was claimed that this was done without 'due regard to the possibility of finding other accommodation' for those affected.[28] The general policy was that married quarters be vacated within one month of an officer or airman's departure for overseas duties and the accommodation given over to the WAAFs.

Alarmingly for Caldwell, these allegations were made in Parliament, along with the assertion that those airmen who complained were threatened with being posted to another station. Herbert Kyle, the MP for Riccarton in Christchurch, advised those 'bullied' not to quit their houses: 'I have pointed out that a private landlord cannot compel a tenant to quit, and that I would defy the Government to put me out of one of the homes . . . The houses, I am given to understand, are needed for the members of the Women's Auxiliary Air Force. I do not say that they should be put into tents, although no doubt some of them will go out many times on holiday and live in tents . . .'[29]

In a draft explanatory report to Goddard for eventual submission to the prime minister, Caldwell explained that there was insufficient accommodation on the station and that this was exacerbated by some wives refusing to quit their accommodation after their husbands' departures. Goddard felt that the report supplied 'a convincing answer for the Prime Minister'.[30]

In the second week of November 1943, Caldwell was told of murmurings among some of the Electrical and Wireless School trainees about Christmas leave provisions. It was a seemingly innocuous matter that quickly escalated. To allow training and other functions to proceed without interruption over Christmas and New Year, the officers and men were informed that only a percentage of personnel could have seven days off. Most would be granted just their regular three-day Christmas leave. As the officer in charge of the school, Squadron Leader John Todd, explained to Caldwell, although the Air Department order made 'no specific mention of the trainees . . . unfortunately the E. & W. Wing almost without exception immediately assumed they would have seven days' leave at Christmas'.

To clarify the matter, a second memo stated that the trainees could take only three days and that 'no exception would be permitted'. Some took this philosophically, but a hard core, driven by 'bitter disappointment' and the belief that the limited leave provisions were a local and arbitrary initiative, dug in.[31]

Within days, Todd reported that they were holding clandestine meetings and planning to strike if they were not granted more leave.[32] Caldwell, who had presided over numerous previous court martials and courts of inquiry, could not recall such ridiculous demands that had such serious implications for those involved.[33] It was hard to believe these trainees considered this was a battle worth fighting *and* one they could win. That these demands were being made during a time of war when many of their compatriots were facing serious hardships overseas was even more galling. Caldwell suspected that not a few of the conspirators were members of the Communist Party.[34]

On 16 November, he descended from his office with Todd to address the students of the Electrical and Wireless School and then the Elementary Radio Training School. He reminded his listeners of their solemn attestation oath — to the king and before God — to faithfully serve in the RNZAF, and to 'observe and obey all orders' of the officers set over them until they were lawfully discharged.

Although any further meetings 'would be considered mutinous',[35] Caldwell indicated that, if they wished, four trainee delegates could see Todd the following morning, when he would endeavour to answer any questions. It was an astute means of defusing the situation but also of perhaps identifying the insurrectionists were further action required. At first, the meeting proved fruitful: the 'four delegates spent the remainder of Wednesday disseminating the explanations given to them and in attempting to assure the remainder of the personnel that any action would lead to more trouble'. By late afternoon the matter was resolved and Caldwell could spend the evening with Dorothy and Virginia safe in the knowledge that 'no further trouble would eventuate'.[36]

That night, however, there was a meeting at the YMCA hut, and a notice appeared on the hut's blackboard informing the men of the scheduled rally, 'Tomorrow 0720 hours'. Later investigations revealed that one or more airmen went from house to house on the station informing personnel of the gathering in 'the paddock' the following morning. By lights out, a considerable number of men knew of the plan and that, should enough personnel attend, the intention was 'to stand fast until a discussion about Christmas leave satisfactory to them was given'.[37]

In the morning, personnel began assembling in groups in the paddock and several men yelled for others to join in, including a flight of airmen being marched to work. A group of Caldwell's NCOs, led by Flight Sergeant Nelson, then arrived and moved among the men, speaking to them in 'an endeavour to persuade them to disperse'. Within five minutes, they were able to scatter the crowd. As Caldwell later noted, Nelson's quick intervention was 'lucky for the personnel concerned . . . serious Courts Martial would otherwise inevitably have followed. [They] would have had the rope round their necks for all time.'[38]

Caldwell initiated a thorough investigation of the 'Christmas Leave Unrest'. Approximately 100 men were associated with the meeting, but a good number claimed to either be unaware of its purpose or simply waiting to see what happened.[39] Although the full extent of the problem was never confirmed, two aircraftsmen second class were singled out in the subsequent report. One identified as posting the meeting notice in the YMCA hut and yelling out to the marching flight was charged for both offences. During interrogation, the other claimed to possess information on the ringleaders and the dissenters but, after being warned, was unwilling to disclose more details. He was brought before Caldwell and charged.

Caldwell managed to keep the fiasco out of the newspapers and made reforms to prevent future problems arising. NCOs were reminded of their responsibilities and encouraged to manage order in the Wireless Wing more closely. To achieve this, some NCOs who lived off-station were moved onto Wigram.

I n January 1944, Caldwell completed a two-week inspection of RNZAF units in the Pacific. He found the New Caledonian capital, Nouméa, bustling with Allied uniforms. At the RNZAF base depot on the New Hebrides island of Espiritu Santo, he located numerous Blenheim and Wigram graduates, all stripped to the waist and very tanned. Everyone looked thinner as the result of the high humidity and the effects of various tropical illnesses. During the tour, which also encompassed the Solomons, Caldwell travelled some 12,000 miles and 'went as far forward as possible', passing within 2 miles of Japanese positions, and was gratified to witness 'our fellows and Yanks going off on a sweep of Rabaul'.[40]

This was part of the continuing Allied attempt to neutralise the major Japanese naval and air power installations on New Britain. Although sleep was difficult in the humidity, with 'all sorts of noises from birds and flying foxes to screeches, whistles and calls like the human voice and the cicadas keep[ing] up a steady accompaniment all the time', Caldwell was fascinated.

Went to the site where A/C Buckley's camp is called 'Bloody Knoll'. Very bitter fighting went on round this spot and the bushman and demolition parties have dug up many dead Japs and much equipment. This was in the fight for the landing strip which the Allies needed and finally won at some cost. Apart from hundreds of rusty broken Jap landing barges all along the coast of certain islands and some large, damaged Jap ships, there is now little evidence of recent fighting. Shell and bomb holes are quickly filled in and the progress . . . is astonishing.

He was very impressed by the Americans' 'simply amazing' equipment and the use they made of it. 'The stoutest fellows of all I would say are the "Seabees" or construction Battalions who land with the striking forces to make our landing strips with their heavy machinery under fire from snipers . . . and shell fire. They say they just raise their grader blades as a part protective shield and drive into the sniper's trees and dislodge them and drive over them.'[41]

In June 1944, Caldwell faced his final and biggest test at home. It began with allegations made in a relatively minor case before an armed forces appeal court — a flight sergeant's petition for release from the RNZAF on the grounds of undue hardship. After 10 years in the air service, James Lloyd was hastily posted from Wigram to RNZAF Station Ohakea. This, he claimed, would leave him unable to support himself at Ohakea *and* keep his home in Christchurch. The story hit the newspapers with accusations that Lloyd's posting was part of a much larger depopulating of Wigram in advance of a visit by the Parliamentary Manpower Committee.[42] Lloyd's lawyer was forthright:

> It seems a serious thing, when manpower services are being investigated, that the Air Force should comb out suddenly skilled personnel and send them to other districts . . . It seems extraordinary that these men should be shifted away with the excuse that they have to get off the station, and that, if they cannot get away they must, at least take part of their leave, but be off the station when the manpower committee is there.[43]

The insinuation that the RNZAF was overstaffed and was trying to cover this up was reported with relish. After nearly five years of war, and with the threat of Japanese invasion greatly diminished, support for the Labour Government was in decline. Both the Opposition and the nation's press were more than willing to highlight the failings and inadequacies of Prime Minster Peter Fraser's leadership and his ministers.[44] Opposition MPs made claims in the House that New Zealand's entire fighting force was overstaffed, but the RNZAF was particularly 'top-heavy' and its leadership 'absolutely impossible' to deal with.[45] Airmen with grievances, some real, some imagined, came forward to assert that resources were being squandered and complainants were posted overseas to shut them up. Also noted were such minor misdemeanours as using trucks and aircraft to deliver flowers for mess functions.[46]

Although much of this could be dismissed, the overstaffing claims were not without merit. The success of EATS and lower-than-anticipated air casualties in the Normandy landings in June had produced a surfeit of aircrew who could not be absorbed into the RAF.[47] Locally, the expanding RNZAF was struggling to find places for its personnel at home and in the Pacific. The planned extensive operations in the latter theatre had stalled, partly due to Fraser's difficulties with the American Secretary of State, Cordell Hull, after the signing of the Canberra Pact, a treaty of mutual cooperation between Australia and New Zealand, in January 1944. Efforts to reduce strengths throughout the RNZAF were proving difficult to achieve. As a local station commander in New Zealand, Caldwell was having to deal with a problem that was not of his own making.

His immediate concern was the decline in relations between RNZAF personnel and the people of Christchurch. 'Many civilians were ready to believe what they read in the newspapers,' he wrote, 'although much of it was obviously illogical and unfair.'

> For a time when the attacks were at their hottest, Air Force personnel, especially officers, felt embarrassed and uncomfortable when off Station, and were at times the subject of outspoken criticism in the streets of Christchurch. This feeling against the Air Force has also been very apparent at football matches when Air Force teams have played local teams in Club competition. Members of our Service have been referred to as 'blue orchids', and our opponents have been encouraged by [cries of] 'come on the workers'.[48]

The players endured the jeering and heckling in silence, but the criticism was keenly felt. Caldwell believed that many denunciations were ill-founded and that staff with grievances should address them within the service. In early August, he responded with a speech to the Wigram staff that was broadcast over the Tannoy speaker system. He encouraged those who felt they were underemployed to hand in their names to the 'Wing Adjutant by 1200 hours tomorrow' so that they could be given 'full and useful employment . . . on this Station'. Alternatively, individuals could be posted to stations 'where vacancies occur' or released from service with the air force for civilian life if the army did not want them. He did not think that the Parliamentary

Manpower Committee had been 'displeased with what they saw, in fact, they gave rather the opposite impression'.

> The story that appeared in the local newspapers that men had been hurriedly posted away from Wigram just because the Committee was coming is all tommy-rot, and not the case. I believe that the opinion was held in some quarters on the Station that these men would all be posted back again after the Committee had left — well they did not come back, and the Committee knew the postings were to reduce our strength to the new reduced Establishment and they had full information about this before they arrived, and again when they arrived.[49]

The administrative and non-flying staff in New Zealand might appear top-heavy to an outsider, or even to an uninformed RNZAF officer, but would appear less so when the upcoming 'in theatre' commitments were made known. 'It might be pointed out', said Caldwell, 'that every effort is being made by the Chief of the Air Staff to ensure that our Air Force is given a man-sized job so that we shall be in at the kill.'[50] (Behind closed doors the RNZAF hierarchy was less certain. On 14 August, the chief of the air staff informed Caldwell 'that more than 6 RNZAF squadrons in the forward area would be an embarrassment to the Americans. It is not that the Americans do not want us with them, it is a question of ways and means of using us.')[51]

Caldwell told his men that he had been 'glad to hear' of a letter sent to the Anglican Bishop of Christchurch, Campbell West-Watson, from Padre Eric Osmers, formerly of Wigram, 'who stated that the men in the Pacific area were fed up to the teeth with press articles that had been appearing in New Zealand and would like some of those gallant critics to see the holes in some of our aircraft which return to base from operations'. Caldwell ended with a rallying cry:

> In the meantime, it is up to every one of us to carry on and give his best. The [Air] Service is still a good one, there must be no slackening of effort — the war is not over yet. To those few (I hope), who are ready to lap up all the adverse press remarks against the Air Force, I would say, there is one quality above all others that should be topmost in our Service and that is LOYALTY [emphasis in the original], and I would ask you to remember that word.[52]

After the speech, only seven individuals indicated that they felt 'underemployed', although Caldwell conceded 'that there are a great many more than this but they probably dislike the thought of a posting and were happy in their Air Force occupation and pay'. On 12 August, Caldwell reported to Wellington that 'our strength is only 21 over establishment, which is not a bad state of affairs'.[53]

But in a confidential report to the Air Department in September, Caldwell was candid: morale had taken a substantial blow. It was not lost on him that some of the criticism was coming from within the ranks. He noted that the majority of the 750 personnel who lived off-station in Christchurch 'regard Wigram largely as a factory and place of work to which they must come each day to earn their keep'.

> While they may admit its purpose and worth as a Station, it is doubtful if the majority of them would be prepared to defend its good name. A parallel can be found in a boarding school where the spirit of loyalty amongst the boarders is so much better than that amongst the day boys who have outside influences to disturb them and have not had the opportunity of absorbing the atmosphere and traditions of their school.[54]

Another parallel for Caldwell had been the small, close-knit squadrons on the Western Front. But that kind of common cause, esprit de corps and teamwork was difficult to maintain on a home-front station, where complacency had infected some of the longer-serving individuals.

The mounting pressure was relieved by the defence minister's announcement, early in September, of a reorganisation of the RNZAF. Several fighter and bomber squadrons were to have operational roles in forward areas against the Japanese, and other transport and patrolling units were being deployed to guard bases and lines of communication. The government was also closing the redundant group headquarters in Auckland.[55] Wigram continued a programme of releasing men and woman of a certain age back into civilian life, which Caldwell called 'weeding out personnel surplus to requirements'.[56]

By the second week of September, as a result of his own efforts and announcements 'in the House of Parliament and the press by the Minister of Defence and the Prime Minister', Caldwell could report that morale 'is now quite up to, if not higher, than a year ago'.[57] The leader of the Opposition, Sidney Holland, had even written to Caldwell saying he was disassociating himself from the criticism levelled at Wigram Station, since he had seen first hand the 'splendid training that was being provided in the workshops and training centres established and maintained by the Air Force'.[58]

For his own efforts in the crisis, Caldwell received a glowing report card from

Clark-Hall in an assessment that covered the period October 1943 to September 1944: 'One of the best station commanders . . . I have known. Extreme devotion to duty. Despite bad health, he drives himself to the limit. A born leader. A thoroughly sound organiser. Extremely loyal to his seniors. Takes greatest interest in welfare of his men.'[59] The station had been extremely productive during Caldwell's tenure. Over 2000 pilots had been trained, 'sufficient', he stated, 'to man a National Air Force'.[60] He calculated that, in training, the men had flown over 35,000,000 miles with a relatively low number of accidents, and in operations overseas had received more than 200 decorations.

Caldwell was particularly proud of the mechanics, whose work had been praised by overseas experts as the 'highest in the Empire Training Organisation'.[61] In recognition of his exceptional work, Caldwell was made a Commander of the Most Excellent Order of the British Empire in the 1945 New Year Honours and 'rewarded' with lengthy postings overseas to India and Britain.[62]

Savoy

I n late 1944, Caldwell was dispatched to India for special duties. Officially it was
a mission to confer with various Allied headquarters regarding a 'new liaison
establishment for the RNZAF in India . . . and to tour RAF units in India with the
purpose of contacting RNZAF personnel on service and welfare matters'.[1] In reality,
it was an operation to quell a growing chorus of discontent among the hundreds of
New Zealanders serving under the RAF in India and Ceylon (now Sri Lanka), who felt
largely abandoned and poorly treated by their superiors in Wellington and London.

Nursing a summer cold, he flew out of Whenuapai aerodrome in a Transport
Command Consolidated B-24 Liberator on 3 December. His immediate destination
was Sydney, followed by Melbourne, Perth and Exmouth in north-west Australia,
before going on to the subcontinent. In Australia he met his New Zealand liaison
officers and was only too happy to be invited to a few Royal Australian Air Force
(RAAF) officers' clubs. In Perth, still with 'a rotten cold', he recorded in his diary
that he had intended to go to bed early, 'but instead spent most of the night with
a bunch of Merchant Service Officers who mixed their drinks properly and became
very interesting on their wartime experiences. I think all of them had been torpedoed
or wrecked in some way and they gave graphic accounts of the tough convoying to
Russia.'[2]

On the 3000-mile flight from Exmouth to Colombo over the Indian Ocean in a

Qantas Liberator, 'We were given certificates saying that this was the longest non-stop flight over water in the world and postcards to fill in giving our impressions of the trip.' Caldwell's was 'critical rather [than] complimentary, except full marks for the tired crew'.[3] He found the bucket seats too upright and the blaring engines made sleep difficult. The final leg was from Colombo to Delhi, 1800 miles up the centre of India, and he was almost deaf from the long flights with a heavy cold.

Caldwell's mission was broken into three stages: January and February in eastern India and forward areas; March in northern and north-western India; and April and May in Ceylon and southern India.[4] He found traditional Delhi bewildering and rather confronting. As he made his way 'at a snail's pace through this mess of life', he was 'almost at times, walking on crippled beggars who were sitting or lying along the narrow pavements. Some . . . were merely blind, others were much worse with crippled limbs twisted in all directions, while others . . . had raw stumps for legs and hands . . .' He was told that it was 'a common thing for parents to maim children when very young to increase their begging value later in life . . . I don't think I want to see the Old Delhi markets again.'[5]

Other parts of his journey were inspiring — Delhi's Old Fort 'with its pure white smooth stone mosques, marble baths, jewelled facades' and the large estates near Kandy in Ceylon, with the 'air scented with sweet smells from many exotic flowers . . . cut out of the jungle'.[6] Over Christmas and New Year, he managed to get in a game of golf with a 'terrible' set of hired clubs. 'The ground was hard and dry and the fairways narrow with dense scrub on both sides, real Tiger country.' One hole ahead of his party was the viceroy, General Archibald Wavell, and a parade of very 'royal looking bearers in attendance, marking his ball'.[7]

Caldwell also discovered that the region was an extremely demanding operational theatre, the heat, disease and difficulties with staffing all conspiring to erode the efficiency and morale of the New Zealanders serving there. Given the large area his mission had to cover, Caldwell spent a good deal of his time flying between locations, either in the ubiquitous Dakota C-47s of the transport unit, or, more commonly, in an Auster L5 allocated for his own personal use. This single-engine liaison and observation machine was ideal for hopping between various small airstrips surrounded by seas of tropical foliage, especially in neigbouring Burma, which was, he wrote, 'mostly jungle and consequently navigation was most difficult at times, but small clouds of dust in the distance usually indicated an airstrip'. While most of his endeavours were administrative and managerial, Caldwell did follow some of the fighting from the air; this was a highlight of his time in the region.

By 1945, the Allies held aerial superiority over great swathes of Burma, allowing Caldwell to fly over the battlefield in relative safety from airborne attack. In this way, he witnessed several active operations. On one occasion, flying low in his Auster L5, he followed the assault on a Japanese-held village not far from the former royal capital of Mandalay in northern Burma. It was a well-organised attack not entirely dissimilar to those in which he had participated during the latter stages of the First World War, successfully combining air power, armour and infantry.

On the ground, tanks and infantry formed up, awaiting the arrival of air power. The RAF was using Hawker Hurricanes and American Republic P-47 Thunderbolts as fighter-bombers. The aircraft delivered bombs and strafed ground targets as tanks broke from their jungle hideaways, and infantry armed with Lee–Enfield rifles and Bren light machine guns fell in behind their armoured cover.[8]

The mission's investigations confirmed the worst. As Caldwell reported to London and Wellington, 'Some of our chaps have now been 3 years in India and have just about had it.'[9] At Bangalore, Caldwell was greeted by New Zealander Wing Commander James Garfield Stewart who, as senior medical officer for 225 Group RAF, was responsible for 'RAF health in a disease-ridden area almost six times the size of his homeland'.[10]

Caldwell learnt that he was 'very worried at the lack of co-operation he was receiving from his senior in his efforts to try and improve the general health of the thousands of Air Force personnel under his care. The sickness incidence was as high as 50% in the monsoon period, due to poor camp facilities, especially poor food, [and] poor bathing arrangements.'[11] Due to the demands of Caldwell's work and travel regime, his diary was abandoned after a month. On 18 December he recorded that he had run 'out of steam', though he did add an addendum summarising all he had done in the preceding months.[12]

> During the rest of my duty in India, until the end of May 1945, we were busy with travel and office administration matters; we moved our Accounts Section to Bombay to follow the RAF move; we increased the size of our small Delhi Office a little. Wing Commander de Lange was brought over from RNZAF NZ to relieve Squadron Leader Twigge, I borrowed a light aircraft from RAF Transport Command and flew it all over India and Burma plus an ass'tn Officer visiting RAF Squadrons

Keith Caldwell's mission to India in late 1944 was designed to assess and organise relief for the large numbers of New Zealanders who had been overshadowed by their countrymen serving in the RAF in Europe and the RNZAF in the Pacific.

where there were NZders serving, several hundred of them. This was worthwhile, as many were due and ready for postings and transfers, some back to NZ.[13]

By the end of the mission, Caldwell was struggling with both health and sleep in a country where the temperature could reach 45°C in the shade. 'Yesterday was 108.8 percent [humidity], it was like a furnace,' he told Dorothy at the beginning of May.[14] Cold lemon drinks, copious cups of tea and bottles of soda water fended off dehydration, but when he lay down to sleep it was like taking a bath in the sea. Caldwell concluded his diary with: 'not sorry to leave'.[15] The RNZAF posted him to Britain to run its London headquarters. In recognition of his work in India and his new responsibilities he was promoted to air commodore.

The conflict with Japan continued, but Germany had surrendered unconditionally on 8 May 1945. But even as the VE Day celebrations lingered and millions of Allied men occupied Germany, plans were being finalised for the largest demobilisation in the history of warfare. Included were thousands of Caldwell's countrymen and women. Of the some 12,000 New Zealanders who had served with the RAF during the war, about a third were still in uniform in Britain.[16] Manning machines across Fighter, Coastal, Transport and Bomber Command, they were a sizable part of the dominion's contribution to the war effort. The management, welfare and repatriation of these New Zealanders was Caldwell's responsibility.

He hit the ground running at the RNZAF headquarters, Halifax House on the Strand, and his first day in the office was 25 May. '[A]mong others, [he] called on Bill Jordan, NZ High Commissioner and exchanged pleasantries. Sid Holland, who returns to NZ tomorrow, called in to say hello and goodbye.'[17] His offices were crowded with piles of paperwork. He apologised to Dorothy that his letter writing was not up to his previous standard, 'but have been awfully busy'.

The amount of work was not dissimilar to 'Wigram at its busiest, but much more weighty things to deal with'. Moreover, he initially lacked much of the support staff who smoothed out his work at Wigram, which meant he had to do an 'awful lot of research and backreading of innumerable files to get the picture'.[18] Early in his posting,

Keith Caldwell, seated third from left in the front row, with New Zealand air force personnel troops in India. Despite their smiles, many rightly felt they had been forgotten in a country in which the climate and disease wreaked havoc on even the strongest of individuals.

he often returned to the office after dinner and worked until 10 p.m. or brought files home to his small flat in Vincent House in Notting Hill.

One month in, Caldwell was still struggling to get everything completed in the office while also carrying out official duties and visiting New Zealand airmen in the field. Nonetheless, on Monday, 25 June, he managed to update Dorothy:

> Since writing last have had a very busy time in the office with many callers and interviews and meetings with semi-political communications with NZ. It is all a bid muddy at the moment and NZ is slow making up its mind over aircrew employment policy. Too many of our chaps idle over here. The adjustment period following VE day is becoming too long and indefinite. However, [the] RAF are very helpful in our affairs and pleasant to work with . . . If I come home in a hurry, it will be because I think the RNZAF should be run by the [Foreign] Service and the Politicians!

The previous Saturday he had made a 'very hurried visit' to Brussels, returning the next day. 'Visited our NZ Sqdn 487 and gave them a talk, they are at a lovely spot near Brussels and the weather was scorching. Thought they seemed a pretty fair bunch, but the Station buildings, messes . . . are so dirty after Wigram.' He had been flown back to a Surrey aerodrome 'in 4 Mosquitos doing 300 mph in close formation'. As he drove to London 'through perfect country', the roads were 'packed with car traffic now that the petrol ration increased. Have seen some lovely Rolls, Bentleys, Aston Martins, and a 140 mph Bugatti in Brussels . . . Brought back 2 bottles of Champagne for 15/., worth £6–£7 here [in England].'[19]

Caldwell's biggest problem was the government's inability to decide about the future of New Zealand air force personnel in Europe and what should be done with those who returned to New Zealand: Would they be demobilised or sent into the Pacific to fight the Japanese? 'The other dominions have made up their minds,' he told Dorothy. 'It is all very unsettling and bad for morale, as we have some 4000 practically idle and I am not able to speak with a firm voice.' He was exchanging long communiqués with Wellington outlining his own solution to the problem.

Caldwell hoped to 'entice' the dominion government to allow 'our fellows to stay in against the Jap[anese], especially all those who have been away some time and have not had a chance to go to war, to give them a chance to ease their consciences and justify the cost and effort put into training'.[20] The only decision made so far was 75 Squadron's insertion into Tiger Force, a British Commonwealth long-range bomber formation selected for Okinawa and bombing targets in Japan. 'Am going up to Lincoln in a day or so to see 75 Squadron and tell the chaps about their new job which is coming . . . soon. They at least have a job to do.'[21]

In the third week of July, Caldwell finally received solid instructions from the New Zealand government: a 'revised policy for employment and repatriation for our fellows over here . . . It will amount to the larger half of RNZAF aircrew in Europe being returned to NZ within the next 6–8 months', with the possibility of a reduced London headquarters and his replacement by a more junior person. The 200-odd aircrew of 75 Squadron destined for Japan took the news well and Caldwell fielded questions for an hour, but less pleased were some 500 trainees at Brighton who had missed their chance to test their mettle in operations. 'Poor devils have been hanging around doing nothing for some months.'[22]

Caldwell's letter to Dorothy on 9 August 1945 was full of the atomic bombs that the United States had dropped on Hiroshima and Nagasaki and Russia's declaration of war against Japan.[23] He hoped that it all meant a quick resolution to the war and an early return to New Zealand. Six days later, when Japan surrendered, and the war was finally over, he wrote to her again.

> All the papers have been full of large headlines for several days and during this time there have been a succession of installments of victory. It was not until late last night that Japan had accepted the Allies [sic] terms unconditionally and today was a day of great festivity. Million or so people crowded . . . London streets, singing, waving flags, and jostling one another. Hotels all full did a roaring trade and I hear the beer in London is nearly all sold out. Tomorrow is also a public holiday . . . We drove along the Mall at 11 am and found about 200,000 people to see the King and Queen and entourage . . . on their way to Parliament. They were in an open carriage in spite of heavy rain. Both looked well — he in Naval uniform and the Queen in light blue looking quite radiant . . .[24]

Caldwell had gone 'sedately to bed' at 10 p.m., though he expected that '90% of the people in London are out celebrating. I have a slight sore throat and am generally too tired after a series of latish nights to do any more celebrating.' On the following Sunday, at the St Paul's Cathedral thanksgiving service, Caldwell had a good view of the proceedings and dignitaries. One in particular caught his attention: 'Winston Churchill . . . looks pretty old and stooped but pugnacious and grim. I am told [he] received the warmest welcome of all the celebrities.'

With repatriation plans in full swing, Caldwell roamed the countryside looking for temporary housing centres to gather hundreds of air personnel before sending them home through the ports of Southampton and Liverpool.[25] With the help of the British Air Ministry, he secured at least one vacant military camp near Brighton. Several embarkations were completed in August ahead of the larger drafts in September. To accommodate the extensive logistical and organisational demands of the task, Caldwell's staff grew considerably. It was challenging work that became particularly stressful when servicemen, used to comfortable accommodation, a well-provisioned mess and access to the comforts and attractions of Britain's towns and cities, resisted being wedged into the bleak confines of a troopship for the month-long journey to New Zealand. This problem first became evident during a Liverpool embarkation in August when Caldwell received a phone call.[26]

RMS *Orion* was loaded with servicemen, including over 1300 New Zealand former prisoners of war and significant numbers of Australian and Royal Navy officers and men. When the RNZAF airmen saw the conditions, around 70 of them, and more than 200 of the New Zealand Expeditionary Force, walked off. In the end, the desire to get home outweighed their dislike of the overcrowded conditions on the ship and most returned to the vessel. Only 147 refused to sail and were taken back to the reception centres.[27] It was fortunate for Caldwell, and Major General Howard Kippenberger, who was overseeing the repatriation of prisoners, that those below deck were unaware of what had happened, as many later asserted that they, too, would have departed, given the onboard privations.

Originally designed for 1400 passengers, the single-funnel ocean liner was requisitioned by the British government at the beginning of the war and converted to accommodate as many as 5000. The hammocks in which men slept were slung over mess tables, and non-fraternisation orders between officers and men restricted most of the soldiers to a section of the lower promenade deck that was too small for exercise. The menu alternated between fish and bully beef, bully beef and fish; the ship's canteen was overpriced; and one part of the ship, home to 500 men, had only 'two conveniences and six basins'. As one man noted, 'I have been a prisoner for a long time, but it shook me.'[28]

Caldwell wanted to avoid future problems but had little control over the vessels chosen for the task. When preparing for the next embarkation, Caldwell wrote home: 'Last time there was some trouble about the standard of accommodation but it will probably be better this time.'[29] He would ensure this by attending future embarkations and personally liaising with the airmen to forestall difficulties.

In the third week of September, Caldwell's efforts to smooth out the problems of the previous month tested his team's endurance. Two large embarkations from Liverpool and Southampton were scheduled.

> I went down to Brighton which was on Wednesday to speak to 900 officers and NCOs who are to leave on 22 Sept from Liverpool for NZ. Had a microphone otherwise it would have been a shouting match . . . All our staff, 95 of them and the Brighton [crew] . . . are very busy finalising arrangements for getting the big draft of 1500 away next week and Gerry Beale and some of the others are nearly cot cases. My sleeping has been affected a little as I have been busier than ever before but am pretty fit all the same and it will be easier going later on.[30]

The larger draft of 1500 RNZAF officers left through Southampton aboard RMS *Andes*, another fast and elegant pre-war cruise ship converted into a cramped troop carrier. The New Zealanders found they were sharing the vessel with a variety of uniformed Commonwealth men, including 1000 RAAF aircrew. With Caldwell managing expectations and promising visions of a glorious springtime New Zealand, there was no baulking at the gate and he was relieved to see *Andes* slip its moorings as an RAF band played on the quay.

The ship was escorted down the Solent by two large bombers — a Short Sunderland and an Avro Lincoln from 75 (NZ) Squadron — and the only Allied jet-powered fighter to see combat in the war, a majestic silver-liveried Gloster Meteor.[31] It travelled via the Suez Canal and Melbourne, then delivered its cargo to Lyttelton and Wellington, where disembarked officers crossed the threshold of homes that some had not seen for over half a decade.[32]

'Life's very full at the moment as busy with conferences with Air Ministry on post-war problems as well as the usual HQ Administration,' Caldwell wrote to Dorothy at the end of November, 'but still find time for odd lunches and dinners and things.'[33] As officer commanding at RNZAF headquarters, he was regularly invited to events where he met or observed at close quarters many leading lights, some of whom featured in the pages of *Burke's Peerage*. Among these, surprisingly, was his new young driver, 'a Lady Southwell — who called me "Sir" in respect for rank and old age which is [a] little disconcerting. Her father, Lord Southwell, died recently and left a large but impoverished estate and so his family have to seek jobs. [She has to] . . . do nothing except drive a car which she does quite well.'[34]

Early in his posting, Caldwell was able to combine his golf obsession with his enjoyment of fine dining and social events at a dominion golf tournament and dinner held by the famous Lucifer Golfing Society, a golf-centred gentleman's club established in 1921. Despite a rough-round-the-edges performance on the greens, he enjoyed a wonderful evening at the palatial Savoy Hotel. '[It] was a grand occasion. There were some very good speeches after dinner — one by Judge [Robert] Jackson the well-known criminal lawyer who is over from the USA to preside over the war-criminals Judicial Committee.'[35]

Former prime ministers, now high commissioners, for Australia and Canada also offered toasts, while Lord Cranborne, secretary of state for dominion affairs, presided over the occasion. That same week Caldwell attended an agreeable cocktail party at the Dorchester, his favourite hotel, organised by the Air Council. At another Savoy dinner, written up in *The Times*, Caldwell sat next to Lord Balfour and an Australian senator while the influential and accomplished orator, Ernest Bevin, delivered, in his strong West Country accent, an informative speech on global affairs.[36]

Caldwell also attended a party at the home of Sir Bernard Freyberg, who had commanded the 2nd New Zealand Division during the war and was soon to become New Zealand's governor-general; supped with his countryman and superior, Chief of the Air Staff Len Isitt — who 'gave an interesting account . . . of his trip to Japan to sign the surrender terms'; and joined Viscount Trenchard's party for an RAF pageant.[37]

As he told his wife and elder daughter, Caldwell supplemented these pleasant official duties with evenings at London's local theatres and cinemas, often in the company of his office staff.

> There is always time to work in a show however, and the other night went to 'Private Lives' (John Clements) which was very good indeed and also to Noel Coward's new show 'Sigh no More' with Cyril Ritchard and Madge Elliot, this was a typical N[oel] C[oward] affair — very clever and unusual . . . Mary would like it too and so would you . . . Tonight, it is my turn and I am taking them to 'A Night in Venice' (musical) and supper at the Boulestin Café after — a small level dining place with good food. So, you can see an effort is being made to see some shows while the chance offers.[38]

Based at RNZAF headquarters in London, Keith Caldwell organised and managed the repatriation of thousands of New Zealand airmen from the European theatre at the end of the war.

Some of the films and shows were direct products of the war, including the premiere of *The Way to the Stars*, an 'excellent film showing RAF, USAF in Station life, [with] good acting by John Mills, Michael Redgrave and others . . . All sorts of big wigs were there', including Air Chief Marshal Charles Portal and Marshal Arthur Harris and 'their ladies'. One of the more unusual thespian efforts was a play staged entirely by Air Force ex-prisoners of war from Stalag III called *Home Away*.

> This was about the most amazing play or series of skits I have been to: it was considered to be right up to professional standard as they had practised and played it for a year or so in prisoner theatres. One Michael Ormond from Hawkes Bay [sic] made a most glamorous girl and sang like one. I gathered a small party . . . and we had a [theatre] box (free thank goodness) and supper after at the Waldorf which is not the best but was handy.[39]

At White City, London, he joined some 80,000 people to watch and bet on the wildly popular greyhound races, and at Albert Hall cheered along with a rowdy 7000 spectators as the bull-necked Bruce Woodcock knocked out his Scottish heavyweight challenger.[40] 'One could easily get involved in a series of social activities, but this would be hopeless for anyone with a lot of work to do,' he told Dorothy.[41]

He did make time, though, to catch up with present and past members of 74 Squadron in Britain. Some of the squadron's Second World War airmen paid their respects to the unit's legendary former commander, including South African pilot Adolf 'Sailor' Malan. At one of the capital's prestigious clubs, Caldwell and Malan were joined by another Battle of Britain ace, New Zealander Alan Deere. 'Had a great talk with these chaps — fine fellows and quiet and modest types.'[42]

First World War brothers-in-arms periodically appeared at RNZAF headquarters. He reminded Dorothy to inform her brother of the recent Tiger gatherings:

> When you write to Freddy next time tell him I have seen [Reginald] Hobhouse, 'Gibspring' Coverdale . . . 'Hank' Goudie came into the office today, a S[quadron] L[eader] in the RCAF and looking blooming, if the owner of a somewhat red nose. All these people and Glynn asked after Freddy — 'The Queen of Sheba' — and sent their love. I have not seen Taffy Jones yet; he owns a Hotel in Wales somewhere. Everyone knows him or something about him.[43]

Many were prospering but some had fallen on hard times. In mid-October, Hobhouse invited Grid to stay with his family in Somerset so they could catch up with Clive Glynn, who needed 'some bucking up'.[44]

On a tour of the garden, Mrs Hobhouse pointed to an old sycamore tree blocking the growth of other trees. She confessed it was beyond her husband's abilities and that they could not get someone in to remove it. Caldwell reckoned that, with a good axe, it was a 10-minute job, but 'unfortunately all we could find were a small chopper and an ordinary small wood-saw'. Undeterred, he took off his jacket and attacked the tree. 'The English people or many of them are hopeless about tools and doing things themselves. So we hacked and sawed and down came the tree . . . and at the end of 1½ hours all told the tree was cut up and in the woodshed. A simple job for an old gardener in NZ but the fuss they made over this feat was amazing.'[45]

After a round of golf on the sandy links at Burnham-on-Sea, Caldwell and Hobhouse met Glynn at the train station. The years had not been kind to Grid's former flight commander and 74 Squadron ace. 'He now has snow-white hair and only 4 teeth left and is generally in a mess. From £3000 a year [he] now earns £4.10/. a week as a clerk in a motor transport business.' Caldwell and Hobhouse hatched a plan to return their 53-year-old former teammate to better times: 'We are getting him some teeth for a start and will try to get him a better job.' In the meantime, the 'drinks went round as we reminisced'.[46] Glynn died two months later.

I n the second half of October, Caldwell led a small party on a five-day whirlwind tour of the British occupation zone in Germany. Alighting from their Avro Anson at Bückeburg airfield, Lower Saxony, Caldwell and his staff were met by one of his countrymen, well-known test pilot and record-breaking RAF officer Group Captain Arthur Clouston. The Motueka-born airman wined and dined Caldwell's party at Air Chief Marshal William Sholto Douglas's plush chalet — 'the place was full of old masters and it was all rather like one of those films [full] of eastern splendour.'

The following day, they blasted along a five-lane autobahn in a large German Horch car, booty from the defeat of the Third Reich, before taking a tour of the remains of Hanover. Here Caldwell saw at close quarters the handiwork of the men he had trained at Wigram. An important regional transport hub and industrial centre, Hanover had been targeted as part of the Allied strategic bombing campaign. The city was flattened — 'evidence of the efficiency of total bombing'. Some 90 per cent of the city's medieval and administrative heart had gone, and over half of all its buildings were damaged or destroyed.

Caldwell had seen towns like Ypres reduced to rubble in the First World War, but it was difficult to grasp the breadth and severity of the all-too-recent bombing campaign that had swept across Germany's towns and cities. Five months after the end of the war, Hanover was a ghost town: 'Hardly a soul except a few sightseers like ourselves.'[47]

That evening, Caldwell flew to Berlin, where he ventured outside his hotel into the 'serene darkness' of a clear and peaceful autumn night. Among the ruins and rubble, he 'noticed light shining in the ground floor of a building which had lost its roof and went in to find a small restaurant and bar place'. The occupants, scattered among tables under an open sky, were uniformed men and fräuleins 'seeking company'.

The next morning, his team seconded an RAF car and traversed the heart of the scarred German capital.

> Berlin must have been one of the most beautiful cities in the world . . . but now it is a ruined and dead city and the people who are still existing there live in cellars and tents in the parks and hovels of all kinds. It is surprising how many German people there still are and most of them [are] old or very young, or women; [they] look ill and half-starved and without expressions in their faces and one cannot help but feel sorry for them. Very few men to be seen, as they are still under Allied control and treated still as prisoners and made to work in restoring essential services such as railways, roads etc. and rebuilding aerodromes for the Allied Air Force's occupational squadrons.

Because Caldwell and his companions had only the morning, they 'kept to the centre of the city and explored the Wilhelmstrasse area which is mainly fallen rubble and skeleton buildings. We found Hitler's chancellery, the Reichstag, Goering's Luftwaffe HQ and Goebbels' Administration HQ too. All magnificent, imposing buildings or had been, but now of course bombed to blazes.'[48]

Early in the afternoon, he was once again in the air, the Anson winging its way to Copenhagen. What impressed Caldwell, from above, was the contrast between the bombed-out shells of Hanover and Berlin, and the pastoral orderliness of the productive Germany countryside with its well-kept farms with their tiny clusters of buildings, so different from the rugged hills of Glen Murray. The country around Hanover was 'really beautiful — the fields are a patchwork of crops and the landscape dotted with forests and woods in autumn tints and the standard of farm building is higher than I have seen before anywhere'. He wondered at the lack of cattle: were they housed against the cold or had they all been consumed under the exigences of the Allied blockade?

The pilot flew Caldwell over the pockmarked Dutch fields of Arnhem and circled over the great German port of Kiel, another victim of Bomber Command. Caldwell took photographs of the capsized heavy cruiser *Admiral Scheer*, its great grey hull belly-up in abject surrender.[49]

Unlike post-war Germany, Copenhagen lacked neither livestock nor produce. After the bland cuisine of Britain under rationing, the Danish capital's restaurants were a pleasant shock to Caldwell's palate. His first meal was a three-hour extravaganza. '[We] settled down to a generous meal of soup, lobster, steak and many vegetables and raspberries and real cream — an enormous meal after England's austere fare.' Breakfast did not disappoint either: for almost the first time 'since leaving New Zealand', he consumed lashings of bacon and eggs. The only downside to Denmark was the high prices.

> I priced dinner sets and crockery generally, but the prices were beyond my resources although the quality was attractive. I could only officially take £10 out of England and had in fact £16, so had to go carefully and just pick up oddments. Collected some silk stockings, a pipe for Peter, a rather nice coloured mirror (hand) and powder box for you or Mary, odd curios, a cig[arette] lighter, a shirt, some handkerchiefs, fur slippers for Virginia and something for David, but it all did not amount to much really as the circumstances were against me.[50]

On the trip he also acquired a nice Swiss watch, a gift from one of his staffers, purchased with 150 of Europe's most valuable currency: cigarettes. Caldwell thought he might, 'if he felt generous', bequeath it to either Peter or David upon his return to New Zealand. After an overnight stay in Brussels it was finally back to England, and that night he was once again ensconced in London and Vincent House.

I n winter's embrace, Caldwell was consumed with the last of the large repatriations. His difficulties began with an embarkation in the second week of November, on the recently returned *Orion*, which had acquired a reputation among the New Zealanders and Australians for overcrowding and poor sanitary conditions. When Caldwell made a thorough inspection of the ship at Southampton, he discovered that little had changed and that there would likely be trouble if they attempted to sail 4300 men west of Suez. He made representations to the Air Ministry and the War Office and successfully got this number reduced by 777. It was a major achievement. Caldwell drove down to Brighton to address the nearly 500 New Zealanders due to leave in an embarkation that included a sizable RAAF contingent. As the *Auckland Star* reported, 'He . . . fully explained to the airmen the action he had taken and the reasons why as many personnel as possible were drafted into each ship in accordance with policy to repatriate servicemen at the earliest opportunity.'

> He pointed out, that with the reduction agreed to, conditions would be better than in other ships, and explained that, in addition to the further 800 to 900 members of the RNZAF still awaiting repatriation from England, there were also nearly 1200 dependents [sic] awaiting passage. Many of these were wives and children of airmen who had now returned to civilian life in New Zealand and who had to send money to England at disadvantageous rates of exchange to support them. He emphasised that the most careful thought was given by the authorities and those experienced in providing shipping accommodation to ensure that nobody would suffer in health.[51]

As was his custom with several drafts, he stayed on, trying to improve the lot and morale of the officers, and received deputations from concerned RNZAF and RAAF personnel until midnight, but found he was unable to corral a sizable group of disgruntled men who had walked off the vessel to go back on board before the *Orion* sailed the following day.[52] Most of the malcontents, some 400, were Australians. Much to his relief, his good standing with the New Zealanders restricted their exodus to only 14 individuals. 'We took disciplinary actions against ours,' wrote a frustrated Caldwell to Dorothy, 'and some of the [British] papers of the *Truth* and *Star Sun* standard printed bolshy articles.'[53] He confessed that morale was falling and that it was taking all 'my tact and persuasion to get men on the boats'. To make matters worse, the *Orion* was plagued with engine trouble and forced to return to port and the men to the repatriation camps.[54]

More sailings followed in December, including one about which Caldwell was apprehensive.

> One boat, the Rangitata I am not worried about, but the Athlone Castle which is carrying 2500 Australian Air Force, as well as our 500 RNZAF, is an anxiety as 400 of the Aussies who walked off the Orion are included in this draft and they

tend to influence our fellows. However, have had a good talk to our chaps and hope they won't let us down by walking off ship. I don't think they will. I go down to Southampton early tomorrow morning to the boats and will be years younger when the boats pull out with our complete draft on board.[55]

Caldwell worked overtime to improve the lot of the passengers. 'The Athlone Castle's berths will be allotted in accordance with mess capacity' and 'warrant officers will be given saloon or cafeteria messing, other ranks travelling in normal troop deck conditions'.[56] East of Suez, the total number of passengers was reduced from 4300 to 3500. Caldwell's efforts were rewarded with an incident-free departure.

As the remaining drafts, including those of the dependants — wives with children and many pregnant war brides — were completed, Caldwell was honoured with an invitation to deliver the 11 December toast at 'a very posh luncheon at the Simpson Services Club'.[57] Founded at the beginning of the war, the much-admired Piccadilly club was established to create goodwill and friendship among the officers of the fighting forces of Britain, the dominions and other Allied countries.[58] 'Lords and Ladies in all directions,' said Caldwell of the nearly 80 guests.[59] He sat with Lady Barnby — the American wife of English aristocrat, soldier and politician Lord Barnby — and the elderly Field Marshal Lord Birdwood, the British commander of the Australian and New Zealand Corps during the 1915 Gallipoli campaign. Other guests included the famous New Zealand plastic surgeons Sir Harold Gillies and Archibald McIndoe; Churchill's personal doctor, Lord Moran, and his wife; and a collection of players from the New Zealand Army rugby team.

With his hair combed back and resplendent in his air commodore's plumage, Caldwell delivered his speech with one hand resting in a pocket and a cigarette and glass in the other.[60] Cameras flashed as he thanked the previous speakers for their references to New Zealand's war effort and its determination to defend the empire. Unable to sidestep the widely discussed *Orion* troubles, he acknowledged the ship's quarters were crowded but also playfully suggested the event 'indicated a reluctance to leave the hospitality of England'. He concluded by saying, 'We are now returning to New Zealand [and] shall take back a lasting impression of a charming country and a charming people, and I want to assure you that we shall continue to refer to England as Home.'[61] 'I had to follow two very distinguished speakers who were most fluent and polished, am glad it is over', he later wrote modestly to Dorothy.[62]

With Caldwell's job all but completed, Leonard Isitt confirmed that his replacement was in hand and he could plan his departure. Caldwell arranged sea freight for the large quantity of goods and gifts he had accumulated in his travels and began drafting an itinerary for his final weeks in Britain. He wanted to say goodbye to his London friends and Air Ministry contacts with a little affair at the Savoy before travelling to Scotland to play golf at St Andrews and visit relatives in Perth, but his eyes were firmly set on summer in New Zealand. 'Still bitterly cold and am huddled in front of the small electric heater writing this,' he told Dorothy. 'If you feel like it and can manage it, I would very much like to spend a holiday at some quiet seaside spot — Waiheki [sic] or Bay of Islands sort of thing plus a boat.'[63]

On 23 December, he handed over the command of the headquarters to Wing Commander Frank Gill and left London to spend Christmas with family friends, before travelling on to Scotland to visit relatives and check out some local farms and their stock. He stayed in a 30-room, four-storey 'old baronial hall sort of castle' on Scotland's east coast.

> St Andrews golf links are only 5 miles away and I had 3 games there being cleaned up by the local Scots in 2 of them. It was bitterly cold there on this coastal course and I had so much clothing on I could hardly swing a club and in fact when I was 5 down to an old man of nearly 70 I removed several layers in spite of the intense cold and got him down to 2 up before he beat me. However, as he was on scratch in 1930, I did not feel too helpless about it. St Andrews is an attractive old town and I met a number of older men who live there just for the golf and fishing.[64]

Caldwell then took the four-hour train journey north to Aberdeen to a second cousin's house at Cults. He stayed with elderly relatives before heading north to Forres on the Moray coast, taking with him a letter of introduction from the director of the New Zealand stock and station agency Wright Stephenson. With a view to improving the cattle on his Papatoetoe property, he visited some of Scotland's best Pollard Angus stud farms. 'I saw some very fine cattle,' he informed Dorothy, 'the highest price[d] one being a 2 year bull bought at £3200 recently. Most of these breeders run about 100 head of cattle only, but only the best and they sell their yearling bulls and heifers for £300–£1000 each . . . I was tempted to buy a bull, but decided not to be too hasty, one can always import later.'[65]

After looking over the operations of five farms, he ended his stay at a party hosted by an elderly Miss Grant, the owner of a 300-acre estate. Extensive culinary preparations in the morning were followed by an afternoon out shooting over her farm and surrounding country: 'We got 1 hare and 2 partridges . . . Suffice to say, I shot nothing and I know Peter and David will be amazed at this! Knowing my deadly marksmanship.'[66] He spent his last evening in Scotland with a dozen newly acquired friends in front of a large open fire, feasting on turkey and cream-smothered trifle.

CHAPTER TWENTY-TWO

More Gravy

C aldwell's second post-war return to New Zealand was a quiet affair. He was no longer the young fighter pilot and squadron commander of the Great War, but a middle-aged air commodore who craved nothing more than slipping out of uniform and into Dorothy's arms, and easing back into life on his Papatoetoe farm under a warm antipodean sun.[1] The family gathered at Forres, where Caldwell gave each of them gifts, with the promise of more treasures — assorted furnishings and kitchenware — which were being shipped separately. His last-minute purchase of a 'large seascape picture' from Harrods had been 'on impulse for £60 by [a] good chap'.[2]

His children had sprouted during his wartime service. The eldest, Mary, was closing in on her twenty-first birthday and the youngest, Virginia, was entering her teenage years. Peter and David were no longer boys, but young men. Like most fathers of the era, Caldwell wanted to set his sons into successful careers and marry off his daughters to worthy suitors.

Peter had completed his flight training but, with limited prospects in an over-

Keith Caldwell's eldest son, Peter, trained with the RNZAF in New Zealand but completed his instruction too late to serve overseas. With the demobilisation and downsizing of the RNZAF there were few places in the peacetime air service, so he turned to farming. Caldwell divided the Glen Murray farm between Peter and his brother, David.

subscribed and shrinking RNZAF, had returned to the farm at Glen Murray, where his father found the sun-tanned 19-year-old well ensconced and working with the farm's stock manager. It was a good fit and, as Caldwell had told Dorothy, 'Peter will at best have some flying to look back on and he can always follow up with aero club flying later on if he wishes.'[3] A farming course, though, would be a good idea: at either 'Lincoln or Massey [universities] for a year or so, then I would say one more year with a good farmer and then go as manager at Glen Murray for a further spell before taking over completely'.[4]

David was more complicated. Caldwell felt that his second son, nearing the completion of his schooling at Wanganui Collegiate, was more academically and artistically minded and floated the idea of dispatching him to the University of Cambridge or a local university. In the weeks before his return to New Zealand, he instructed Dorothy to have David 'get a list of all the occupations from the Auck[land] University ready for us to go through and discuss. There must be some 30–40 professions to choose from.'[5] But David appeared to have some interest in cars. During his last year at school, he and a consortium of boys bought a vehicle for £7, which they proposed to drive to Auckland and resell at a profit.[6] 'David may care to become a car salesman,' ruminated his bemused father.

In fact, though David would go on to race cars, he remained undecided about his future vocation, with flying or agriculture foremost in his thinking. The latter surprised Caldwell, who had not 'thought David was particularly interested in farming'.[7] In the end, David joined his brother at Massey, and in the 1950s the Glen Murray property was divided between the two young men.

When the Korean War sent wool prices to stratospheric heights, the brothers reaped the benefits of their father's backbreaking interwar efforts.[8] More generally, improved regional infrastructure, advanced machinery, including pumps, and the advent of aerial topdressing, lifted the productivity of both farms. This last agricultural marvel was aided by the establishment of an airstrip on David's property, which, when not accommodating small aeroplanes, doubled as a polo field for families and local players. A small lake was formed to aid both water management and duck shooting.[9] On his regular visits to Glen Murray, Keith could only quietly shake his head at the transformation of the land he had once farmed largely by horse and hand.[10]

Mary was three years into a physiotherapy degree at the University of Otago when she met medical student Geoffrey Gordon. Her father was unimpressed. The Gordons

Keith Caldwell's mother, Mary.

did not travel in the same circles as the Caldwells, and his daughter's suitor bore no resemblance to the clean-cut men of Caldwell's air force world or the conservative farms of the northern Waikato. With longish hair and languid habits acquired in the student flats of Dunedin, Gordon was singularly independent and in no mood to conform to the expectations of a retired air commodore who was not shy about correcting misapprehensions or 'facts' and could be impatient.[11] As his future son-in-law later confessed:

> He and I didn't get off to the best of starts with each other. There were, I suppose, faults on both sides but mostly mine. He had just returned from the UK and after 5 years of service in the Air Force and he really was a bit short in the fuse and I was a penniless medical student who had had no war service and was courting his daughter which he found rather hard to accept. He also had a very strong personality and an aura of authority and the only way I could come to terms with this was to act the rebel. When he and his helpers were haymaking or digging potatoes, I would be inside reading a book and smoking innumerable cigarettes. In short, behaving very badly.[12]

Caldwell's elderly mother, who was still living in the family's Remuera house, was more accommodating. When a financially strapped Geoff Gordon came up to Auckland to visit and buy an engagement ring, she told him, 'You don't have to buy one. Have one of these', and gave him one from her jewellery box.[13] Gordon finally mustered the courage to ask Caldwell for his daughter's hand in marriage while throwing a rugby ball around.[14] Geoff and Mary were married in the garden of the Papatoetoe property and the Caldwells were generous in funding the wedding and those of their other children. In the 1950s, the other three children also got married. Peter met his future wife, Judy McNaughton, playing tennis on a neighbouring farm, David met Elizabeth Lambe at a polo tournament, and Virginia knew Wallace Macky as a long-standing family friend. Much to Caldwell's delight, by the end of the decade all of the couples were producing grandchildren.

Keith Caldwell at his eldest daughter Mary's wedding to Geoffrey Gordon. From left: Helen Broad, Keith Caldwell, Virginia Caldwell, Marjorie Carson and Mary Caldwell.

The Papatoetoe farm became the centre of Caldwell's universe and the grand-children the stars upon whom he could lavish his attention. His herd of Aberdeen Angus cattle was bolstered by the purchase of a heifer, Ebony Kira of Rowley, from Scotland, to which he added top females from the Tautane, Beachlea, Tauwhare, Ruapehu and Omakere studs. It was described as a 'small but select herd'.[15] The farm was also home to a menagerie of other animals, including a small dairy herd run by his farm manager Pat Smith, who, with his wife, lived in a small cottage on the property.

Fenced off from all of this, and behind a 'picturesque frontage', was the sprawling homestead, a two-storey white weatherboard house surrounded by Dorothy's large flower beds and a good-sized vegetable garden.[16] Caldwell carved off some of the lawn for a tennis court. Visits to Forres became the stuff of legend for the grandchildren, who, along with the rest of family called Keith and Dorothy 'Werfer' and 'Wawee'.

Caldwell presided over the estate in a relaxed but lordly 'English manner'.[17] When the grandchildren stayed, the day began with Dorothy rising early and giving her husband breakfast in bed before waking the grandchildren in their bedroom adjacent to the large farm kitchen, where they would find freshly made brown bread and homemade butter on the breakfast table.[18] Dorothy would also sometimes take the cream off the milk and let it set on the coal range so they could have 'clotted cream on porridge with brown sugar'.

Their grandfather would arise and descend in silk pyjamas on the way to his study. He could be stern, and even grumpy, but he 'always had magic tricks' to entertain them and possessed a 'good sense of humour'. Then there were the innumerable hours spent playing outdoors with the 'chickens, ducks, pigs (often with piglets), a cat, milking cows . . . and mucking around in the old sheds [and] playing tennis. The old tractor was a crowd favourite. We all drove for feeding out, often sitting on Werfer's knee. "More gravy," he would say to pull the throttle down,' recalled one granddaughter.[19] On other occasions, shrieking and shouting children were towed behind the tractor on toboggan rides.[20]

Lunch, frequently roast meat and vegetables, was the largest meal of the day. The relaxed 'anything goes' evening meal commonly centred on scrambled eggs. As the grandchildren grew older, Caldwell introduced them to a small glass of sherry before Sunday lunches, 'supposedly to teach us sensible drinking habits . . . We felt very grown up.'[21]

In the evening, Caldwell regaled the children with fanciful stories, taught them chess or sometimes got out his film projector to screen homemade movies. Often, he put the record player on and danced around the living room with Dorothy, just as he had done in front of their own children. At Christmas, a magnificent tree in the garden was festooned with decorations and gifts placed at its base that were often personally chosen and purchased by Caldwell.

Then there were the numerous outings in his cherished V8-powered Rover P6: to the movies — at least once a week — and when Mary and Geoff Gordon's children came up to visit from Kaikōura in the summer holidays, they would visit their uncles and cousins at the twin Glen Murray farms. They also regularly headed south-east of Auckland to the family's favourite summer holiday spot, Dorothy's father's beach house at Ōrere Point.

Caldwell also took the grandchildren to numerous sporting events, including the annual New Zealand Grand Prix at Pukekohe, where his son David continued his love affair with motoring, racing a red Alfa Romeo, and to the Stanley Street courts for the Auckland Open tennis championships. The grandchildren, lavished with treats, relaxed in the shadow of their celebrated grandfather, who seemed to know everyone of import in Auckland.

C aldwell, who had been flying since 1915 and had witnessed, first hand, four decades of advances in aviation, was about to grumpily oversee its most recent iteration from his Papatoetoe farm. In the late 1950s, civil aviation and international air travel were on the ascent. Long-haul flying boats were being supplanted by machines of the jet age. Sleek Douglas DC-8s and Boeing 707s popularised jet travel, and by the end of the 1950s more people were crossing the Atlantic by air than by sea. Mass international travel had arrived and plans were under way to bring New Zealand into the long-haul international aviation web.

After acquiring the Australian government's half share of TEAL, the New Zealand government renamed the airline Air New Zealand and ordered DC-8s for its national carrier. To cater for these and other jets, Auckland, as the nation's largest city, was chosen for an airport that would befit its international gateway status. The proposed location of the airfield at Māngere, then the site of a modest aerodrome, and its subsequent use, became a matter of considerable vexation for Caldwell.[22]

He lobbied for the new airport to be built at RNZAF Base Auckland, Whenuapai, but found himself up against a well-resourced group — including former First and Second World War pilot and commander Keith Park — that was advocating strongly for the former Auckland Aero Club's Māngere aerodrome. It was a battle he could not win: the hills adjacent to Whenuapai and the prospect of a much larger, purpose-built airport at Māngere were against him. International airport consultants agreed: 'Mangere is an excellent site — one you would dream about. It would be hard to find a better one anywhere in the world.'[23] And of course the matter was personal: the international airport would be his new neighbour, as Forres was a mere '11,000 ft in direct line with the proposed airfield'.[24]

Construction began on the heavy-duty runway in 1960. With the threat of a road being put through his farm, Caldwell decided to divest himself of the farm's cattle and began a protracted battle with the Auckland City Council and the bureaucrats in Wellington over the noise pollution that would be inflicted on the locals by the large turbojet-powered passenger aircraft. He sold his Aberdeen Angus herd at auction in 1961 for a princely £7000.[25] Other equally concerned landowners and the local East Tāmaki branch of Federated Farmers gathered around Caldwell's agitating efforts, and his large study at Forres — a shed that accommodated a desk, holding his overworked typewriter, two comfortable leather armchairs and the mementoes of his First World War exploits — became campaign headquarters.[26]

The study was a fascinating place. His medals and awards — CBE, MC, DFC and bar, Croix de guerre (Belgium) — were modestly out of sight but the silver SE5a, the gift from 74 Squadron, sat in pride of place on a shelf. (The Sidcot flight suit was tucked away in a cupboard.) The walls were covered with photographs of various sporting teams in which he had played, 74 Squadron on display at Clairmarais and portraits of fellow pilots and adversaries, including a photograph of a dead and bloody von Richthofen.[27] As a sea of newspaper clippings, maps and photographs threatened to overflow his desk, Mick Mannock and Werner Voss watched as, late into the evening, Grid struck the keys in a staccato rattle, firing off letters against the intruders.

Caldwell's missives demonstrated an impressive understanding of the nuances of modern jet-powered flight and its impact on those living in the shadow of arriving and departing aircraft. His detailed letters to Wellington were shuffled on to officials who were mindful of Caldwell's extensive aviation knowledge and exemplary service in two world wars. Many, of course, knew him personally, having served under him in the RNZAF or encountered him via the Auckland Aero Club or the broader aviation community. In May 1964, Jim Taylor of the Department of Civil Aviation replied to a number of these letters.

> It is generally accepted that near an aerodrome is somewhat noisy at times but the accepted criterion must in the end be the opinion of the persons living or

working at a particular spot . . . the effect of aeroplane noise on the communities near aerodromes regularly used by internal airlines in New Zealand has, in fact, been much less than might have been expected, as a result of theoretical comparison with data available from abroad. For example, Wellington Airport is highly utilised by modern turbine powered aircraft and its approaches and departures areas are fringed by dense urban development, yet no complaints are on record from the people living in the area.

Studies seemed to indicate that the frequency and duration of landings and takeoffs were the most important factors for those living close to an airfield. The noise level of 112 PNdB (perceived noise in decibels) for a DC-8 or B707 was 'admittedly high', but the exposure would only last 'for approximately 5 seconds' on an approach speed of 165 knots at 500 feet, Taylor wrote. Based on arrival and departure data from international jet flights currently using Whenuapai, Taylor projected growth at Māngere to reach close to 5200 movements by 1970 — 15 per day or fewer than five minutes of high noise levels.

Taylor concluded his letter with a plea: 'Keith, this letter to you gives my own personal views, and I would like you to treat it as such and it is not for public use. The moment figures are used they become debatable and we would not wish to be involved publicly in this way. However, I hope it will be useful to help you resolve your problem, but don't hesitate to write to me again if you want further elucidation.'[28]

In between writing to Wellington, Caldwell went on a handful of overseas fact-finding visits to other international airports.[29] Early in May 1964, after arriving at Sydney's Kingsford Smith airport, still known by its previous name of Mascot, he wrote to Peter Koch of the Australian Department of Civil Aviation, explaining the reason for his 'short personal visit' and making a request: 'Authorities at Mascot Airport have been most helpful in assistance with relative information, but I understand from the Assistant Airport Manager, Mr. Leonard Crowe, that your department might be able to supply a map of the Mascot Airport showing the noise levels in decibel ratings.'[30] Almost a month later, First Assistant Director-General of Civil Aviation Wilfred Pickford replied, stating that no such map existed, but that in Sydney 'there are many houses much closer' than Caldwell's own would be to the Auckland runway and that 'we believe that your house . . . should not be subjected to excessive noise as a result of aircraft operations'.[31]

This was a variance with Caldwell's findings: 'I spoke to residents two miles at end of runways & most were worried by the noise, but accepted it as they did not want to move . . . [though] residents did say that windows rattled and some older wooden houses shook a little.'[32]

When the Auckland runway was completed the following year, the anxieties of Caldwell and other landowners appeared to be confirmed. The farm was plagued by interminable low-level test flights.[33] For long periods at night, the house shook as planes performed touch-and-go landings in an unending 'circuits and bumps' dance. The roar of the engines prevented any sane conversation at Forres.[34] As the opening of the airport in late 1965 drew near, Caldwell's efforts and those of others resulted in a report on the noise expected in the following years. Its recommendations and conclusions were announced by John McAlpine, Minister of Civil Aviation. While admitting that the test flights were 'producing more noise', McAlpine said they were a short inconvenience and though the 'noise nuisance could never be entirely eliminated, the disturbances at Mangere would be of a minor nature compared with those at other major cities in the world'.[35]

Caldwell raised the white flag of surrender and many of the residents resigned themselves to the inevitable. Some farmers found the noise less intrusive than they had feared but continued lobbying the Manukau County Council regarding the prospect of their land being rezoned as industrial. In the face of rising land rates, would they be able to sustain their farms? Caldwell, who turned 70 on the eve of the airport's official opening, was ready to decamp. He planned to spend his remaining years well away from the airport.

Nonetheless, he had no intention of selling the property immediately. With the likely expansion of the airport, the rezoning of the land in subsequent years and the much-touted Southwestern Motorway locked into the city's transport masterplan, he calculated that the decreasing viability of the farm would be compensated for by the land's increasing monetary value for light industry and airport-related ventures. Delaying the farm's sale would result in a financial windfall. His solution was to place the property in a trust for all 17 grandchildren, with his sons as principal administrative trustees.[36]

Caldwell, ever the pragmatist, was not about to let the airport fracas deter him from feeding his own travel addiction. Within months of its official opening, he and Dorothy were winging their way from Māngere to the world, collecting arrival and embarkation stamps in Kuala Lumpur, Hong Kong, London, Beirut, Cairo and New York during a nearly five-month trip.[37]

Within a few years of this extensive tour, the Caldwells were living in the leafy suburb of Glendowie on the north-eastern end of the Auckland isthmus. The smart, sharp-lined weatherboard house, with its modern 1970s Formica-surfaced kitchen and deep-carpeted hallway in brown and orange tones, was smaller than Forres. But, perched on the side of a hill, the steep quarter-acre section had stunning views of Rangitoto Island and the Waitematā Harbour, the same waters where, some 50 years earlier, Caldwell had learnt to fly at the Walsh brothers' school. To squeeze into his new, more modest office, he divested himself of some of his treasures: the Sidcot suit and the German machine gun found a home at the Auckland War Memorial Museum.[38] These donations did not, however, represent a declining interest in military matters and the air war of the First World War.

After returning from the Second World War, Caldwell officiated at various Anzac Days, appeared in numerous air-power publications, organised regular annual gatherings of New Zealand's First World War airmen and spent a good deal of his time communicating with aviation enthusiasts, researchers and historians around the world. In the early Cold War period, he delivered a commemorative speech to a dawn gathering in the small Waikato town of Tuakau. He spoke of the countrymen who had died in both world wars, and the 'loss of potential leadership . . . to this country', especially 'during these troublous times with such strong disruptive forces at work [when] the need for strong & true leadership has never been greater'. He then asked his audience, including a troop of uniformed Tuakau Boy Scouts, to preserve the values for which so many had given their lives:

> Those of us who are left, the large majority, must not be sidetracked from our duty to the fallen & their relatives to do all we can to retain the ideals of democratic freedom for which they fought . . . We owe it to our dead in war, their next of kin, our children & ourselves to play our part in restoring confidence & goodwill. We have a tremendous task in helping to bring peace again to the world but let us this Anzac Day resolve to face up to the problems with the same spirit which inspired our men who gave their lives in war for the cause of freedom. Let us prove that their sacrifice was not in vain.[39]

Caldwell and a handful of compatriots, notably Leonard Isitt and Sopwith Dolphin ace Ronald Bannerman, were instrumental in formalising the First World War airmen's reunions into the New Zealand 1914–1918 Airmen's Association.[40] At its peak, the national AGM attracted nearly 200 attendees, including Keith Park,

reconnaissance specialist and flying instructor John Seabrook, successful bomber pilot Euan Dickson and New Zealand's highest-scoring RNAS airman, Harold Beamish.[41] Brandishing brandies and cigarettes, the increasingly silver-haired airmen discussed the attributes of their favourite grids, relived old battles and told tall stories that were reported by newspapers under suitably evocative if sometimes corny headlines: 'Warbirds fly back the years' and 'Canvas Kites and Hun in the Sun'.[42]

The booming number of books on the subject showed that fascination with the airmen who had flown fabric-and-wood machines against the feared black-crossed aeroplanes of the Luftstreitkräfte was undiminished. Caldwell popped up in numerous publications and in 1954 was once again at the forefront of a well-received Ira Jones effort: a history of 74 Squadron in two world wars. Nearly half of *Tiger Squadron* was dedicated to a mere nine months in 1918 and Caldwell played a principal role in what was really Taffy's wartime diary spruced up for publication.[43]

In 1966, further interest was revived with the premier of the movie blockbuster *The Blue Max*, starring George Peppard, James Mason and Ursula Andress. The public loved the air-fighting scenes, even as the airmen themselves were critical of the poor adherence to accuracy. Jack D. Hunter, who wrote the book on which the film was based, agreed. During filming he visited Bray Studio on the Thames:

> I was literally left speechless when I saw Fokker D-7s with inverted engines and 1916-style insignia, Dr-1s with radial engines and smoke canisters on their landing gear struts, machine-guns that looked like Space Cadet props spouting flame without benefit of ammo tracks, every pilot wearing an Uhlan uniform and Battle of Britain style goggles, Gypsy Moths pretending to be Albatros D-3s, a Stampe presented as an RE-8 — the anachronisms and goofs compounded. When I asked [former First World War pilot and technical adviser Kurt] Delang about it later, he merely shrugged, rolled his eyes, and sighed resignedly. When I challenged the art director on something so glaring as a D-7 with curve-sided crosses, he shrugged, too. 'That kind of cross photographs better,' he said.[44]

Caldwell's response was succinct: 'Air fighting shots very insipid I thought; it was not quite as easy as that.'[45] Despite its deficiencies, the film returned a handsome profit to

A 1956 Warbirds function at the Brevet Club rooms in Durham Lane, Auckland. From left: William Bloomfield (seated), Tom Mills, Harry Leese, Keith Caldwell, Doug Lillian and Eric Calder. Caldwell is holding a model SE5a.

20th Century Fox. Other films followed, including *The Red Baron* (1971) and *Aces High* (1976). These celluloid depictions allowed the Airmen's Association to bask quietly in the reflected glory of each film and compare notes on the various aspects of each cinematic attempt to capture their lives over the Western Front trenches more than half a century earlier.

With interest still high in First World War aviation, but the numbers of surviving airmen falling, Caldwell became increasingly sought after as a commentator and source of expertise. As he told his old colleague William Fry: 'There are so few of us left to help them.'[46] Typically, Caldwell's answers for information resulted in follow-up letters of appreciation that contained requests for clarification or more information. 'I always appreciate your letters which are full of interest and help me considerably with my researches', wrote one enthusiast. 'Your patience in answering my many questions is quite remarkable.' Then came the inevitable follow-up query:

> May I just ask a last 'technical' point to you concerning the flying of the S.E.? Sometime ago, one of the Canadian pilots, George Dixon, wrote and told me how he first came to fly an SE at Hounslow. It appears a notice came on the board about the time Bishop succeeded in getting 85 converted to S.E.s from Dolphins which instructed all officers having experience on the S.E. to hand their names into the office. Dixon had never flown an S.E. but knew McGregor had, so got 'Mac' to explain the controls to him. This was done and Dixon took a machine up for a short flight on return from which he added his name to the list of those who were already 'qualified'. The rest came with practical experience, not specific training and George Dixon went on to explain that he was a long time in France before he found out that there was a critical point on the throttle control which had to be passed over quickly to get maximum r.p.m. In consequence, he was always experiencing difficulty in 'keeping up' with the patrol when full power was required. Can you comment on this?[47]

Others sent him books, photographs and copies of his old combat in air reports in exchange for his valuable insights. 'I've enclosed pics of [Paul] Billik, [Adolf Ritter von] Tutschek (not a very good one I'm afraid) and others which might interest you,' wrote one correspondent, '[as] small payment for the enjoyment I'm getting research wise in your wonderful letters.'[48]

Many of these requests for help were for articles being submitted to the American and British versions of the *Cross & Cockade*, historical magazines about First World War aviation. 'Enclosed . . . is the first draft of my article on Wilhelm Prien of Jasta Boelcke which I intend to use in the first issue of the *Cross & Cockade Journal*,' wrote editor Marvin Skelton in July 1970. 'Since this is my first "solo" I am particularly anxious that it be interesting, so will appreciate any comments or corrections.'[49] The journal's name came from the black cross and coloured roundel symbols used on the German and British machines. *Cross & Cockade* became a focal point for Great War aviation research during the 1970s and subsequent decades.

They were addictive publications for a global network of devotees and surviving participants, and Caldwell devoured the articles on his Central Power adversaries.[50] 'It has been interesting to read about the various Huns we scrapped with,' he told a correspondent, 'not knowing at the time who was flying what, although one got to note colour schemes & flying ability . . . their leaders were often pretty hot stuff.'[51]

The well-regarded researcher Douglass Whetton was supplying Caldwell with copies of the journal in brown envelopes in return for information on Australia's most successful ace of the war, Arthur Cobby.[52] 'Very pleased to see the *Cross & Cockade* are arriving,' wrote Whetton in 1977. 'There are now six copies on the way to you. Four, of course, for last year, and the first two for this year . . . You may also like a copy of *War Weekly*, December 1977, when it is due. I have an article on [French fighter ace Georges] Guynemer in this, and you are mentioned with reference to your comments on attacks on hostile two-seaters.'[53]

Caldwell also received drafts of books to look over and give his stamp of approval, and the published versions soon found their way into his ever-expanding library of First World War aviation volumes.[54] In reply to a Caldwell missive, aviation writer James Dudgeon wrote: 'One can become a little despondent when working on a project like this, but certain little "gems", such as your letter, can cheer one up enormously. With your help, I will be able to finish my work at last.'[55] The next three pages listed 27 questions regarding his biography of Mannock. Caldwell responded with a densely typewritten letter answering all but the last question, which asked for his thoughts on Mick: 'I would think you can gain enough impressions of my opinion of Mannock from the pretty full list of questions you have posed.' He also pointed Dudgeon to a pithy summary of his thoughts in Whetton's 1977 book on Mannock.[56]

When Dudgeon's book was published, it contained a foreword by Caldwell and a tribute to him: '"Grid" Caldwell, now retired as an Air Commodore in New Zealand, is still actively involved in assisting those who would study that first war in the air.

Without his dedicated help and comprehensive knowledge, few aero-historians would get very far.'[57] As Whetton had told Caldwell, 'Without your personal kindness and guidance in these matters, my material would have lacked the authenticity which is so essential in works of this sort.' Skelton agreed: 'The kind of information you sent can only come from one who was there and in the type of data which makes a particular individual more "real".'[58]

In the 1970s, and much to his delight, Caldwell received numerous letters from elderly First World War veterans. Norman 'Pusher' Birks, a former DH2 pilot and First World War POW, wrote to Caldwell in October 1977.

> My daughter brought me an RFC tie for my [eightieth] birthday . . . so, I asked her to get one for you as well. I don't suppose they are obtainable in the cannibal islands in the mid-Pacific! I don't like being old and birthdays emphasise the position don't they? Last week we had a P.O.W. reunion (1914–1918) and between you and me most of the remaining lot appear to be senile.[59]

Another frequent correspondent was Gwilym 'Cherub' Lewis. Caldwell had experienced his most terrifying moments of the war at the hands of Cherub's father when, in 1918, he was invited to the Lewis home north of London. When Lewis senior, a colonel in the infantry, heard of his son's flying aspirations he took lessons himself at a Hendon flying school and avidly followed his son's aviation career. Lewis recalled many years later how his father also kept an 'open house in Hampstead for my pals, particularly from overseas':

> Later in 1918, a not unusual quartet on leave was Zulu Lloyd (South Africa), Mick Mannock (Ireland?) and Grid Caldwell (NZ). Zulu and Mick were familiar with the house, and one Sunday they brought Grid along too for lunch . . . Anyway my Dad was a firm character and towards the evening, as was usual on Sundays, he proposed we sing family hymns. The Lewis's had no problem in singing; but for the three old heathens, this was really something! And when the time came for the old man to turn to Grid with, 'Grid, perhaps you would sing the next verse?' our New Zealander nearly burst a blood vessel. Well, Grid never turned his tail to a Hun, but he was shaking like a leaf and with a very rough, croaky, shaky, and rather untuneful voice, he gave a rendering of 'Abide with me.'

It was a nightmarish moment that haunted Caldwell for the rest of his life: the interminable verses, a grinning Lloyd. That evening, the 'three of them fell back strongly on the bar of the RFC Club to recover their nerves'.[60]

Lewis's memoir, *Wings over the Somme*, was published in 1976. Of the more than 150 books he had read on First World War aviation, Caldwell considered it to be among the top five — high praise indeed. When he asked Cherub if any more titles were forthcoming, the answer was 'No, no more books, that was my "magnum opus".'[61]

Arthur Gould Lee, a veteran and prolific author, acquired Caldwell's address from former 60 Squadron airman Geoffrey 'Pidders' Piddock.

> I can't recall that we ever met during our RFC/RAF days, though we must have passed pretty close once or twice in 1917–18. Of course, yours is a name well-known since World War I days, with your service in 60 and 74, but I don't suppose you've heard of me unless you happen to come across my last two books, *No Parachute* and *Open Cockpit*, both of which deal with my modest experiences as a Pup and Camel pilot in 46 Squadron in 1917.[62]

Of all the old pals, William 'Willie' Fry became Caldwell's closest confidant in the last decade of his life. The letters between them were warm and detailed, filled with candid discussions about their ailments, family and old times on the Western Front. The two men had flown Nieuports together in Alan Scott's 60 Squadron and had shared a victory over an Albatros DIII in the late spring of 1917. Fry had ended the war with nine credits to his name, flying Sopwith Dolphins, and spent much of the interwar period in the RAF before becoming a wing commander in the Second World War. During the war Caldwell had found Fry a 'quiet shy fellow and it was not until we met again in 1955 and 1966 that I realised what a nice genuine chap he was'.[63]

In 1975, Caldwell told Fry that he had received a phone call 'sometime back advising that a British "ace" (hate the word) named . . . Griffith was coming to NZ'.[64] The reporter arranged a lunch for the few remaining local First World War airmen to meet the former 48 Squadron Bristol F2b Fighter pilot. When he appeared in Auckland, the newspapers boldly claimed that Griffith had shot down the third-highest-scoring German pilot, Erich Loewenhardt. Caldwell was bemused:

> I happened to know from my records that L had died following a collision with one of his pals, Lt [Alfred] Wentz [Wenz] on 10-8-18. Also looked up to find that Griffith had been credited with one Hun between 19 & 25th August [1918]. His

observor'r [sic] name is mentioned too. In the morning Griffith was televised
& claimed that [Squadron] 48's role was to contain Richthofen's Circus. Well, I
took along evidence to the lunch to show that there had been a case of mistaken
identity, to put it mildly, but G seemed such a nice little man, that I held my horse
& said nothing; thought it did not matter much, G would have to live with his
conscience . . . but I hate humbug & again in the paper this morning there was
his photograph with some more blarney & the shooting down of Loewenhardt .
. . & was able to correct some errors in his memory about happenings & thought
he would gather that I knew what I was talking about. He goes off South today
& I should think he would want to avoid us again. What a disappointment, as he
seemed a nice fellow.

In his letter to Fry, Caldwell then launched into a lengthy discussion of the six Bristol
F2b Fighter squadrons in 1918 before catching himself. 'So much for warfare, but this
Griffith man has started me off on the subject,' he confessed.[65]

Books that failed to live up to expectations were opportunities to set the record
straight. When Dorothy brought her husband a copy of *Aces High: The war in the
air over the Western Front 1914–18* (1973), by noted politician and author Alan Clark,
he was disappointed.[66] 'It is quite good, except that he has got most of his material
from hearsay, there are some glaring inaccuracies,' Caldwell told Fry, damning Clark's
account of Albert Ball in 8 Squadron, the exploits of Mannock and the death of Voss.
He enjoyed Bill Lambert's *Combat Report* (1975) but found his estimation of the SE5a
compared with the German machines overgenerous.[67]

> Many of us, who had a fair time in the SEs, found that a Fokker D.7 & their
> triplane could quickly catch up with an SE in vertical turning, which put the SE
> at a decided disadvantage, as so many engagements developed into the circling
> business . . . These Fokkers used to spiral down steeply with lots of motor & an
> SE could not follow, without risking break up. Amazing how one still natters on
> about 1st war days with a contemporary.[68]

An irregular but lively topic of conversation between the pair was Billy Bishop.
Caldwell had liked the Canadian super-ace for his outgoing and lively contributions
to the esprit de corps of 60 Squadron and had appreciated Bishop's fulsome praise
in his much-reprinted *Winged Warfare*. When Bishop died in 1956, Caldwell had
written to his wife, enclosing a monetary gift.[69]

Caldwell was less enamoured with Bishop's penchant for exaggeration — in airmen's parlance, 'shooting a line'. 'Looking at our Encyclopedia last night,' he told Fry, 'I saw Bishop's name as a famous flier, but not Ball, McCudden or Mannock? I ask you! Only a few of us know the story; all very sad.'[70] Foremost in Caldwell's mind was Bishop's much-admired 2 June 1917 'raid' on a German airfield. 'Your remarks re Billy Bishop, I can readily understand,' said Caldwell to Fry.

> It always seemed so unfair that he received so much public acclaim during the years from writers who did not know the facts; so unfair to so many genuine chaps who went unsung bravely doing their best & very often, unrewarded. One does not like damning a man who is dead and gone, but I get sick of reading what a terrific hero he was. I still cannot think what he got up to on his VC jaunt; coming back without his Lewis; why, how, would he want to shed it? [Raymond] Collishaw from Canada in one of his many letters . . . told me there were no losses at any Hun aerodromes that day & [that Bishop's] claims were completely spurious. Do you think he could have landed in some remote place, taken off his gun & shot holes in his wings? I can hardly believe that anyone could go to such awful extremes to try to gain cudos [sic] & chest job [medal].[71]

Caldwell's private comments were rarely publicly aired, but Fry's 1974 memoir, *Air of Battle*, elaborated on this correspondence. Neither believed Bishop. The Canadian's inability to name the airfield attacked, the lack of German corroboration, the implausibly tightly gathered bullet holes and the inexplicably missing machine gun all stretched credulity to breaking point. As Fry argued, this 'must be a very unusual case of a Victoria Cross or any high honour being awarded on the word of the recipient only as to his exploit and without any witnesses or participants'. Fry expanded further on his concerns in a document he deposited with aviation historian Alex Revell for publication in *Cross & Cockade* after his death.[72]

In the decades that followed, Bishop's detractors grew in number, as others, including official historians of the Royal Canadian Air Force, revisited his extensive aerial combat claims, many of which were similarly unwitnessed lone-wolf sorties.[73] It was a painful re-examination of a national hero. 'When his son wrote to me some years back for comment on his Father . . . there was not much to say,' Caldwell confessed to Gwilym Lewis, 'except that he was popular & a cheery bird etc. I could not reveal my opinion to the son. The book about this father was produced by a proud son; & that was as it should be.'[74]

When Caldwell, along with other 60 Squadron veterans, was asked by the RAF Museum to endorse and sign a painting of 'Bishop doing his VC act', he politely declined because 'I have to doubt its authenticity'.[75]

Straight Bat

B y the mid-1970s, the Airmen's Association was in precipitous decline. 'Eight of us, Ex Air Force WWI, are having lunch next month at the local Officers' Club; just an informal "get together", no speeches or nonsense,' Caldwell told Fry in October 1975. 'We are about the only chaps left or mobile, in Auckland.'[1]

When Caldwell was told that an American researcher was arriving in New Zealand to see him, he assembled a couple of other airmen for him to interview, but lamented that the visitor 'won't get much out of them; they are all too far gone, a bit gaga'.[2]

All of this simply made Caldwell, now aged 80, an even more valuable commodity. 'As you say, there is still a great deal of interest in 1st war flying,' he wrote to Gwilym Lewis. 'There seems to be an air of urgency amongst historians & other interested parties to get all the "gen" they can from those of us who are still about.'[3]

Caldwell was also encouraged to put his own experiences down on paper. After a more general discussion on recent war-related publications, Marvin Skelton broached the idea in a January 1977 letter:

> Speaking of books, have you considered the possibility of writing one? I am sure
> you have been approached, and since a book by you has not appeared, I assume
> you are not interested. However, I am sure someone like William Kimber (who

published the books by Fry and Lewis) would be delighted to handle one by you. And I would be honoured to help, with typing etc. One very convenient way to avoid the tedium of writing such an account is to use a tape recorder and have the contents typed. Again, I would be honoured to help with the tapes.[4]

Fry and Lewis also gently raised the prospect with Grid, but he was reluctant. First, he did not relish talking about himself; it assaulted his excessive modesty. When asked by well-known aviation artist Robert E. Carlin whether he could recreate the New Zealander's mid-1917 scrap with Voss on canvas, Caldwell told Fry of his

> reluctance to be a party to this painting, which he expected me to autograph & he would add a caption to it . . . I explained to Carlin, my wish to avoid personal publicity, especially when it had to do with war service, especially if it reflects, skills, courage to some degree etc. One does not talk about these matters to anyone, let alone a man who probably wants to cash in on it . . . The Yanks, or many of them, do not understand the British reluctance to keep away from any form of self-aggrandisement & probably put it down to 'narrow-mindedness' or stuffiness.[5]

Second, such a book would require a public airing of his opinions on others, and 'Bish' loomed large in this regard. He was loath to publicly air his criticisms. Third, though he had made prodigious efforts to reply to questions and look over other's literary efforts, it was an altogether different matter to write a substantial memoir. 'Thank you for the kindly thought that it is my turn to write some memoirs,' he told Lewis. 'Others have suggested this, but it won't be happening. I never kept a diary, only a meagre logbook & have a few letters relating to WWI & I would not trust my memory to be accurate after all these years . . . So, as they say, sorry no dice.'[6]

Besides, the number of letters he was still receiving in the latter part of the decade — at least one a week — was threatening to overwhelm him. 'There has been such a spate of questions & requests from historinian [sic] chaps of the last few years, that it has become a nuisance.'[7]

And old age was sapping the last remnants of his physical prowess. In 1976 the man who had wrestled his Glen Murray hill-country farm into submission was forced to hand his suburban lawn-mowing duties to a younger man at $5 a time. The effort was just 'too tiring and hurtful,' he told Fry.[8]

I know I seem to do a lot of about planning what should be done, yet it never seems to get done. One is just growing older . . . all that excitement we had years ago has probably taken some toll we cannot measure, I know I never expected to be almost 81 years old; thought it would be impossible. Yet at heart or mentally one does not feel at all senile or slow of thought. Many old friends have either died or gone into old people's homes this year, & the topic is often, 'have you booked in anywhere' as there is . . . such a demand. One pair we know well have erected a small 900ft cottage in the grounds of a 'house' where they grow old happily & when they turn their toes up, the house goes into a Home Trust.[9]

The following year, there was a nasty incident while he and Dorothy were gardening, though his description of the event showed his dogged mental acuity.

Dorothy's hand which I attacked with [a] chainsaw some time back has healed completely thank goodness . . . We were cutting up firewood at our beach place when I failed to spot a movement of her hand to pick up a piece. Luckily it needed only a few stiches, but it gave us an awful fright; never again will she be allowed to help with the chainsaw work. She is pretty fit for just on 76. I am the dud of the party, as [I] have to swallow heart pills & cannot take much exercise which is an awful nuisance & my eyes are poor; just wearing out as do others of my age; 82 next month, but mentally I think I am not too senile yet & happy on the whole, really.[10]

He kept up his interest in politics. In 1974, Prime Minister Edward Heath's struggles over the establishment of the European Economic Community and his battles with coal miners had coincided with the departure of the Third Labour Government of New Zealand and the arrival of Robert Muldoon's conservative National government. 'Poor old England is having a dreadful time,' Caldwell lamented in a letter to William Fry, and reckoned New Zealand was in for its own government versus unions trial.[11]

That year, too, he had followed the Christchurch Commonwealth Games on television, delighted by how well all of the colonies of the old Empire 'got on so well with one another . . . The final pictures of all the nations' athletes joining hands & romping around the arena before royalty and all the world to see, was quite emotional.' He slipped into terminology of another era when he told Fry, 'This is undoubtedly a loyal dominion.'[12]

All Blacks tours against 'our old Springbok rivals' and the French were eagerly anticipated, though the hard grounds and tough play of the South Africans would 'probably cause casualties, that we cannot afford' and the French were 'no saints on the rugby field'.[13]

Family events were a highlight and large gatherings with children and grandchildren were anticipated and long remembered. When Lewis informed him of his upcoming fiftieth wedding anniversary, Caldwell recalled his and Dorothy's:

> Golden weddings come eventually to all who wait & we would like to wish you and your wife a very happy day on July 11. Being more ancient than you probably, we had ours two years ago, when the family turned out in force against our wishes & it was a happy time. We have a bunch of 17 starving g/children (4 children of our own) & we see quite a bit of them; they are great fun but sadly they grow so quickly. Ours range from 26 to 7 in years.[14]

Caldwell's only problem lay in keeping track of the comings and goings of such a large and adventurous brood. 'Yes, we will tell our two wandering g/daughters to look you up, if ever up your way,' he wrote to William Fry, who had offered lodgings to Caldwell family members passing through Norwich.

> One is in Switzerland at the moment & the other one, I think, has just arrived in UK from Africa. They will phone first, if they can pop in. We have another g/child, a boy, in the USA at the moment, for some vacation months, yet another g/daughter takes off later this year, I think, for England to take a cooking (Cordon Bleu) course. Seems to be an urge with young people, now a days, to get off somewhere, before they settle down to a married existence & I suppose one can understand their unrest . . .[15]

Younger grandchildren were regular house guests — 'Having a 9 year old g/son staying with us for a week, while his folks are on holiday . . . it is fun having him' — and older teens and young adults were wined and dined at restaurants on Queen Street for celebratory birthdays; there were buffet lunches at the Hotel Intercontinental for

Above: **Attendees of the New Zealand (1914–1918) Airmen's Association reunion in front of the Auckland War Memorial Museum in March 1962. Keith Caldwell is in the front row, third from left. By the 1970s the numbers had dropped markedly.**

Below: **Caldwell and his family at Christmas lunch in Glendowie, Auckland, in 1974.**

those returning to boarding school; and, famously, champagne and oysters for those heading off on that New Zealand rite of passage, the big OE.[16] As young adults the grandchildren eventually became beneficiaries of the Papatoetoe farm trust Caldwell had established.[17]

The family, in turn, regularly organised the couple's trips down to the beach house and hosted them at their homes. The Ōrere Point property was full of memories, and its flat section enabled them to potter in the garden more readily than on the steep Glendowie property. They also went to Glen Murray; the man who had fought with the Germans over the Western Front now lamented the poor prospects of the local waterfowl.

> We had a happy day last weekend out at our sons' farms, which was once our farm. They both have quite large lakes or damned swamps where native birds nest & breed. I sat for an hour near one, watching ducks, swans, pukekos, swallows, pied stilts, shags & some others. Sad to think that in May many of them will be shot when the shooting season starts, but not the swans. I do not shoot any longer; feel too sorry for the birds, but of course, being a dud shot, many escaped.[18]

In the meantime, his old flying comrades were falling fast, among them two retired air vice-marshals. Like Caldwell, Geoffrey Pidcock preferred to keep his thoughts and past exploits to himself. 'I am not a publicity merchant,' he told Grid.[19] Stanley Vincent was one of the few airmen to fly operationally in both wars, even picking up a handful of victories as a station commander during the Battle of Britain. Both men died within a month of each other in 1976. 'What a sad time it is at present & lately,' Caldwell lamented to Fry.

> It was not unexpected really, the news of Pidders going west, but it was pretty devastating all the same & thank you (if I had not already done so), for telling me about his end & for the funeral enclosures from newspapers. Others have sent similar cuttings too. I had a very fine letter from Pidders' wife, Christine, recently, she, of course was desolate, especially as she was with him all the time towards the end & when he died; holding his hand; all very pathetic, poor soul. Now, there are you, Chidlaw & myself of the 'old core', & I read in our local Auckland this morning that Stanley Vincent has also just died. Where, when, does our grief end?[20]

The loss of these men and others over the years was something only those who lived it really understood, but occasionally Caldwell shared his emotions. One day, his granddaughter Jane wandered into his office 'to say hi'.

> I looked at the photo of his old squadron, in amongst all the other photos of the war. I thought some of them could or should have been visiting, as old friends. I asked him where they were, and he just looked completely stricken and so sad. He just looked at me and said, 'they're all dead'. I was sad and gobsmacked, as I had only heard wonderful stories of 'derring-do' and 'jolly good chaps' — more from others than himself. I got a glimmer of what the reality of war perhaps really meant.[21]

The family was also devastated by the death of Virginia's husband, Wallace Macky, who died of cancer in November 1975. Their widowed daughter was now the sole parent of five children. In March 1976, Caldwell told Fry:

> We just said goodbye to Virginia, our youngest daughter who is off with friends to Hong Kong, [and] Singapore for two weeks, the change we hope will help her have a break from a busy, difficult time, coping with so many problems since the death of her husband not long ago. She decided to sell the rather large house they live in for a smaller one & only yesterday, saw one she liked & quite close to us. Dorothy & I had a look plus a valuer friend & we all thought it would be just right for her, if the price is right. So, the haggling has started today & in her absence we shall do the best we can. Her youngest son Robert comes to us during this time, age is 10, so hope we can cope with his homework![22]

Other grandchildren found comfort in Caldwell's orbit, including Mary's son Simon, and another of Virginia's boys, Christopher. Simon's sporting talent was revealed in events Caldwell organised on Boxing Day gatherings at Papatoetoe, when Werfer ran the children through a raucous regime of running races and competitions of all kinds. When Simon demonstrated good athleticism and eye–hand coordination, Caldwell immediately set about teaching him the rudimentary skills of cricket and rugby, placing his handkerchief on the tennis court for Simon to aim for when bowling and correcting his grip on a rugby ball when punting and dropkicking.[23] Over the years, Caldwell added the grubber and chip kick to his grandson's repertoire, which he used to good try-scoring effect.

Like his grandfather, Simon would go on to play schoolboy rugby for Christ's College, and representatively for Marlborough. In 1978, Caldwell made the long trek to Wanganui Collegiate School to support his grandson in the finals of the annual tournament he had played in during his own school days — now a quadrangular event with the inclusion of Nelson College. Christ's College lacked the size of their opponents and Caldwell's alma mater won in a low-scoring match. 'Good game, man,' he consoled his grandson, who had kicked a successful penalty from the sideline.[24]

Christopher Macky was aviation mad and had obtained his private licence while attending Wanganui Collegiate.[25] Flying from south Auckland's Ardmore Airport — built by the United States Army Air Force in the Second World War to accommodate Boeing B-17 Flying Fortresses — Christopher took Werfer up in small four-seater Cessna 172 and 177 machines. These flights roamed over Auckland and often included the Glen Murray farms, Dorothy working in the Glendowie garden and the waters off Mission Bay, where Caldwell had begun his flight instruction in 1915.

The contrast between those early years and his grandson's training experience was stark. The Walsh brothers had had only two troublesome wood-and-fabric seaplanes with ribbons to gauge wind direction. The Rex Manukau Flying School had over 20 all-metal machines whose enclosed cockpits were jam-packed with modern instrumentation and communications gear. And the school's instructors were infinitely superior to the self-taught Vivian Walsh at Kohimarama and the untrained instructors of 1916 Britain. 'We have one grandson, just turned 19 . . . who has about 100 hours on Cessnas etc. and he loves it and is an excellent pilot,' Caldwell told Skelton.

> I often go up with him, which he does not object to, as I am useful in the office after the flight is over when some settling is necessary. He lets me fly it but not land, probably a wise decision. Nowadays, of course, they motor into a landing (sensible) whereas in our early days this would have been considered just 'not on'. One was always expected to come in without engine and make a 'three-pointer'; never resort to engine help. They get so much dual [instruction], which is sensible; we were shot off solo, as soon as we got off, round and down reasonably well. Instructors did not seem to care for their pupils much in those days and there were many first solo crashes.[26]

During their flights, Caldwell, who had survived half a dozen crash-landings in the First World War, imparted hard-earnt knowledge on dealing with engine failures, landing on water and even how to negotiate an emergency landing in a tree.[27] Mostly, though, it was simply the joy of being airborne with his grandson, who recalled that having 'my grandfather Keith sitting in the righthand seat flying the Cessna aircraft . . . [was] the highlight of my flying hours'.[28]

Caldwell had spent a good part of his working life under the strong New Zealand sun, and he was particularly vulnerable to skin cancer. 'So sad that so often old age brings with it illness of some kind or other just at a time when all one wants is peace and serenity . . . There is a lot of skin trouble amongst farmers in this country, especially with those people, like myself who scorned wearing hats in our hot summers,' he told William Fry after a round of radiotherapy in 1975 for a melanoma that had left his face a mess and prevented his attendance at a First World War commemoration event.[29]

At the end of the decade the cancer returned and Caldwell faced his final adversary. In the wake of the news of his illness and an unsuccessful operation, Geoff Gordon visited to see how Dorothy, who had only recently recovered from a surgery of her own, was coping.

> I said to her 'What are you going to do when all this is over?' She said, 'What do you mean?' and I said, 'Well your husband is dying and has only a few weeks to go.' She replied, 'That is the first time that death has been mentioned.' She truly had no thought of death as a possibility and very sadly neither she nor Keith had ever discussed this outcome and made any plans for the future. I think that he in his last few months felt most unwell and couldn't bring himself to talk about it and she didn't want to admit even to herself that people died.[30]

Werfer's family was ever-present in the final weeks. Individuals and groups arrived and Caldwell did his best to encourage them, despite his own pain and medication. Peter appeared on numerous occasions, sometimes in the company of his son Michael, who Caldwell encouraged to 'always play with a straight bat'.[31] His granddaughter Deborah was not far from his thoughts. He managed to write to her to congratulate her on her upcoming nuptials and to apologise for not being able to attend. He wished her and Richard 'every happiness over a very long spell of years'.[32] 'It was such a special letter to me,' she recalled, 'because he was dying and heavily sedated with morphine and he wrote this wonderful letter. Very clear and precise and very much Werf.'[33]

It had been a rich life, characterised by a work ethic modelled by his father; a playfulness and generosity of spirit gleaned from his mother; ideals of Christian sacrifice and service absorbed in the school chapel; manliness and gentlemanliness acquired on the rugby field and cricket pitch; and the enduring importance of family.

The First World War was the defining event of his life, and he never escaped its grasp. Nor did he want to. For all its carnage and personal loss, the war had tested him and had given him a place in the most exhilarating undertaking of the conflict: aerial combat over the Western Front. As an airman, he had known incomparable moments of fear and elation; been part of a league of extraordinary comrades; found considerable, if unlooked for, fame; occupied a prominent post-war role in his country's Territorial Air Force; and held significant commands in the Second World War.

On 28 November 1980, aged 85, and surrounded by his family, the bravest of the brave, Keith 'Grid' Caldwell, died.

Seventy-four

In France there's a damn good old Squadron
Though the drome's on the side of a hill,
It's a Squadron of great reputation,
It is Seventy Four escadrille.

There was Mannock of fame in the Air Force,
Hunarinos he shot down with ease,
As happy as hell round the aerodrome,
As he shouted for, 'All tickets please.'

And Roxburgh, and Taffy and Youngski,
Men who are all in the air,
And all the rest in the Squadron,
The best you could find anywhere.

Now one toast will I offer in closing,
Just one it could easily be more,
A toast to the C.O. who led us,
To Caldwell of Seventy Four.

— *Leonard Richardson*

Keith Caldwell's victories

CAPT landed in Allied lines (may or may not indicate intact)   **FTL** forced to land
DES destroyed   **OOC** out of control

	Date	Enemy	Aircraft	Location	Time	Result
			8 Squadron, RFC			
1.	18 Sep 1916	Roland CII	BE2D 5735	Achiet-le-Petit	1930	DES*
			60 Squadron, RFC			
2.	11 Dec 1916	Albatros C	Nieuport	W Arras	1015	CAPT**
3.	14 Jun 1917	Albatros DIII	Nieuport B1654	Drocourt	0955	OOC
4.	15 Jun 1917	Albatros DIII	Nieuport B1654	N Vitry	2020	DES ***
5.	24 Jun 1917	Albatros DIII	Nieuport B1654	S & SE Douai	2010	DES
6.	24 Jun 1917	Albatros DIII	Nieuport B1654	S & SE Douai	2010	OOC †
7.	3 Jul 1917	Albatros DIII	Nieuport B1654	Graincourt	1750	OOC
8.	15 Jul 1917	Albatros DIII	Nieuport B1654	Vitry	1950	DES ††
9.	25 Sep 1917	Aviatik C	SE5a B534	St Julien	1600	OOC
			74 Squadron, RAF			
10.	12 Apr 1918	Albatros DV	SE5a C5396	S E Deûlémont	1140	DES
11.	7 May 1918	Fokker DrI	SE5a C5396	N E Ypres	1520	OOC †††
12.	21 May 1918	Pfalz DIII	SE5a C5396	E Ypres	1900	DES
13.	28 May 1918	Pfalz DIII	SE5a C5396	Map Ref I 36	1935	OOC
14.	31 May 1918	Pfalz DIII	SE5a C5396	W Ploegsteert Wood	1950	OOC
15.	1 Jun 1918	Pfalz DIII	SE5a C5396	E Dickebusch	1945	OOC
16.	15 Jul 1918	Fokker DVII	SE5a D6864	S Roulers	0850	DES
17.	29 July 1918	Pfalz DIII	SE5aD6864	E Dickebusch	1945	OOC
18.	30 Jul 1918	Fokker DVII	SE5a D6864	W Armentières	1130	OOC
19.	23 Aug 1918	Fokker DVII	SE5a D6864	S E Houthoulst Wood	1925	DES
20.	4 Sept 1918	Fokker DVII	SE5a D6864	S Lille	1930	DES
21.	17 Sep 1918	Fokker DVII	SE5a	N Courtrai	1825	DES
22.	17 Sep 1918	Fokker DVII	SE5a	N W Courtrai	1840	OOC
23.	21 Sep 1918	Fokker DVII	SE5a	W Lille	1845	OOC
24.	24 Sep 1918	SS DIV	SE5a	E Armentières	1030	OOC
25.	14 Oct 1918	Fokker DVII	SE5a C1139	Iseghem	1100	DES
26.	28 Oct 1918	Fokker DVII	SE5a	N E Tournai	0825	DES

* Observer P. E. Welchman

** Shared with E. Grenfell, H. Meintjes, A. P. V. Daley, A. D. Whitehead and L. S. Weedon

*** Shared with W. M. Fry and J. Collier

† Shared with D. G. C. Murray and A. R. Adam

†† Shared with W. E. Jenkins and W. B. Sherwood

††† Shared with B. Roxburgh-Smith

Front lines and airfields, 1918

Dover

English Channel

Ostend

Leffrinckhoucke
Teteghem
Dunkirk
St Pol
Petit Synthe
Calais
Coudekerque

Frontier
Bray Dunes
Hondschoote

Nieuport

Furnes

FLANDERS

Antwerp

Ghent

BRUSSELS

BELGIAN ARMY

La Lovie
Droglandt
Abeele
Clairmarais
Sainte-Marie-Cappel
Boisdinghem
St Omer
Bailleul

Boulogne

SECOND ARMY
Hazebrouck

Drionville
Serny
Reclinghem
Liettres
Estrée Blanche

Étaples

FIRST ARMY

ARTOIS

Auchel
Béthune
Bruay

St Pol

Savy-Berlette
Izel lès Hameau
Arras

Conteville
Abbeville

Doullens
Candas

THIRD ARMY

La Bellevue
Logeast Wood
Bapaume

Villers Bocage
Bertangles
Amiens
Villers- Bretonneux

Lealvillers
Baizieux
Albert
Poulainville

PICARDY

Somme

FIFTH ARMY/FOURTH ARMY

FRANCE

Péronne
Proyart
Bernes
Bouvincourt
Fjez
Estrées-en-Chaussée
St Quentin
Nesle
Ham
Roye

Montdidier

Noyon

Oise

Ypres
Cuerne
Courtrai
Marche
Reckem

Armentières
Lomme
Lille
Froidmont
Hautbourdin
Grand Ennetières
Point-à-Marcq

BELGIUM

Mons

Lens

Valenciennes

Douai
Vitry

Cambrai

Premont

Scheldt
Lys
Escaut
Sambre
Thuilles

Laon

Compiègne

Aisne
Soissons

Reims

FRENCH SIXTH ARMY

Oise

50 km

Seine

Marne

Château-Thierry

Épernay

FRENCH FIFTH ARMY

FRENCH FOURTH ARMY

PARIS

N

- Airfield
- National border
- Front line March 1918
- Limit of German advances, Spring 1918

0

Keith Caldwell donated his Sidcot flying suit, made in Regent Street, London, to the Auckland War Memorial Museum. He also donated this captured German Spandau machine gun, retrieved from a Fokker DVII, which he brought back with him from Europe.

Notes

Abbreviations

AFMNZ Air Force Museum of New Zealand
ANZ Archives New Zealand
ATL Alexander Turnbull Library
MOTAT Museum of Transport and Technology
TNA The National Archives, UK

Introduction

1 Victories and losses vary between sources, but most fall in close agreement with 'Grid' Caldwell's 'D.F.C.' Squadron', Air Historical Branch, author's collection, p. 1; cf. History of No. 74 Squadron, RAF, Air Historical Branch, The National Archives (TNA), AIR 27-644.

2 'Grid' Caldwell's 'D.F.C.' Squadron, Air Historical Branch, Authors Collection, pp. 2–3.

3 Christopher Shores, Norman Franks and Russell Guest, *Above the Trenches: A complete record of the fighter aces and units of the Brtish air forces, 1915-1920* (London: Grub Street, 1990), pp. 94–95; Keith Caldwell, Logbook, Airforce Museum of New Zealand (AFMNZ), 1992/038.1.

4 Keith Caldwell to Marvin Skelton, n.d., Andrew Caldwell Family Collection.

5 Keith Caldwell to Marvin Skelton, n.d., Andrew Caldwell Family Collection.

Chapter One: Very Lucky Still

1 When I decided to write this biography, I immediately regretted my prior use of its opening story as the start of my earlier book *Fearless: The extraordinary story of New Zealand's Great War Airmen*. It rightly belongs here with Caldwell, it is part of his iconography, and it needed to be front and centre in a book devoted to him. And so it is that I have used it again. The story has gathered accretions over the years, the plausible mingling with the impossible in its many retellings. Caldwell himself refuted the idea that after the collision with Sydney Carlin he flew his damaged aeroplane down to the ground while standing either entirely on the wing or half in and half out of the cockpit. Abandoning the rudder pedals would have hastened his demise, and the cockpit depth of an SE5a makes it impossible for a pilot to have one foot on the rudder inside cockpit and one outside on the wing. 'What happened was that I found that I could get the machine

under some control by putting my left foot hard on the right rudder and leaning out to the right as far [as] I could,' Caldwell wrote in the 1970s. 'So much for that episode. But I am glad to have another opportunity to correct an error which has worried me a bit.' See Marvin L. Skelton, *Callahan, the Last War Bird* (Manhattan, Kansas: Air Force Historical Foundation, 1980), pp. 95–96.

2 Mary Gordon, interview with author, 15 March 2019; *Waikato Independent*, 8 December 1923; Hugh Dickey, *The Growth of New Zealand Towns* (Auckland: Hugh Dickey, 2017), pp. 78–9. The Caldwells paid rates on four sections on Hamilton Road, Cambridge, in 1914. Karen Payne, Cambridge Museum, to author, 13 March 2019.

3 *New Zealand Mail*, 4 December 1891; Keith Caldwell, Personnel File, The National Archives, UK [TNA], WO339/57844; Mary Gordon interview.

4 The company went through a string of iterations as partners retired over its lengthy existence. *New Zealand Herald*, 26 September 1900; *New Zealand Herald*, 29 September 1900.

5 Trish Macky (ed.), *The Darlimurla Letter: Love and loss portrayed in a New Zealand family's correspondence, 1875 to the* Lusitania *disaster 1915* (Te Awamutu: Tui Press, 2015), p. 239.

6 *Free Lance*, 27 December 1913; *Greymouth Evening Star*, 17 November 1911.

7 Macky (ed.), *The Darlimurla Letter*, p. 267.

8 Anne Caldwell, interview with author, 15 March 2019.

9 *New Zealand Herald*, 26 November 1906.

10 *New Zealand Times*, 8 January 1903; *Auckland Star*, 8 January 1903; Macky (ed.), *The Darlimurla Letter*, pp. 64, 245.

11 A. E. Campbell, *Educating New Zealand* (Wellington: Department of Internal Affairs, 1941), p.1; F. B. Malim, *Almae Matres: Recollections of some schools at home and abroad* (Cambridge: Cambridge University Press, 1948), p. 160.

12 Bruce and Don Hamilton, *Never a Footstep Back: A history of the Wanganui Collegiate School, 1854–2003* (Whanganui: Whanganui College Board of Trustees, 2003), p. 153.

13 Hamilton, *Never A Footstep Back*, pp. 79–143.

14 *Wanganui Collegian*, April 1910, pp. 1–2.

15 Frances Gibbons, archivist, Whanganui Collegiate School, to author, 14 March 2019.

16 *Wanganui Collegian*, April 1912, p. 22. This was from Stott's preceding Easter sermon. Wendy Pettigrew, *Heart of a Great School: The chapel of Wanganui Collegiate School* (Whanganui: Whanganui Collegiate School Museum Trust, 2012), p. 14.

17 *Wanganui Collegian*, April 1911, p. 3.

18 *Wanganui Collegian*, April 1911, pp. 6, 7; April 1914, p. 15.

19 *Wanganui Collegian*, April 1914, p. 5; Elizabeth Vandiver, *Stand in the Trench: Achilles: Classical receptions in British poetry of the Great War* (Oxford: Oxford University Press, 2010), p. 36.

20 Pettigrew, *Heart of a Great School*, p. 9.

21 *Wanganui Collegian*, April 1901, p. 1; Hamilton, *Never a Footstep Back*, p. 111.

22 In the twentieth century, the title, the Dying 'Gladiator', gave way to the Dying 'Gaul' or 'Galatian', after classicists more accurately identified the subject matter.

23 *New Zealand Herald*, 29 October 1910; *Wanganui Collegian*, December 1911, p. 11.

24 *Wanganui Collegian*, April 1912, p. 5.

25 *Wanganui Collegian*, April 1913, p. 5.

26 *Wanganui Collegian*, April 1913, p. 4.

27 *Wanganui Collegian*, December 1913, p. 5.

28 *Wanganui Collegian*, April 1913, p. 4.

Chapter Two: Favoured Ones

1 *Manawatu Standard*, 22 September 1902.

2 Caroline Daley, 'Modernity and Leisure in Early Twentieth-Century New Zealand', *New Zealand Journal of History* 34, no. 2 (2000): p. 241.

3 *New Zealand Graphic*, 15 November 1902.

4 *Weekly Press*, 24 December 1902.

5 Bruce and Don Hamilton, *Never a Footstep Back: A history of the Wanganui Collegiate School, 1854–2003* (Whanganui: Whanganui College Board of Trustees, 2003), pp. 107–8; *Wanganui Collegian*, April 1903, p. 3, April 1913, p. 2.

6 *Otago Daily Times*, 1 January 1902.

7 Daley, 'Modernity and Leisure', pp. 241, 253.

8 Hamilton, *Never a Footstep Back*, p. 112.

9 Ibid.

10 Greg Ryan, 'Cricket and the Moral Curriculum of the New Zealand Elite Secondary Schools c1860–1920', *The Sports Historian* 19, no. 2 (November 1999): pp. 61–79.

11 *Wanganui Collegian*, April 1912, p. 2; Hamilton,

Never a Footstep Back, pp. 157–8.

12 Henry Newbolt's poem was introduced to the boys in 1901. *Wanganui Collegian, March 1933*, p. 17. For the influence of this poem in empire schools see: Elizabeth Vandiver, *Stand in the Trench: Achilles: Classical receptions in British poetry of the Great War* (Oxford: Oxford University Press, 2010), pp. 48–52.

13 Ryan, 'Cricket and the Moral Curriculum', p. 61; Greg Ryan, *The Making of New Zealand Cricket: 1832–1914*, (London: Frank Cass Publishers, 2004), pp. 106–7.

14 *Wanganui Collegian*, December 1913, p. 5; April 1914, p. 9; December 1914, p. 4.

15 Hamilton, *Never a Footstep Back*, p. 165.

16 *Wanganui Collegian*, December 1913, p. 3; December 1914, p. 3, March 1933, p. 26.

17 *Wanganui Collegian*, August 1912, p. 17.

18 https://nzhistory.govt.nz/media/video/hms-new-zealand-great-war-story (retrieved 4 March 2018).

19 *West Coast Times*, 17 June 1913.

20 *West Coast Times*, 17 June 1913; *Wanganui Collegian*, August 1913, p. 5.

21 *Wanganui Collegian*, August 1913, p. 5; *West Coast Times*, 17 June 1913; Hamilton, *Never A Footstep Back*, p. 165.

22 *Wanganui Collegian*, December 1913, pp. 15–16.

23 *Wanganui Collegian*, April 1914, p. 17.

24 *Dominion*, 22 April 1914; *Wanganui Collegian*, August 1914, p. 12.

25 *Wanganui Collegian*, April 1912, p. 3.

26 *Evening Post*, 5 August 1914.

27 *Wanganui Collegian*, December 1914.

28 *Wanganui Collegian*, 1933, p. 25.

29 *Whanganui Chronicle*, 12 August 2014; *Whanganui Chronicle*, 29 April 2015.

Chapter Three: Clear-eyed Young Men

1 Bruce and Don Hamilton, *Never a Footstep Back: A history of the Wanganui Collegiate School, 1854–2003* (Whanganui: Whanganui College Board of Trustees, 2003), p. 129; *Wanganui Collegian*, April 1913, p. 5.

2 Seton Montgomerie to his mother, Anne Montgomerie, 9 August 1914, Susanna Montgomerie Norris Collection. Like Caldwell, Montgomerie served as an airman in the war. Adam Claasen, *Fearless: The extraordinary untold story of New Zealand's Great War airmen* (Auckland: Massey University Press, 2017),

pp. 345–7; Susanna Montgomerie Norris with Anna Rogers, *Annie's War: A New Zealand woman and her family in England 1916–19* (Dunedin: Otago University Press, 2014).

3 *Wanganui Collegian*, April 1933, p, 25.

4 Keith Caldwell, Personnel File, TNA WO339/57844.

5 *New Zealand Times*, 19 January 1914. For a detailed discussion on New Zealand's pre-war aviators see: Errol Martyn, *A Passion for Flight: New Zealand aviation before the Great War, Volume Two, aero clubs, aeroplanes, aviators and aeronauts 1910–1914* (Christchurch: Volplane Press, 1999), and *Volume Three, the Joe Hammond story and military beginnings 1910–1914* (Christchurch: Volplane Press, 1999), p. 149.

6 *Sun*, 14 March 1914.

7 *Wanganui Collegian*, 1933, p. 25.

8 *Press*, 22 May 1915.

9 Wendy Pettigrew to author, 14 April 2014.

10 *Auckland Star*, 17 July 1915; Keith Caldwell, Personnel File, TNA WO339/57844.

11 Trish Macky (ed.), *The Darlimurla Letter: Love and loss portrayed in a New Zealand family's correspondence, 1875 to the* Lusitania *disaster 1915* (Te Awamutu: Tui Press, 2015), p. 410.

12 Tony Bridgland, *Outrage at Sea: Naval atrocities of the First World War* (Barnsley, South Yorkshire: Leo Cooper, 2002).

13 Macky (ed.), *The Darlimurla Letter*, p. 412.

14 *Evening Post*, 20 May 1915.

15 *New Zealand Herald*, 11 December 1915.

16 *New Zealand Herald*, 12 May 1915.

17 *Auckland Star*, 17 July 1915.

18 E. F. Harvie, *George Bolt: Pioneer aviator* (Wellington: A. H. Reed & A. W. Reed, 1974), p. 20.

19 *Manawatu Times*, 14 December 1917.

20 Eric Paton, 'Paper by E. Paton (incomplete)', p. 5, Museum of Transport and Technology [MOTAT], Walsh Memorial Library, Box 71 04/077/131A.

21 H. H. Russell & W. R. Puglisi, '"Grid" Caldwell of 74', *Cross & Cockade* 10, no. 3 (Autumn 1960): p. 195.

22 Eric Paton, 'Paper', p. 8.

23 L. Sherriff, 'Notes on Walsh Brothers Flying School, 1915–1924', p. 2, MOTAT, Walsh Memorial Library, Box 72, Envelope 13, 04/077/102B, C + D146.

24 Unknown author, 'Walsh Brothers and Dexter, NZFS, 1915–1924', p. 4, MOTAT Box 71 04/077/146; Sherriff, 'Notes on Walsh Brothers Flying School', pp. 2–3; *Auckland Star*, 14 February 1918.

25 Official imperial recognition did not come through until 21 February 1916. War Office to Minister of Defence, Wellington, 22 April 1916; Candidates for Commissions in Royal Flying Corps, 5 February 1917, ANZ, ACHK 8604 G1:218 1917/903. For a comprehensive discussion of the New Zealand government's attitude towards the establishment of a military flying school in this period see Claasen, *Fearless*.

26 *Timaru Herald*, 4 December 1915; *Evening Post*, 27 November 1915.

27 Harvie, *George Bolt*, p. 18.

28 Werner Eugene Langguth, Personnel File, ANZ, AABK 7291 W5614 25/D. 2/487; Langguth's father was made the consul for Austria-Hungary at Auckland in 1897. *New Zealand Times*, 16 March 1916.

29 *Northern Advocate*, 26 September 1906, 17 June 1910, 9 November 1901; *Auckland Star*, 21 August 1903; *New Zealand Herald*, March 1906; *Wanganui Herald*, 2 May 1912; *New Zealand Herald*, 27 June 1913.

30 *New Zealand Herald*, 6 December 1915.

31 Werner Eugene Langguth, Personnel File.

32 Harvie, *George Bolt*, pp. 61, 63; Russell and Puglisi, '"Grid" Caldwell of 74', p. 195, fn. 2.

33 Keith Logan Caldwell, Logbook, inside front cover. AFMNZ, 1992/038.1.

34 Keith Logan Caldwell, Personnel File, TNA WO file WO 339/57844.

Chapter Four: Magnificent

1 *New Zealand Times*, 6 January 1918.

2 *Evening Post*, 8 January 1916.

3 Susanna Montgomerie Norris with Anna Rogers, *Annie's War: A New Zealand woman and her family in England 1916–19* (Dunedin: Otago University Press, 2014), p. 15.

4 *Ashburton Guardian*, 12 January 1916

5 *Wanganui Collegian*, December 1914, p. 6.

6 Ibid., December 1915, pp. 7–8.

7 Ibid., December 1915, p. 1.

8 Ibid., December 1915, pp. 2–3; Richard Bourne and Francis Gibbons, Whanganui Collegiate School Museum and Archives, to author, 7 February 2023.

9 *Wanganui Collegian*, December 1915, pp. 4–5.

10 Ibid., December 1915, p. 16.

11 Keith Caldwell, Personnel File, TNA WO 339/57844.

12 Ibid.

13 *Wanganui Collegian*, December 1916, p. 14.

14 H. W. B. Joseph, 'Oxford in the Last War', *The Oxford Magazine* LIX, no. 2 (May 1941): p. 309; 'The Royal Flying Corps on the Home Front, 1914–1918', Imperial War Museum, photograph Q 302283, www.iwm.org.uk/collections/item/object/205025859 (retrieved 17 June 2018).

15 Judith Curthoys, *The Stones of Christ Church: The story of the buildings of Christ Church, Oxford* (London: Profile, 2017), p. 298; Geoffrey Wall, *Letters of an Airman* (Melbourne: Australian Authors' Agency, 1918), p. 97.

16 John Grider, *War Birds: Diary of an unknown aviator* (Sydney: Cornstock, 1928), p. 18; The quality of the food declined in 1918 when rationing was established. Judith Curthoys, *The Cardinal's College: Christ Church, chapter and verse* (London: Profile, 2012), p. 298.

17 Joseph, 'Oxford in the Last War', p. 309.

18 War Office Memorandum, 3 June 1914, TNA, AIR1/117/15/40/23, in Michael Molkentin, 'The Dominion of the Air: The Imperial dimension of Britain's war in the air, 1914–1918,' *The British Journal for Military History* 4, no. 2 (February 2018): p. 76.

19 Molkentin, 'The Dominion of the Air', p. 76; *Waikato Independent*, 2 May 1916.

20 Adam Claasen, *Fearless: The extraordinary untold story of New Zealand's Great War airmen* (Auckland: Massey University Press, 2017, pp. 139–41.

21 William Stanley Shirtcliffe, Service Record, TNA AIR76/460/0/0549-51; *Auckland Star*, 11 January 1918.

22 Originally simply titled No. 2 School of Instruction, but changed in October 1916 to 2 School of Military Aeronautics.

23 Alex Revell, *Brief Glory: The life of Arthur Rhys Davids DSO MC* (Barnsley, South Yorkshire: Pen & Sword, 2010), p. 68.

24 *Evening Star*, 12 October 1917.

25 Wall, *Letters of an Airman*, p. 98.

26 'Syllabus for short courses, 1 March 1917', Schools of Military Aeronautics, RFC Reading and Oxford, TNA AIR 1/1830/204/204/1.

27 Melville White to 'Brethren', 5 April 1917, ATL, MSY-7036.

28 Grider, *War Birds*, pp. 20, 31.

29 Joseph, 'Oxford in the Last War', p. 309.

30 Revell, *Brief Glory*, pp. 69–70.

31 Grider, *War Birds*, p. 27.

32 Joseph, 'Oxford in the Last War', p. 327 .

33 *New Zealand Herald*, 28 September 1916.

Chapter Five: Wings

1 Spragg was named after his father, Wesley, but was generally known by his second name: Neal. Jeff Jefford, '45 Squadron: The early years', *Cross & Cockade International* 30, no. 4 (Winter 1999): p. 192; For Spragg see, Errol Martyn, *A Passion for Flight: New Zealand aviation before the Great War, Volume Three, the Joe Hammond story and military beginnings 1910–1914* (Christchurch: Volplane Press, 1999), p. 449; Sandra Coney, *Gone West: Great War memorials of Waitakere and their soldiers* (Auckland: Protect Piha Heritage Society, 2017), p. 99.

2 Wesley Neal Spragg, Brent Mackrell scrapbook relating to early British military aviation (II). ATL, MSZ-1581.

3 Keith Logan Caldwell, Logbook, 14 May 1916, AFMNZ 1992/038.1.

4 *New Zealand Times*, 29 March 1917.

5 Duncan Grinnell-Milne, *Wind in the Wires* (London: Panther, 1957), p. 11.

6 Edgar Garland, quoted in *Evening Post*, 23 May 1917.

7 Grinnell-Milne, *Wind in the Wires*, p. 11.

8 Jefford, '45 Squadron: The early years', p. 182.

9 Adam Claasen, *Fearless: The extraordinary untold story of New Zealand's Great War airmen* (Auckland: Massey University Press, 2017), p. 163.

10 Sir Gordon Taylor, *The Sky Beyond* (Sydney: Cassell, 1963), p. 8.

11 Ibid., p. 7.

12 Melville White to 'Brethren', 5 April 1917, ATL, MSY-7036.

13 Thomas Quarles Back to Keith Caldwell, 25 June 1977, Andrew Caldwell Family Collection.

14 Keith Logan Caldwell, Logbook, 14 May 1916, AFMNZ 1992/038.1.

15 *Auckland Star*, 14 September 1916.

16 Report on Cpt. S. M. Webb by Maj. Ludlow-Hewitt, No 1 RAS, Farnborough. HQRFC Central Flying School, Confidential Reports on Officers. TNA AIR 1/758/204/4/117.

17 Jefford, '45 Squadron: The early years', p. 192.

18 Ibid., p. 182.

19 Ian Mackersey, *No Empty Chairs: The short and heroic lives of the young aviators who fought and died in the First World War* (London: Weidenfeld & Nicolson, 2012), p. 177.

20 Jefford, '45 Squadron: The early years', p. 182.

21 Rhodes-Moorhouse was the son of Mary Ann Rhodes (Ngāti Tama, Ngāti Ruanui and Te Ātiawa). His maternal grandfather was a successful Wellington businessman and politician. Claasen, *Fearless*, pp. 87–89.

22 *Star*, 17 June 1915.

23 *Evening Post*, 22 October 1915.

24 Alfred de Bathe Brandon, Unpublished memoir, Errol Martyn Collection; Full report on the information gathered from the crew of L15, April–May 1916, TNA, AIR 1/2596–2620; Ridged Airship Committee Meeting. Reports received relative to Zeppelin No. 15., TNA Air 1/2566; Christopher Cole and E. F. Cheesman, *The Air Defence of Britain* (London: Putnam, 1984), p. 105.

25 *Daily Sketch* (Britain), 3 April 1916. AFMNZ; *Northern Advocate*, 31 May 1916; *Free Lance*, 7 April 1916; *Dominion*, 4 April 1916. In September 1916, Brandon was instrumental in bringing down another Zeppelin over England, *L33*. See Claasen, *Fearless*, pp. 220–23.

26 Eric Fox Pitt Lubbock, Logbook, 9 June 1916, Imperial War Museum; Keith Caldwell, Logbook, 9 June 1916, AFMNZ.

27 Grinnell-Milne, *Wind in the Wires*, pp. 13, 15, 16.

28 *Waikato Independent*, 24 August 1916.

29 Keith Logan Caldwell, Logbook, 14 July 1916. AFMNZ 1992/038.1.

30 *New Zealand Times*, 22 March 1917.

31 Arthur Gould Lee, *Open Cockpit: A pilot of the Royal Flying Corps* (London: Grub Street, 2012).

32 Jefford, '45 Squadron: The early years', p. 182.

33 *Waikato Independent*, 24 August 1916.

34 *Waikato Independent*, 21 September 1916.

35 Harold Francis Beamish, Service Record, TNA AIR 76/29/220; Harold Francis Beamish, Logbook, AFMNZ 1994/209.1.

36 *Wanganui Collegian*, April 1916, p. 4.

37 Claasen, *Fearless*, pp. 198–203.

38 *Wanganui Collegian*, April 1916, p. 5.

Chapter Six: Flaming Onions

1 Gwilym H. Lewis, *Wings over the Somme, 1916–1918* (Bristol: Bridge Books, 1994), pp. 188–89.

2 H. A. Jones, *The War in the Air: Being the story of the part played in the Great War by the Royal Air Force, Vol. 2* (Oxford University Press: London, 1928), p. 189; Ray Sturtivant, *Flying Training and Support Units since 1912* (Staplefield, West Sussex: Air-Britain, 2007), p. 41.

3 Lewis, *Wings over the Somme*, p. 35.

4 Trevor Henshaw, *The Sky Their Battlefield: Air fighting and air casualties of the Great War. British Commonwealth and United States Air Services 1912–1919* (London: Fetubi Books, 2014), pp. 30–1.

5 Clive Collet to Claude Collet, 21 March 1916, ATL MSZ-1583.

6 Keith Caldwell to William Fry, 20 September 1971, Andrew Caldwell Family Collection; Chaz Bowyer, *Albert Ball, VC: The story of the 1st World War Ace* (Manchester: Crécy, 2001), pp. 113–14.

7 Keith Caldwell to William Fry, 18 January 1975, Andrew Caldwell Family Collection.

8 A. A. Nicod, 'Re-union Memories', *Popular Flying*, January 1936, p. 538.

9 Peter Hart, *Somme Success: The Royal Flying Crops and the Battle of the Somme, 1916* (Barnsley, South Yorkshire: Leo Cooper, 2001), p. 148.

10 Bowyer, *Albert Ball, V.C.*, pp. 68–69.

11 History of 8 Squadron, TNA AIR 1/1671/206/109/25.

12 Sir Patrick Playfair and John Jarvis, *'Pip' Playfair: A founding father of the RAF* (Ilfracombe, Devon: Arthur H. Stockwell, 1979), p. 29. Playfair later cowrote *Warfare Today: How modern battles are planned and fought on land, at sea, and in the air* (London: Odhams Press, 1944) with Reginald Bacon and J. F. C. Fuller.

13 Playfair and Jarvis, *'Pip' Playfair*, pp. 29–30.

14 Playfair was succeeded by Major Ernest Leslie Gossage later in August 1916. History of 8 Squadron, AIR 1/1671/206/109/25.

15 Keith Caldwell to William Fry, 25 October 1975, Andrew Caldwell Family Collection; Percy Gilbert Ross-Hume, Casualty Card, RAF Museum Hendon.

16 Keith Caldwell to William Fry, 20 September 1971, Andrew Caldwell Family Collection.

17 Although Caldwell did not play an active role in photographic work, 2260 negatives were exposed and 58,500 prints made by 8 Squadron between May and November 1916. History of 8 Squadron, AIR 1/1671/206/109/25; Sgt Fred Hartly, 8 Squadron narrative. X003-7871 RAF Hendon.

18 Playfair and Jarvis, *'Pip' Playfair*, pp. 45–46.

19 History of 8 Squadron, TNA AIR 1/1671/206/109/25.

20 J. M. Bruce, *The Aeroplanes of the Royal Flying Corps: Military Wing* (London: Putman, 1992), pp. 360–61.

21 8 Squadron, Record Book, 1 August 1916. TNA AIR 1/1668/204/109/3.

22 Keith Caldwell, Logbook, 1 August 1916. AFMNZ 1992/038.1. 8 Squadron, Record Book, 1 August 1916. TNA AIR 1/1668/204/109/3.

23 Keith Logan Caldwell, Logbook, 14 July 1916, AFMNZ 1992/038.1.

24 Francis William Crawford, Logbook, 11 March 1917, AFMNZ 1981/149.2.

25 Sgt Fred Hartly, 8 Squadron narrative, RAF Museum, Hendon, X003-7871.

26 Major James T. B. McCudden VC DSO MC MM, *Five Years in the Royal Flying Corps* (London: Aeroplane and General, 1918), p. 61.

27 History of 8 Squadron, TNA AIR 1/1671/206/109/25.

28 Henshaw, *The Sky Their Battlefield*, p. 347; Edward B. Westermann, *Flak: German anti-aircraft defences 1914–1945* (Lawrence, KS: University of Kansas Press, 2001), p. 24.

29 8 Squadron Record Book, 4 August 1916, TNA AIR 1/1668/204/109/3; Keith Caldwell, Logbook, 4 August 1916, AFMNZ 1992/038.1; *Waikato Independent*, 21 September 1916.

30 The starting procedure for the BE2 was provided by pilot David Horrell, The Vintage Aviator. David Horrell to author, 2 and 11 March 2020.

31 Cecil Lewis, *Sagittarius Rising* (London: Greenhill Books, 1993), p. 66.

32 III Brigade RFC, War Diary, 4 August 1916, TNA AIR 1/2245/209/42/30.

33 *Waikato Independent*, 21 September 1916.

34 *Waikato Independent*, 17 October 1916; III Brigade RFC, War Diary, 7 August 1916, TNA AIR 1/2245/209/42/30; 8 Squadron Record Book, 7 August 1916, TNA AIR 1/1668/204/109/3.

35 *Waikato Times*, 17 October 1916; Keith Caldwell, Logbook, 13 August 1916, AFMNZ 1992/038.1.

36 III Brigade RFC, War Diary, 13 August 1916, TNA AIR 1/2245/209/42/30.

Chapter Seven: Maniacs

1 Cecil Lewis, *Sagittarius Rising* (London: Greenhill Books, 1993), p. 64.

2 *Wanganui Collegian*, April 1916, p. 4.

3 Lewis, *Sagittarius Rising*, p. 67.

4 *Wanganui Collegian*, December 1916, p. 11; John Davis Canning, Service Record, TNA AIR 76/75.

5 Keith Caldwell, Logbook, 1 August to 31 August 1916, AFMNZ 1992/038.1.

6 Lt Evans, 3 Squadron RFC, quoted in Peter Hart, *Somme Success: The Royal Flying Corps and the Battle of the Somme, 1916* (Barnsley, South Yorkshire: Leo Cooper, 2001), pp. 107–8.

7 Lieutenant Leslie Horridge, 7 Squadron RFC, in Hart, *Somme Success*, p. 108.

8 Lyn MacDonald, *Somme* (London: Michael Joseph, 1983), p. 143.

9 www.iwm.org.uk/history/voices-of-the-first-world-war-war-in-the-air (retrieved 27 March 2020).

10 Hart, *Somme Success*, p. 153.

11 *Waikato Independent*, 17 October 1916; David Franklin, Casualty Card, RAF Museum Hendon.

12 H. B. R. Rowell, 'Memoir of Service with the Royal Flying Corps 1915 & 1916, Farnborough, No. 1 Reserve Aeroplane Squadron BEF, France, No. 8 & 12 Squadrons', p. 19, RAF Museum Hendon B3021.

13 MacDonald, *Somme*, p. 78.

14 Rowell, 'Memoir of Service with the Royal Flying Corps', p. 19.

15 MacDonald, *Somme*, pp. 78–9.

16 Rowell, 'Memoir of Service with the Royal Flying Corps', p. 20.

17 Keith Caldwell, Logbook, 5 & 22 August 1916, AFMNZ 1992/038.1.

18 There is some disagreement about when this occurred, with 13, 14 and 16 August all suggested in Caldwell's letters and logbook. However, the flight with Corbishley and the dislodging of the machine gun is only possible on 16 August. See *Waikato Independent*, 17 October 1916; Keith Caldwell Logbook, 16 August 1916, AFMNZ 1992/038.1; Keith Caldwell to William Fry, 20 September 1971, Andrew Caldwell Family Collection.

19 A. J. L. Scott, *Sixty Squadron RAF: On the Western Front during the First World War* (Leonaur, 2010), p. 33.

20 Charles Vaughan Clayton, Casualty Card, RAF Museum Hendon.

21 *Waikato Independent*, 21 September 1916.

22 Norman Bradford Harris, Casualty Card, RAF Museum Hendon.

23 Caldwell's logbook states that this event occurred on 24 August 1916, but the 8 Squadron Record Book has him flying with Harris on an artillery patrol on 25 August 1916. Keith Logan Caldwell, Logbook, 24 August 1916, AFMNZ 1992/038.1; 8 Squadron Record Book, 7 August 1916, TNA AIR 1/1668/204/109/3.

24 *Waikato Independent*, 11 November 1916; Paul Sortehaug with Keith Caldwell, quoted in Paul Sortehaug, 'Major Keith Logan Caldwell', *Pacific Wings* (December 2012–January 2013): p. 49.

25 Patrick Eliot Welchman, Casualty Card, RAF

Museum Hendon; quoted in Sortehaug, 'Major Keith Logan Caldwell', p. 49.

26 Quoted in Sortehaug, 'Major Keith Logan Caldwell', p. 49.

27 *Waikato Independent*, 11 November 1916.

28 Ibid.; *Wanganui Collegian*, December 1916, p. 12.

29 See also his 10 November 1916 attack. Keith Caldwell, Combat in Air Report, 10 November 1916, TNA AIR 1/2246/209/42/33.

30 Keith Caldwell, Logbook, August–November 1916, AFMNZ 1992/038.1.

31 Playfair was given command of 13 Wing on 24 August 1916.

32 Keith Caldwell to William Fry, 20 September 1971, Andrew Caldwell Family Collection.

33 Keith Caldwell, Logbook, 12–16 November 1916, AFMNZ 1992/038.1.

34 Trevor Henshaw, *The Sky Their Battlefield: Air fighting and air casualties of the Great War. British Commonwealth and United States Air Services 1912–1919* (London: Fetubi Books, 2014), p. 50.

35 *Ibid.*, p. 347.

36 H. A. Jones, *The War in the Air: Being the part played in the Great War by the Royal Air Force, Vol. 2* (Uckfield, East Sussex: Naval and Military Press, 1928), pp. 296–97.

37 Ibid., pp. 304–5.

38 E. R. Hooton, *War Over the Trenches: Air power and the Western Front campaigns 1916–1918* (Hersham, Surrey: Ian Allan, 2010), p. 105.

39 Henshaw, *The Sky Their Battlefield*, p. 60.

Chapter Eight: Fire Eaters

1 A. J. Insall, *Observer: Memoirs of the RFC, 1915–18* (London: William and Kimber, 1970), p. 113.

2 11 Squadron History, TNA AIR 1/166/15/150/1.

3 A. J. Young and D. W. Warne, *Sixty Squadron: A history of fifty years' service* (Singapore: Eurasia Press, 1967), pp. 14, 17.

4 Enzo Angelucci and Paolo Matricardi, *World Aircraft: Origins — World War 1* (Maidenhead, Berkshire: Sampson Low, 1977), pp. 128–29; Lee Kennett, *The First Air War: 1914–1918* (New York: The Free Press, 1991).

5 Alex Revell, *No 60 Squadron RFC/RAF* (Oxford: Osprey Publishing, 2011), pp. 19–20; Joe Warne, '60 Squadron: A detailed history, part 1', *Cross & Cockade Great Britain International* 11, no.1 (Spring 1980): p. 34.

6 F. D. Tredrey, *Pioneer Pilot: The great Smith Barry who taught the world how to fly* (London: Peter Davis, 1976), pp. 27–28.

7 A. J. L. Scott, *Sixty Squadron RAF: On the Western Front during the First World War* (Milton Keynes: Leonaur, 2010), p. 26.

8 Young and Warne, *Sixty Squadron*, p. 13.

9 'Comments from Keith L. Caldwell (compiled and annotated by Marvin L. Skelton)', 15 August 1977, p. 7, Andrew Caldwell Family Collection. In this draft Caldwell states that William Sowden was his flight commander at this time. Soon after he came under the leadership of Eustace Grenfell.

10 W. M. Fry, *Air of Battle* (London: William Kimber, 1974), pp. 81–82.

11 Scott, *Sixty Squadron RAF*, p. 26.

12 Fry, *Air of Battle*, p. 84; Russell and Puglisi state this was 'B Flight', see H. H. Russell and W. R. Puglisi, '"Grid" Caldwell of 74', *Cross & Cockade* 10, no. 3 (Autumn 1969): p. 195. See also *Air of Battle*, p. 91; Keith Caldwell, Logbook, 25 December 1916, AFMNZ 1992/038.1. It is possible that he was initially placed with this flight under the command of William Sowery, but soon came under the leadership of Grenfell. See 'Comments from Keith L. Caldwell (compiled and annotated by Marvin L. Skelton)', 15 August 1977, p. 7, Andrew Caldwell Family Collection.

13 Fry, *Air of Battle*, p. 81.

14 Revell, *No 60 Squadron*, p. 33.

15 Fry, *Air of Battle*, p. 91.

16 *Waikato Independent*, 17 October 1916.

17 Fry, *Air of Battle*, p. 84.

18 *Ibid.*, pp. 100–1.

19 David Horrell, pilot, The Vintage Aviator, to author, 6 May 2020.

20 Ibid.

21 Paul Sortehaug, 'Major Keith Logan Caldwell', *Pacific Wings* (December 2012–January 2013): p. 50.

22 Russell and Puglisi, '"Grid" Caldwell of 74', p. 196, fn. 3.

23 Keith Caldwell, Logbook, 19 November 1916, AFMNZ 1992/038.1.

24 Sortehaug, 'Major Keith Logan Caldwell', p. 50.

25 Lewis, *Sagittarius Rising* (London: Greenhill Books, 1993), pp. 149–52.

26 Russell and Puglisi, '"Grid" Caldwell of 74', p. 196, fn. 3.

27 David Tappin, '"Chidlaw": Robert Leslie Chidlaw-Roberts MC Hampshire Regt and RFC: Just an ordinary humdrum pilot', *Cross & Cockade International Journal* 20, no. 2 (1989): p. 60.

28 Keith Caldwell, Logbook, 4 December 1916, AFMNZ 1992/038.1.

29 Fry, *Air of Battle*, p. 105.

30 13 Wing Operational Orders, 11 December 1916. NAUK AIR 1/1808/204/161/3.

31 Henry Meintjes, Combat in Air Report, 11 December 1916, TNA AIR 1/2246/209/42/34; Lindsey Spence Weedon, Combat in Air Report, 11 December 1916, TNA AIR 1/2246/209/42/34; Lewis Edward Whitehead, Combat in Air Report, TNA AIR 1/2246/209/42/34; Keith Caldwell, Combat in Air Report, 11 December 1916, TNA AIR 1/2246/209/42/34.

32 Eustace Osborne Grenfell, Combat in Air Report, 11 December 1916, TNA AIR 1/2246/209/42/34

33 Keith Caldwell, Combat in Air Report, 11 December 1916, TNA AIR 1/2246/209/42/34.

34 Grenfell communicated his short combats in the air report from a local casualty clearing station. Obviously disoriented from being struck on the head, he mistakenly told Smith-Barry that the German observer had been killed. Playfair was not convinced: 'I do not think Captain Grenfell's statement re the German observer is correct,' he wrote at the bottom of the report. Eustace Osborne Grenfell, Combat in Air Report, 11 December 1916, TNA AIR 1/2246/209/42/34; Eustace Osborne Grenfell, Personnel File, TNA WO 339/36268.

35 Lindsey Spence Weedon, Combat in Air Report, 11 December 1916, TNA AIR 1/2246/209/42/34.

36 Henry Meintjes, Combat in Air Report, 11 December 1916, TNA AIR 1/2246/209/42/34; Linsey Spence Weedon, Combat in Air Report, 11 December 1916, TNA AIR 1/2246/209/42/34.

37 Keith Caldwell to W. R. Puglisi, 1963.

38 Fry, *Air of Battle* (London: William Kimber, 1974), pp. 102–3.

39 Keith Caldwell, Combat in Air Report, 16 December 1916, TNA AIR 1/2246/209/42/34.

40 The logbook and combat report disagree on the date this occurred. Keith Caldwell, Logbook, 21 December 1916, AFMNZ 1992/038.1; Keith Caldwell, Combat in Air Report, 20 December 1916, AFMNZ 1992/038.1.

41 *Evening Post*, 4 June 1917.

42 James T. B. McCudden, *Flying Fury: Five years in the Royal Air Flying Corps* (London: Greenhill, 2000), p. 149.

43 Revell, *No 60 Squadron*, p. 63.

44 Young and Warne, *Sixty Squadron*, p. 19.

45 Fry, *Air of Battle*, p. 105.

46 A. A. Nicod, 'Memories of 60 Squadron', *Popular Flying* 3, no. 9 (December 1934): p. 466.

47 Young and Warne, *Sixty Squadron*, p. 20.

48 *Waikato Independent*, 14 November 1916.

49 *New Zealand Herald*, 12 September 1916; *Wanganui Chronicle*, 15 September 1916.

50 *Taranaki Herald*, 4 November 1916.

51 20 Squadron History, pp. 15, 17, TNA AIR 2 2/12026.

52 Geoffrey Callender, Combat in Air Report, 20 October 1916, TNA AIR 1/991/204/5/835; Report on Casualties to Personnel and Machines, Geoffrey Callender, 20 October 1916, TNA AIR 1/845/204/5/374.

53 *Northern Advocate*, 12 January 1918; Geoffrey Callender, Casualty Form, RAF Museum Hendon; Geoffrey Callender, Base Records, ANZ, AABK 22525/W5712/1/BR.37/996.

54 Medical Report on Fly Officer, 12 February 1918, Geoffrey Callender, Personnel File, TNA WO 339157846.

Chapter Nine: Black Crosses

1 Evelyn Paget Graves, Casualty Form, RAF Museum Hendon; A. J. L. Scott, *Sixty Squadron RAF 1916–1919* (London: Greenhill Books, 1990), pp. 23–24; www.hambo.org/lancing/view_man.php?id=68 (retrieved 30 April 2020).

2 A. J. Young and D. W. Warne, *Sixty Squadron: A history of fifty years of service* (Singapore: Eurasia Press, 1967) p. 22.

3 W. M. Fry, *Air of Battle* (London: William Kimber, 1974), p. 106; Scott, *Sixty Squadron*, p. 24.

4 Fry, *Air of Battle*, p. 106.

5 Lee Kennett, *The First Air War, 1914–1918* (New York: The Free Press, 1991), p. 106.

6 Young and Warne, *Sixty Squadron*, p. 9.

7 Paul Sortehaug, 'Major Keith Logan Caldwell', *Pacific Wings* (December 2012–January 2013): p. 50.

8 Joe Warne, 'Sixty Squadron: A detailed history, Part 2', *Cross & Cockade Great Britain* 11, no. 2 (Summer 1980): p. 54.

9 Leonard Rochford, Confidential Reports, TNA ADM 273/9/61; he got lost on 25 February 1917.

10 Leonard Rochford, *I Choose the Sky* (London: William Kimber, 1977), pp. 64–65.

11 Russell Miller, *Trenchard: Father of the Royal Air Force* (London: Weidenfeld & Nicolson, 2017), pp. 114–15.

12 Fry, *Air of Battle*, p. 102; *Timaru Herald*, 7 March 1919.

13 John Milne, *Footprints of the 1/4th Leicestershire Regiment: August 1914 to November 1918* (Leicester: Edgar Backus, 1935).

14 13 Wing, Operational Orders, 27–30 January 1917, AIR 1/1808/204/161/3.

15 Fry, *Air of Battle*, p. 108.

16 Fry states, 'Our armament officer was always beseeching us to keep and return the empty double-sized Lewis ammunition drums as they were specially made for the RFC and were scarce, but to save time we nearly always threw them overboard as we feared being caught with our guns down.' Fry, *Air of Battle*, p. 110.

17 Keith Caldwell, Combat in Air Report, 29 January 1917, TNA AIR 1/2238/209/42/1.

18 H. H. Russell and W. R. Puglisi, '"Grid" Caldwell of 74', *Cross & Cockade* 10, no. 3 (Fall 1969): p. 198.

19 Fry, *Air of Battle*, p. 108.

20 The aircraft was in fact repaired and reassembled only to be lost by A. D. Whitehead, POW, on 11 March 1917.

21 Fry, *Air of Battle*, pp. 108–10.

22 Caldwell to Collishaw, 30 October 1965; Fry, *Air of Battle*, pp. 107, 109.

23 13 Wing headquarters, 10 February 1917, TNA AIR 1/1555/204/79/75.

24 Henry Meintjes, Service Record, TNA AIR 76/343/199; William Fry, Casualty Form, RAF Museum Hendon. Caldwell's logbook recorded no entries between 16 and 25 February, and Fry records that he and Meintjes had leave around the same time. Keith Caldwell Logbook, 16–25 February 1917, AFMNZ 1992/038.1; Fry, *Air of Battle*, p. 112.

25 Recommendation, General Officer Commanding III Brigade RFC, NA AIR 1/1158/204/5/2488; 'Mentioned in Dispatches', *Flight*, 17 May 1917, p. 485.

26 J. M. Bruce, *The Aeroplanes of the Royal Flying Corps* (London: Putnam, 1992), p. 522–23.

27 Bruce, *The Aeroplanes of the Royal Flying Corps*, p. 523.

28 Keith Logan Caldwell, Logbook, 26 February 1917, AFMNZ 1992/038.1.

29 Fry, *Air of Battle*, pp. 94–95.

30 H. B. R. Rowell, 'Memoir of Service with the Royal Flying Corps 1915 & 1916, Farnborough, No. 1 Reserve Aeroplane Squadron BEF, France, No. 8 & 12 Squadrons', p. 19, RAF Museum Hendon B3021. Lyn MacDonald, *Somme* (London: Michael Joseph, 1983), pp. 22–23.

31 Terrence J. Finnegan, *Shooting the Front: Allied reconnaissance in the First World War* (Stroud, Gloucestershire: Spellmount, 2011), pp. 74–75.

32 Keith Logan Caldwell, Logbook, 1 February– 6 March 1917, AFMNZ 1992/038.1.

33 13 Wing, Operational Orders, 6 March 1917, TNA AIR 1/1808/204/161/3. Philip Solomon Joyce, Casualty Form, RAF Museum Hendon; Philip Solomon Joyce, TNA AIR 1/267/141.

34 Keith Caldwell, 6 March 1917, AFMNZ 1992/038.1.

35 Norman L. R. Franks, Frank W. Baily and Russell Guest, *Above the Lines: A complete record of the fighter aces of the German Air Service, Naval Air Service and Flanders Marine Corps, 1914–1918* (London: Grub Street, 1993), p. 95; Trevor Henshaw, *The Sky Their Battlefield, II: Air fighting and air casualties of the Great War* (High Barnet, Hertfordshire: Fetubi Books, 2014), p. 71.

36 Young and Warne, *Sixty Squadron*, p. 22.

37 Keith Logan Caldwell, Logbook, August 1916– March 1917, AFMNZ 1992/038.1.

38 Keith Caldwell, Personnel File, TNA WO 339/57844.

Chapter Ten: Hot Stuff

1 A. J. L. Scott, *Sixty Squadron RAF, 1916–1919* (London: Greenhill Books, 1990), p. 34.

2 Alex Revell, *No 60 Squadron RFC/RAF* (Oxford: Osprey, 2011), p. 35.

3 Trevor Henshaw, *The Sky Their Battlefield, II: Air fighting and air casualties of the Great War* (High Barnet, Hertfordshire: Fetubi Books, 2014), p. 74.

4 Alan Scott to Officer Commanding 13th Wing, 31 March 1917, TNA AIR1/1555/204/79/75. Joe Warne, 'Sixty Squadron: A detailed history, Part 2', *Cross & Cockade Great Britain* 11, no. 2 (Summer 1980): pp. 55–56.

5 Scott, *Sixty Squadron RAF*, pp. 45–46.

6 Ibid., p. 46.

7 A. Binnie, quoted in N. Franks and H. Giblin, *Under the Guns of the German Aces* (London, Grub Street, 1997), pp. 141–42.

8 Alan Scott to 13th Wing headquarters, 5 June 1917, Missing Officers, 60 Squadron, Dec 1916–Sept 1917, TNA AIR 1/1552/204/79/50; Adam Claasen, *Fearless: The extraordinary untold story of New Zealand's Great War airmen* (Auckland: Massey University Press, 2017), pp. 249–50; April list of causalities extracted from German document, 5 August 1917, Missing Officers, 60 Squadron, Dec 1916–Sept 1917, TNA AIR 1/1552/204/79/50.

9 Henshaw, *The Sky Their Battlefield*, p. 347.

10 Alan Scott, commanding officer 60 Squadron, to headquarters, 13th Wing, 6 May 1917, TNA AIR1/1555/204/79/75.

11 G. F. Pretyman, Commanding 13th Wing, RFC, 9 May 1917, TNA AIR1/1555/204/79/75.

12 William Sholto Douglas, *Years of Combat: The first volume of the autobiography of Sholto Douglas, Marshal of the Royal Air Force Lord Douglas of Kirtleside, G.C.B., M.C., D.F.C.* (London: Collins, 1963), p. 163.

13 Unknown author, 'Jack Scott: Cripple of the air', typed obituary, 13 February 1922, Andrew Caldwell Family Collection.

14 Air Historical Branch, 43 Squadron, p. 6. TNA AIR 1/692/21/20/43; Sholto Douglas, *Years of Combat*, p. 163

15 *London Gazette*, 24 July 1917, Supplement 30204, p. 7639; Alan Scott, Combat in Air Report, 31 March 1917, TNA AIR 1/1225/204/5/2634.

16 Alan Scott, Combat in Air Report, 28 May 1917, TNA AIR 1/1225/204/5/2634.

17 This anecdote has been retold many times and with great variation, including whether it took place in late May or early June. The author has chosen to follow Scott's own telling of the event: Scott, *Sixty Squadron*, pp. 53–7. Cf Revell, *No 60 Squadron*, p. 52; Ian Mackersey, *No Empty Chairs: The short and heroic lives of the young aviators who fought and died in the First World War* (London: Weidenfeld & Nicolson, 2012), p. 207; A. A Nicod, 'Re-union Memories', *Popular Flying* (January 1936): p. 568; Claasen, *Fearless*, p. 245.

18 Scott, *Sixty Squadron RAF*, p. 57.

19 Ibid., p. 39.

20 Ibid., p. 49.

21 Ibid., pp. 61–62.

22 Ibid., pp. 81–82.

23 Arthur Gould Lee, *Open Cockpit* (London: Grub Street, 2012), p.148.

24 Scott, *Sixty Squadron RAF*, p. 83.

25 Keith Caldwell to Willie Fry, 5 July 1976, Andrew Caldwell Family Collection.

26 Unknown to Alan Scott, 1 April 1917, TNA AIR1/1555/204/79/75.

27 Scott, *Sixty Squadron RAF*, pp. 73–74.

28 Denis Winter, *The First of the Few: Fighter Pilots of the First World War* (London: Allen Lane, 1982), pp. 70–71.

29 Billy Bishop, quoted in Winter, *The First of the Few*, p. 71.

30 William Molesworth, OC (temp) 60 Squadron to headquarters 13th Wing, RFC, 21 June 1917, TNA AIR1/1555/204/79/75.

31 John Collier, Casualty Form, RAF Museum Hendon; Henshaw, *The Sky Their Battlefield*, p. 162.

32 Keith Caldwell, Combat in Air Report, 25 May 1917, TNA AIR 1/2239/209/42/5 Pt. 2.

33 James T. B. McCudden, *Flying Fury: Five Years in the Royal Flying Corps* (New York: Ace, 1968), pp. 147–48.

34 Barry Diggens, *September Evening: The life and final combat of the German World War One ace Werner Voss* (London: Grub Street, 2003), pp. 11–12.

35 Diggens, *September Evening*, pp. 58–9.

36 There is a small possibility that Caldwell in fact fought with another element of Jasta 5 and that his protagonist in what followed was Kurt Schneider, but Caldwell and most chroniclers of the First World War favour Voss. See Revell, *No 60 Squadron*, p. 52; Diggens, *September Evening*, pp. 57–58.

37 Keith Caldwell, Combat in Air Report, 28 May 1917, TNA AIR 1/1225.

38 Keith Caldwell, Logbook, 28 May 1917, AFMNZ 1992/038.1.

39 Dennis Hylands, 'Werner Voss, The Last Hussar', *Cross & Cockade Great Britain* 6, no. 3 (Autumn 1975): pp. 97–104.

40 Revell, *No 60 Squadron*, p. 52.

41 Hylands, 'Werner Voss', pp. 97–104.

42 Keith Caldwell to William Fry, 5 July 1976, Andrew Caldwell Family Collection.

43 Alex Revell, 'Grid Caldwell', *Aeroplane Monthly* (December 2016): p. 47.

44 Caldwell quoted in H. H. Russell and W. R. Puglisi, '"Grid" Caldwell of 74', *Cross & Cockade Journal* 10, no. 3 (Autumn 1969): p. 199.

45 Keith Caldwell, Logbook, 28 May 1917, AFMNZ 1992/038.1.

46 Scott, *Sixty Squadron*, pp. 63–64.

47 William Fry, 'William Avery Bishop VC: Statement by Wing Commander William Fry MC', 2 August 1988, p. 5, RAF Museum Hendon.

48 Ibid., p. 9.

49 William H. Bishop, *Winged Warfare: The experiences of a Canadian 'ace' of the RFC during the First World War* (Milton Keynes: Leonaur, 2011), pp. 110–11.

50 W. M. Fry, *Air of Battle* (London: William Kimber, 1974), p. 135.

51 Bishop, *Winged Warfare*, p. 111; Fry, 'William Avery Bishop', p. 11; Revell, *No 60 Squadron*, p. 55.

52 Fry, *Air of Battle*, pp. 135–36; Fry, 'William Avery Bishop', p. 10.

53 Fry, 'William Avery Bishop', p. 10.

54 Cf Fry wrote in his 1974 memoirs that 'Our CO knew Bishop so well as to believe in him

implicitly, as did the whole squadron and higher authority. Keith Caldwell to William Fry, 20 September 1970, Andrew Caldwell Family Collection; Fry, *Air of Battle*, p. 136.

55 Keith Caldwell (acting) OC, 60 Squadron to 13th Wing, RFC, 30 June 1917, TNA AIR 1/1555/204/79/75.

56 Brereton Greenhous, *The Making of Billy Bishop: The First World War exploits of Billy Bishop VC* (Toronto: Dundurn Press, 2002), pp. 123–128. Greenhous's claim that Caldwell's temporary command led to a decline in Bishop's claims does not appear to consider the lower number of sorties undertaken by the Canadian during this 10-day period. William Avery Bishop, Logbook, 16 June–27 July 1917, CWM 19760521-002.

57 Peter Kilduff, *Billy Bishop VC Lone Wolf Hunter: The RAF ace re-examined* (London: Grub Street, 2014), p. 111.

58 William Bishop, Combat in Air Report, 28 June 1917, AIR 1/1225/204/5/2634/60; Greenhous, *The Making of Billy Bishop*, pp. 136–37; Kilduff, *Billy Bishop VC*, pp. 113–14.

59 Chaz Bowyer, *Royal Flying Corps Communiques, 1917–1918* (London: Grub Street, 1998), p. 74; Greenhous, *The Making of Billy Bishop*, pp. 135–36.

60 Fry, 'William Avery Bishop VC', p. 6. The action in question was on 4 May 1917, see Christopher Shores, Norman Franks and Russell Guest, *Above the Trenches: A complete record of the fighter aces and units of the British air forces, 1915–1920* (London: Grub Street, 1990), pp. 76–78, 161.

Chapter Eleven: Leading Lights

1 Keith Caldwell, Logbook, 8 June 1917, AFMNZ 1992/038.1.

2 A. J. L. Scott, *Sixty Squadron RAF, 1916–1919* (London: Greenhill Books, 1990), pp. 61–2.

3 Keith Caldwell, William Gunner, Frank Soden and Robert Steele, Combat in Air Report, 15 June 1917, TNA AIR 1/2239/209/42/6.

4 William Fry, undated Letter, RAF Museum Hendon, AC86/77/4/3.

5 G. F. Pretyman to headquarters, III Brigade, 17 July 1917, TNA AIR 1/1516/204/58/58.

6 Keith Caldwell, Combat in Air Report, 14 June 1917, TNA AIR 1/2239/209/42/6; Keith Caldwell, Logbook, 14 June 1917, AFMNZ 1992/038.1.

7 Keith Caldwell, Combat in Air Report, 14 June 1917, TNA AIR 1/1225/204/5/2634.

8 The squadron's report book, Caldwell's Combat in Air Report and logbook all record this occurring

on 15 June 1917. Sixty Squadron Officers' Record Book, Keith Caldwell, 15 June 1917, AIR 1/1553/204/79/56; Keith Caldwell, Combat in Air Report, 15 June 1917, TNA AIR 1/2239/209/42/6; Keith Caldwell, Logbook, 15 June 1917, AFMNZ 1992/038.1. However other documentation and many secondary publications state 16 June. Cf Alex Revell, *No 60 Squadron RFC/RAF* (Oxford: Osprey, 2011), p. 55. A typographical error in the generally reliable *Above the Trenches* says this action occurred on 4 June 1917. Christopher Shores, Norman Franks and Russell Guest, *Above the Trenches: A complete record of the fighter aces and units of the British air forces, 1915–1920* (London: Grub Street, 1990).

9 William Fry, Combat in Air Report, 15 June 1917, TNA AIR 1/2239/209/42/6; John Collier, Combat in Air Report, 15 June 1917, TNA AIR 1/2239/209/42/6.

10 Keith Caldwell, Logbook, 15 June 1917, AFMNZ 1992/038.1; Keith Caldwell, Combat in Air Report, TNA AIR 1 1225/204/5/2634

11 Keith Caldwell, Logbook, 24 June 1917, AFMNZ 1992/038.1; H. H. Russell and W. R. Puglisi, '"Grid" Caldwell of 74', *Cross & Cockade Journal* 10, no. 3 (Autumn 1969): p. 200.

12 Keith Caldwell, Combat in Air Report, 24 June 1917, TNA AIR 1/2240/209/42/7.

13 Keith Caldwell, Combat in Air Report, 3 and 15 July 1917, TNA AIR 1/2240/209/42/7.

14 Gerald Parkes, Casualty Form, RAF Museum Hendon.

15 William Molesworth, quoted in Scott, *Sixty Squadron*, pp. 56–68.

16 William Molesworth, quoted in Revell, *No 60 Squadron RFC/RAF*, p. 58.

17 Alan Scott to 13th Wing HQ, 16 July 1917, TNA AIR 1/1555/204/79/75.

18 John Higgins, 19 July 1917, TNA AIR 1/1032/204/5/434.

19 William Molesworth, quoted in Scott, *Sixty Squadron RAF*, p. 99.

20 A. A. Nicod, 'Memories of 60 Squadron RFC', *Popular Flying* 3, no. 9 (December 1934): p. 494; Keith Caldwell to William Fry, 5 July 1976, Andrew Caldwell Family Collection.

21 William Arthur Bishop, *The Courage of the Morning: A frank biography of Billy Bishop, the great ace of World War I* (New York: David McKay Company, 1967), pp. 64–65.

22 A. J. Insall, 'Lanoe Hawker, VC: Recollections and reflections (II)', *Popular Flying* (January 1936): p. 550.

23 Arthur Gould Lee, *Open Cockpit: A pilot of the Royal Flying Corps* (London: Grub Street, 2012, 1st published 1969), p. 158.

24 Ibid., pp. 149–50

25 Bishop, *The Courage of the Morning*, pp. 96–97.

26 Revell, *No 60 Squadron RFC/RAF*, p. 53.

27 William Molesworth, quoted in Scott, *Sixty Squadron RAF*, p. 60.

28 Nicod, 'Memories of 60 Squadron', p. 494.

29 William Molesworth, quoted in Scott, *Sixty Squadron RAF*, p. 60.

30 William Molesworth, quoted in Scott, *Sixty Squadron RAF*, pp. 63–64.

31 Robert Graves, *Goodbye to All That* (London: Jonathan Cape, 1931), p. 163; Lee, *Open Cockpit*, p. 95.

32 David Tappin, '"Chidlaw": Robert Leslie Chidlaw-Roberts MC Hampshire Regt and RFC: Just an ordinary humdrum pilot', *Cross & Cockade International Journal* 20, no. 2 (Summer 1989): p. 64.

33 Cecil Lewis, *Sagittarius Rising* (London: Greenhill Books, 1993), p. 74.

34 William Fry, *Air of Battle* (London: William Kimber, 1974), p. 100.

35 T. J. Mitchell and G. M. Smith, *Medical Services: Casualties and medical statistics of the Great War* (London: His Majesty's Stationery Office, 1931), pp. 164, 174.

36 Ian Mackersey, *No Empty Chairs: The short and heroic lives of the young aviators who fought and died in the First World War* (London: Weidenfeld & Nicolson, 2012), p. 201.

37 William Kennedy Cochran-Patrick, Personnel File, TNA WO 339/50031; Tappin, '"Chidlaw"', p. 62.

38 G. F. Pretyman, Commanding 13th Wing, 'Leaving squadrons during operations & flying over the lines', 2 February 1917, TNA.

39 Ralf Leinburger, *Fighter: Technology, facts, history* (London: Parragon, 2008), p. 30.

40 James T. B. McCudden, *Flying Fury: Five years in the Royal Air Flying Corps* (London: Greenhill, 2000), p. 168.

41 Joe Warne, 'Sixty Squadron, a detailed history, part 2', *Cross & Cockade International Journal* 11, no. 2 (Summer 1980): pp. 61–62.

42 William Molesworth, quoted in Scott, *Sixty Squadron RAF*, p. 101.

43 Tappin, '"Chidlaw"', p. 62.

44 Keith Caldwell, Logbook, 27 July 1917, AFMNZ AFMNZ 1992/038.1.

45 Alan Scott, O.C. 60 Squadron, to headquarters 13th Wing, RFC, 3 June 1917, Confidential reports on officers, Dec 1916 to April 1918, No 60 Squadron, TNA AIR 1/1555/204/79/75.

46 William A. Bishop and Stanley M. Ulanoff (eds), *Winged Warfare* (Folkstone: Bailey Brothers and Swinfen, 1975), pp. 205–6.

47 Bishop, *The Courage of the Morning*, p. 177.

48 Bishop and Ulanoff, *Winged Warfare*, p. 206.

49 Adam Claasen, *Fearless: The extraordinary untold story of New Zealand's Great War airmen* (Auckland: Massey University Press, 2017), pp. 292, 294, 302–4; Alex Revell, *High in the Empty Blue: The history of 56 Squadron, RFC, RAF 1916–1919* (Mountain View, CA: Flying Machines Press, 1995), p. 415; Revell, *No 60 Squadron*, p. 86.

50 Alexander Adam, 3 July 1917, Officers' Record Book, TNA AIR 1/1553/204/79/56.

51 Warne, 'Sixty Squadron', p. 60; Revell, *No 60 Squadron*, p. 59.

52 William Henry Gunner, 1 August 1917, Personnel File, WO 339/8572; William Henry Gunner, Service Record, TNA AIR 76/199/187; Missing and Wounded Officers, 60 Squadron, Sept 1917–March 1918, TNA AIR 1/1552/204/79/51.

53 Recording Officer for the OC 60 Squadron, 4 September 1917, Missing Officers 60 Squadron, Dec 1916–Sept 1917, TNA AIR 1/1552/204/79/50.

54 William Henry Gunner, 18 November 1917, Personnel File, TNA WO 339/8572.

55 Ibid.

56 David Caldwell arrived in England via Liverpool on 12 August and left on 31 October 1917. His arrival coincided with his son's brief furlough of 4–18 August 1917.

57 *Wanganui Collegian*, December 1917, p. 4.

58 Mackersey, *No Empty Chairs*, pp. 176–7.

Chapter Twelve: Clever Caldwell

1 A. J. L. Scott, *Sixty Squadron RAF, 1916–1919* (London: Greenhill Books, 1990), p. 86.

2 Robert Chidlaw-Roberts, Service Record, TNA AIR 76/429/50; Spencer Horn, Service Record, TNA AIR 76/238/40.

3 David Tappin, '"Chidlaw": Robert Leslie Chidlaw-Roberts MC Hampshire Regt and RFC: Just an ordinary humdrum pilot', *Cross & Cockade International Journal* 20, no. 2 (1989): p. 61.

4 Report of attacks of Enemy Infantry, 22 August 1917, TNA AIR 1/1225/204/5/2634/60; Keith Caldwell, 22 August 1917, Officers' Record Book, TNA AIR 1/1553/204/79/56.

5 Joe Warne, 'Sixty Squadron, a detailed history, part 2', *Cross & Cockade International Journal* 11, no. 2 (Summer 1980): p. 63.

6 Lieutenant Norman Macmillan, 45 Squadron, quoted in Nigel Steel & Peter Hart, *Tumult in the Clouds: The British experience of the war in the air, 1914–1918* (London: Coronet Books, 1997), pp. 232–33.

7 Winter, *The First of the Few*, pp. 129–30.

8 Ibid., pp. 127–28.

9 H. H. Russell, 'Rhys Davids of 56 Sqdn, RFC', *Cross & Cockade* (Fall 1976): p. 394; Alex Revell, *Brief Glory: The life of Arthur Rhys Davids DSO, MC and bar* (London: William Kimber, 1984), pp. 168–69.

10 Alex Revell, *No 60 Squadron* (Oxford: Osprey, 2011), p. 71; Tappin, '"Chidlaw"', p. 63.

11 James McCudden, *Flying Fury: Five Years in the Royal Flying Corps* (New York: Ace, 1968; first published 1918), p. 222.

12 Alex Revell, *Fall of Eagles* (Barnsley, South Yorkshire: Pen and Sword Books, 2011), pp. 114–15; Revell, *Brief Glory*, p. 174.

13 Keith Caldwell to Alex Revell, 5 March 1975, Alex Revell Collection.

14 Rothesay Stuart Wortley, quoted in Revell, *Fall of Eagles*, pp. 115–16.

15 Alex Revell, *Fall of Eagles*, p. 117.

16 Bowman, quoted in Revell, *Fall of Eagles*, p. 117.

17 McCudden, *Flying Fury*, p. 223; H. A. Jones, *The War in the Air: Being the story of the part played in the Great War by the Royal Air Force*, Vol. 4, pp. 189–90.

18 Tappin, '"Chidlaw"', p. 63.

19 Russell, 'Rhys Davids', p. 395.

20 Revell, *Brief Glory*, p. 208.

21 Chaz Bowyer, *Royal Flying Corps Communiqués, 1917–1918* (London: Grub Street, 1998), pp. 139–40.

22 Keith Caldwell, Combat in Air Report, 25 September 1917, TNA AIR 1/1225.

23 Keith Caldwell, 6 September–10 October 1917, Officers' Record Book, TNA AIR 1/1553/204/79/56.

24 William Kennedy-Cochran-Patrick to 11th Wing headquarters, 6 October 1917, TNA AIR 1/1551/204/79/75.

25 *Auckland Star*, 16 August 1917.

26 *Evening Mail* (UK), 7 September 1917.

27 *New Zealand Herald*, 20 December 1917.

28 *Waikato Independent*, 4 September 1917.

29 *New Zealand Herald*, 4 October 1917.

30 *Feilding Star*, 28 November 1917.

31 *Wanganui Collegian*, December 1917, p. 4.

32 Ibid., p. 6.

33 *Wanganui Collegian*, August 1917, p. 6.

34 Ibid., p. 8.

35 Keith Caldwell, Logbook, 11 November 1917, AFMNZ.

36 F. D. Tredrey, *Pioneer Pilot: The great Smith Barry who taught the world how to fly* (London: Peter Davies, 1976), p 89; Gwilym H. Lewis, *Wings Over the Somme, 1916–1919* (Bristol: Bridge Books, 1994), p. 95.

37 Quoted in Tredrey, *Pioneer Pilot*, pp. 52–53.

38 Tredrey, *Pioneer Pilot*, p. 40.

39 Ibid., p. 90.

40 Smith Barry, Report on French Flying Schools, 1917, TNA AIR 20/598.

41 Russell Miller, *Trenchard. Father of the Royal Air Force: The biography* (London: Weidenfeld & Nicolson, 2017), p. 169.

42 *Wanganui Collegian*, April 1918, p. 8.

43 Ira Jones, *Tiger Squadron: The story of 74 Squadron, RAF, in Two World Wars* (London: W. H. Allen, 1954), pp. 63–64.

44 Henry Hamer, Logbook, 6 March 1918, AFMNZ, 1988/004.1b.

45 Keith Caldwell to Mary Caldwell, 15 and 25 December 1917, Deborah Stovell Family Collection.

46 Keith Caldwell to Mary Caldwell, 20 January 1918, Deborah Stovell Family Collection.

47 Keith Caldwell to Gwilym Lewis, c.1975, Alex Revell Collection.

48 Keith Caldwell to Gwilym Lewis, 18 August 1975, Alex Revell Collection.

49 Keith Caldwell to Mary Caldwell, 20 January 1918, Deborah Stovell Family Collection.

50 Winter, *The First of the Few*, pp. 43–44.

51 H. H. Russell and W. R. Puglisi, '"Grid" Caldwell of 74', *Cross & Cockade Journal* 10, no. 3 (Autumn 1969): p. 202.

52 Keith Caldwell to Mary Caldwell, 25 January 1918, Deborah Stovell Family Collection.

Chapter Thirteen: Dentist's Chair

1 H. A. Jones, *The War in the Air: Being the part played in the Great War by the Royal Air Force*, Vol. 4 (Uckfield, East Sussex: Naval and Military Press, 1934), pp. 275–6.

2 Jones, *The War in the Air*, p. 273.

3   H. A. Jones, *The War in the Air: Being the story of the part played in the Great War by the Royal Air Force, Vol. 6* (Uckfield, East Sussex: Naval and Military Press, 1937), pp. 11–12.

4   The mobilisation of the squadron in early March was started by Caldwell's predecessor, Major Alan Sidney Whitehorn Dore. History of 74 Squadron RAF, Air Historical Branch, Air Ministry, TNA Air 27/644. Aside from this brief internal Air Ministry history, 74 Squadron has a handful of books dedicated to it: Ira Jones, *Tiger Squadron: The story of 74 Squadron, RAF in two world wars* (London: W. H. Allen, 1954); Bob Crossey, *Tigers: The story of 74 Squadron RAF* (London: Arms and Armour, 1992); Douglas Tidy, *I Fear No Man: The history of No. 74 Squadron, Royal Air Force 1917–1997* (Hailsham, East Sussex: J & KH Publishing, 1998).

5   Hesperus van Ryneveld, Commanding 11 Wing, RAF, Routine Orders, 14 April 1918, TNA AIR 1/982/204/5/1160.

6   Hesperus van Ryneveld, Commanding 11 Wing, RAF, Routine Orders, 13 April 1918, TNA AIR 1/982/204/5/1160; Report: procedures laid down for administration of these units, also approximate cost of a squadron (10 August 1917–5 February 1918), Australian Flying Corps, TNA AIR 1/1142/204/5/2339.

7   James Dudgeon, *Mick: The story of Major Edward Mannock VC, DSO, MC, RFC, RAF* (London: Robert Hale, 1981), pp. 122–23; Jones, *Tiger Squadron*, p. 64; Ira Jones, *King of the Air Fighters: The biography of Major 'Mick' Mannock VC* (London: Nicolson & Watson, 1935), p. 168.

8   Wilfred Young, Personnel File, TNA WO 339/30902; Wilfred Young, Proceedings Medical Board, 29 November 1917, TNA WO 339/30902.

9   Dudgeon, *Mick*, p. 123.

10 Frederick Oughton, *The Personal Diary of Mick Mannock VC DSO (2 bars), MC (1 bar)* (Neville London: Spearman, 1966), p. 17.

11 Oughton, *The Personal Diary of Mick Mannock*, p. 17.

12 William Sholto Douglas, *Years of Combat* (London: Collins, 1963), p. 202.

13 MacLanachan, quoted in Norman Franks and Andy Saunders, *Mannock: The life and death of Major Edward Mannock VC, DSO, MC, RAF* (London: Grub Street, 2008), p. 30.

14 Radio recording, quoted in Franks and Saunders, *Mannock*, p. 84.

15 Dudgeon, *Mick*, p. 123.

16 Jones, *Tiger Squadron*, p. 69.

17 Ibid., pp. 65–66.

18 Arthur Gordon Lewis was briefly the recording officer until he was replaced by Everard. Franks and Saunders, *Mannock*, p. 89. Nonetheless, there is some uncertainty as to the identity of the squadron adjutant at the time of its departure to France. As some of the images reproduced in this book indicated Caldwell's photographs state it was a 'Jarrard' who served as adjutant. The author was unable to locate support for this but records demonstrate William Everard was with the squadron in November 1917. TNA AIR 76/154/177.

19 Elizabeth Richardson-Whealy (ed.), *Pilot's Log: The log, diary letters and verse of Lt. Leonard A. Richardson, Royal Flying Corps, 1917–1918* (St. Catherine's, ON: A Lilywood Book, 1999), pp. 107–8.

20 Major K. L. Caldwell, Commanding 74 Squadron, London Colney, 8 February, 13 March 1918, 74 Squadron Orderly Room Record Book, RFC London Colney, 19 December 1917–22 March 1918, RAF Hendon X0067001.

21 Major Dores, Commanding 74 Squadron, 4 March 1918, 74 Squadron Orderly Room Record Book, RFC London Colney, 19 December 1917–22 March 1918, RAF Hendon X0067001.

22 Major K. L. Caldwell, Officer Commanding, 19 & 20 March 1918: 74 Squadron Orderly Room Record Book, RFC London Colney, 19 December 1917–22 March 1918, RAF Hendon X0067001.

23 Winston Churchill, *The World Crisis, 1911–1918* (New York: Free Press, 2005), p. 768.

24 Richardson-Whealy (ed.), *Pilot's Log*, pp. 110, 138, 139.

25 Keith Caldwell to William Fry, 21 Sept 1978, Alex Revell Collection; cf 'Comments from Keith L. Caldwell (compiled and annotated by Marvin L. Skelton)', 15 August 1977, pp. 7–8, Andrew Caldwell Family Collection.

26 Keith Caldwell to William Fry, 21 Sept 1978, Alex Revell Collection.

27 Keith Caldwell to Mary Caldwell, March 1918, Deborah Stovell Family Collection.

28 History of 74 Squadron, RAF, TNA AIR 27/644.

29 Jones, *Tiger Squadron*, p. 66.

30 www.crossandcockade.com/StOmer/TheAircraftDepot.asp (accessed 10 April 2021).

31 Arthur Gould Lee, *No Parachute: A fighter pilot in World War I* (New York: Harper & Row, 1970), p. 4.

32 William Fry, *Air of Battle* (London: William Kimber, 1974), p. 19.

33 Denis Winter, *The First of the Few: Fighter pilots of the First World War* (Harmondsworth, Middlesex: Penguin, 1983), pp. 58–59; Gwilym H. Lewis, *Wings over the Somme, 1916–1918* (Bristol: Longdunn Press, 1994), p. 42.

34 Jones, *Tiger Squadron*, pp. 66–67.

35 Winter, *The First of the Few*, pp. 58–59.

36 Lee, *No Parachute*, p. 95.

37 Jones, *Tiger Squadron*, p. 67.

38 Keith Caldwell to Mary Caldwell, 5 April 1918, Deborah Stovell Family Collection.

39 Keith Caldwell to Mary Caldwell, 5 April 1918, Deborah Stovell Family Collection.

40 Jones, *Tiger Squadron*, pp. 68–69.

41 74 Squadron History, TNA AIR 27/644; Jones, *Tiger Squadron*, p. 68.

42 Jones, *Tiger Squadron*, pp. 69–70.

43 Ibid., pp. 69, 70.

44 War Diary, II Brigade RAF, 11 April 1917, TNA AIR 1/2231.

45 Richardson-Whealy (ed.), *Pilot's Log*, p. 147.

46 Jones, *Tiger Squadron*, p. 72.

47 Hesperus Andrias van Ryneveld, 11 Wing, Routine Orders, 13 April 1918, TNA AIR 1/982/204/5/1160. Initially 74 Squadron arrived in France as part of 64th Wing. See 74 Squadron History, TNA AIR 27/644.

48 Richardson-Whealy (ed.), *Pilot's Log*, p. 147.

49 Jones, *The War in the Air*, p. 375.

50 Ibid., p. 380.

51 Jones, *Tiger Squadron*, p. 73.

52 Richardson-Whealy (ed.), *Pilot's Log*, p. 148.

53 Jones, *Tiger Squadron*, p. 73.

Chapter Fourteen: Day of Days

1 War Diary, II Brigade, 12 April 1918, TNA AIR 1/2232/209/41/16.

2 Ira Jones, *Tiger Squadron: The story of 74 Squadron, RAF, in two world wars* (London: W. H. Allen, 1954), p. 73.

3 Ibid., p. 74.

4 Ira Jones, *King of the Air Fighters: The biography of Major 'Mick' Mannock VC* (London: Nicolson & Watson, 1935), pp. 178–79.

5 Jones, *Tiger Squadron*, p. 77.

6 Ibid., p. 78.

7 Henry Dolan, Combat in Air Report, 12 April 1918, TNA AIR 1/2232/209/41/16.

8 There is some confusion in the secondary sources over whether Dolan or Mannock secured the squadron's first credit, though most sources go with the latter. For a recent assessment see Norman Franks and Andy Saunders, *Mannock: The life and death of Major Edward Mannock VC, DSO, MC, RAF* (London: Grub Street, 2008), p. 92.

9 Marvin L. Skelton, *Callanan, the Last War Bird* (Manhattan, KS: Air Historical Foundation, 1980), p. 102.

10 Skelton, *Callanan*, p. 172.

11 Keith Caldwell, Combat in Air Report, 12 April 1918, TNA AIR 1/226/204/5/2634; Keith Caldwell, Logbook, 12 April 1918, AFMNZ.

12 H. A. Jones, *The War in the Air: Being the part played in the Great War by the Royal Air Force, Vol. 4* (Uckfield, East Sussex: Naval and Military Press, 1934), pp. 381.

13 Ibid., pp. 381–82, fn. 1.

14 Jones, *King of the Air Fighters*, p. 181.

15 74 Squadron History, Air Historical Branch, p. 2, TNA AIR 27/644.

16 Jones, *King of the Air Fighters*, p. 182.

17 Jones, *Tiger Squadron*, p. 80.

18 Hesperus 'Pierre' Andrias van Ryneveld, Personnel File, TNA AIR 76/441/122.

19 Jones, *King of the Air Fighters*, p. 184.

20 Jones, *The War in the Air*, p. 378 fn. 1.

21 Elizabeth Richardson-Whealy (ed.), *Pilot's Log: The log, diary letters and verse of Lt. Leonard A. Richardson, Royal Flying Corps, 1917–1918* (St. Catherine's, ON: A Lilywood Book, 1999), pp. 152–53, 149.

22 Jones, *King of the Air Fighters*, p. 185.

23 Richardson-Whealy (ed.), *Pilot's Log*, p. 148.

24 Ibid., p. 150.

25 Jones, *Tiger Squadron*, p. 84.

26 Keith Caldwell to Mary Caldwell, 23 April 1918, Deborah Stovell Family Collection.

27 Trevor Henshaw, *The Sky Their Battlefield, II: Air fighting and air casualties of the Great War* (High Barnet, Hertfordshire: Fetubi Books, 2014), p. 167.

28 Jones, *Tiger Squadron*, p. 85.

29 James Dudgeon, *Mick: The story of Major Edward Mannock VC, DSO, MC, RFC, RAF* (London: Robert Hale, 1981), pp. 130–31.

30 Keith Caldwell to Mary Caldwell, 23 April 1918, Deborah Stovell Family Collection.

31 Jack Treacy, quoted in Nigel Steel and Peter Hart, *Tumult in the Clouds: The British experience of the war in the air, 1914–1918* (London: Coronet Books, 1997), p. 322.

32 Jones, *King of the Air Fighters*, p. 188; Edward

Mannock, quoted in Peter Vansittart (ed.), *Voices from the Great War* (London: Penguin Books, 1963), p. 230.

33 Ian Mackersey, *No Empty Chairs: The short and heroic lives of the young aviators who fought and died in the First World War* (London: Weidenfeld & Nicolson, 2012), pp. 293–94.

34 Jones, *Tiger Squadron*, p. 84.

35 Adam Claasen, *Fearless: The extraordinary untold story of New Zealand's Great War airmen* (Auckland: Massey University Press, 2017), pp. 229–30; Russell Miller, *Trenchard: Father of the Royal Air Force* (London: Weidenfeld & Nicolson, 1917); Arthur Gould Lee, *No Parachute: A fighter pilot in World War I* (New York: Harper & Row, 1970), pp. 219–25.

36 Jones, *King of the Air Fighters*, p. 169.

37 Keith Caldwell to Mary Caldwell, 26 April 1918, Deborah Stovell Family Collection.

38 Richardson-Whealy (ed.), *Pilot's Log*, p. 154.

39 Jones, *The War in the Air*, p. 399.

40 Richardson-Whealy (ed.), *Pilot's Log*, pp. 155–56.

41 Jones, *The War in the Air*, p. 399.

42 54 Squadron History, Air Historical Branch, TNA AIR 1/693/21/20/54.

43 Keith Caldwell to Mary Caldwell, 5 May 1918, Deborah Stovell Family Collection. For a period the squadron was recognised by the British air service as 71 Squadron, but the Australians preferred to retain their AFC numbering and always referred to it as 4 Squadron AFC. Van Ryneveld, Routine Orders, 11 Wing, RAF, 30 April 1918, TNA AIR 1/1825/204/202/6. II Brigade, War Diary, 29 April 1918, TNA AIR 1/223/209/41/61.

44 Keith Caldwell to Gwilym Lewis, 22 March 1977, Alex Revell Collection.

45 Jones, *Tiger Squadron*, p. 90.

46 Ibid., p. 93.

47 Keith Caldwell to Mary Caldwell, 30 April 1918, Deborah Stovell Family Collection.

48 Jones, *The War in the Air*, pp. 402–3.

49 Keith Caldwell to Mary Caldwell, 30 April 1918, Deborah Stovell Family Collection; Jones, *Tiger Squadron*, p. 93.

50 Richardson-Whealy (ed.), *Pilot's Log*, p. 166; Keith Caldwell to Mary Caldwell, 12 May 1918, Deborah Stovell Family Collection.

51 Jones, *Tiger Squadron*, p. 99.

52 Ibid., p. 99.

53 Richardson-Whealy (ed.), *Pilot's Log*, p. 166; Jones, *Tiger Squadron*, p. 95; Keith Caldwell to

Mary Caldwell, 12 May 1918, Deborah Stovell Family Collection.

54 John Robert Piggott, Casualty Form, RAF Hendon; John Robert Piggott, Personal File, TNA AIR 76/404/137.

55 Franks and Saunders, *Mannock*, pp. 101–2.

56 II Brigade War Diary, 12 May 1918, TNA AIR 1/2231/209/41/17; Henry Eric Dolan, Personnel File, TNA WO 339/14532, Henry Eric Dolan, Casualty Card, RAF Hendon.

57 Franks and Saunders, *Mannock*, pp. 102–3.

58 Jones, *Tiger Squadron*, p. 92.

59 Franks and Saunders, *Mannock*, p. 103.

60 Wilfred Giles quoted in Bob Cossey, *Tigers: The story of No. 74 Squadron RAF* (London: Arms and Armour, 1992), pp. 30–31.

61 Jones, *King of the Air Fighters*, p. 193.

62 Jones, *Tiger Squadron*, pp. 102–3.

63 Leigh Morphew Nixon, Service Record, AIR 76/374/114.

64 Jones, *Tiger Squadron*, p. 107.

65 www.thegreatsilence.co.uk/the-great-silence-blog/choristers (retrieved 25 May 2021).

66 Lambert Francis Barton, Personnel File, TNA AIR 76/26/97; www.militaryimages.net/media/lambert-francis-barton.82128 (retrieved 26 May 2021).

67 II Brigade War Diary, 17 May 1918, TNA AIR 1/2231/209/41/17.

68 Van Ryneveld, Routine Orders, 11 Wing, RAF, 18 May 1918, TNA AIR 1/1825/204/202/6.

69 Jones, *Tiger Squadron*, pp. 105–6.

70 Wilfred Giles quoted in Cossey, *Tigers*, pp. 30–31; the routine orders emanating from 11 Wing Head Quarters detailed the men attached to and struck off its squadrons, see TNA AIR 1/982/204/5/1160.

Chapter Fifteen: Bravest of the Brave

1 Elizabeth Richardson-Whealy (ed.), *Pilot's Log: The log, diary letters and verse of Lt. Leonard A. Richardson, Royal Flying Corps, 1917–1918* (St. Catherine's, ON: A Lilywood Book, 1999), p. 170.

2 Andrew Cameron Kiddie, Personnel File, TNA WO 339/6771. Melaena referred to dark, tarry faeces resulting from gastrointestinal bleeding.

3 Christopher Shores, Norman Franks and Russell Guest, *Above the Trenches: A complete record of the fighter aces and units of the British Empire Air Forces, 1915–1920* (London: Grub Street, 1990), p. 222.

4 Ira Jones, *Tiger Squadron: The story of 74*

Squadron, RAF, in two world wars (London: W. H. Allen, 1954), p. 116.

5 Ira Jones, Combat in Air Report, 19 May 1918, TNA AIR 1/1829/204/202/20.

6 Jones, Tiger Squadron, p. 115.

7 Kiddie, Combat in Air Report, 19 May 1918, TNA AIR 1/1829/204/202/20.

8 Jones, Tiger Squadron, pp. 115–16.

9 Keith Caldwell to Mary Caldwell, 20 May 1918, Deborah Stovell Family Collection.

10 Richardson-Whealy (ed.), Pilot's Log, p. 175.

11 Jones, Tiger Squadron, p. 116.

12 Edward Mannock, Combat in Air Report, 21 May 1918, TNA AIR 1/1829/204/202/20.

13 Frederick Oughton, The Personal Diary of Mick Mannock VC DSO (2 bars), MC (1 bar) (Neville London: Spearman, 1966), p. 190.

14 Keith Caldwell to Mary Caldwell, 16 May 1918, Deborah Stovell Family Collection.

15 Jones, Tiger Squadron, pp. 88, 110.

16 Keith Logan Caldwell, Combat in Air Report, 21 May 1918, TNA AIR 1/1829/204/202/20; Keith Caldwell to Mary Caldwell, 22 May 1918, Deborah Stovell Family Collection.

17 Keith Caldwell to Mary Caldwell, 22 May 1918, Deborah Stovell Family Collection.

18 Jones, Tiger Squadron, p. 121; Keith Caldwell to Mary Caldwell, 20 May 1918, Deborah Stovell Family Collection.

19 Keith Caldwell to Mary Caldwell, 20 May 1918, Deborah Stovell Family Collection.

20 Keith Caldwell to Mary Caldwell, 22 May 1918, Deborah Stovell Family Collection.

21 Keith Caldwell, Combat in Air Report, 28 May 1918, TNA AIR 1/1829/204/202/20.

22 Jones, Tiger Squadron, p. 127.

23 Jones, Tiger Squadron, p. 128; Keith Caldwell, Logbook, 28 April 1918, AFMNZ.

24 Keith Caldwell, 31 May 1918, Combat in Air Report, TNA AIR 1/1829/204/202/20.

25 Richardson-Whealy (ed.), Pilot's Log, p. 183.

26 Jones, Tiger Squadron, p. 111.

27 Oughton, The Personal Diary of Mick Mannock, p. 183.

28 Richardson-Whealy (ed.), Pilot's Log, pp. 151–52.

29 Ibid., p. 180.

30 Ibid., p. 184.

31 Ira Jones, King of the Air Fighters: The biography of Major 'Mick' Mannock VC (London: Nicolson & Watson, 1935), pp. 208–9.

32 Ibid., p. 209.

33 Jones, Tiger Squadron, p. 123; Jones, King of the Air Fighters, pp. 204–5.

34 Richardson-Whealy (ed.), Pilot's Log, pp. 177–78.

35 Jones, Tiger Squadron, p. 124.

36 Joe Gleeson, Irish Aces of the RFC and RAF in the First World War (United Kingdom: Fonthill, 2015), pp. 38–39.

37 Jones, Tiger Squadron, p. 136.

38 Richardson-Whealy (ed.), Pilot's Log, p. 187.

39 Keith Caldwell, Combat in Air Report, 1 June 1918, TNA AIR 1/1829/20/204/202/20.

40 Ira Jones, An Air Fighter's Scrapbook (London: Greenhill Books, 1990), pp. 77–78.

41 Jones, Tiger Squadron, p. 141.

42 Ibid., p. 141.

43 Peter Yule (ed.), Sergeant Lawrence Goes to France (Melbourne: Melbourne University Press, 1987), p. 168. Lawrence may be referring to Caldwell or Cobby. In Tiger Squadron, Ira Jones has Caldwell as the first assailant, but in An Air Fighter's Scrapbook he has Cobby. In his autobiography, Cobby makes no mention of the presence of 74. Caldwell's logbook inexplicably has large gaps over this period of operations. Jones, Tiger Squadron, p. 141; Jones, An Air Fighter's Scrapbook, pp. 79–80; A. H. Cobby, High Adventure: The autobiography of Australia's most famous WW1 Flying Ace (Melbourne: Kookaburra Technical Publications, 1981), pp. 67–68; Keith Caldwell, Logbook, 12 May–June 1918.

44 Jones, Tiger Squadron, p. 142.

45 A 29 Squadron pilot also made a claim on Mertens. Jones, Tiger Squadron, p. 142.

46 Cobby, High Adventure, pp. 67–68; Jones, Tiger Squadron, p. 142; 'Tail skid from a Pfalz D IIIa Scout shot down by Flying Officer A H Cobby, No. 4 Squadron, Australian Flying Corps', www.awm.gov.au/collection/C111420 (retrieved 22 July 2021).

47 Cobby, High Adventure, p. 68.

48 Jones, Tiger Squadron, p. 142; cf Jones, An Air Fighter's Scrapbook, p. 80.

Chapter Sixteen: Immolation

1 Routine Orders, van Ryneveld, 11 Wing, RAF, 10 June 1918 TNA AIR 1/982/204/5/1160.

2 Keith Caldwell to Mary Caldwell, 5 May 1918, Deborah Stovell Family Collection.

3 Routine Orders, van Ryneveld, 11 Wing, RAF, 13 June 1918 TNA AIR 1/982/204/5/1160.

4 Ira Jones, Tiger Squadron: The story of 74 Squadron, RAF, in two world wars (London: W. H. Allen, 1954), p. 140.

5   Keith Caldwell, quoted in James Dudgeon, *Mick: The story of Major Edward Mannock VC, DSO, MC, RFC, RAF* (London: Robert Hale, 1981), p. 127.

6   Dudgeon, *Mick*, p. 155.

7   Keith Caldwell to Skelton, quoted Marvin L. Skelton, *Callahan, the Last War Bird* (Manhattan, Kansas: Air Force Historical Foundation, 1980), p. 101.

8   Elizabeth Richardson-Whealy (ed.), *Pilot's Log: The log, diary letters and verse of Lt. Leonard A. Richardson, Royal Flying Corps, 1917–1918* (St. Catherine's, ON: A Lilywood Book, 1999), p. 204.

9   Laura Spinney, *Pale Rider: The Spanish Flu of 1918 and how it changed the world* (London: Vintage, 2018), pp. 39, 248–49.

10 Richardson-Whealy (ed.), *Pilot's Log*, p. 205.

11 Jones, *Tiger Squadron*, p. 148.

12 Keith Caldwell to Mary Caldwell, June 1918, Deborah Stovell Family Collection.

13 Richardson-Whealy (ed.), *Pilot's Log*, p. 212; Keith Caldwell to Mary Caldwell, June 1918, Deborah Stovell Family Collection.

14 Combats 11 Wing RAF, June–July 1918, TNA AIR 1/1829/204/202/21.

15 Jones makes this claim on 21 June 1918; Richardson on 25 June 1918. Jones, *Tiger Squadron*, p. 142; cf Ira Jones, *An Air Fighter's Scrapbook* (London: Greenhill Books, 1990), p. 144; Richardson-Whealy (ed.), *Pilot's Log*, p. 204.

16 Ira Jones, *King of the Air Fighters: The biography of Major 'Mick' Mannock VC* (London: Nicolson & Watson, 1935), p. 236.

17 Sydney Carlin, Personnel File, TNA WO 374/12384.

18 Jones, *King of the Air Fighters*, p. 125.

19 *New Zealand Times*, 17 January 1918.

20 Jones, *King of the Air Fighters*, p. 158.

21 Caldwell tried to get Auckland farmer Maurice Sinclair added to the roster but lost him to 56 Squadron. Keith Caldwell to Mary Caldwell, 30 June 1918, Deborah Stovell Family Collection; Maurice Denman Sinclair, Casualty Card, RAF Hendon; Maurice Denman Sinclair, Service Record, TNA AIR 76/464/54.

22 Keith Caldwell to Mary Caldwell, 30 June 1918, Deborah Stovell Family Collection.

23 Richardson-Whealy (ed.), *Pilot's Log*, 19 July 1918.

24 Harold Shoemaker to father, 3 July 1918, www. theaerodrome.com/forum/showthread. php?t=71550&highlight=shoemaker (retrieved 29 March 2023).

25 Frederick Ernest Luff, Service Record, TNA AIR 76/310/18; Conrad Henry Matthiessen, Service Record, TNA AIR 76/339/127; Archibald Martin Roberts, TNA AIR 76/428/91. Although Roberts was born in Britain, he appears to have spent time in the United States and Cuba and on his service record he is an 'American Cadet.' Jones mistakenly substitutes 'Alexander' for 'Archibald'. Jones, *King of the Air Fighters*, p. 139.

26 *London Gazette*, 14 June 1918, p. 7068; Keith Caldwell to Mary Caldwell, 5 June 1918, Deborah Stovell Family Collection.

27 Jones, *King of the Air Fighters*, p. 149.

28 Jones, *King of the Air Fighters*, p. 149; Percy Howe, Service Record, TNA AIR 76/240; Percy Howe, Casualty Form, RAF Museum, Hendon.

29 Richardson-Whealy (ed.), *Pilot's Log*, pp. 218–19.

30 Ibid., p. 219

31 War Diary, II Brigade, 26 July 1918, TNA AIR 1/2231/209/41/19.

32 *London Gazette*, 26 November 1915; Donald Clyde Inglis, Service Record, TNA AIR 76/249/40; Donald Clyde Inglis, Personnel File, ANZ AABK 18805 W551 44/0058859.

33 G. H. Cunningham, *Mac's Memoirs: The flying life of Squadron-Leader McGregor* (Wellington: A. H. & A. W. Reed, 1937), pp. 57–8.

34 Frederick Oughton (ed.), *The Personal Diary of 'Mick' Mannock, V.C., D.S.O., M.C., D.F.C., M.C. (1 bar)* (London: Oakfield Press, 1966), pp. 197–99.

35 Donald Clyde Inglis, Combat in Air Report, 26 July 1918, TNA 1/1227/204/5/2634; *Sun*, 6 October 1919.

36 Donald Inglis, 'Mannock's Last Flight', *Popular Flying*, July 1938, p. 188; Oughton, *The Personal Diary of Mick Mannock*, p. 200.

37 Oughton, *The Personal Diary of Mick Mannock*, p. 201. This is at variance with Jones's claim to have flown over the 'charred remains' of Mannock's machine, Jones, diary, p. 26, July 1918. In the decades that followed, numerous stories regarding Mannock's state of mind and the events surrounding his death were popularised and, in some cases, embellished, see Adrian Smith, *Mick Mannock Fighter Pilot: Myth, life and politics* (London: Palgrave, 2001), pp. 125–31. Much has also been written about Mannock's final resting place. For a recent consideration, see Norman Franks and Andy Saunders, *Mannock: The life and times of Major Edward Mannock, VC, DSO, MC, RAF* (London: Grub Street, 2008), pp. 149–72.

38 Cunningham, *Mac's Memoirs*, p. 63.

39 Jones, *King of the Air Fighters*, p. 252. Regarding Arthur 'Mary' Coningham, see Adam Claasen, *Fearless: The extraordinary untold story of New Zealand's Great War airmen* (Auckland: Massey University Press, 2017), pp. 277–81, 390–94, 425.

40 Jones, *King of the Air Fighters*, pp. 251–52.

41 Elliot White Springs, *War Birds: Diary of an unknown aviator* (New York: George H. Doran Company, 1926), pp. 236–39.

42 Jones, *King of the Air Fighters*, p. 161.

43 *Bridgeton Evening News* (New Jersey), 26 August 1918.

44 'Bags his first plane: Lieut. Harold G. Shoemaker, [19]15, tells of his experience', *Alumni Bulletin of Lehigh University*, pp. 32–33; Harold Shoemaker, Combat in Air Report, 30 July 1918, TNA AIR 1/1829/204/202/21.

45 Keith Caldwell, Combat in Air Report, 30 July 1918, TNA AIR 1/1829/204/202/2; Keith Caldwell, Logbook, 30 July 1918, AFMNZ 1992/038.1; Russell and Puglisi state that Caldwell 'gained a double on the 30th', but there is only one combat in the air report and in his logbook Caldwell stated of this second enemy machine. 'don't think I got him'. H. H. Russell and W. R. Puglisi, '"Grid" Caldwell of 74', *Cross & Cockade Journal* 10, no. 3 (Autumn 1969), pp. 206, 212; Keith Caldwell, Logbook, 30 July 1918, AFMNZ 1992/038.1. Cf Christopher Shores, Norman Franks and Russell Guest, *Above the Trenches: A complete record of the fighter aces and units of the British air forces, 1915–1920* (London: Grub Street, 1990), p. 94. In addition to the two Fokker DVIIs of July, he was credited with a victory against a Pfalz on 29 July 1918. Keith Caldwell, Combat in Air Report, 29 July 1918, TNA AIR 1/1829/204/202/2; Keith Caldwell, Logbook, 29 July 1918, AFMNZ 1992/038.1.

46 'Bags his first plane', p. 33.

47 This total is underreported: Caldwell's and two of Jones's well-documented 30 July successes are inexplicably missing from the tabulation. 'Summary of work done by 11 Wing, RAF during July 1918', TNA AIR 1/1829/204/202/2.

48 Young's posting took effect on 3 August 1918. Wilfred Ernest Young, Casualty Form, RAF Hendon.

49 Jones, *Tiger Squadron*, p. 148.

50 *Wanganui Collegian*, April 1918, pp. 2–4.

51 *Auckland Star*, 11 January 1918; Sandra Coney, *Gone West: Great War memorials of Waitakere and their soldiers* (Auckland: Protect Piha Heritage Society, 2017), pp. 102–3; William Neal Spragg, Personnel File, TNA WO 339/57833.

52 *New Zealand Herald*, 29 November 1918.

53 For a contemporary appreciation of St Paul's from a New Zealand airman see House of Harkness, *A World War 1 Adventure: The life and times of RNAS bomber pilot Donald E. Harkness* (Bloomington, Ind.: AuthorHouse, 2014), p. 61.

54 L. J. Collins, *Theatre at War 1914–18* (London: Macmillan, 1998), p. 3; Gordon Williams, *British Theatre in the Great War: A re-evaluation* (London: Continuum, 2003), pp. 18–19; *Tatler*, 12 September 1917.

55 Jones, *King of the Air Fighters*, p. 161.

56 II Brigade, Routine Orders, 16 August 1918, TNA AIR 1/1826/204/202/9.

57 Howard Vincent Coverdale, Service Record, TNA AIR 76/109/16.

58 *Wanganui Collegian*, December 1918, p. 4.

Chapter Seventeen: Great Escape

1 Philip Gibbs, quoted in 'British Victories on the Somme: Triumphant progress towards and beyond the Hindenburg Line from Lens to St. Quentin', *Current History* 9, no. 1 (October 1918): pp. 21–22.

2 H. A. Jones, *The War in the Air: Being the part played in the Great War by the Royal Air Force*, Vol. 6 (Uckfield, East Sussex: Naval and Military Press, 1937), pp. 473–74.

3 Harris Clements quoted in James Dudgeon, *Mick: The story of Major Edward Mannock VC, DSO, MC, RFC, RAF* (London: Robert Hale, 1981), pp. 148–49.

4 Andy Powell, 'The Use of Wireless at the Battle of Amiens 8–11 August 1918', Western Front Association. www.westernfrontassociation. com/world-war-i-articles/ma-dissertations/ the-use-of-wireless-at-the-battle-of-amiens-8-11-august-1918 (retrieved 3 February 1918).

5 Operation Order, No. 206, 11 Wing, 22 August 1918, TNA AIR 1/1794/204/153/24.

6 Keith Logan Caldwell, Logbook, 23 August 1918, AFMNZ 1992/038.1.

7 Keith Caldwell and Benjamin Roxburgh-Smith, Combat in Air Report, 23 August 1918, TNA AIR 1/1829/204/202/22.

8 Summary of Work done by 11 Wing during August 1918, AIR 1/1829/204/202/22; cf Combat in Air reports of War Diary, II Brigade, August 1918, TNA 1/2231/209/41/20.

9 Jones, *The War in the Air*, pp. 434–36. The RAF's numerical advantage was even stronger than these figures suggest: there were nearly

1000 additional machines at its disposal on the Western Front. Trevor Henshaw, *The Sky Their Battlefield, II: Air fighting and air casualties of the Great War* (High Barnet, Hertfordshire: Fetubi Books, 2014), pp. 195–96.

10 Norman Franks, Russell Guest and Frank Baily, *Bloody April . . . Black September: An exciting and detailed analysis of the two deadliest months in the air in World War One* (London: Grub Street, 1995).

11 Jones, *The War in the Air*, p. 445.

12 H. H. Russell and W. R. Puglisi, '"Grid" Caldwell of 74', *Cross & Cockade Journal* 10, no. 3 (Autumn 1969): 1968, p. 202.

13 Keith Caldwell and Frederick Hunt, Combat in Air Report, 4 September 1918, TNA AIR 1/1829/204/202/22.

14 Sydney Carlin and Frederick Stanley Gordon, Combat in Air Report, 4 September 1918, TNA AIR 1/1829/204/202/22.

15 Ira Jones, *King of the Air Fighters: The biography of Major 'Mick' Mannock VC* (London: Nicolson & Watson, 1935), p. 226.

16 Richmond Mayson, unpublished memoir, https://sites.google.com/site/cahsreginachapter/richmond-mayson-74-squadron (retrieved 16 February 2022). Richard Mayson, Personnel File, TNA AIR 76/341/261.

17 Rea Isaiah Hagenbuch to Annie 'Winnie' W. Jones, 11 September 1918, Ted Harwood Collection; Rea Isaiah Hagenbuch, Service Record, TNA AIR 76/201/98.

18 Henshaw, *The Sky Their Battlefield*, p. 218.

19 Operation Order No. 229, 11 Wing, 15 September 1918, TNA AIR 1/1794/204/153/24.

20 Hagenbuch to Annie 'Winnie' W. Jones, 28 September 1918.

21 Keith Caldwell and Frederick Hunt, Combat in Air Report, 17 September 1918, TNA AIR 1/1829/204/202/22.

22 Shores et al. posit that the second victory was over Vzfw Popp of Jasta 77. Christopher Shores, Norman Franks and Russell Guest, *Above the Trenches: A complete record of the fighter aces and units of the British air forces, 1915–1920* (London: Grub Street, 1990), p. 95.

23 T. I. Webb-Brown's recommendation was for *either* a 'DSO or DFC'. Brigade headquarters, 20 September 1918, TNA AIR 1/1033/204/5/1434; Form of recommendation for the Order of the British Empire, 7 October 1918, TNA AIR 1/1157/204/5/2473.

24 Keith Caldwell, Benjamin Roxburgh Smith, Clive Glynn and Frederick Hunt, Combat in Air Report, 21 September 1918, TNA AIR 1/1829/204/202/22.

25 Russell and Puglisi, '"Grid" Caldwell of 74', p. 210.

26 Operation Order No. 236, 11 Wing, 23 September 1918, TNA 1/1794/204/153/24.

27 Keith Caldwell, Benjamin Roxburgh Smith and George Rensbury Hicks, Combat in Air Report, 24 September 1918, TNA AIR 1/1829/204/202/22; Keith Caldwell, Logbook, 24 September 1918, AFMNZ 1992/038.1.

28 https://sites.google.com/site/cahsreginachapter/richmond-mayson-74-squadron (retrieved 30 March 2023).

29 11 Wing Operation Orders, 27 September 1918, TNA 1/1794/204/153/24.

30 https://sites.google.com/site/cahsreginachapter/richmond-mayson-74-squadron (retrieved 30 March 2023).

31 *Daily Reporter*, Dover, Ohio June 19, 1961, p. 8.

32 Ibid.

33 https://sites.google.com/site/cahsreginachapter/richmond-mayson-74-squadron (retrieved 30 March 2023).

34 Ibid.

35 Combat in Air Report, 1 September–30 September 1918, TNA AIR 1/1829/204/202/22.

36 Keith Caldwell, Logbook, 24 September 1918, AFMNZ 1992/038.1.

37 Keith Caldwell to Raymond Collishaw, 20 October 1965, Alex Revell Collection.

Chapter Eighteen: Richthofen's Bed

1 John Baltzly Garver, Diary, 1 October 1918, Garver Family Collection.

2 Albert Montague Sanderson, Service Record, TNA AIR 76/443; Frank Edger Bond, Casualty Card, RAF Hendon; William Edward Bardgett, Service Record, TNA AIR 76/21/207.

3 Keith Caldwell to 11th Wing headquarters, 8 October 1918, TNA AIR 1/1024/204/5/1410; Keith Caldwell to 11th Wing headquarters, 19 October 1918, TNA AIR 1/1024/204/5/1410.

4 Routine Orders, 11 Wing, 3 September, 29 August 1918, TNA AIR 1/1826/204/202/7.

5 Keith Caldwell, Logbook, 25 September to 13 October 1918, AFMNZ 1992/038.1.

6 'Grid' Caldwell's 'D.F.C.' Squadron, Air Historical Branch History, p. 1, Errol Martyn Collection. Reginald Oliver Hobhouse, TNA AIR 76/231/81.

7 https://sites.google.com/site/cahsreginachapter/richmond-mayson-74-squadron (retrieved 30 March 2023).

8   Garver Diary, 11 October 1918.

9   Ibid., 7 October 1918.

10 H. A. Jones, *The War in the Air: Being the part played in the Great War by the Royal Air Force, Vol. 6* (Uckfield, East Sussex: Naval and Military Press, 1937), pp. 539–40.

11 Richmond Mayson, https://sites.google.com/site/cahsreginachapter/richmond-mayson-74-squadron (retrieved 30 March 2023).

12 Mayson's diary suggests that Caldwell's victory was secured on this early morning patrol but Caldwell's Combat in Air Report states that it was at 11.00am. Keith Caldwell, Combat in Air Report, 14 October 1918, TNA AIR 1/1829/204/202/23; Keith Caldwell, Logbook, 14 October 1918, AFMNZ 1992/038.1.

13 Richmond Mayson, Diary, 14 October 1918.

14 Garver Diary, 14 October 1918.

15 Benjamin Roxburgh-Smith, Sydney Stidolph, Eugene Roesch, Combat in Air Report, 14 October 1918, TNA AIR 1/1829/204/202/23.

16 Richmond Mayson, Diary, 14 October 1918.

17 II Brigade War Diary, 14 October 1918, TNA AIR 1/2232/209/41.21.

18 Garver Diary, 15 October 1918.

19 Elliot Springs to mother, 19 October 1918, quoted in David K. Vaughan (ed.), *Letters from a War Bird: The war correspondence of Elliot White Springs* (Columbia: University of South Florida Press, 2014).

20 Garver Diary, 24 October 1918.

21 Wilfred Bertie Giles, Diary, 29 October 1918, Bob Cossey 74 (F) Tiger Squadron Association.

22 'Comments from Keith L. Caldwell', Compiled and annotated by Marvin L. Skelton, Revised 15 August 1977, Andrew Caldwell Family Collection, p. 4.

23 Garver Diary, 25 October 1918.

24 Garver Diary, 24, 25 October 1918.

25 11 Wing, Operational Orders, 25 October 1918, TNA AIR 1/1794/204/153/24/.

26 Richmond Mayson Diary, n.d.

27 Jules Ferrand, 26 October, Combat in Air Report, TNA AIR 1/1829/204/202/23.

28 Murdo MacLean, Service Record, TNA AIR 76/325/27.

29 Garver Diary, 26 October 1918.

30 Jones, *The War in the Air*, p. 544; Trevor Henshaw, *The Sky Their Battlefield, II: Air fighting and air casualties of the Great War* (High Barnet, Hertfordshire: Fetubi Books, 2014), p. 240

31 11 Wing, Operational Orders, 27, 28 and 29 October 1918, TNA AIR 1/1794/204/153/24.

32 Eugene Roesch, Andrew Kiddie, Frederick Gordon, Reginald Hobhouse, 28 October 1918, TNA AIR 1/2232/209/41/21.

33 Shores et al. place this victory on 30 October, but Caldwell's logbook states that it occurred on 28 October. Their source is a Wing Summary, but this shows no claim for Caldwell on 30 October. Moreover, Caldwell's reference to Gilbert Murlis Green of 70 Squadron ties in with Combat in Air reports made by that unit for 28 October: Caldwell and 70 Squadron were in the air at the same time on the same day as the 28 October logbook entry. Keith Caldwell, Logbook, 28 October 1918, AFMNZ 1992/038.1; cf Christopher Shores, Norman Franks and Russell Guest, *Above the Trenches: A complete record of the fighter aces and units of the British air forces, 1915–1920* (London: Grub Street, 1990), p. 95; 11 Wing, Operational Orders, 27 October 1918, AIR 1/1794/204/153/24.

34 Keith Caldwell, Logbook, 28 October 1918, AFMNZ 1992/038.1; Russell and Puglisi, '"Grid" Caldwell of 74', p. 212.

35 The routine orders state that Jones returned to the squadron 10 November, and this is supported by Giles' diary entry for 12 November 1918. However, in *Tiger Squadron*, Jones states he witnessed the bombing on 30 October 1918. Daily Routine Orders, 11 Wing RAF, 13 November 1918, TNA AIR 1/1825/204/202/3; Giles Diary, 12 November 1918. Cf Ira Jones, *Tiger Squadron: The story of 74 Squadron, RAF, in Two World Wars* (London: W. H. Allen, 1954), p. 169.

36 Jones, *Tiger Squadron*, p. 169.

37 Andrew Kiddie, George Gauld, William Carlton Woods, Combat in Air Report, 1 November 1918, TNA AIR 1/1829/204/23.

38 Jones, *Tiger Squadron*, p. 169.

39 Andrew Kiddie, Combat in Air Report, 4 November 1918, TNA AIR 1/1829/204/23.

40 Giles Diary, 3 November 1918.

41 Ibid., 5–8 November 1918.

42 Ibid., 10 November 1918.

43 G. H. Cunningham, *Mac's Memoirs: The flying life of Squadron Leader McGregor* (Wellington: A. H. & A. W. Reed, 1937), p. 69.

44 Giles Diary, 11 November 1918.

45 Jones, *Tiger Squadron*, pp. 169–70.

46 Giles Diary, 11 November 1918.

47 Ibid., 30 November 1918.

48 Ibid., 2 December 1918.

49 Ibid., 22 November 1918, 23 January 1919.

50 Jones, *Tiger Squadron*, p. 175; Keith Caldwell, Service Record, TNA AIR 76/73/33; Jones, *The War in the Air*, p. 146.

51 Giles Diary, 11, 29 December 1918.

52 Ibid., 27 December 1918.

53 Ibid., 1 January 1919.

54 The aircraft were initially sent to Germany as part of the Army Occupation and subsequently to England. Giles Diary, 24 January 1919.

55 Giles Diary, n.d.

56 Ibid., 23 January 1919.

57 Keith Caldwell, Service Record, TNA AIR 76/73/33.

58 Giles Diary, 9 February 1919.

59 Cunningham, *Mac's Memoirs*, p. 71.

Chapter Nineteen: Tea for Two

1 *New Zealand Herald*, 1 August 1919; *Auckland Star*, 1 August 1919; *Waikato Independent*, 2 August 1919; *Otago Daily Times*, 9 August 1919; *Feilding Star*, 15 August 1919; *Hawera and Normanby Star*, 20 August 1919.

2 Barbara Ewen, interview with author, 1 April 2022.

3 Judy Caldwell, interview with author, 4 April 2022.

4 Judy Caldwell interview, 2 April 2022.

5 G. H. Cunningham, *Mac's Memoirs: The flying life of Squadron Leader McGregor* (Wellington: A. H. & A. W. Reed, 1937), p. 73.

6 *Northern Advocate*, 23 June 1921.

7 *Northern Advocate*, 23 and 27 June 1921.

8 Roger Gordon, interview with author, 31 March 2022; *Northern Advocate*, 6 August 1921.

9 *Auckland Star*, 11 August 1921.

10 *Auckland Star*, 11 August 1921; *New Zealand Herald*, 11 August 1921.

11 For an excellent discussion on the future of military aviation in New Zealand see, Alex M. Spencer, *British Imperial Air Power: The royal air forces and the defense of Australia and New Zealand between the world wars* (West Lafayette, Indiana: Purdue University Press, 2020).

12 Spencer, *British Imperial Air Power*, p. 33–34.

13 *Hawke's Bay Tribune*, 20 October 1922.

14 Errol Martyn, *Swift to the Sky: New Zealand's military aviation history* (Auckland: Penguin, 2010), p. 76; Geoffrey Cyril Ellis, *Tool Box on the Wing: My life in the air force* (Wellington: Mallinson Rendel, 1983), p. 141.

15 Ellis, *Tool Box on the Wing*, p.142.

16 *New Zealand Herald*, 28 June 1923; *Waikato Times*, 29 June 1923.

17 Simon Moody, interview with author, 19 April 2022.

18 *Star* (Christchurch), 24 January 1924.

19 *New Zealand Herald*, 25 June 1927.

20 *New Zealand Herald*, 14 February 1922.

21 Barbara Ewen interview, 1 April 2022.

22 *Star* (Christchurch), 3 May 1920.

23 Barbara Ewen interview, 1 April 2022.

24 *Star* (Christchurch), 3 May 1920.

25 Christine Futter, interview with author, 30 March 2022.

26 *Waikato Independent*, 22 July 1922; *New Zealand Times*, 24 July 1922; *Auckland Star*, 16 May 1923.

27 *Auckland Star*, 16 May 1923.

28 Elizabeth Caldwell, unpublished notes on David Caldwell at Glen Murray, n.d., Andrew Caldwell Family Collection; Roger Gordon, 29 March 2022.

29 Roger Gordon interview, 31 March 2022.

30 Ernie Alexander, *Glen Murray's Incredible Pioneers: Over 100 years of amazing history* (Glen Murray: Glen Murray School and District Centennial Committee Publication, 1996), p. 17.

31 Sarah MacKenzie to author, 12 April 2022.

32 Elizabeth Caldwell, unpublished notes on David Caldwell at Glen Murray, n.d., Andrew Caldwell Family Collection.

33 Mary Caldwell, interview with author, 2020; Alexander, *Glen Murray's Incredible Pioneers*, p. 17.

34 Judy Caldwell interview, 31 March 2022; Mary Gordon interview, 2020; Keith Logan Caldwell, Base Record, ANZ Item Code R24589276 Series Code 18805, Providence AABK.

35 Mary Gordon interview, 29 March 2022.

36 *Waikato Times*, 2 December 1939.

37 Alexander, *Glen Murray's Incredible Pioneers*, pp. 16–17.

38 *Auckland Star*, 22 January 1935; *Auckland Star*, 22 January 1936.

39 *New Zealand Herald*, 2 January 1937.

40 *Auckland Star*, 20 September 1934; *Auckland Star*, 12 August 1936; *New Zealand Herald*, 30 July 1937; *Auckland Star*, 5 July 1938.

41 *Waikato Times*, 26 January 1931; *Auckland Star*, 27 November 1934; *New Zealand Herald*, 8 March 1937.

42 *New Zealand Herald*, 27 March 1933.

43 Ibid.

44 *Nelson Evening Mail*, 15 January 1936; *Hawke's Bay Tribune*, 4 August 1934; *Grey River Argus*, 13 April 1935.

45 Reunion dinner order of service and menu, 1 June 1935, C. K. Mills Collection, MOTAT 14/004/020.

46 *New Zealand Herald*, 3 June 1935.

47 Reunion dinner order of service and menu.

48 *Franklin Times*, 7 May 1935.

49 *New Zealand Herald*, 3 June 1935.

50 *New Zealand Herald*, 20 July 1936.

51 *Manawatu Herald*, 22 February 1936; *Auckland Star*, 18 March 1936

52 *Manawatu Herald*, 22 February 1936.

53 Ira Jones, *King of the Air Fighters: The biography of Major 'Mick' Mannock V.C.* (London: W. H. Allen, 1934).

54 *News of the World*, 11 October 1936.

55 *N.Z. Truth*, 25 November 1936, newspaper clipping, Deb Stovell Family Collection.

56 Ira Jones, *An Air Fighter's Scrapbook* (London: Nicholson & Watson, 1935); *New Zealand Herald*, 14 January 1939, Brett Mackrell, Scrapbooks relating to early British and New Zealand military aviation (I) and (III), MSZ-1583, ATL Collection; *Auckland Star*, 13 January 1940; *Otago Daily Times*, 19 January 1940.

57 J. M. S. Ross, *Royal New Zealand Air Force* (Wellington: Historical Publications Branch, 1955), pp. 21–22.

58 Martyn, *Swift to the Sky*, p. 76; Ellis, *Tool Box on the Wing*, p. 147.

59 Keith Caldwell, 26 August 1937, Base Records, NZDF, ANZ Item Code R24589276, Series Code 18805, AABK.

Chapter Twenty: Mutiny

1 Keith Caldwell to R. F. Coldham, Harrison and Grierson and Partners, 30 June 1976, Andrew Caldwell Family Collection.

2 *New Zealand Herald*, 2 December 1939.

3 David Robert Caldwell, ANZ R9393121 Series Code 1570 Provenance 'Transferred by agency BBAE.

4 RNZAF Medical Board, 6 October 1944, Keith Logan Caldwell, Base File, ANZ R24589276, Series Code 18805, Provence AABK, File 106.

5 J. M. S. Ross, *Royal New Zealand Air Force* (Wellington: Historical Publications Branch, 1955), p. 45.

6 *Franklin Times*, 15 May 1940.

7 Ross, *Royal New Zealand Air Force*, p. 59.

8 Keith Caldwell to Wing Commander R. W. K.

Stevens, Air Force headquarters, 14 July 1942, Confidential File, Wigram Commanding Officer 14 November 1940–10 March 1942, AFMNZ 1992/038.5.

9 Margaret McClure, *Fighting Spirit: 75 Years of the RNZAF* (Auckland: Random House, 2012), p. 62.

10 McClure, *Fighting Spirit*, p. 62; Bee Dawson, *Wigram: The birthplace of military aviation in New Zealand* (Auckland: Random House, 2012), pp. 183–90.

11 Notes from Flight Lieutenant A. George, 31 December 1943, Wigram Commanding Officer, Notes for talks to airman 2 March 1943–16 September 1943, AFMNZ 1992/038.6.

12 Leonard Isitt, 'Notes taken on address given by Air Commodore L. M. Isitt CBE to airmen pilots passing out', 9 April 1943, Wigram Commanding Officer, Notes for talks to airmen 2 March 1943–16 September 1943, AFMNZ 1992/038.6. For the formation of the 'New Zealand Squadrons' or 'Article XV Squadrons', as they were also known, see Wing Commander H. L. Thompson, *New Zealanders with the Royal Air Force, Vol. I* (Wellington: Historical Publications Branch, 1956), pp. 209–11; Wing Commander H. L. Thompson, *New Zealanders with the Royal Air Force, Vol. II* (Wellington: Historical Publications Branch, 1956), pp. 456–62.

13 Dawson, *Wigram*, pp. 114–16, 122.

14 R. H. and J. L. Clark-Hall, *Air Marshal Sir Robert Clark-Hall, KBE, CMG, DSO* (Christchurch: Raven Press, 1995), pp. 127, 135; Dawson, *Wigram*, pp. 223–24.

15 Keith Caldwell to R. V. Goddard, Chief of Air Staff, 3 November 1942, Confidential File, Wigram Commanding Officer 14 November 1940–10 March 1942, AFMNZ 1992/038.5.

16 Conference, Whenuapai, November 1942, Confidential File, Wigram Commanding Officer 14 November 1940–10 March 1942, AFMNZ 1992/038.5.

17 Group Captain Keith Logan Caldwell to Mrs Margaret Brown, 10 September 194, Confidential File, Wigram Commanding Officer 14 November 1940–10 March 1942, AFMNZ 1992/038.5.

18 Dr S. R. Cattell to Group Captain Keith Caldwell, 16 July 1943, Confidential File, Wigram Commanding Officer 14 November 1940–10 March 1942, AFMNZ 1992/038.5; Harley Cattell to Sydney Cattell, 26 May 1943, Confidential File, Wigram Commanding Officer 14 November 1940–10 March 1942, AFMNZ 1992/038.5; *Press*, 22 September 1942; Harley Rivers Cattell, New

Zealand, World War II Army Nominal Rolls, 1 January 1945–31 December 1945.

19 *Ellesmere Guardian*, 27 March 1945.

20 Air Commodore R. V. Goddard to Group Captain Keith Caldwell, 4 July 1942, Confidential File, Wigram Commanding Officer 14 November 1940–10 March 1942, AFMNZ 1992/038.5.

21 Group Captain Keith Caldwell to R. V. Goddard, 10 July 1942, Confidential File, Wigram Commanding Officer 14 November 1940–10 March 1942, AFMNZ 1992/038.5.

22 R. V. Goddard to Caldwell, 2 May 1942, Confidential File, Wigram Commanding Officer 14 November 1940–10 March 1942, AFMNZ 1992/038.5.

23 Group Captain Keith Logan Caldwell to Clark-Hall, 19 May 1943, Confidential File, Wigram Commanding Officer 14 November 1940–10 March 1942, AFMNZ 1992/038.5.

24 Keith Logan Caldwell, 'Wings Presentation, Wigram', 16 March 1944, Wigram Commanding Officer Notes for talks to airmen, 2 March 1943–16 August 1943, AFMNZ 1992/038.6.

25 Wing Commander K. L. Caldwell, Standing Orders, Part 1, May 1941, Confidential File, Wigram Commanding Officer 14 November 1940–10 March 1942, AFMNZ 1992/038.5.

26 Conference: Whenuapai, November 1942, Confidential File, Wigram Commanding Officer 14 November 1940–10 March 1942, AFMNZ 1992/038.5.

27 Dawson, *Wigram*, pp. 207–8.

28 Memorandum for the Minister of Defence from the Air Ministry, 19 March 1943, Confidential File, Wigram Commanding Officer 14 November 1940–10 March 1942, AFMNZ 1992/038.5.

29 House of Representatives, 17 March 1943, #496. pp. 470–71.

30 Memorandum for the Minister of Defence from the Air Ministry, 19 March 1943, Confidential File, Wigram Commanding Officer 14 November 1940–10 March 1942, AFMNZ 1992/038.5; Air Commodore Robert Goddard to Group Captain Keith Logan Caldwell, 26 November 1943, Confidential File, Wigram Commanding Officer 14 November 1940–10 March 1942, AFMNZ 1992/038.5.

31 'Report on unrest re Christmas Leave', J. W. Todd, Officer Commanding, Electrical and Wireless School, to Group Captain Keith Logan Caldwell, 26 November 1943, Confidential File, Wigram Commanding Officer 14 November 1940–10 March 1942, AFMNZ 1992/038.5.

32 Ibid.

33 Caldwell's base file shows that he was 'President' at Court Martial and Court of Inquiry on over a dozen occasions, Keith Logan Caldwell, Base File, ANZ R24589276, Series Code 18805, Provence AABK, File 106.

34 Simon Moody, Research Curator, AFMNZ, to author, 13 June 2022. Security Occurrence Register, RNZAF Station Wigram, 1942–1945, AFMNZ 2009/753

35 'Parade of Certain E & W School Personnel in the Institute at 1345 hrs, Friday, 26 November 1943', Wigram Commanding Officer Notes for talks to airmen 2 March 1943–16 August 1943, AFMNZ 1992/0.38.6; 'Report on unrest re Christmas Leave', J. W. Todd, Officer Commanding, Electrical and Wireless School, to Group Captain Keith Logan Caldwell, 26 November 1943, Confidential File, Wigram Commanding Officer 14 November 1940–10 March 1942, AFMNZ 1992/038.5.

36 'Report on unrest re Christmas Leave'.

37 Ibid.

38 Parade of Certain E & W School Personnel in the Institute'.

39 Ibid.

40 Keith Caldwell, Pacific Tour Diary, January–February 1944, Andrew Caldwell Family Collection.

41 Ibid.

42 For discussions on manpower issues see: Nancy M. Taylor, *The Home Front, VII* (Wellington: Historical Publications Branch, 1986), pp 663–741.

43 *New Zealand Herald*, 24 June 1944.

44 House of Representatives, 26 July 1944, #10. p. 2.

45 House of Representatives, 2 August 1944, #107, p. 99; House of Representatives, 27 July 1944, #37, p. 29.

46 House of Representatives, 2 August 1944, #108, p. 100.

47 Operation Overlord air casualties were under 1 per cent, much lower than the anticipated 8 per cent. 'Notes from a talk given by CAS to AOC and Station Commanders Southern Group at Harewood 16 August 1944', Wigram Commanding Officer Notes for talks to airmen 2 March 1943–16 August 1943, AFMNZ 1992/0.38.6.

48 Keith Caldwell confidential report to Intelligence Security Officer, Air Department, Wellington, 12 September 1944, Confidential File, Wigram Commanding Officer 14 November 1940–10 March 1942, AFMNZ 1992/038.5.

49 Keith Caldwell, Tannoy talk to Wigram Staff, 3 August 1944, Confidential File, Wigram Commanding Officer 14 November 1940–10 March 1942, AFMNZ 1992/038.5.

50 Keith Caldwell Tannoy talk to Wigram Staff, 3 August 1944; Notes from a talk given by CAS to AOC and Station Commanders Southern Group at Harewood 16 August 1944', Confidential File, Wigram Commanding Officer 14 November 1940–10 March 1942, AFMNZ 1992/038.5.

51 Notes from talk given by C.A.S. to A.O.C. and Station Commanders.

52 Keith Caldwell speech to Wigram Staff, 3 August 1944; Confidential File, Wigram Commanding Officer 14 November 1940–10 March 1942, AFMNZ 1992/038.5.

53 Keith Caldwell to A. de T. Nevill, 7 August 1944, Confidential File, Wigram Commanding Officer 14 November 1940–10 March 1942, AFMNZ 1992/038.5; Keith Logan Caldwell to Ronald Bannerman, 12 August 1944, Confidential File, Wigram Commanding Officer 14 November 1940–10 March 1942, AFMNZ 1992/038.5.

54 Keith Caldwell confidential report to Intelligence Security Officer, Air Department, Wellington, 12 September 1944, Confidential File, Wigram Commanding Officer 14 November 1940–10 March 1942, AFMNZ 1992/038.5.

55 *New Zealand Herald*, 7 September 1944.

56 Notes from talk given by C.A.S. to A.O.C. and Station.

57 Keith Caldwell confidential report to Intelligence Security Officer, Air Department, Wellington, 12 September 1944, Confidential File, Wigram Commanding Officer 14 November 1940–10 March 1942, AFMNZ 1992/038.5.

58 Leader of the Opposition to Keith Caldwell, 21 August 1944, Confidential File, Wigram Commanding Officer 14 November 1940–10 March 1942', AFMNZ 1992/038.5.

59 Robert Clark-Hall, confidential report, Keith Caldwell, 20 November 1944, ANZ R24589276, Series Code 18805, Providence AABK.

60 Keith Caldwell speech to Wigram Staff, 3 August 1944, Confidential File, Wigram Commanding Officer 14 November 1940–10 March 1942', AFMNZ 1992/038.5.

61 Keith Caldwell confidential report to Intelligence Security Officer, Air Department, Wellington, 12 September 1944, Confidential File, Wigram Commanding Officer 14 November 1940–10 March 1942, AFMNZ 1992/038.5.

62 F. Jones, Minster of Defence telegram to Dorothy Caldwell, 2 January 1945, Andrew Caldwell Family Collection; *The Times* (UK), 1 January 1945; *Wanganui Chronicle*, 2 January 1945. In early 1944, Caldwell had a short 14-day posting to the Solomons and New Hebrides. Keith Logan Caldwell, Base File, ANZ Item Code R24589276, Series Code 18805, AABK.

Chapter Twenty-one: Savoy

1 Memorandum 3 January 1945, Keith Caldwell, Base File, ANZ R24589276, Series Code 18805, Provence AABK.

2 Keith Caldwell, unpublished diary, 6 December 1944, Andrew Caldwell Family Collection.

3 Ibid., 8 December 1944, Andrew Caldwell Family Collection.

4 Memorandum 3 January 1945, Keith Caldwell, Base File, ANZ R24589276, Series Code 18805, Provence AABK, File 106.

5 Caldwell, unpublished diary, 17 December 1944, Andrew Caldwell Family Collection.

6 Ibid., 17, 20 December 1944.

7 Ibid., 30 December 1944.

8 Ibid., n.d.

9 Ibid., 13 December 1944.

10 *New Zealand Herald*, 31 March 1945.

11 Caldwell, unpublished diary, 18 December 1944.

12 Ibid., n.d.

13 Ibid., n.d.

14 Keith Caldwell to Dorothy Caldwell, 2 May 1945, Sally Gordon Family Collection.

15 Caldwell, unpublished diary, n.d.

16 Caldwell to Dorothy Caldwell, 10 July 1945.

17 Keith Caldwell to Dorothy Caldwell, 26 May 1945.

18 Keith Caldwell to Dorothy Caldwell, 7 June 1945.

19 Keith Caldwell to Dorothy Caldwell, 25 June 1945.

20 Keith Caldwell to Dorothy Caldwell, 10 July 1945.

21 Keith Caldwell to Dorothy Caldwell, 10 July 1945; H. L. Thompson, *New Zealanders with the Royal Air Force, Vol. II* (Wellington: Historical Publications Branch, 1956), p. 442; Margaret McClure, *Fighting Spirit: 75 Years of the RNZAF* (Auckland: Random House, 2012), p. 87.

22 Keith Caldwell to Dorothy Caldwell, 27 July 1945.

23 Keith Caldwell to Dorothy Caldwell, 9 August 1945.

24 Keith Caldwell to Dorothy Caldwell, 15 August 1945.

25 Keith Caldwell to Dorothy Caldwell, 23 August 1945; Keith Caldwell to Dorothy Caldwell, 24 August 1945.

26 Keith Caldwell to Dorothy Caldwell, 9 August 1945.

27 *New Zealand Herald*, 6 September 1945.

28 Ibid.

29 Keith Caldwell to Dorothy Caldwell, 25 August 1945.

30 Keith Caldwell to Dorothy Caldwell, 15 September 1945.

31 *New Zealand Herald*, 25 September 1945.

32 *New Zealand Herald*, 22 October 1945.

33 Keith Caldwell to Dorothy Caldwell, 29 November 1945.

34 Keith Caldwell to Dorothy Caldwell, 9 August, 1945.

35 Keith Caldwell to Dorothy Caldwell, 21 July 1945.

36 Keith Caldwell to Dorothy Caldwell, 29 July 1945.

37 Keith Caldwell to Dorothy Caldwell, 9 August, 8 October 1945; *Bay of Plenty Times*, 5 November 1945.

38 Keith Caldwell to Dorothy Caldwell, 15 September 1945.

39 Keith Caldwell to Dorothy Caldwell, 2 August 1945.

40 Keith Caldwell to Dorothy Caldwell, 29 November 1945.

41 Keith Caldwell to Dorothy Caldwell, 26 October 1945.

42 Keith Caldwell to Dorothy Caldwell, 15 October 1945.

43 Keith Caldwell to Dorothy Caldwell, 9 November 1945.

44 Keith Caldwell to Dorothy Caldwell, 15 October 1945.

45 Ibid.

46 Ibid.

47 Keith Caldwell to Dorothy Caldwell, 26 October 1945.

48 Ibid.

49 In his letter Caldwell mistakenly identified the vessel as *Scharnhorst*.

50 Keith Caldwell to Dorothy Caldwell, 26 October 1945.

51 *Auckland Star*, 13 November 1945.

52 Keith Caldwell to Dorothy Caldwell, 5 November 1945; *Auckland Star*, 13 November 1945.

53 Keith Caldwell to Dorothy Caldwell, 25 November 1945.

54 *Evening Post*, 26 November 1945.

55 Keith Caldwell to Dorothy Caldwell, 29 November 1945.

56 *Evening Post*, 26 November 1945.

57 Keith Caldwell to Dorothy Caldwell, 11 December 1945; 'Simpson Services Club: Wartime Record', undated pamphlet, Andrew Caldwell Family Collection.

58 Various, The Rt. Hon. A. V. Alexander, *The Simpson Services Club during the Second World War, 1939–1945* (1947).

59 Keith Caldwell to Dorothy Caldwell, 11 December 1945.

60 Newspaper clipping, Andrew Caldwell Family Collection.

61 *New Zealand News*, 18 December 1945.

62 Keith Caldwell to Dorothy Caldwell 11 December 1945.

63 Keith Caldwell to Dorothy Caldwell, 15, 11, 5 December 1945.

64 Keith Caldwell to Dorothy Caldwell, 3 January 1946.

65 Ibid.; Keith Caldwell to Dorothy Caldwell, 4 January 1918.

66 Keith Caldwell to Dorothy Caldwell, 3 January 1946.

Chapter Twenty-two: More Gravy

1 Keith Caldwell to Gwilym Lewis, 22 March 1977, Alex Revell Collection.

2 Keith Caldwell to Dorothy Caldwell, 29 November 1945, 3 January 1946, Sally Gordon Family Collection.

3 Keith Caldwell to Dorothy Caldwell, 2 August 1945.

4 Keith Caldwell to Dorothy Caldwell, 12 August 1945.

5 Keith Caldwell to Dorothy Caldwell, 11 December 1945; Anna Brown to author, 27 April 2022.

6 Keith Caldwell to Dorothy Caldwell, 9 August 1945.

7 Keith Caldwell to Dorothy Caldwell, 11 December 1945.

8 Andrew Caldwell, interview with author, 7 April 2022; Barbara Ewen to author, 1 April 2022; Anna Brown to author, 27 April 2022.

9 Judy Caldwell, interview with author, 2 April 2022; Anna Brown to author, 27 April 2022.

10 Andrew Caldwell, interview with author, 7 April 2022; Roger Gordon, interview with author, 31 March 2022.

11 Judy Caldwell interview, 2022.

12 Geoffrey Gordon, unpublished family vignettes, n.d., Sally Gordon Family Collection.

13 Mary Gordon and Sally Gordon, interview with author, 9 September 2022; Geoffrey Gordon, unpublished family vignettes.

14 Christine and Malcolm Futter, interview with author, 2021.

15 Auction booklet: 'Complete "Forres" Aberdeen Angus Herd', 23 May 1961, Andrew Caldwell Family Collection.

16 *Press*, November 1951.

17 Jane Foote to author, 19 April 2022.

18 Deborah Stovell, interview with author, 21 December 2022.

19 Jane Foote to author, 19 April 2022.

20 Deborah Stovell to author, 17 June 2022.

21 Ibid.

22 Judy Caldwell to author, 23 July 2022.

23 *Press*, 14 May 1959.

24 Keith Caldwell to Peter Koch, Department of Civil Aviation, c/- Tasman Empire Airways Limited, 7 May 1964, Andrew Caldwell Family Collection.

25 Auction Booklet, 'Complete dispersal Forres Aberdeen Angus Herd on account of K. L. Caldwell, Esquire, Puhinui Road, Papatoetoe, 23 May 1961', Andrew Caldwell Family Collection.

26 The Chairman, East Tamaki Branch, Federated Farmers to Chairman, Manukau County Council, Manurewa, 29 May 1964, Andrew Caldwell Family Collection.

27 Jane Foote to author, 19 July 2022.

28 Jim Taylor to Keith Caldwell, 15 May 1964, Andrew Caldwell Family Collection.

29 Judy Caldwell, interview with author, 23 July 2022.

30 Keith Caldwell to Peter Koch 7 May 1964, Andrew Caldwell Family Collection.

31 W. H. Pickford to Keith Caldwell, 5 June 1964, Andrew Caldwell Family Collection.

32 Keith Caldwell, 'Visit to Mascot Airport: 4–8 May 1964', Andrew Caldwell Family Collection.

33 *Press*, 9 November 1965.

34 Judy Caldwell interview with author, 23 July 2022.

35 *Press*, 9 November 1965.

36 Keith Caldwell to Peter Caldwell, 4 November 1973, Andrew Caldwell Family Collection; Newspaper clipping with Caldwell's annotations: John Stackhouse, 'Land Rezoning: a profitable way around airport noise', *Australian Financial Review*, 16 February 1970, Andrew Caldwell Family Collection.

37 Keith Caldwell, Passport, issued 4 March 1966, Andrew Caldwell Family Collection; Dorothy

Caldwell, Passport, issued 4 March 1966, Andrew Caldwell Family Collection.

38 The Sidcot suit was received by the museum in 1971 and the machine gun in 1977. www.aucklandmuseum.com/collections-research/collections/record/am_humanhistory-object-740214?k=sidcot&ordinal=0 (retrieved 22 December 2022).

39 Keith Caldwell, Anzac Day speech, n.d., Andrew Caldwell Family Collection; Keith Caldwell, notes for Anzac Day Speech, n.d., Andrew Caldwell Family Collection.

40 'How the Society Began', Historical notes by K. L. Caldwell (1914–1918) (NZ) Airmen's Association Papers', AFMNZ 204/133.11

41 Simon Moody, 'Kiwi Rising: New Zealand and the War in the Air', in John Crawford, David Littlewood and James Watson (eds.), *Experience of a Lifetime: People, personalities and leaders in the First World War* (Auckland: Massey University Press, 2016), p. 210.

42 *Auckland Star*, 27 October 1956, Andrew Caldwell Family Collection; *New Zealand Herald*, 17 June 1972, AFMNZ.

43 Ira Jones, *Tiger Squadron: The story of 74 Squadron in two world wars* (London: W. H. Allen, 1954).

44 Jack D. Hunter, 'The Blue Max Revisited', *Over the Front* 13, no. 3 (Fall 1998): pp. 197–202.

45 Keith Caldwell to unknown, 16 November 1966, Alex Revell Collection.

46 Keith Caldwell to William Fry, 6 September 1977, Andrew Caldwell Family Collection.

47 Douglass Wheaton to Keith Caldwell, 14 October 1977, Andrew Caldwell Family Collection.

48 Unknown author to Keith Caldwell, 17 November 1964, Andrew Caldwell Family Collection.

49 Marvin Skelton to Keith Caldwell, 23 July 1970, Andrew Caldwell Family Collection.

50 Marvin Skelton to Keith Caldwell, 5 Jan 1976, Andrew Caldwell Family Collection.

51 Keith Caldwell to Gwilym Lewis, n.d. (1970s), Alex Revell Collection.

52 Douglass Whetton to Keith Caldwell, 14 October 1977, Andrew Caldwell Family Collection; Alex Revell to author, 21 January 2023.

53 Douglass Whetton to Keith Caldwell, 14 October 1977, Andrew Caldwell Family Collection.

54 Mervin Skelton to Keith Caldwell, 5 January 1976, Andrew Caldwell Family Collection.

55 James Dudgeon to Keith Caldwell, 14 November 1978, Andrew Caldwell Family Collection.

56 Keith Caldwell to James Dudgeon, 25 November 1978, Andrew Caldwell Collection; Douglass Whetton, *Mannock: Patrol leader supreme* (Falls Church, VA: Ajay Enterprises, 1977), p. 26.

57 James M. Dudgeon, *Mick: The story of Major Edward Mannock, VC, DSO, MC, RFC, RAF* (London: Robert Hale, 1981), p. 182.

58 Douglass Whetton to Keith Caldwell, April 1978, Andrew Caldwell Family Collection. Marvin Skelton to Keith Caldwell, 2 June 1976, Andrew Caldwell Family Collection.

59 Norman Birks to Keith Caldwell, 31 October 1977, Andrew Caldwell Collection.

60 Gwilym Lewis to Marvin Skelton, quoted in 'Comments From Keith Caldwell (Compiled and Annotated by Marvin Skelton)', 15 August 1977, Andrew Caldwell Family Collection.

61 Keith Caldwell to Gwilym Lewis, 22 March 1977, Alex Revell Collection; Gwilym Lewis to Keith Caldwell, 26 January 1978, Andrew Caldwell Collection.

62 Arthur Gould Lee to Keith Caldwell, 13 August 1970, Andrew Caldwell Family Collection; Arthur Gould Lee, *No Parachute: A fighter pilot of the Royal Flying Corps* (New York: Harper & Row, 1970); Arthur Gould Lee, *Open Cockpit: A pilot of the Royal Flying Corps* (London: Jarrolds, 1969).

63 Keith Caldwell to Gwilym Lewis, n.d. (1970s), Alex Revell Collection.

64 Keith Caldwell to William Fry, 1975, Andrew Caldwell Family Collection; Edward Noel Griffith, Casualty Form, RAF Hendon.

65 Keith Caldwell to William Fry, 1975, Andrew Caldwell Family Collection.

66 Alan Clark, *Aces High* (London: Ballantine, 1974).

67 Bill Lambert, *Combat Report* (London: Corgi, 1975).

68 Keith Caldwell to William Fry, 3 July 1975, Andrew Caldwell Family Collection.

69 William Avery Bishop, *Winged Warfare* (London: Hodder & Stoughton, 1918); Margaret Bishop to Keith Caldwell, 11 October 1956, Andrew Caldwell Family Collection.

70 Keith Caldwell to William Fry, 25 October 1975, Andrew Caldwell Family Collection.

71 Keith Caldwell to William Fry, 20 September 1971, Andrew Caldwell Family Collection.

72 William Fry, *Air of Battle* (London: William Kimber, 1974), p. 136; '"The Bishop Affair", A previously unpublished document by Wing Commander William Mays Fry, MC, entrusted for publication to Alex Revell.' *Cross & Cockade*

International Journal 32, no. 1 (Spring 2001): pp. 38–45. Revell noted that the document 'is entirely Willie Fry's work. There are no additions, deletions, or omissions.'

73 Brereton Greenhous, *The Making of Billy Bishop: The First World War exploits of Billy Bishop VC* (Toronto: Dundurn, 2002); cf. Lieutenant-Colonel David Bashow, 'The incomparable Billy Bishop: The man and the myths', *Canadian Military Journal* (Autumn 2002): pp. 55–60.

74 Keith Caldwell to Gwilym Lewis, 1975, Alex Revell Collection. Bishop's son had sent a questionnaire for Caldwell to complete, see Keith Caldwell to Raymond Collishaw, 13 December 1965, Alex Revell Collection; William Arthur Bishop, *The Courage of the Early Morning: A son's biography of a famous father, the story of Billy Bishop* (Toronto: McClelland and Stewart, 1965).

75 Keith Caldwell to William Fry, 16 June 1977, Alex Revell Collection.

Chapter Twenty-three: Straight Bat

1 Keith Caldwell to William Fry, 25 October 1975, Andrew Caldwell Family Collection. The last meeting of the association was in 1975. Keith Caldwell to William Fry, 18 January 1975, Andrew Caldwell Collection.

2 Keith Caldwell to William Fry, 4 February 1978, Andrew Caldwell Family Collection.

3 Keith Caldwell to Gwilym Lewis, 1975, Alex Revell Collection.

4 Marvin Skelton to Keith Caldwell, 18 January 1977, Andrew Caldwell Family Collection.

5 Keith Caldwell to William Fry, 11 February 1979, Andrew Caldwell Family Collection.

6 Keith Caldwell to Gwilym Lewis, 3 February 1977 Alex Revell Collection.

7 Keith Caldwell to William Fry, 11 February 1979, Andrew Caldwell Family Collection.

8 Keith Caldwell to William Fry, 18 November 1976, Andrew Caldwell Family Collection.

9 Keith Caldwell to William Fry, 5 July 1976, Andrew Caldwell Collection.

10 Keith Caldwell to William Fry, 6 September 1977, Andrew Caldwell Family Collection.

11 Keith Caldwell to William Fry, 14 February 1974; Keith Caldwell to William Fry, 27 November 1975, Andrew Caldwell Family Collection.

12 Keith Caldwell to William Fry, 14 February 1974, Andrew Caldwell Family Collection.

13 Keith Caldwell to William Fry, 1976, Andrew Caldwell Family Collection; Keith Caldwell to

William Fry, 6 September 1977, Andrew Caldwell
Family Collection.

14 Keith to Gwilym Lewis, 1975, Alex Revell
Collection.

15 Keith Caldwell to William Fry, 18 Jan 1975,
Andrew Caldwell Family Collection.

16 Deborah Stovell to author, 17 June 2022.

17 The grandchildren received a payment at the ages
of 21 and 30. In 1976 the farm was valued at over
$3 million. Harrison and Grierson and Partners
to Keith Caldwell, 5 July 1976, Andrew Caldwell
Family Collection; Keith Caldwell to Peter
Caldwell, 4 November 1973, Andrew Caldwell
Family Collection.

18 Keith Caldwell to Gwilym Lewis, 1975, Alex Revell
Collection.

19 Geoffrey Pidcock to Keith Caldwell, 26 August
1960, Andrew Caldwell Family Collection.

20 Keith Caldwell to William Fry, 17 March 1976.
Andrew Caldwell Family Collection.

21 Jane Foote to author, 19 April 2022.

22 Keith Caldwell to William Fry, 17 March 1976,
Andrew Caldwell Family Collection.

23 Simon Gordon, interview with author,
25 February 2023.

24 Simon Gordon, interview with author,
25 February 2023; Simon Gordon to author,
1 March 2023.

25 Chris Macky, interview with author, 16 February
2023.

26 Marvin Skelton (ed.), 'Comments from Keith L.
Caldwell, Andrew Caldwell Family Collection',
unpublished manuscript, 15 August 1977, Andrew
Caldwell Family Collection.

27 Christopher Macky to author, 16 February 2023.

28 Christopher Macky to author, 26 January 2023.

29 Keith Caldwell to William Fry, 3 July 1975, Andrew
Caldwell Family Collection.

30 Geoffrey Gordon, unpublished family vignettes,
n.d., Sally Gordon Family Collection.

31 Michael Caldwell, interview with author, January
2023.

32 Keith Caldwell to Deborah Macky, 15 May 1980,
Deborah Stovell Family Collection.

33 Deborah Stovell to author, 17 February 2023.

Select bibliography

Alexander, Ernie. *Glen Murray's Incredible Pioneers: Over 100 years of amazing history.* Glen Murray: Glen Murray School and District Centennial Committee Publication, 1996.

Bashow, David. 'The incomparable Billy Bishop: The man and the myths'. *Canadian Military Journal* (Autumn 2002): pp. 55–60.

Bishop, William Arthur. *The Courage of the Morning: A frank biography of Billy Bishop, the great ace of World War I.* New York: David McKay Company, 1967.

Bishop, William A. & Stanley M. Ulanoff (eds). *Winged Warfare.* Folkstone, Bailey Brothers and Swinfen, 1975.

Bishop, William H. *Winged Warfare: The experiences of a Canadian 'ace' of the RFC during the First World War.* Milton Keynes: Leonaur, 2011.

Bridgland, Tony. *Outrage at Sea: Naval atrocities of the First World War* (Barnsley, South Yorkshire: Leo Cooper, 2002).

Bowyer, Chaz. *Albert Ball VC.* London: William Kimber, 1977.

Bowyer, Chaz. *Albert Ball VC: The story of the 1st World War ace.* Manchester: Crécy, 1994.

Bowyer, Chaz. *Royal Flying Corps Communiques, 1917–1918.* London: Grub Street, 1998.

'British Victories on the Somme: Triumphant progress towards and beyond the Hindenburg Line from Lens to St. Quentin'. *Current History* 9, no. 1 (October 1918): pp. 20–3.

Bruce, J. M. *The Aeroplanes of the Royal Flying Corps: Military Wing.* London: Putman, 1992.

Campbell, A. E. *Educating New Zealand.* Wellington: Department of Internal Affairs, 1941.

Claasen, Adam. *Fearless: The extraordinary untold story of New Zealand's Great War airmen.* Auckland: Massey University Press, 2017.

Clark, Alan. *Aces High.* London: Ballantine, 1974.

Clark-Hall, R. H. & J. L. *Air Marshal Sir Robert Clark-Hall, KBE, CMG, DSO.* Christchurch: Raven Press, 1995.

Cole, Christopher & E. F. Cheesman. *The Air Defence of Britain.* London: Putnam, 1984.

Churchill, Winston. *The World Crisis, 1911–1918.* New York: Free Press, 2005.

Coney, Sandra. *Gone West: Great War memorials of Waitakere and their soldiers.* Auckland: Protect Piha Heritage Society, 2017.

Cossey, Bob. *Tigers: The story of 74 Squadron RAF.* London: Arms & Armour, 1992.

Crawford, John & Matthew Buck. *Phenomenal and Wicked: Attrition and reinforcements in the New Zealand Expeditionary Force at Gallipoli.* Wellington: New Zealand Defence Force, 2020.

Crawford, John, David Littlewood & James Watson (eds). *Experience of a Lifetime: People, personalities and leaders in the First World War.* Auckland: Massey University Press, 2016.

Cunningham, G. H. *Mac's Memoirs: The flying life of Squadron-Leader McGregor.* Wellington: A. H. & A. W. Reed, 1937.

Curthoys, Judith. *The Stones of Christ Church: The story of the buildings of Christ Church, Oxford.* London: Profile, 2017.

Daley, Caroline. 'Modernity and Leisure in Early Twentieth-Century New Zealand'. *New Zealand Journal of History* 34, no. 2 (2000): pp. 241–61.

Dawson, Bee. *Wigram: The birthplace of military aviation in New Zealand.* Auckland: Random House, 2012.

Dickey, Hugh. *The Growth of New Zealand Towns.* Auckland: Hugh Dickey, 2017.

Diggens, Barry. *September Evening: The life and final combat of the German World War One ace Werner Voss.* London: Grub Street, 2003.

Douglas, William Sholto. *Years of Combat: The first volume of the autobiography of Sholto Douglas, Marshal of the Royal Air Force Lord Douglas of Kirtleside, G.C.B., M.C., D.F.C.* London: Collins, 1963.

Dudgeon, James. *Mick: The story of Major Edward Mannock VC, DSO, MC, RFC, RAF.* London: Robert Hale, 1981.

Ellis, Geoffrey Cyril. *Tool Box on the Wing: My life in the air force.* Wellington: Mallinson Rendel, 1983.

Finnegan, Terrence J. *Shooting the Front: Allied reconnaissance in the First World War.* Stroud, Gloucestershire: Spellmount, 2011.

Franks, Norman & Andy Saunders. *Mannock: The life and death of Major Edward Mannock VC, DSO, MC, RAF.* London: Grub Street, 2008.

Franks, Norman L. R., Frank W. Baily & Russell Guest. *Above the Lines: A complete record of the fighter aces of the German Air Service, Naval Air Service and Flanders Marine Corps, 1914–1918.* London: Grub Street, 1993.

Franks, Norman, Russell Guest & Frank Baily. *Bloody April . . . Black September: An exciting and detailed analysis of the two deadliest months in the air in World War One.* London: Grub Street, 1995.

Franks, N. & H. Giblin. *Under the Guns of the German Aces.* London, Grub Street, 1997.

Fry, W. M. *Air of Battle.* London: William Kimber, 1974.

Graves, Robert. *Goodbye to All That.* London: Jonathan Cape, 1931.

Greenhous, Brereton. *The Making of Billy Bishop: The First World War exploits of Billy Bishop VC.* Toronto: Dundurn Press, 2002.

Grider, John. *War Birds: Diary of an unknown aviator.* Sydney: Cornstock, 1928.

Grinnell-Milne, Duncan. *Wind in the Wires.* London: Panther, 1957.

Hamilton, Bruce & Don. *Never a Footstep Back: A history of the Wanganui Collegiate School, 1854–2003.* Whanganui: Whanganui College Board of Trustees, 2003.

Harvie, E. F. *George Bolt: Pioneer aviator.* Wellington: A. H. Reed & A. W. Reed, 1974.

Harper, Glyn. *Johnny Enzed: The New Zealand soldier in the First World War 1914–1918.* Auckland: Exisle Publishing, 2015.

Harrison, Brian. *The History of the University of Oxford: Volume VIII: The twentieth century.* Oxford: Oxford University Press, 2011.

Hart, Peter. *Somme Success: The Royal Flying Crops and the Battle of the Somme, 1916.* Barnsley, South Yorkshire: Leo Cooper, 2001.

Henshaw, Trevor. *The Sky Their Battlefield, II: Air fighting and air casualties of the Great War.* High Barnet, Hertfordshire: Fetubi Books, 2014.

Hooton, E. R. *War Over the Trenches: Air power and the Western Front campaigns 1916–1918.* Hersham, Surrey: Ian Allan, 2010.

Hunter, Jack D. 'The Blue Max Revisited'. *Over the Front* 13, no. 3 (Fall 1998): pp. 197–202.

Hylands, Dennis. 'Werner Voss, The Last Hussar'. *Cross & Cockade Great Britain* 6, no. 3 (Autumn, 1975): pp. 97–104.

Insall, A. J. 'Lanoe Hawker, VC: Recollections and reflections (II)'. *Popular Flying* (January 1936): p. 550.

Insall, A. J. *Observer: Memoirs of the RFC, 1915–18.* London: William Kimber, 1970.

Jefford, Jeff. '45 Squadron: The early years'. *Cross & Cockade International* 30, no. 4 (Winter, 1999): pp. 181–95.

Jones, H. A. *The War in the Air: Being the part played in the Great War by the Royal Air Force,* Vols 2–6 and Appendices. Uckfield, East Sussex: Naval and Military Press, 1928–1937.

Jones, Ira. *An Air Fighter's Scrapbook.* London: Greenhill Books, 1990.

Jones, Ira. *King of the Air Fighters: The biography of Major 'Mick' Mannock VC.* London: Nicolson & Watson, 1935.

Jones, Ira. *Tiger Squadron: The story of 74 Squadron, RAF, in two world wars.* London: W. H. Allen, 1954.

Joseph, H. W. B. 'Oxford in the Last War'. *The Oxford Magazine* LIX, no. 2 (May 1941): pp. 327–309.

Kennett, Lee. *The First Air War, 1914–1918.* New York: The Free Press, 1991.

Kilduff, Peter. *Billy Bishop VC Lone Wolf Hunter: The RAF ace re-examined*. London: Grub Street, 2014.

Lambert, Bill. *Combat Report*. London: Corgi, 1975.

Lee, Arthur Gould. *No Parachute: A fighter pilot in World War I*. New York: Harper & Row, 1970.

Lee, Arthur Gould. *Open Cockpit: A pilot of the Royal Flying Corps*. London: Grub Street, 2012.

Leinburger, Ralf. *Fighter: Technology, facts, history*. London: Parragon, 2008.

Lewis, Cecil. *Sagittarius Rising*. London: Greenhill Books, 1993.

Lewis, Gwilym H. *Wings over the Somme, 1916–1919*. Bristol: Bridge Books, 1994.

Mackersey, Ian. *No Empty Chairs: The short and heroic lives of the young aviators who fought and died in the First World War*. London: Weidenfeld & Nicolson, 2012.

Malim, F. B. *Almae Maters: Recollections of some schools at home and abroad*. Cambridge: Cambridge University Press, 1948.

MacDonald, Lyn. *Somme*. London: Michael Joseph, 1983.

Macky, Trish (ed.). *The Darlimurla Letter: Love and loss portrayed in a New Zealand family's correspondence, 1875 to the* Lusitania *disaster 1915*. Te Awamutu: Tui Press, 2015.

Martyn, Errol. *A Passion for Flight: New Zealand aviation before the Great War, Volume Two, aero clubs, aeroplanes, aviators and aeronauts 1910–1914*. Christchurch: Volplane Press, 1999.

Martyn, Errol. *A Passion for Flight: New Zealand aviation before the Great War, Volume Three, the Joe Hammond story and military beginnings 1910–1914*. Christchurch: Volplane Press, 1999.

McClure, Margaret. *Fighting Spirit: 75 years of the RNZAF*. Auckland: Random House, 2012.

McCudden VC DSO MC MM, Major James T. B. *Five Years in the Royal Flying Corps*. London: Aeroplane and General, 1918.

McCudden, James T. B. *Flying Fury: Five years in the Royal Air Flying Corps*. London: Greenhill, 2000.

Miller, Russell. *Trenchard: Father of the Royal Air Force*. London: Weidenfeld & Nicolson, 2017.

Milne, John. *Footprints of the 1/4th Leicestershire Regiment: August 1914 to November 1918*. Leicester: Edgar Backus, 1935.

Molkentin, Michael. 'The Dominion of the Air: The Imperial dimension of Britain's war in the air, 1914–1918'. *The British Journal for Military History* 4, no. 2 (February 2018): pp. 2–7.

Nicod, A. A. 'Memories of 60 Squadron'. *Popular Flying* (December 1934): pp. 464–95.

Nicod, A. A. 'Memories of 60 Squadron'. *Popular Flying* (January 1935): pp. 540–2.

Nicod, A. A. 'Re-union Memories'. *Popular Flying* (January 1936): pp. 536–40, 568.

Norris, Susanna Montgomerie, with Anna Rogers (eds). *Annie's War: A New Zealand woman and her family in England, 1916–19*. Dunedin: Otago University Press, 2014.

Oughton, Frederick. *The Personal Diary of Mick Mannock VC DSO (2 bars), MC (1 bar)*. London: Spearman, 1966.

Pettigrew, Wendy. *Heart of a Great School: The chapel of Wangunui Collegiate School*. Whanganui: Whanganui Collegiate School Museum Trust, 2012.

Playfair, Sir Patrick & John Jarvis. *'Pip' Playfair: A founding father of the RAF*. Ilfracombe, Devon: Arthur H. Stockwell, 1979.

Pugsley, Christopher. *The Anzac Experience: New Zealand, Australia and Empire in the First World War*. Auckland: Reed, 2004.

Raleigh, Walter. *The War in the Air: Being the part played in the Great War by the Royal Air Force, Vol. 1*. Uckfield, East Sussex: Naval and Military Press, 1922.

Revell, Alex. *Brief Glory: The life of Arthur Rhys Davids DSO, MC and bar*. London: William Kimber, 1984.

Revell, Alex. *Fall of Eagles*. Barnsley, South Yorkshire: Pen and Sword Books, 2011.

Revell, Alex. *No 60 Squadron RFC/RAF*. Oxford: Osprey, 2011.

Revell, Alex. 'Grid Caldwell'. *Aeroplane Monthly* (December 2016): pp. 44–9.

Richardson-Whealy, Elizabeth (ed.). *Pilot's Log: The log, diary letters and verse of Lt. Leonard A. Richardson, Royal Flying Corps, 1917–1918*. St. Catherine's, ON: A Lilywood Book, 1999.

Rochford, Leonard. *I Choose the Sky*. London: William Kimber, 1977.

Ross, J. M. S. *Royal New Zealand Air Force*. Wellington: Historical Publications Branch, 1955.

Russell, H. H. 'Rhys Davids of 56 Sqdn, RFC'. *Cross & Cockade* (Autumn 1976): pp. 382–99.

Russell, H. H., & W. R. Puglisi. '"Grid" Caldwell of 74'. *Cross and Cockade Journal* 10, no. 3 (Autumn 1969): pp. 193–212

Ryan, Greg. 'Cricket and the Moral Curriculum of the New Zealand Elite Secondary Schools c1860–1920'. *The Sports Historian* 19, no. 2 (November 1999): pp. 61–79.

Ryan, Greg. *The Making of New Zealand Cricket: 1832–1914*. London: Frank Cass Publishers, 2004.

Scott, A. J. L. *Sixty Squadron RAF: On the Western Front during the First World War*. Milton Keynes: Leonaur, 2010.

Scott, A. J. L. *Sixty Squadron RAF, 1916–1919*. London: Greenhill Books, 1990.

Shores, Christopher, Norman Franks & Russell Guest. *Above the Trenches: A complete record of the fighter aces and units of the British air forces, 1915–1920*. London: Grub Street, 1990.

Skelton, Marvin L. *Callahan, the Last War Bird*. Manhattan, Kansas: Air Force Historical Foundation, 1980.

Sortehaug, Paul. 'Major Keith Logan Caldwell'. *Pacific Wings* 80, no. 11 (December 2012–January 2013): pp. 48–53.

Sortehaug, Paul. 'Flight Lieutenant Thomas Grey Culling'. *Pacific Wings* 81, no. 12 (December 2013–January 2014): pp. 50–5.

Spencer, Alex M. *British Imperial Air Power: The royal air forces and the defense of Australia and New Zealand between the world wars*. West Lafayette, Indiana: Purdue University Press, 2020.

Spinney, Laura. *Pale Rider: The Spanish Flu of 1918 and how it changed the world*. London: Vintage, 2018.

Steel, Nigel & Peter Hart. *Tumult in the Clouds: The British experience of the war in the air, 1914–1918*. London: Coronet Books, 1997.

Sturtivant, Ray. *Flying Training and Support Units Since 1912*. Staplefield, West Sussex: Air-Britain, 2007.

Tappin, David. '"Chidlaw": Robert Leslie Chidlaw-Roberts MC Hampshire Regt and RFC: Just an ordinary humdrum pilot'. *Cross & Cockade International Journal* 20, no. 2 (1989): pp. 57–67.

Taylor, Sir Gordon. *The Sky Beyond*. Sydney: Cassell, 1963.

Thompson, H. L. *New Zealanders with the Royal Air Force, Vols I and II*. Wellington: Historical Publications Branch, 1956.

Tredrey, F. D. *Pioneer Pilot: The great Smith Barry who taught the world how to fly*. London: Peter Davies, 1976.

Vandiver, Elizabeth. *Stand in the Trench, Achilles: Classical receptions in British poetry of the Great War*. Oxford: Oxford University Press, 2010.

Wall, Geoffrey. *Letters of an Airman*. Melbourne: Australian Authors' Agency, 1918.

Warne, Joe. 'Sixty Squadron: A detailed history, Parts 1–5'. *Cross & Cockade Great Britain* 11, no. 1–4; 12, no 1 (Spring 1980–Summer 1981): pp. 29–34; 49–65; 120–31; 171–85; 30–46.

Westermann, Edward B. *Flak: German anti-aircraft defences 1914–1945*. Lawrence, KS: University of Kansas Press, 2001.

Whetton, Douglass. *Mannock: Patrol leader supreme*. Falls Church, Virginia: Ajay Enterprises, 1977.

Winter, Denis. *The First of the Few: Fighter pilots of the First World War*. London: Allen Lane, 1982.

Young, A. J., & D. W. Warne. *Sixty Squadron: A history of fifty years service*. Singapore: Eurasia Press, 1967.

Acknowledgements

T his book would not be possible without assistance from my publisher and academic institution. Nicola Legat and her Massey University Press team patiently saw the book through to its glorious completion. Massey University assisted with research at various archives and its library staff were tireless in tracking down books and obscure articles.

Numerous members of the extended Caldwell family generously furnished me with materials and answered interminable questions. Sally Gordon, Andrew Caldwell and Deborah Stovell supplied the all-important family documents and photographs without which this biography would have been much poorer. I was also fortunate to interview and/or correspond with Mary Gordon, Roger Gordon, Simon Gordon, Judy Caldwell, Jane Foote, Christine and Malcolm Futter, Anna Caldwell, Chris Macky, Barbara Ewen, Angus Gordon, Kate Caldwell, Sarah McKenzie and Michael Caldwell.

Several people with knowledge in the field of military aviation were extremely generous with their time and expertise. Great War air-power historian Alex Revell provided me with photographs, a collection of letters between Caldwell and other airmen in the 1960s and 1970s, and helpfully read over much of my text dealing with Caldwell's aerial exploits. Simon Moody at the New Zealand Air Force Museum answered numerous emails about Caldwell's career and those he worked with in the Royal New Zealand Air Force during the Second World War, and ran an expert eye over the chapters covering RNZAF stations Woodbourne and Wigram and Caldwell's postings to India and the United Kingdom.

Aviation researcher and writer Errol Martyn generously gave me a copy of his draft 'Caldwell' entry for his upcoming multi-volume biographical series dedicated to New Zealand Great War personnel, a string of primary documents, and he answered many questions on miscellaneous matters.

Staff at the following archives were extremely helpful: the Air Force Museum of New Zealand; Archives New Zealand Te Rua Mahara o te Kāwanatanga; the Alexander Turnbull Library; the Museum of Transport and Technology; the Auckland War Memorial Museum Tāmaki Paenga Hira; the Navy Museum; Whanganui Collegiate School Museum and Archives; the Royal Air Force Museum; The National Archives (UK); and the Imperial War Museum.

Allan Udy of the Historical Aviation Film Unit arranged an important visit to The Vintage Aviator Limited, Hood Aerodrome, Masterton. It was a wonderful and informative day facilitated by chief engineer David Cretchley and Scott Thomson. Many thanks to pilot Dave Horrell, who took me up in the BE2c. On the ground, pilot Mike Williams got me in a SE5a cockpit and instructed me on the various controls and instruments and the performance parameters of the machine. Chief pilot John Lanham carried out an 'on the ground' reenactment to determine whether a pilot of Caldwell's height and stature could stand half-in and half-out of the cockpit of an SE5a — they could not — and during the preparation of this book answered many questions on the quirks and features of the various machines. Of course, many thanks to Sir Peter Jackson, who has made such a great collection of First World War aeroplanes possible.

More generally, others who assisted, in no particular order: Trevor Henshaw, Jeff Jefford, Victoria Whealy, John Saunders, Christine Clement, Richard Bourne, Glyn Harper, Francis Gibbons, Bob Cossey, Andrew Hagenbuch, John Garver, Ted Hardwood, Matthew O'Sullivan, Allan Kendrick, Anna Rogers, Emily Goldthorpe, Michael Wynd, Dave Homewood, Graeme Neale, Peter Connor, Gail Romano, John Arnold, John Crawford, Bee Dawson, Hal Harding, Sarah Harding, Mathew Williams, Mike Cunningham, John Chapman, Mike Roche, Ralph and Robyn Gardiner, Glenn Reddiex, Anastasia Bakogianni, Michael Belgrave, Kerry Taylor, Tina Sheehan, Chelsea Renshaw, Jenny Clark, Karen Payne, Roger Smith, Carol Garver, Alex Spencer, Peter Millward, Chris Clifford, Anna Brown, Charlotte Bennett, Martin Chapman, Ken Arnold, Michael Greene, Dave Holmwood, Jonathan Moffat, and members of the Great War Forum (www.greatwarforum.org/forum/25-air-personnel-and-the-war-in-the-air). My apologies if I have missed anyone.

My wife, Sandra, and my family have been long-suffering about this project, which ran longer in time and length than initially envisaged. One of my sons, Nathanael, was instrumental in getting many of the photographs together. His expertise as a concept artist and his proficiency with image repair and enhancement were invaluable. One of his siblings, Josiah, looked over various sections of text. To the Claasen tribe, young and old, many thanks for all your encouragement. It's finished!

A special acknowledgement must go to two successive chiefs of the Air Force: Air Vice-Marshal Andrew Clark and Air Vice-Marshal Darryn Webb, RNZAF. As the book neared the finish line, both gentlemen saw the importance of a book on Keith Caldwell and generously made funds available to complete the volume you now hold in your hands. I am honoured to have Darryn Webb write the foreword.

About the author

Dr Adam Claasen is an historian at Massey University, New Zealand. He is a Smithsonian Institution Fellowship grantee, a Fulbright Scholarship (Georgetown University) awardee and a Massey University research team medallist. Adam teaches on the Second World War and American foreign policy and is a Vice-Chancellor's award recipient for sustained excellence in teaching. He has presented conference papers and published on military intelligence, air power and geostrategy. His books include *Hitler's Northern War: The Luftwaffe's ill-fated campaign, 1940–1945*; *Dogfight: Anzacs in the Battle of Britain*; and *Fearless: The extraordinary untold story of New Zealand's Great War airmen*.

Image credits

pp. 3–4: Imperial War Museums, Q 12053; p. 22: courtesy of Deborah Stovell; p. 25: courtesy of Sally Gordon; p. 29: courtesy of the Whanganui Collegiate School Museum and Archives; p. 31: courtesy of Sally Gordon; pp. 34–35: National Museum of the Royal New Zealand Navy, ABT 0056; p. 43: Museum of Transport and Technology, 04/077/058; pp. 44–45: Museum of Transport and Technology, PHO-2004-77.11; p. 48: David Mulgan, *The Kiwi's First Wings: The story of the Walsh Brothers and the New Zealand Flying School 1910–1924* (Wellington: The Wingfield Press, 1960), p. 48; p. 55: Imperial War Museums, HU94502; p. 59: Imperial War Museums, Q 27249; p. 63: courtesy of the Vintage Aviator; p. 66: Spragg family papers, MSS-Archives-A-264, folder 9. Special Collections, University of Auckland Libraries and Learning Services; p. 69: courtesy of Andrew Caldwell; p. 78: Imperial War Museums, Q 69593; p. 81: San Diego Air and Space Museum Archive, 01_00079945; p. 84: courtesy of Andrew Caldwell; p. 93: courtesy of Drake Goodman; p. 95: Air Force Museum of New Zealand; pp. 98–99: courtesy of Kees Kort; p. 104: courtesy of Andrew Caldwell (above); W. M. Fry, *Air of Battle* (London: William Kimber & Co Limited, 1974), p. 51 (below); p. 114: courtesy of Andrew Caldwell; p. 121: Imperial War Museums, Q 42284; p. 123: Imperial War Museums, Q 50328; p. 129: Air Force Museum of New Zealand (above); courtesy of Drake Goodman (below); p. 135: courtesy of Andrew Caldwell; p. 136: Air Force Museum of New Zealand; p. 143: courtesy of Drake Goodman; pp. 146–47: Alamy; p. 154: courtesy of the Vintage Aviator; p. 164: Royal Aero Club Trust; p. 167: courtesy of Sally Gordon; p. 170: courtesy of Alex Revell; p. 172: courtesy of Angus Gordon; p. 175: Imperial War Museums, Q 46099; pp. 182–83: courtesy of Andrew Caldwell; p. 189: Imperial War Museums, Q 73408; pp. 192–93: Air Force Museum of New Zealand; p. 199: Air Force Museum of New Zealand (above); courtesy of Sally Gordon (below); p. 203: courtesy of Victoria Whealy; p. 206: Imperial War Museums, Q 12067 (above); courtesy of Sally Gordon (below); p. 212: courtesy of Micheal Welch; p. 222: Air Force Museum of New Zealand; p. 232: Museum of Transport and Technology, 04/071/040; pp. 234–35: Imperial War Museums, Q 12109; p. 243: Australian War Memorial, A03697; p. 246: Imperial War Museums, Q 12052; p. 252: Air Force Museum of New Zealand; p. 255: Air Force Museum of New Zealand; pp. 258–59: courtesy of Angus Gordon; pp. 264–65: courtesy of Gavin Webster; p. 267: John Grider and Clayton Knight (illustrator), *War Birds: Diary of an unknown aviator* (New York: George H. Doran Company), 1926; pp. 270–71: Air Force Museum of New Zealand; pp. 277–77: courtesy of Kees Kort; p. 282: courtesy of Sally Gordon; p. 289: courtesy of Angus Gordon; p. 296: courtesy of Sally Gordon; p. 298: courtesy of Andrew Caldwell; p. 303: courtesy of Sally Gordon (above); Air Force Museum of New Zealand (below); p. 307: courtesy of Andrew Caldwell; p. 309: Air Force Museum of New Zealand; p. 311: courtesy of Andrew Caldwell; p. 320: courtesy of Andrew Caldwell; p. 323: Air Force Museum of New Zealand; pp. 324–25: Air Force Museum of New Zealand; pp. 328–29: Air Force Museum of New Zealand; p. 331: courtesy of Andrew Caldwell; p. 342: RNZAF Official; p. 344: Air Force Museum of New Zealand; p. 351: Air Force Museum of New Zealand; p. 361: courtesy of Deborah Stovell; p. 363: courtesy of Andrew Caldwell; p. 364: courtesy of Andrew Caldwell; p. 372: Air Force Museum of New Zealand; p. 384: Air Force Museum of New Zealand (above); courtesy of Chris Macky (below); p. 393: map, Roger Smith; p. 394: Auckland War Memorial Museum Tāmaki Paenga Hira; photo section: courtesy of Allan Udy, Historical Aviation Film Unit (HAFU), photographs by Alex Mitchell (HAFU); Fokker DrI photograph by Les Bushell (HAFU).

Index

First published in 2024 by Massey University Press
Private Bag 102904, North Shore Mail Centre
Auckland 0745, New Zealand
www.masseypress.ac.nz

Cover design by Nathanael Claasen and Kate Barraclough
Internal design by Kate Barraclough
Cover photograph: Courtesy of Richard Stowers
Back cover photograph: Tiger Squadron on full display. Keith
Caldwell occupies the cockpit of the SE5a at far right. Courtesy of
the Air Force Museum of New Zealand

A catalogue record for this book is available from
the National Library of New Zealand

Printed and bound in Singapore by Markono Print Media Pte Ltd

ISBN: 978-0-9951029-3-4
eISBN: 978-1-99-101691-1